POLITICAL REPRESSION IN U.S. HISTORY

Previously published in this series:

For more details, see www.vuuitgeverij.nl

*   These volumes have been produced for the European Association for American Studies (E.A.A.S.).

**   This volume is produced with assistance of the Historical Documentation Center for Dutch Protestantism, Vrije Universiteit Amsterdam.

POLITICAL REPRESSION
IN U.S. HISTORY

edited by

Cornelis A. van Minnen and Sylvia L. Hilton

VU UNIVERSITY PRESS
AMSTERDAM 2009

EUROPEAN CONTRIBUTIONS TO AMERICAN STUDIES

This series is published for the Netherlands American Studies Association
(N.A.S.A.) and the European Association for American Studies (E.A.A.S.)

Founding editor:
Rob Kroes

General editor:
Ruud Janssens
University of Amsterdam

VU University Press is an imprint of
VU Boekhandel/Uitgeverij bv
De Boelelaan 1105
1081 HV Amsterdam
The Netherlands

E-mail: info@vu-uitgeverij.nl
Website: www.vuuitgeverij.nl

ISBN 978 90 8659 319 4 (ECAS no. 68)
NUR 686

Design cover: De Ontwerperij (Marcel Bakker), Amsterdam

CONTENTS

INTRODUCTION:
REVISITING THE HISTORICAL ROLE
OF POLITICAL REPRESSION IN THE UNITED STATES

Sylvia L. Hilton and Cornelis A. van Minnen

This book of essays aims to discuss the relationship between political repression and democracy in the history of the United States. The fact that there *is* a relationship is something of a paradox, because although modern democracy purports to defend individual rights and freedoms within a state based on equality under the law, the historical and ongoing existence of political repression in the United States cannot be ignored, much less denied. Political repression has been called "the seamy side" of USAmerican democracy,[1] "the nether side of the American tradition of constitutional liberties,"[2] and many other similarly negative descriptions. Part of the problem in dealing with political repression lies in the tendency to overrate or overstate the capacity of democratic regimes to eradicate its existence. Mythologizing versions of USAmerican history (both in the United States and abroad) have set the standard too high, by persistently overplaying the celebratory message that superior, legally instituted democratic processes guarantee the exercise of political rights and enjoyment of individual freedoms for all bonafide citizens. This has fostered the widespread notion that democracy and repression are or should be incompatible, so that the evidence of historical and ongoing political repression is often considered to "prove" that the USAmerican democracy is a farce or a failure. However, the existence of political repression in the United States does not necessarily mean that democracy has failed. Success or efficacy, in this regard, could be measured more realistically as a matter of degree by comparison with other political regimes, in the context of the historical evolution of the nation-state, and taking into account social scientific research into the nature of power within states. Christian Davenport points out that almost all quantitative analyses published in the past thirty-five years have been "overwhelmingly supportive" of the proposition that: "Through an alteration of incentives and the very functioning of the process by which policies are enacted, democracy makes the political system more accountable to constituents and decreases the likelihood that repressive behavior (especially the most lethal forms) will be used." In short, this author maintains that "democracy is

---

[1] Alan Wolfe, *The Seamy Side of Democracy: Repression in America* (New York: D. McKay Co., 1973). Authors who have used the term "USAmerican" are Charles Bright and Michael Geyer, "Where in the World is America? The History of the United States in the Global Age," in Thomas Bender, ed., *Rethinking American History in a Global Age* (Berkeley: University of California Press, 2002), 63-98, and Richard Ellis, "USAmerican Studies in the United Kingdom," *European Journal of American Studies* 1 (2006), online at http://ejas.revues.org. The term USAmerican is more respectful of other American neighbors than either "American" or "North American," and at the same time it is economical and not unduly clumsy.

[2] Bud Schultz and Ruth Schultz, eds., "Preface" in *It Did Happen Here: Recollections of Political Repression in America* (Berkeley: University of California Press, 1989), xi.

seen to decrease state repression ... institutions associated with democracy play an important and perhaps *the* major role in decreasing state repressive behavior."[3]

In this introductory essay, we propose to offer some thoughts on the concept of political repression, aiming to open up the discussion of its nature, the different agents that have been responsible for its practice or application, the arguments used to justify it, its aims, the diverse means deployed to make it effective, and its individual and collective targets. The first theoretical problem that arises when attempting to examine political repression within specific historical contexts is the debate among sociologists and political scientists regarding its proper scope and definition. Marxists and social scientists influenced by Freud and psychological approaches expanded the definition of repression to practically every aspect of political activity and everyday life in society.[4] Another problem arises from the ambiguity of liberalism itself in its theoretical defence of both individual rights and those of the state, which imposes the practical necessity of reaching and maintaining negotiated compromises. After pointing out the inadequacies of too much theory in a social and historical vacuum and of too much factual description without a theoretical framework, Alan Wolfe posited that political repression in liberal democracies actually forms part of the operations of the state, and therefore must be seen as part of a theory of the state.[5] More recently, Christian Davenport has developed the same idea, affirming that all states practise repression to some degree: "To the specialist ... repression can be rare or frequent, it can be legitimate or illegitimate, but is is always essential to the very definition of the state—one of the most basic functions of the institution."[6] Given that the United States has been a liberal democracy, in one form or another, since its origins as an independent state, this premise means that political repression has not necessarily been an abnormality (however much it may seem to be incompatible with abstract theories of democracy), but is actually a systemic feature of the USAmerican political regime. Indeed, a case might even be made that repression is not only an inherent and therefore inevitable part of any state, but that it might serve an essential role in creating and maintaining the political system.[7] In this book, for example, Thomas

---

[3]   Christian Davenport, ed., *State Repression and the Domestic Democratic Peace* (New York: Cambridge University Press, 2007), in his "Introduction," 10-11.

[4]   For example, Herbert Marcuse, *Eros and Civilization* (New York: Vintage, 1955), *One Dimensional Man* (Boston: Beacon Press, 1968), and "The Movement in a New Era of Repression," *Berkeley Journal of Sociology* 16 (1971): 1-14, whose ideas are summarized in Wolfe, *The Seamy Side*, 20: "repression, in both its psychological and political aspects, is an essential feature of advanced, industrial society, affecting its every aspect, including language." For his part, Henri Lefebvre, *Everyday Life in the Modern World* (New York: Harper Torchbooks, 1971), 145, declared: "it is inexact to restrict an analysis of repression to economic conditions ... or to institutions and ideologies; both attitudes omit the important factor of everyday life, of the pressures and repressions at all levels, at all times and in every sphere of experience including sexual and emotional, private and family life, childhood, adolescence and maturity."

[5]   Wolfe, *The Seamy Side*, 21.

[6]   Davenport, *State Repression*, 35.

[7]   This idea was famously put forward by Niccolò Machiavelli, *Il principe* (1513), Nuova edizione a cura di Giorgio Inglese (Torino: Einaudi, 1995), and Thomas Hobbes,

Clark argues that James Fenimore Cooper's ideas were not as contradictory as some critics have suggested, but that repression and exclusion were necessary to the definition of liberty and democracy in his day and age.

The essays in this book amass considerable historical evidence illustrating various forms of political repression at different times in the United States. However, most of the authors present their examples and discussions within highly critical interpretive frameworks.[8] This tendency points to a third problem for the historical study of political repression, which resides in the powerful interposition of ideology in the definition of the object of study.[9] What for some people constitutes political repression, for others might merely be the legitimate exercise of government authority in the better interests of the majority. In short, the definition of the causes, forms, means, aims and consequences of political repression depends largely on personal ideology. Some definitions are fairly narrow, confining "political repression" to repression *of* political rights *by* government or state agencies only. Whereas some authors distinguish between illegal and legal, violent and non-violent behavior, others do not, affirming that such variables do not change the nature of repression, which is always the same.[10] The phrase government (or state) repression puts emphasis on the agency and the means of repression, and not on its objectives. Early theorists like Max Weber and more recent authors, including Christian Davenport, maintain that state repression is "a generally 'neutral' mechanism of influence, simply one strategy among many employed by political authorities against those within their territorial jurisdiction."[11] Some authors broaden the definition to include coercion by non-governmental actors, and diverse kinds of social pressure which can be repressive of individual and group freedoms, whereas others consider this more inclusive sphere should be more properly described as "social control."[12] According to Anne Edwards, "Social control includes all social measures which involve the management, containment, punishment, repression,

---

8   *Leviathan, or Matter, Form, and Power of a Commonwealth Ecclesiastical and Civil* (1651), A Critical Edition by G.A.J. Rogers and Karl Schuhmann (London: Continuum, 2005), or both works in vol. 21 of the series edited by Mortimer J. Adler, *Great Books of the Western World* (Chicago: Encyclopaedia Britannica, Inc., 1993), but many modern social scientists agree that a degree of repression is necessary and justified even in democratic regimes.

    Their view belongs to the social scientific and historiographical traditions that argue that repression indicates "systemic malfunction, deficiency, and/or pathology," in the words of Davenport, *State Repression*, 37.

9   Wolfe, *The Seamy Side*, 5, noted: "repression is a value-laden word."

10   For example, Michael Stohl and George A. Lopez, eds., *The State as Terrorist: The Dynamics of Governmental Violence and Repression* (Westport, CT: Greenwood Press, 1984) and Christian Davenport, ed., *Paths to State Repression: Human Rights Violations and Contentious Politics* (Lanham, MD: Rowman & Littlefield Publishers, 2000).

11   Max Weber, *From Max Weber: Essays in Sociology* (New York: Oxford University Press, 1946), in Davenport, *State Repression*, 37.

12   Davenport, *State Repression*, 36, "Whereas repression concentrates on the coercive behavior of the state, research on social control highlights nonstate actors and so is deemed quite different."

direction or redirection of individuals and groups who are perceived to constitute a
threat or a problem for society. Social control can use a variety of means—physical,
psychological, economic, moral, ideological, political—and can adopt positive or
negative forms. It is a component of all social relations...."[13] Clearly there is a great
deal of overlap, although a case can be made that political repression should be
considered as one form of social control, since the latter can include inducements in
the form of rewards and opportunities whereas repression is limited to more punitive
and generally negative strategies.[14] Adjectival qualification can describe different
kinds of "repression," according to its specific object of attention, as for example in
psychological repression, cultural repression or ideological repression.[15] It can also
refer to its aim and methods, as in preventive repression (measures taken *before*
dissidence is formed or organized and not as a reaction to its manifestation), or to a
specific agent of repression. For example, in his work on the role of the police,
Frank Donner states: "Political repression ... in the context of policing, may be
defined as police behavior motivated or influenced in whole or in part by hostility to
protest, dissent and related activities perceived as a threat to the status quo."[16] In this
book, Kevern Verney points out that political repression can adopt a "variety of
subtle forms," and the contributing authors have certainly given evidence of that.
Verney refers to "overt political oppression" by the federal government. Several
other authors associate political repression in general terms with varying degrees of
oppression by the government. Ole Moen has preferred to speak of specific
repressive and restrictive measures or practices as policies of "oppressive
government." The synonyms and descriptions of political repression most frequently
used refer to the curtailment, suppression or restriction of rights and liberties.
Specific subjects also lend themselves to the use of many other terms loaded with
negative connotations, such as coercion, discrimination, exploitation, imperialism,
injustices, persecution, destruction, and suffocation.

The discussion of the nature of political repression seems to hang on three
different but intimately intertwined explanatory pegs: reason, emotion, and illness.
All the contributors in this volume take for granted that repressive measures
enforced by government agencies spring from deliberate, premeditated, consciously
self-serving strategies. This self-interested character of political repression prompts
Serge Ricard to suggest that it is a function of "calculating cynicism" and
"realpolitik," thus underscoring the rationality that informs and sustains political
repression. In other words, although coldly rational motivations may not be the only
driving force behind political repression, they certainly play a major role. In the
cases of self-censorship and other forms of (more or less voluntary) individual or
group acquiescence or forbearance in the repression of their own political interests, a

---

[13]   Anne R. Edwards, *Regulation and Repression: The Study of Social Control* (Sydney:
        Allen and Unwin, 1988), 65.

[14]   See idem, 66.

[15]   For example, some chapter titles in Wolfe, *The Seamy Side*, are: "Violent Repression,"
        "Legal Repression," "Private Ideological Repression" (which includes "Corporate
        Ideological Repression"), and "Public Ideological Repression."

[16]   Frank Donner, *Protectors of Privilege: Red Squads and Police Repression in Urban
        America* (Berkeley: University of California Press, 1990), 1.

different aspect of rationality comes into play. The cases examined by Daniela Rossini, Maria Luz Arroyo, and Kevern Verney show that the adoption of such decisions required a certain intensity of intellectual engagement, in order to prioritize objectives in difficult contexts of changing circumstances, resulting in internal struggles which could pain individuals and cause rifts within groups.

Many authors ponder the involvement of emotional factors. Serge Ricard allows that passion must be considered as an ingredient of human history. Catherine Lejeune points to the passionately emotional character of the debate over immigration. Daniela Rossini notes the "emotional appeals" of propaganda during World War I. Clive Webb focuses on "hate speech" and the role of the "hatemonger" as well as the "impassioned public reaction" to Stoner's campaign. Ole Moen argues forcefully that U.S. governments and society are motivated by a fearful sense of insecurity, and inspired by "basic instincts of a conformal pack creature." His language leaves no room for compromise. He speaks of "a deep-seated, unspecified but unadulterated fear," a "basic fear of the undermining national unity," a fear that is "inherent," "pervasive," and "profound." Mark Ellis's study of early twentieth-century southern society also describes its response to efforts to promote racial reform as "an instinctive repressive reaction." More problematic are attitudes of intolerance based on diverse kinds of prejudice, which arguably spring from both rational and emotional sources. Clive Webb speaks of "racial and religious prejudice." Fanaticism—as in this author's reference to fanatical anti-Semitism, or in Alex Goodall's quotation of Walter Lippman on "fanatical jingoism and fanatical pacifism"—is dangerous precisely because of its capacity to harness powerful emotions within rigid rationalizations. Kevern Verney mentions "ethnic prejudices" against Japanese Americans in California. Another kind of prejudice informs the popular anti-elitism or democratic anti-intellectualism identified by Richard Hofstadter and discussed in Ole Moen's essay.

The tendency to use similes and metaphors of mental illness actually reflects the difficulties inherent in trying to separate the rational from the emotional in human motivations and actions. Health-related keywords can be useful when historians seek to offer non-judgemental explanations of certain unpalatable psycho-sociological phenomena; that is, declaring the undesirability of the ailments, but non-commital regarding the source of the problem. On the other hand, when dealing with the motivations of individuals or small identifiable groups, the discourse of psychological illness and disease tends to suggest that their conduct cannot be judged by "normal" standards; a strategy which tends to put such individuals beyond (and therefore not representative of) the "healthy" general body of society. In this volume Kevern Verney's description of the "emotive political climate" of the World War II years as being one of uncertainty, apprehension, and public anxiety is mildly suggestive of psychological distress. Serge Ricard refers to the war "fever" of the 1790s, John Adams's opinion that Jefferson suffered from a "delirium" of ambition, and Richard Hofstader's thesis that USAmerican society participated in the general "panic" arising from the threat posed by the French Revolution. Clive Webb defines J.B. Stoner's racial and religious prejudices as a form of "rabidity," and his reference to "atavistic rhetoric" conjures up images of recurring disease after the intermission of several generations. Ole Moen sees an immature nation readily submitting to what he calls the "strong man syndrome."

Several authors in this volume cite Richard Hofstadter's study of "the paranoid style" in USAmerican politics in order to introduce consideration of national, popular or mass paranoia. David Brion Davis, Barry Glassner and many other historians are also cited as authorities on the much-discussed psycho-sociological problems of both politicians and "ordinary" USAmericans, such as a tendency to suffer bouts of political hysteria, lack of self-confidence, or obsession with conspiracy theories regarding threats to U.S. security, national integrity or the USAmerican way of life. Frank Donner lamented "our national obsession with conspiracy and with scapegoating evil forces in our earthly paradise," and feared that "all that may be needed to stir a traditional countersubversive response in a society programmed for fear and quick to forget the costly and repressive follies of the past ... is the mythification of the extent and gravity of the threat."[17] In the late 1980s, Bud and Ruth Schultz opined: "Political repression ... has become institutionalized in American life, an unwelcome legacy from the sometimes brutal, sometimes hysterical attacks on political dissidents," affirming that the repression fed by anti-communism has been "a mania that suspends rationality."[18] Ole Moen argues in his essay that "this seemingly endemic and pervasive national paranoia," especially when it affects the conduct of U.S. foreign policy, has repeatedly revealed "a need for self-assertion which borders on the pathological."

Government authorities or the "state" are considered to be the main agents responsible for political repression by most of the authors in this volume. The executive branches of the federal and state governments have been found especially culpable, but accusations also pinpoint other government agencies at all levels and in different historical periods. Nonetheless, several essays show that there has often been a murky relationship between repressive government policies and repressive public opinion and social pressures, that make it difficult to discern the flow of mutual influences between state or government initiatives and social or cultural factors. Anne Edwards clarifies that "The obviously hardline punitive and repressive control institutions (police, courts, the law, government departments, 'the state') are not the only ones engaged in the business of regulating society. This task is the responsibility also of socialisation agencies, such as the family, the school, religion and the media, which rely on the 'softer' techniques of education and persuasion."[19] In effect, families, neighborhood and local communities, employers, professional associations, labor unions and diverse business interests, religious and social organizations, and special interest groups can all exert various kinds and intensities of pressure on the attitudes and behavior of individuals. They can all establish boundaries and rules, and punish perceived transgressions, as well as encourage and reward acquiescence and compliance. The complicity of non-governmental agencies in repressive activities has been amply documented. Frank Donner observes that "the American political scene has historically been a fertile breeding ground for

---

[17]   Donner, *Protectors of Privilege*, 4 and 364.
[18]   Schultz and Schultz, *It Did Happen Here*, ix and 411.
[19]   Edwards, *Regulation and Repression*, 7.

countersubversive vigilantism, punitive self-help, and scapegoating during periods of social tension."[20] Ellen Schrecker is especially struck by "the collaborative nature of public and private forces," which she considers "is really a very unique and important element in American political repression."[21] In this book, Adam Fairclough and Mark Ellis discuss the social pressures that worked against African American progress in the south in different historical periods. Serge Ricard and Ole Moen point out the repressive tendencies demonstrated at different times by political parties, the media, and religious leaders. Social support of political repression can also take the form of physical aggressions, or what Clive Webb calls "extralegal violence," including mob lynching, violent protest against civil rights demonstrations, and fires and bombs in synagogues and churches. Daniela Rossini's study of the Committee on Public Information finds that government agency during World War I was responsible for the "fabrication of consent," but that this created popular attitudes that amounted to a "dictatorship of the majority." Clive Webb's discussion of the hate-speech used by J.B. Stoner and conservative elites against African-Americans and Jews highlights the social origins of political repression, and underscores the paradox inherent in the decision of the NAACP and the Anti-Defamation League of B'nai B'rith to seek legal restrictions on free speech in order to combat hatemongers. Similarly, Ole Moen argues that the "Israeli Lobby" in Congress has hindered free speech by pursuing a strong dissuasionary strategy of protest, political pressure and public refutation of opinions deemed to be anti-Semitic.

The general purpose of political repression is to prevent, control or destroy effective challenges to the retention of power in all its forms by existing governing elites. It therefore aims to restrict the freedoms of individuals and social groups that, by their acts or expressions of opinion, actually or potentially challenge and threaten the established social and political order, which is generally conflated with the concept of the greater social good. The essays in this book deal with efforts, made mostly but not only by government agencies, to prevent actions and to silence dissent, criticism, unpalatable truths, political opposition or, indeed, any kind of opinions that threatened or in any way inconvenienced powerful and privileged groups in the United States.

Among the most effective means of political repression, legislation has been a major method employed throughout U.S. history, and the essays in this volume discuss a considerable number of laws that have legitimized repressive policies. Nonetheless, the law has certainly not been the only means by which political repression has been historically instituted and practiced. The means and processes of political repression have been extremely varied. If one considers them as methods of ensuring the continuation and reproduction of existing power relationships in both the short and the long terms, the concept of "reproductive mechanism" developed by

---

20 Donner, *Protectors of Privilege*, 362.
21 Victor Cohen, "Our History of Political Repression: An Interview with Ellen Schrecker." *Reconstruction: Studies in Contemporary Culture* 8.1 (2008): 3 at http://reconstruction.eserver.org/081/cohen.shtml.

Karl Marx can be usefully applied.[22] Government and private agencies in society may use different methods most convenient to their own systemic characteristics, but their repressive aims and strategies may also converge or overlap. Unlawful methods include denial of legal rights, intimidation and physical violence, illegal surveillance and searches, wrongful detention and incarceration, false charges, and excessive punishment, but the central point made by Ellen Schrecker and other authors in this book is that most repressive policies and actions are actually carried out within the limits of the law. Government authorities at all levels, whether legislative, executive or judicial, have used legal prohibitions, impediments, multiple forms of social control, and an array of varied types of punishment. Law-enforcement agencies such as the police, the armed forces, the prison system, the courts and secret intelligence services have worked effectively in support of repressive policies without breaking the letter of the law. In addition, Adam Fairclough, Mark Ellis, Daniela Rossini, Melvyn Stokes and others show that there was often nothing illegal about the repressive pressures exerted by social actors or non-governmental agencies. Several essays in this book discuss legal discrimination, censorship of the periodical press and other mass media, censorship of the opinions of specific individuals, the development of mass propaganda by means of government control of the main sources of news and of the film industry, the control of public opinion by special interest groups, the legal persecution of dissent and the silencing of criticism at home in peacetime and during wars. Delays, segregation, harassment, intimidation, arrest, formal accusations, prosecution and costly trials, fines, imprisonment, deportation, and criminalization all form part of the arsenal of legal ways and means employed to control a host of otherwise-minded citizens such as political and ideological opponents, racial and ethnic minorities, immigrants, anti-war protesters, labor activists, and civil rights demonstrators.

More subtle and more socially pervasive means of achieving political repression are closely connected with the discourses used to justify government policies. Systematic efforts to influence and control public opinion rely not only on direct action to repress minority dissent or criticism, but even more heavily on persuasion of the general public by appeals to self-interest and/or from the "high" moral ground. The arguments used in justification of repressive attitudes and policies tend to fall into a few broad categories, all of which pertain in a general sense to the notion of the greater public good. Since evolving ideas of social justice subject that concept to endless and intense debates, the historiographical discussion of specific examples of political repression requires especially careful attention to context. The most common justifications of repression refer to the need and/or obligation to ensure and protect internal social stability and personal security, the existing constitutional order, national unity and identity, and national security. This last justification has lent itself to very broad definitions, that refer not only to the national military defense against foreign enemies, but to international relations

---

[22]   "Repression can best be understood as a reproductive mechanism ... methods of ensuring that existing power relationships will be reproduced from generation to generation, as well as from day to day." Karl Marx, *Pre-Capitalist Economic Formations* (New York: 1965), cit. in Wolfe, *The Seamy Side*, 262.

generally, as well as certain economic and ideological interests of the United States. Official declarations appeal to principles of honor, justice, and other ethical values associated with good citizenship and patriotism or with religious creeds. This method aims to encourage voluntary self-censorship, self-denial, and self-sacrifice, for the sake of a greater collective good. The more or less voluntary cooperation of certain individuals and groups that might exert a powerful influence over public opinion is especially sought. Consequently, government agencies have often cultivated, legally restricted or put other kinds of pressure on the periodical press and other publishing ventures, the film industry, radio and television channels, leaders and other representives of generally respected churches, associations and movements, and individuals whose opinions are generally perceived to be based on inside knowledge or first-hand experience. Such means may actually be deployed legitimately for the collective good, and therefore cannot always be considered to be harmful. The problem is that government and other social agencies have often been guilty of demagogic interpretation and instrumentalization of high moral principles and national interests for non-legitimate ends, by simultaneously appealing to the prejudices and/or cupidity of the masses.

One of the most frequent means of repressing political rights, particularly in wartime or during periods of intense international tension, is by accusing certain groups or individuals of being enemies of the national community. The Federalists studied by Serge Ricard accused the Jeffersonians of being un-American "Jacobin" traitors who were guilty of conspiracy, sedition and subversion against the constitution, the government and the nation. This author's reference to "martial histrionics" suggests that, while patriotism may be a socially valued virtue, its political uses have often revealed little more than theatrical posturing for the purpose of mobilizing popular feeling. Alex Goodall and Daniela Rossini examine the labelling of political opponents as unpatriotic during World War I, and Goodall introduces the issue of social groups that seek to "influence the state's choice of enemy." More or less voluntary self-censorship may certainly be an expression of patriotism, honor and loyalty, but Rossini and Catherine Lejeune consider that it may also be seen as a form of political repression, and as such it is discussed by Kevern Verney and María Luz Arroyo.[23] Social pressures which were brought to bear in the name of patriotism led many to act not from conviction but, according to Verney, from "moral cowardice at the thought of appearing unpatriotic." The political repression of socialists and communists had considerable social backing because these groups were successfully labelled unpatriotic. Ole Moen reminds us that socialists in the 1920s were accused of promoting "insubordination, disloyalty and refusal of duty in the military and naval forces." The suspicion, real or pretended, that Japanese American loyalty was not to be trusted during World War II clouded the better judgement not just of Roosevelt's administration but of USAmerican society generally.

Demanding manifestations of loyalty in times of grave international tension and war may be seen as an understandable social response to the perception of real

---

[23]   Schultz and Schultz, *It Did Happen Here*, 413, suggest that self-censorship caused by fear "might be the worst intrusion of all."

collective danger. However, Clive Webb reminds us that attempts to mobilize deep human fears have also often been in evidence in peacetime. J.B. Stoner's efforts to create public disorder were comparable to "falsely shouting fire in a theater and causing a panic." In other words they were a classic case of scare tactics. Fear of collective danger can take many forms. In this book, communism and Soviet expansionism, racial and ethnic differences, the national origins and cultural traits of immigrants, and terrorism are all discussed as perceived threats to the collective security and wellbeing. Their political repression has historically been effected not merely by government policies and propaganda, but has also been founded on psycho-sociological insecurities. Another kind of expression of the fearful perception of a collective danger is the victim syndrome examined by Clive Webb. The persecution and punishment of leaders or representatives of particular social groups has often resulted in the creation of martyrs, who have then become powerful symbols that strengthen the resistance of the victims of political repression, whether they be Indians, blacks, women, or any other historically oppressed group. This author interprets that white racists, recognizing the possible usefulness of self-portrayal as "victims of oppression," in the 1950s began to develop a discourse of "white victimization."

The general war of words in varied social contexts involves seeking the moral high ground by denigration and debasement of others in both verbal and written forms. Opprobrium, aspersions, rumors, demeaning language and vilification are all means of depriving others of human dignity and, in this way, of persuading that their political repression is justified. Government recourse to propaganda has no doubt exerted a great deal of influence on public opinion, but this method of repressing undesirable opinions and actions also melds into the efforts of different social groups that reflect or support government positions for reasons of their own, or that effectively exert their own independent influences on public opinion. A particularly vicious form of repression involves the character assassination of individuals and groups alike. Emphasis might be put on condemning what an individual or group has *done or said*, if it can be put in a bad light and bring general discredit. Examples would be certain accusations made against Thomas Jefferson discussed by Serge Ricard, against Martin Luther King, Hosea Williams, Sam Massell discussed by Clive Webb, or those made against Stephen M. Walt and John J. Mearsheimer discussed by Ole Moen. When the denigration refers to what a person or group *is*, negative stereotypes are reinforced. Thus, communists have been portrayed as subversive revolutionaries, African-Americans have been classed as inferior and possibly less than human, black males have been cast as violent criminals and sexual predators, and immigrants have been deemed unworthy to enjoy civil rights and deportable. A special version of character assassination as a means of justifying repression involves the mobilization of deeply felt religious convictions, in order to associate the individual or group with evil forces. This may also be considered another way of tapping into human fears and irrationality, and has historically caused a number of outbreaks of collective repressive hysteria which present similarities. References to evil forces, witches and witch-hunting, hell, the devil, Satan, God, divine vengeance, crusades, and the like demand repression as the obligation of a society which sees itself on the right side of the eternal war of good against evil. When discoursive disparagement is extreme, it can lead to demonization/ satanization of perceived foreign and internal enemies, with the use of "hate speech" that not only aspires to have an inflammatory effect on public opinion but attempts to intimidate by advocating discriminatory policies, persecution and violent action against the chosen targets.

The targets and victims of political repression can be individuals and social groups. The chapters in this book discuss many individuals whose freedom of action or speech was curtailed in some degree: John Peter Zenger, William Duane, Albert Gallatin, Benjamin F. Bache, Matthew Lyon, Thomas Jefferson, Junius Scales and a host of other plaintiffs in Supreme Court cases, socialist leader Eugene Debs and the producer of the film *Spirit of '76*, draft-dodgers and advocators against military service in World War I, Claude G. Bowers, Walter White, William Sentner, named communists and sympathizers during the early Cold War, Martin Luther King, and professors Stephen M. Walt, John J. Mearsheimer and Norman Finkelstein. Targeted groups might be political or ideological opponents like the Jeffersonian Republicans in the 1790s, anarchists, socialists, "Bolsheviki" and pacifists during World War I, the radical Communist Labor Party during the 1920s and 1930s, communists and "fellow-travelers" during the Cold War, civil rights activists, or certain protesters against the Vietnam War in the 1960s and early 1970s. Racial, ethnic and religious minorities have also been collective victims targeted by political repression. Immigrants and refugees of all races, ethnicities, nationalities and religions at different times, African Americans, Jews, Japanese Americans, and since 11-S foreign Muslim scholars and artists seeking resident or immigration status in the United States. Writers, newspaper editors, publishing houses, communications agencies, and movie companies have not only collaborated with government agencies in encouraging social acquiescence in repressive policies, but they themselves have also often been victims of repression when governing elites have sought to control freedom of expression. Frank Donner fears that "if the past is a guide, 'terrorist' may well be converted into an all-purpose taint or stigma against an expandable body of targets—potential terrorists, fronts, suspects, supporters, and sympathizers."[24] Since 9-11, Ole Moen points out that anybody using a public library, if deemed to be seeking information of use to terrorists, may be subjected to control by means of National Security Letters.[25]

* * *

In his essay on Thomas Jefferson and the Revolution of 1800, Serge Ricard discusses the Alien and Sedition Acts as an episode in domestic power struggles, in the light of the political and international developments of the 1790s. Political

---

[24]   Donner, *Protectors of Privilege*, 367.

[25]   A vast amount of bibliographical, media and special interest materials relevant to the discussion of political repression in the United States and round the world can be found on many internet sites. See for example, http://www.publiceye.org, or http://www.thirdworldtraveler.com.

repression is defined here as the unconstitutional curtailment of individual freedom. Feeding on the paranoid fear of the enemy "within our gates," while international conspiracy theory pointed to the possibility of a dangerous Jacobinical plot threatening USAmerican security, the tools of political repression by the federal goernment were press censorship, arrest, imprisonment, and deportation of aliens. Seeking national "unanimity" and "acquiescence" in the government's measures, authoritarianism flourished as war mongering rhetoric reached fever pitch. Foreign enemies and domestic opponents of the government were said to threaten national integrity and constitutional government. Anybody maintaining opposing views was quickly accused of being anti-patriotic, seditious, subversive, and traitorous. In a classical instrumentalization of international wars and domestic fears, the Federalist Party saw "a glorious opportunity to destroy faction." Nonetheless, while popular opinion might have shown some paranoid tendencies, Serge Ricard is careful to point out that the calculating cynicism displayed by some Federalists suggests that they themselves were actually more inspired by realpolitik than by paranoia.

In attempting to answer the initial question of whether political repression has been an unfortunate, corrigible aberration from USAmerican democracy, or is a systemically inherent product, Thomas Clark's essay focuses on the ideas of James Fenimore Cooper as a representative of classical Jeffersonian-Jacksonian republican democratic thought in the 1820s-1830s. Some authors argue that Cooper saw but did not endorse the deficiencies of USAmerican liberty, and aimed in his work to critically reflect them. Others strongly dissent, holding that Cooper's attitudes were, in fact, "racist, sexist and anti-democratic; based on an ethnocentric, culturally imperialist and hierarchal view of society." Thomas Clark argues that Cooper was indeed comfortable with the idea that democracy and the liberty of some (the few) rested on the political repression of the many (especially Africans and foreign immigrants), and their exclusion from the benefits of equality and political rights. The explanation for these contradictions lies in the prevalence in USAmerican society of deep anxieties about the possible failure, internal subversion or foreign destruction of U.S. democracy. A widespread belief in the inequality of humans and a paranoid fear of the nation's corruption by sinister forces were deeply rooted in the USAmerican mainstream. Cooper's illiberal and contradictory thought was not the product of fanaticism, but was based on his classical republican belief in the inevitability of inequalities and hierarchies. Black inequality was just one of many. In short, in Cooper's view, liberty actually depended on repression, and democracy depended on exclusion. The standard liberal view propagates the enduring myth that historical examples of exclusion and repression in the United States have been accidental and temporary aberrations from the essential democratic principles of liberty, equal rights and universal suffrage. On the contrary, Clark argues that Cooper's case may represent a USAmerican intellectual tradition in which repression and exclusion repeatedly become the keys to liberty and democracy.

In Adam Fairclough's view, political repression in the United States has not relied primarily upon widespread violence, but on a relatively "clean-shirted and kid-gloved variety" of intimidation. Arguing that political repression does not have to be total to be effective, this author points out that the post-civil war South did not need to be a fascist or totalitarian regime in order to be successfully repressive. In fact, in his study of political repression in Louisiana, he affirms that white southern Democrats employed only as much force as was necessary to render the Republican Party impotent. In this essay, Adam Fairclough examines the repressive tactics used by southern white Democrats against black Republicans in the town of Natchitoches during the Reconstruction years. The old historiographical narrative of oppressed whites, gullible blacks, and thieving carpetbaggers was a logical product of the public discourse of Democrat newspaper editors posing as lonely crusaders against northern and republican political oppression. In their view, the White League was created in order to defend the legitimate rights of oppressed whites, portrayed as victims groaning under excessive taxation, and to redeem the state of Louisiana from Republican misrule. Consequently, throughout the South, black voters were disfranchised en masse, and black population was generally oppressed. This systematic destruction of the southern Republican Party underpinned the system of white supremacy, entrenching a racially repressive system that endured into the 1960s, and according to the author, "may well be the most sweeping instance of political repression in American history."

Mark Ellis's essay about racial reformism in the early twentieth-century South does not focus on the different forms of repression employed against African Americans, nor is it a discussion of political repression by government agencies. It aims instead to examine the repressive nature of social pressures against white dissent on racial issues and against reform for black progress. Arguing that the southern race settlement of the 1890s had overwhelming intellectual and popular endorsement, Mark Ellis says the promotion of segregation was seen as a device for preserving both peace and racial integrity. A repressive consensus reflecting "a persistent sense of grievance" among white southerners was reinforced by a "habit of hate" which was inspired by the organized propaganda of World War I, effectively preventing divergence from white supremacist ideas and policies. Many white dissenters were deterred by the pervasive white supremacist tendency from challenging the status quo until at least the 1930s. It became a question of loyalty. White racial solidarity was conflated with the idealism of USAmericanism and southern or national patriotism, and the curtailment of free speech on race issues became a general attitude of government, law enforcement agencies, patriotic organizations and the press. The many forms of social pressures included disapproval, scorn, scepticism, vilification, ostracism, isolation, and witness intimidation by the Ku Klux Klan. Even the mildest dissenters were forced into silence or exile by the intensely hostile language used against any internal criticism. Gossip, newspapers, books, sermons, and "scientific" discourse disseminated a "subtle and continuous propaganda" that was especially hurtful "in a regional culture in which reputation and social standing were paramount." The aim was to make reformers and dissenters, or indeed anyone adopting moderate views on racial issues, feel that they were social outcasts because of their own unnatural and disloyal attitudes. This form of repression did not necessarily entail material hardship or physical pain, but it was meant to cause real social and mental discomfort. As a result, southern white moderates constantly censored themselves to avoid unpleasant social responses, and showed some courage (or madness) when they dared to challenge the status quo.

The entanglement of foreign and domestic affairs can often be found at the heart of repressive attitudes and policies. Alex Goodall addresses this theme in connection with Woodrow Wilson's perplexing role in the development of USAmerican anticommunism. He does not dwell on the issue of "primacy," trying to determine whether foreign or domestic concerns were the major driving force, but prefers simply to stress the interconnectedness of foreign and domestic spheres. Wilson proclaimed that the United States had an exceptional civilizing mission to promote human liberty around the world. In his view, this required the United States to join forces with European and other states in a League of Nations, as well as a commitment to a policy of spreading democratic ideals and forms of government. Nonetheless, arguing that any represssive action against the Bolsheviks in Russia would only strengthen their appeal, Wilson consistently refused to intervene to oppose their push for power, justifying this policy in the name of anti-imperialism and Russian national self-determination. He purported to believe that the popular will of the Russian people would eventually overcome the repressive rule of the Bolshevik minority without U.S. intervention. This apparently liberal stance contrasted sharply with Wilson's domestic policies aimed at the political repression of communism in the United States, indicating an ideological inconsistency that leads Alex Goodall to maintain that Wilson's new globalising ideology of liberation was contradicted by the repressive measures put into practice by his administration at home, and for which this author holds Wilson responsible. By a process of rationalization, Wilson's crusading idealism of universal human liberation became merged on the domestic front with traditional forms of USAmerican antiradicalism, to produce anticommunist attitudes that would find later expression in McCarthyism. After 1917, Congress, the federal government, and Wilson himself began to take a more aggressive role in campaigns against radicalism, exploiting repressive wartime attitudes in order to regulate dissenting public discourse and suppress the radical left. Free speech, socialism, communism, strikes, and other expressions of social and political dissent were repressed by legislation, the use of the armed forces, and other means. The radical left was subject to arrests and police harassment, and the federal postal service refused to deliver socialist publications. Plans for massive repression were illustrated by the excessive violence of the Palmer raids. The left was already deeply divided over the war and, in Goodall's opinion, was further damaged as a result of Wilsonian domestic policies. The repression implied that there could be no accommodation with liberal capitalism, and consequently strengthened the hand of the radical left. In sum, this author concludes that Woodrow Wilson must be held responsible not only for the anti-democratic political repression of dissent at home, but for the growth of xenophobia, ultra-patriotism, and conservative anti-radicalism in the United States.

The Committee on Public Information was created by Woodrow Wilson during World War I as a government instrument for the management of public opinion during wartime. Headed by George Creel, the CPI quickly dominated two key and intertwined aspects of mass communications: censorship and propaganda. Praised as "a nationalizing force at home and an Americanizing agent abroad," the Committee's overall goal was to promote the circulation of positive images of the United States and to counter or prevent the spread of negative perceptions of the

USA or of Great Britain and other Allied Powers. Daniela Rossini sees in the CPI's activities "a crusading attitude and a skillful combination of selective repression, centralization of information, control of the media and propaganda," that enabled Wilson's administration to manage public opinion in an unparalleled way. Censorship was not simply imposed by the government. The press, the film industry, other mass media, and the general public were urged, for the sake of honor and patriotism, to comply with CPI guidelines. In other words, the government sought to mobilize a general "self-imposed conformism" in order to achieve what amounted to a high level of voluntary censorship. The CPI also undertook missions abroad. Charles Merriam led one such mission in Italy, organizing the first mass propaganda campaign in favor of the United States in that country, and offering a plan to improve Italian propaganda in the United States. Noting John Dewey's observation on the efficacy of mass methods in manufacturing popular sentiment for all kinds of causes (worthy or not), this essay argues that the fabrication of consent was in fact achieved by repression of democratic rights. Daniela Rossini is careful to point out that U.S. censorship and propaganda were not so heavy handed as they were at that time in Italy, France or other European countries, but she echoes arguments similar to those used by Alex Goodall regarding the contradictory nature of Wilsonian policies and their adverse effects on the functioning of democracy in the United States. The capacity of government-inspired censorship and propaganda to fabricate majority consent was proven by the CPI and the reactions of USAmerican society during World War I. This experience undermined basic U.S. assumptions about enlightened public opinion. It shed doubts on the capacity and willingness of an intelligent general public to maintain independent and diverse rational opinions. Furthermore, the author argues, it created a social atmosphere which was unfavorable to the expression of dissent, while sowing the seeds of reactionary postwar hysteria which encouraged antidemocratic attitudes of "isolationism, illiberalism, and intolerance."

Self-censorship or the voluntary limitation of free speech is the subject of Kervern Verney's study of the NAACP and Walter White's role during World War II. During the "King-centric" 1960s, historians neglected the early development of militancy in African American communities as a field of research, but in the 1970s this became a central theme in civil rights historiography, and since the 1980s scholars have often contended that World War II prepared the way for the postwar civil rights movement by heightening racial consciousness among African Americans. Once again, it is seen that war in defense of democracy and human rights had negative effects on democratic processes and progress within the United States. NAACP leader Walter White showed an unprecedented interest in race relations outside the United States, attaching great importance to international developments, such as Nazi racism and the postwar decolonization of Africa and Asia. In the author's opinion, this new international focus was "the most notable departure in NAACP strategy during the war years." Meanwhile, on the home front, the NAACP not only declined to support a legal challenge waged by an African American serviceman, in protest against being drafted into a segregated regiment, but actually urged him to drop the case. When he rejected this advice, the national NAACP leadership justified the expulsion of his lawyer brother from the NAACP branch in Jamaica, Long Island, by saying that pursuance of the issue was unpatriotic in wartime. The leadership was supported in these decisions by Special Legal Counsel Thurgood Marshall, leaving the feisty Conrad brothers to face FBI harassment under suspicion that they were Communist fellow travelers. Such self-censorship or "accommodationism" among NAACP leaders, under the influence of President Roosevelt and government advisors, is presented here as one form of political repression. Kevern Verney merely suggests without affirming that White may have been partly motivated by personal ambitions on the international stage, and he stops short of concluding that the NAACP was in this case not the victim but the perpetrator of repression. He does, however, make it clear that White subordinated the domestic objectives of the NAACP to the needs of the war effort, on the grounds that any action that might seem disloyal or assist in any way the Nazi war effort imposed temporary but unavoidable limitations on legitimate NAACP activities at home.

In her study of the long-delayed publication of the Spanish memoirs of U.S. Ambassador Claude G. Bowers, María Luz Arroyo explores the relationship between the repression of freedom of speech in the United States and voluntary censorship. Claude Bowers was the U.S. ambassador in Spain from 1933 to 1939. His memoirs, entitled *My Mission to Spain: Watching the Rehearsal for World War II*, not only documented the crisis of the Second Spanish Republic and the Civil War, but also criticized the attitude and policies of the democratic nations during those crucial years. Bowers believed that their failure to support the Spanish Republic and adoption of the appeasement policy had terrible consequences for both Spain and the whole of Europe. He planned to publish his memoirs immediately after his recall, but ended up waiting for fourteen years to see his manuscript in print. His initial voluntary forbearance was based on the premise that it would be temporary, but the later suggestion that the state department might subject his manuscript to their censorship led him to resist publication on those terms. María Luz Arroyo analyzes the circumstances and reasons for this long delay, as well as some of the responses in Spain, the United States and other countries when it was finally published in 1954. The essay also examines the international context of this case, especially as regards the foreign policies of Spain and the United States. The available evidence leads the author to conclude that the long delay resulted from Bowers' acquiescence, but that he was subjected to diverse personal and political pressures from several quarters at different times, and that some of those pressures were less palatable to him than others, suggesting that his self-censorship might be considered a subtle form of political repression.

Ellen Schrecker's study of government persecution of communist William Sentner and his wife in 1952-1954 portrays this couple as victims of "the repressive machinery of the state," emphasizing that the political repression to which they and the United Electrical workers were subjected was not only within the law, but often *was* the law. In the early years of the Cold War all levels of government contributed to "the seamless nature" of political repression. In the federal sphere, as in most of the states, lawmakers customarily deferred to the executive, while judges and juries remained passive in the face of the political harassment of defendants, rarely standing up in protest. Multiple jurisdictions did not lead to diversity of attitude and conduct, but only intensified the repression. State repression of political dissent was justified in the name of national security, and targeted communists, union organizers and members, striking workers, left-wing radicals, African Americans, civil rights workers in the South, aliens, jobless vagrants, and in the 1960s opponents of the Vietnam War, the Black Panthers and other left-wing activists. Legislation was a favorite method of controling political dissent and activities. The author discusses major repressive laws such as the Smith Act, the 1940 Hatch Act, the McCarran Internal Security Act of 1950, the Anti-Riot Act of 1968, the Iowa criminal syndicalism law, and other anti-sedition, criminal anarchy, or criminal syndicalism laws passed by states, but she also points out that even presumably neutral regulations were used to counter threats to the status quo. Old vagrancy laws, those against disturbing the peace or disorderly conduct, and ordinary laws might be enforced in politically discriminatory ways, while minor crimes could bring excessive punishments if committed by racial minorities or political dissenters. Government authorities enforced the law selectively, made use of informers, witness perjury and illegal evidence, committed abuses of due process, and sometimes simply manufactured criminal charges. Other legal measures included congressional investigations, FBI surveillance, criminal prosecutions and conspiracy indictments. Judges often handed down injunctions as a way of preventing strikers from picketing, leafleting, or encouraging other workers to walk off the job. Proceedings against immigrants and deportation are not subject to constitutional constraints on criminal prosecutions, and are therefore exempt from due process, which means that they can be used for politically repressive purposes. Sentner's immigrant wife was arrested, held without bail for several days, required to report regularly to immigration authorities, submit to physical and mental examinations, and renounce all political activities and associates, including her spouse. Ellen Schrecker concludes that "the legal harassment of William Sentner was completely in keeping with the American tradition of political repression," finding no cause for celebration in her reluctant recognition that in the end "the nation's avowed respect for individual rights reasserted itself."

Positing that political repression, conspiracy theories and popular hysteria and have often gone hand in hand in USAmerican history, Melvyn Stokes examines these phenomena in connection with the U.S. film industry in the years 1951-1952. Following Robert J. Goldstein's work on political repression in Europe and in the United States, the author maintains that ruling USAmerican elites have rarely embraced repression as a means of protecting their own political power and status on the same systematic scale or with the continuous intensity as have European elites. He does accept, with some reserves and citing examples studied by Murray Levin, that elites in the United States have sometimes fostered conspiracy theories, seeking to fan irrational fears that U.S. values and way of life were threatened. However, Melvyn Stokes cautions against views that overrate the capacity of politicians and other influential groups to manufacture national panics without any real cause and in their own interest. Any success such groups may have in using political hysteria as a mode of repression depends on popular approval and mass acquiescence, the deep roots of which must be sought in USAmerican culture and in the collective psyche. In the early 1950s, anti-communism was a mainstream phenomenon with much institutional support, leading this author to suggest that the political repression of that period was supported by a broad democratic consensus, and to offer an interpretation of the Hollywood inquisition that seeks other factors instead of the standard version of political repression carried out by HUAC under government orders. He contends that many USAmericans have supported crusades against spectral enemies for reasons of their own, and different organized groups have led campaigns to repress subversion and sedition. Such groups have sometimes formed part of government agencies, like police forces in certain cities. Others have been private groups and organizations. Melvyn Stokes focuses specifically on the use of repression and the instrumentalization of popular hysteria by the bosses of the Hollywood studio system in the early 1950s. The U.S. film industry has operated at different times under several apparently restrictive regimes, but this author affirms that such restrictions have been welcomed or actually pioneered by the film industry itself to avoid more serious external scrutiny. Most scholars have interpreted the Hollywood inquisition as one manifestation of political repression carried out by HUAC, but this essay argues that HUAC activities might be seen as serving the repressive designs of Hollywood bosses. Modifying the usual image of HUAC as a government agency repressing the entire Hollywood community, Melvyn Stokes contends that the Committee was acting in many ways as an instrument of one section of that community—the studio elite—in its own campaign to repress union militancy.

Clive Webb's contribution analyzes the controversy surrounding the disputed right to free speech of white racists in the 1970s. In the first half of the twentieth century, U.S. courts sustained a narrow interpretation of the individual right of free speech. In the 1919 case of *Schenck v. United States*, Justice Oliver Wendell Holmes held that repression of free speech was legally justified if the words used represented a "clear and present danger." Application of this standard led to significant government repression of political dissent. However, in the 1950s and 1960s, under the leadership of Earl Warren, the Supreme Court broadened its interpretation of the First Amendment guarantee of free speech, in order to protect civil rights activists. In 1964, the Court upheld the individual right to express "vehement, caustic and sometimes unpleasantly sharp attacks on government and public officials." Furthermore, accusations of libel would have to meet the new "actual malice" standard, by which a plaintiff must prove that the author of a statement knew that it was false or acted in "reckless disregard" of the truth. This expansion of First Amendment protection culminated in the 1969 case of *Brandenburg v. Ohio*, in which the Supreme Court recognized the right of free speech of a Cincinnati Klansman, definitively abandoning the 1919 "clear and present danger" test. Protected by this broad interpretation of the freedom of expression, "hate speech" became increasingly common. One example was the racist campaign of J.B. Stoner in his bid for a seat in the U.S. Senate in 1972. His language was so offensive that it led to a policy shift in the NAACP, the ADL and other groups that, despite internal divisions, attempted to use the power of the state to silence political opponents. Without explicitly mentioning Stoner's crude stereotyping of blacks, but arguing that "racial epithets" caused irremediable "psychological harm," they petitioned the courts for restrictions on free speech when it threatened the security and/or equal rights of other citizens. Clive Webb concludes that the shift from defending free speech for all, in the 1950s and 1960s, to attempting to impose government censorship, in the 1970s, represented a major turning point in the strategies of the NAACP, the ADL and other organizations representing racial and ethnic minorities.

Focusing on legislation and policies that have increasingly limited alien and illegal immigrants' civil rights since the 1990s, Catherine Lejeune's essay argues that the most recent trend is not just about social control, but about creating a new form of political repression. Citing anthropologist De Genova, the author contends that U.S. government authorities cultivate popular fears regarding the existence of a pervasive and imminent external threat to the stability and security of the United States, as a means of silencing political dissent. During the Cold War, communism was identified as the main source of the threat, but since 1990 (and with greater force since 9/11) that ideological role has been assigned to international terrorism. Government agencies such as the FBI, the DHS and others carry out the repressive policies, but civil society, too, plays a part, inasmuch as individuals internalize repression and self-censor their political opinions. The notion that illegal aliens contribute to the corrosion of law and order has led to the adoption of increasingly severe laws and policies aimed specifically at depriving immigrants of their political rights, and which may affect not just illegal or undocumented immigrants, but also lawful permanent residents. Many non-citizens may be subjected to repressive treatment, including preventive detentions, deportations, surveillance of individuals and organizations, and diverse other measures of discipline, intimidation and control. Citing Sunaina Maira, the author considers that deportation is possibly the most problematic form of political repression because it not only serves the U.S. government's aims of political repression and domination but it also supports U.S. economic interest in strategies of liberal capitalism. Detentions and deportations may be based on "guilt by association," and deportation hearings may be held in secret, without access to a lawyer, and without the right to appeal. In conclusion, and contending that, far from being exceptional situations, political repression at home and war overseas represent the everyday state of emergency throughout the U.S. empire, Catherine Lejeune argues that deportation is a technology of subjection for the regulation by the state of citizens, migrants and workers.

In his analysis of twentieth-century examples of legal restrictions imposed by the U.S. government on the freedom of expression, Ole Moen examines the continuing legal and constitutional evidence of a trait observed by Alexis de Tocqueville in the 1830s: "I know no country where there is so little true independence of mind and freedom of expression as in America." The essay "Free Speech vs. Fear: A Constitutional Ideal and the Tyranny of the Majority in the American Tradition" is a detailed discussion of judicial cases arising from repressive legislation and other governmental measures which were taken during the Red Scare of the 1920s and 1930s, the McCarthy era, the Vietnam War, and the reaction to international terrorism since 2001. The author maintains a strong focus on the theme of political repression and the difficulties of its definition. Despite making a very strong liberal critique of the Bush administration, he also looks at government swings *against* repression, a political fact which few liberal authors are willing to address. The study shows that individuals have not always found it easy to express dissent, and have often been punished, persecuted or stygmatized for doing so. In all of the examples analyzed in this study, the common denominator has been the official justification that national security was in danger. For this reason, the author concentrates on the evolution and application of the "clear and present danger" criterion since its enunciation by Justice Oliver Wendell Holmes in 1919. Citing Richard Hofstadter, Michael Moore, and Barry Glassner, Ole Moen believes that USAmerican society is not, as is often affirmed, an individualistic society. He argues, on the contrary, that the United States as a nation is still immature, lacking in self-confidence, and easily targeted by demagoguery that appeals to "a deep-seated, unspecified but unadulterated fear," bordering at times on hysteria and paranoia. While recognizing the formidable USAmerican track record in favor of peace and civil liberties, and conceding that the world tends to hold the United States to a higher democratic standard than that expected of other countries, Ole Moen suggests that this basic fearfulness regarding national unity and security is the root cause of the readiness, arrogance and relative impunity with which U.S. government officials have violated democratic principles, rights and liberties that theoretically lie at the very heart of USAmerican political values.

In 1973, Alan Wolfe gave us this definition: "Repression is a process by which those in power try to keep themselves in power by consciously attempting to destroy or render harmless organizations and ideologies that threaten their power."[26] Robert Goldstein's definition is more specific: "Political repression consists of government action which grossly discriminates against persons or organizations viewed as presenting a fundamental challenge to existing power relationships or key government policies, because of their perceived political beliefs."[27] As the twenty-first century dawned, Christian Davenport ventured that political repression can be defined as "behavior that is applied by governments in an effort to bring about political quiescence and facilitate the continuity of the regime through some form of restriction or violation of political and civil liberties. This encompasses behavior that is violent (executions and torture) and nonviolent (mass arrests, detention, intimidation), legal (sanctioned by law) and illegal, as well as behavior that is specifically and diffusely targeted."[28] The essays in this volume aim to contribute to the historical documentation and discussion of these ideas.

---

[26]   Wolfe, *The Seamy Side*, 6.
[27]   Robert J. Goldstein, *Political Repression in Modern America: 1870 to the Present* (Cambridge, MA: Schenkman, 1978), xvi, cit. in Schultz and Schultz, *It Did Happen Here*, xi, and by Melvyn Stokes in this book.
[28]   Davenport, *Paths to State Repression*, 6.

SUPPRESSING DISSENT IN THE EARLY REPUBLIC: ADAMS, JEFFERSON, THE ALIEN AND SEDITION ACTS, AND "THE REVOLUTION OF 1800"

Serge Ricard

In the United States, foreign conflicts have almost always had domestic repercussions. And on several occasions, war with other nations has led to the curtailment of civil liberties. The paranoid fear of a fifth column, of the enemy "within our gates," has often prompted repressive measures against suspected foes. Albeit for brief periods, authoritarianism has been known to make inroads on democracy. Press censorship and imprisonment for sedition, arrest and deportation of aliens have featured prominently in the paraphernalia of repression, as during World War I and World War II.

The first instance in U.S. history of such onslaughts on alleged radicals, anti-patriots and critics of the government, in violation of habeas corpus and the First Amendment, occurred during the "Quasi-War" with France in 1798-1800. It was a time of national and international turmoil that led to a confrontation between Federalists and Jeffersonians and resulted in the showdown of 1800-1801 and the ensuing Republican victory that Jefferson famously labeled "The Revolution of 1800." "To an extraordinary extent," it may be argued, "developments in the French revolutionary and Napoleonic wars thus determined the course of American politics."[1] The infamous Alien and Sedition Acts, passed in the wake of the XYZ affair, were supposedly designed to ensure national security, but they also aimed at stifling dissent and specifically targeted the Federalists' political enemies and their radical protégés, many of whom came from Ireland, England, and France. The episode would be instrumental in the rise of political parties, Jefferson's accession to the presidency—an electoral triumph of which the Republicans for a while thought they might be robbed—and the ultimate demise of the Federalists. And it ended a long-time friendship between two great revolutionary leaders, John Adams and Thomas Jefferson. But the so-called "revolution" was no upheaval, inasmuch as it corresponded to the peaceful devolution of power from one party to another, an unprecedented democratic feat in the eighteenth-century world.

Relations between the two friends were to deteriorate shortly after Adams's inauguration in March 1797, when partisanship got the better of the Federalists during the Quasi-War with France, as historians now call it. A sense of crisis would pervade the whole of Adams's presidency.[2] The story is well known. The French government was angered by the Jay Treaty which it interpreted as a rapprochement with Great Britain, if not a breach of the 1778 alliance, and began to interfere with American shipping. Charles Cotesworth Pinckney was sent to Paris to try to pacify the Directory but was turned down. Adams was facing a serious crisis and his

---

[1]   James Horn, Jan Ellen Lewis, and Peter Onuf, eds., *The Revolution of 1800: Democracy, Race, and the New Republic* (Charlottesville: University of Virginia Press, 2002), xiii.

[2]   James E. Lewis, Jr., "What Is to Become of Our Government?" in Horn, Lewis, and Onuf, *The Revolution of 1800*, 8.

cabinet instantly favored a confrontation. They objected to the president's proposal to send a bipartisan commission to Paris but relented when they discovered that Hamilton agreed. After convening Congress to a special session two months later he urged extensive military preparations—short of the creation of the provisional army that Hamilton recommended—and appointed, on 31 May 1797, Pinckney, John Marshall, and Elbridge Gerry, a Republican, as commissioners, with instructions to negotiate a treaty of commerce and amity with France. The Republicans who had vociferously agitated for war when Britain tampered with American commerce just as loudly lambasted Adams's aggressive policy toward France. Jefferson, now a convert to neutrality as the safest course for the United States, mustered the opposition in Congress, which contributed to whittling down the Federalist military-preparedness program. But he remained convinced that American independence, two decades after its proclamation, was in jeopardy owing to the nation's pro-British economic policies.[3]

Envoys Marshall and Gerry joined Pinckney in Paris in early October and all three were unofficially received by Foreign Minister Charles-Maurice de Talleyrand-Périgord on 8 October 1797. Ten days later they were visited by three secret agents of Talleyrand—who later became known anonymously as X, Y, and Z—who suggested a U.S. loan to France together with a $240,000 bribe. The American commissioners refused and eventually reported to their government. Meanwhile partisanship ran high in Philadelphia and there was more in store. On 4 March 1798, exactly one year after his inauguration, President Adams was apprised of the failure of the envoys' mission and of the slight they had suffered. He then urged defensive measures anew, as well as the enactment of new taxes, but he kept his head, despite his anger, and did not ask Congress for a declaration of war; nor did he reveal the XYZ episode, only informing Congress of the French refusal to receive the delegation officially. Hamilton was jubilant, even though Adams had not requested the creation of a provisional army that he advocated; Jefferson was appalled and believed war to be inevitable. Because the Republicans thought that Adams had deliberately painted a dark picture to persuade Congress to put the country on a war footing, they committed a major blunder by forcing him to divulge the contents of the dispatches. Adams complied and the ploy that was meant to expose the president's suspected duplicity backfired, the irony of it all being that the whole country was soon clamoring for war. The ensuing patriotic mood boosted Adams's popularity tremendously and ensured, between March and July 1798, the easy adoption by Congress of the Federalist defense program and even its strengthening beyond what the president had recommended, notably the tripling of the existing army and the creation in addition of a provisional army, should the fears of an invasion materialize. George Washington declared himself ready, if this happened, to serve as commanding general, but insisted on having the army placed under the active field direction of Alexander Hamilton, who was to be named inspector general, and second in command. A department of the Navy was established, an embargo was put on trade with France, and the Franco-American

---

[3]   John Ferling, *Adams vs. Jefferson: The Tumultuous Election of 1800* (New York: Oxford University Press, 2004), 102-104.

Alliance of 1778 was terminated. Congress further authorized the seizure of any French vessel that endangered American commerce, which was tantamount to an undeclared naval war.

The Republicans, who had been taken by surprise by the XYZ affair, were in a quandary; Jefferson hoped the Federalists would overreach themselves and John Adams tried not to be engulfed in the war fever maelstrom. The summer drama hit them both in different ways. The Ultra-Federalists struck with a vengeance: the Alien and Sedition Acts of June-July 1798 both targeted those radical European refugees who were Republican publicists and aimed at curtailing civil liberties; and more specifically at muzzling opposition newspapers by criminalizing any anti-government writing of a "false, scandalous and malicious nature." Jefferson knew the idea had been hatching since April at least:

> One of the war party, in a fit of unguarded passion, declared some time ago they would pass a citizen bill, an alien bill, and a sedition bill; accordingly, some days ago, Coit laid a motion on the table of the House of Representatives for modifying the citizen law. Their threats point at Gallatin, and it is believed they will endeavor to reach him by this bill. Yesterday Mr. Hillhouse laid on the table of the Senate a motion for giving power to send away suspected aliens. This is understood to be meant for Volney and Collot. But it will not stop there when it gets into a course of execution. There is now only wanting, to accomplish the whole declaration before mentioned, a sedition bill, which we shall certainly soon see proposed.[4]

The Naturalization Act (18 June) extended to fourteen years, instead of five, the required period of residence; the Alien Act (25 June) authorized the president to deport suspicious aliens in the name of public peace and safety; the Alien Enemies Act (July 6) authorized the president in time of declared war to arrest, imprison, or banish aliens subject to an enemy power. Worst of all because of its domestic implications, the Sedition Act, "An Act for the Punishment of Certain Crimes against the United States" (14 July) was the most oppressive of the four measures. Passed by the House of Representatives by a vote of 44 to 41, and signed into law by President Adams four days later, this Act made it a high misdemeanor punishable by a fine and by imprisonment

> 1) For "any persons [to] unlawfully combine or conspire together, with intent to oppose any measure or measures of the government of the United States, which are or shall be directed by proper authority, or to impede the operation of any law of the United States, or to intimidate or prevent any person holding a place or office in or under the government of the United States, from

---

[4]   Jefferson to James Madison, 26 April 1798, General Correspondence, 1651-1827, series 1, Thomas Jefferson Papers, Manuscript Division, Library of Congress, Washington, DC; John P. Foley, ed., *The Jeffersonian Cyclopedia: A Comprehensive Collection of the Views of Thomas Jefferson* (New York and London: Funk and Wagnells Company, 1900), quote no. 277, at http://etext.lib.virginia.edu/jefferson/.

undertaking, performing or executing his trust or duty"; for "any person or persons, with intent aforesaid, [to] counsel, advise or attempt to procure any insurrection, riot, unlawful assembly, or combination, whether such conspiracy, threatening, counsel, advice, or attempt shall have the proposed effect or not";

2) For "any person [to] write, print, utter or publish, or ... cause or procure to be written, printed, uttered or published, or ... knowingly and willingly assist or aid in writing, printing, uttering or publishing any false, scandalous and malicious writing or writings against the government of the United States, or either House of the Congress of the United States, or the President of the United States, with intent to defame the said government, or either house of the said Congress, or the said President, or to bring them, or either of them, into contempt or disrepute; or to excite against them, or either or any of them, the hatred of the good people of the United States, or to excite any unlawful combinations therein, for opposing or resisting any law of the United States, or any act of the President of the United States, done in pursuance of any such law, or of the powers in him vested by the constitution of the United States, or to resist, oppose, or defeat any such law or act, or to aid, encourage or abet any hostile designs of any foreign nation against the United States, their people or government, then such person, being thereof convicted before any court of the United States having jurisdiction thereof, shall be punished by a fine not exceeding two thousand dollars, and by imprisonment not exceeding two years.[5]

The Ultras had got out of control. The "Gag-bill," as Republicans labeled it, had not been requested by Adams, and he was powerless to stop it. Even Hamilton, fearing a backlash, had been unable to contain the Ultras.[6] "Unanimity" was the new catchword,[7] which echoed in a sense George Washington's insistence in his Farewell Address on "acquiescence" in the government's measures and "the duty of every Individual to obey the established Government," so that citizens were left only the freedom to obey.[8] Most Federalists, like James Lloyd who proposed the first draft of the Sedition Act, could not accept criticism of and opposition to the State, as if the party in power thought "there should be just one party, one truth, one foreign policy, and one notion of the common good—its own."[9] They believed or feigned to believe that their opponents sought to subvert constitutional government. "*He that is*

---

[5]   Ricard Peters, ed., *The Public States at Large of the United States of America* (Boston: Charles C. Little and James Brown, 1845), 5th Congress, 2nd Session, 1:566-568, 570-571, 577, 596.

[6]   Ferling, *Adams vs. Jefferson*, 111-112; Susan Dunn, *Jefferson's Second Revolution: The Election Crisis of 1800 and the Triumph of Republicanism* (Boston: Houghton, 2004), 105, 119.

[7]   Dunn, *Jefferson's Second Revolution*, 100, 310.

[8]   Ibid., 117-118, 314.

[9]   Ibid., 102.

not for us, is against us," warned Fenno's *Gazette of the United States.*[10] "I believe faction and Jacobinism," Wolcott wrote to Hamilton, "to be the natural and immortal enemies of our system." Many Ultra-Federalists made no bones about their ultimate goal and agreed with Theodore Sedgwick of Massachusetts that the war fever afforded "a glorious opportunity to destroy faction."[11] And what better way was there to suffocate the Republican Party and suppress its influence than to silence it by targeting its newspapers? In other words, as perceptively noted by James E. Lewis, Jr., "Men acted together in parties, but they did not accept the legitimacy of a party system."[12]

Ironically, despite allegations to the contrary, in the spring of 1798 only a quarter of the nation's papers supported the Republicans and few—Benjamin Franklin Bache's *Aurora*, the Boston *Independent Chronicle*, the New York *Journal*, the Vermont *Gazette*, and half a dozen others—took aggressive stands. True enough, some newspaper editors reveled in abusive ad hominem attacks, which by 1795 had become commonplace, but Hamilton's followers really had little to fear given the imbalance in their favor.[13] Few prominent Federalists opposed the Sedition Act, and when they did it was for the wrong reasons, as in the case of John Marshall who thought it useless or Sedgwick who thought it too mild. Basically, the law protected Federalists from opposition and enabled "one party to oppress the other," as perspicaciously noted by Albert Gallatin, the leader of the Republican opposition in the House.[14] Yet in doing so, as a despondent Jefferson remarked, they were emulating the French Jacobins that they hated and reproached Republicans for sympathizing with. Indeed, the Jacobins offered a model for political repression. The "purification" of the country, however, would be a bloodless one in the United States.[15] Adams for his part had changed his mind about freedom of speech and let partisanship get the better of him. Had he not back in 1770 given to the old *Boston Gazette* its motto, "*A Free Press maintains the Majesty of the People,*" and would he not in later years defend the constitutionality and salutariness of the Alien and Sedition Acts? Although historians disagree as to the extent of his responsibility, there is little doubt that he cooperated in the enforcement of the Alien and Sedition Acts, subsequently seen as a blot on his presidency, and that he was comfortable with them at the time inasmuch as they fettered those who in his eyes imperiled national security.[16]

---

[10] Ibid., 100; Ferling, *Adams vs. Jefferson*, 111. This quote may have inspired George W. Bush when he launched his "war on terror" after 9/11: "You're either with us or against us in the fight against terror," he declared on 6 November 2001, at http://archives.cnn.com/2001/US/11/06/gen.attack.on.terror.

[11] Dunn, *Jefferson's Second Revolution*, 104-105; Ferling, *Adams vs. Jefferson*, 111.

[12] Lewis, Jr., "What Is to Become of Our Government?" 22.

[13] Dunn, *Jefferson's Second Revolution*, 105; Frank L. Mott, *American Journalism: A History of Newspapers in the United States through 260 Years: 1690 to 1950*, rev. ed. (1941; repr., New York: Macmillan, 1950), 147-148.

[14] Dunn, *Jefferson's Second Revolution*, 107, 109.

[15] Ferling, *Adams vs. Jefferson* 112; Dunn, *Jefferson's Second Revolution*, 109.

[16] Dunn, *Jefferson's Second Revolution*, 108; Ferling, *Adams vs. Jefferson* 111.

Had the country gone berserk in the summer of 1798? How could it switch sympathies so quickly and turn violently Francophobe and anti-Republican so unexpectedly and unexplainably? Even Adams was puzzled by his own party's warmongering. Some Federalists even dreamt of using military force against America's alleged domestic enemies, the Republicans, those fifth columnists. Abigail Adams saw a "close connection between the Infernals of France & those in our own Bosoms."[17] Liberties were taken with the lexicon: political opposition became synonymous with anti-patriotism, sedition, subversion, and treason. "It is Patriotism to write in favor of our government," the *Columbian Centinel* thundered, "it is Sedition to write against it."[18] In retrospect the whole crisis looks like the first illustration of Richard Hofstadter's 1964 essay on "The Paranoid Style in American Politics."[19] Actually, Hofstadter traces this political pathology to the early history of the United States and finds it for example in the anti-Masonic movement of the 1790s:

> A suitable point of departure is the panic that broke out in some quarters at the end of the eighteenth century over the allegedly subversive activities of the Bavarian Illuminati. This panic, which came with the general Western reaction to the French Revolution, was heightened here by the response of certain reactionaries, mostly in New England and among the established clergy, to the rise of Jeffersonian democracy.[20]

One of his examples throws light on the volatile political climate of the times:

> In May 1798, a prominent minister of the Massachusetts Congregational establishment in Boston, Jedidiah Morse, delivered a timely sermon of great import to the young country, which was then sharply divided between Jeffersonians and Federalists, Francophiles and Anglophiles. After reading Robison, Morse was convinced that the United States too was the victim of a Jacobinical plot touched off by Illuminism, and that the country should be rallied to defend itself against the machinations of the international conspiracy. His warnings were heeded throughout New England wherever Federalists brooded about the rising tide of religious infidelity or Jeffersonian democracy.[21]

---

[17]   Dunn, *Jefferson's Second Revolution*, 101.

[18]   Ibid., 98-99, 101.

[19]   Cf. ibid., 101.

[20]   Richard Hofstadter, *The Paranoid Style in American Politics and Other Essays* (1965; repr., New York: Random-Vintage, 1967), 10. The original article was published as "The Paranoid Style in American Politics," *Harper's Magazine* (November 1964): 77-86.

[21]   Hofstadter, *The Paranoid Style in American Politics*, 13. According to Hofstadter, Americans first learnt of Illuminism through a book by John Robison, a well-known Scottish scientist. Ibid., 10-11.

Scholars are not of one mind about paranoia and the conspiracy fantasies. In view of some Federalists' calculating cynicism it may be argued that realpolitik was more likely than paranoia. Yet, there is also evidence that Adams and his party believed that "the Republicans were Jacobin conspirators seeking a French-style revolution in the United States" and that their rhetoric was "no mere scare tactics."[22]

Although Jefferson, despite his misgivings, remained imperturbable and unshakably optimistic throughout the crisis, he reflected gloomily on the turn of events, on what he regarded not only as an unconstitutional curtailment of individual freedom but also as a legislative offensive against his friends and supporters:

> They have brought into the lower House a sedition bill, which, among other enormities, undertakes to make printing certain matters criminal, though one of the amendments to the Constitution has so expressly taken religion, printing presses, &c. out of their coercion. Indeed this bill, and the alien bill are both so palpably in the teeth of the Constitution as to show they mean to pay no respect to it.[23]

In point of fact, he was personally targeted by the Sedition Act as vice president inasmuch as the president and various officials were to be protected from criticism, but *not* the vice president, who was left off the statute's list.[24] During the public debate while the sedition bill was being examined he was the butt of many Federalist attacks: he was the "Chief Juggler" and financial backer—which he was, indeed, and would continue to be for printers and indicted editors—behind the most important Republican newspapers,[25] "the grandest of all Villains," an "infernal Scoundrel," and a "traitor to his country." A number of Republicans, including Jefferson, feared that General Hamilton might be planning to use the army to enforce the Alien and Sedition Acts and possibly invade Virginia; given his ambition and love of glory, they thought he came dangerously close to resembling Napoleon, "our Buonaparte," as Jefferson put it. Interestingly, the Adamses also disliked and distrusted him. Abigail called him "a second Buonaparty" and her husband detected in him "a delirium of Ambition." Actually the second president joined his vice-president in nicknaming him "Caesar" in private.[26]

The witch-hunter in chief was Secretary of State Timothy Pickering. He was frustrated in his enforcement of the Alien Acts for curiously Adams was reluctant to sign orders of deportation. All in all Pickering banished only three Frenchmen, after

---

[22]   Dunn, *Jefferson's Second Revolution*, 104-105; Jeffrey L. Pasley, "1800 as a Revolution in Political Culture: Newspapers, Celebrations, Voting, and Democratization in the Early Republic," in Horn, Lewis, and Onuf, *The Revolution of 1800*, 122-123.

[23]   Jefferson to James Madison, 7 June 1798, Jefferson Papers; Foyley, *Jeffersonian Cyclopedia*, quote no. 278. Cf. Madison on the unconstitutionality of the Sedition Act in 1800 in Dunn, *Jefferson's Second Revolution*, 167.

[24]   R.B. Bernstein, *Thomas Jefferson* (2003; repr., New York: Oxford University Press Paperbacks, 2005), 124.

[25]   For example the New London *Bee* (Connecticut) or the *Albany Register*. Cf. Dunn, *Jefferson's Second Revolution*, 110-111.

[26]   Ferling, *Adams vs. Jefferson*, 110-111, 114-115.

they left the country! Under the Sedition Act, however, some twenty-five people were arrested and about fifteen were prosecuted—mostly Republican printers and editors, with a few silly cases involving isolated individuals. Many of those indicted were English or Irish refugees who, significantly, were also targeted by the Alien Acts, like the most famous of them all, William Duane, an English citizen born in America and brought up in Ireland. There were eleven trials resulting in ten convictions; fifteen if actions under the common law are included, of which eight concerned newspapers. About half a dozen leading Republican newspapers were attacked: the *Aurora* in Philadelphia, the *Argus* in New York, the *Independent Chronicle* of Boston, the Richmond *Examiner*, the *Vermont Gazette*, the *Bee* of New London, Connecticut. Most of the prosecutions occurred in Federalist New England. One of the first to be prosecuted was the *Aurora*'s editor, Benjamin Franklin Bache, Franklin's grandson, who died before he could be tried. Duane, his assistant, carried on the fight against the Alien and Sedition Acts, was the defendant in several libel actions, and twice avoided a prison sentence.[27] The most spectacular affair involved a colorful politician-journalist, Matthew Lyon of Vermont, founder of *The Scourge of Aristocracy and Repository of Important Political Truths*, best known for a riotous incident on the floor of the House of Representatives, who was indicted and imprisoned for libelous attacks on the president and reelected to Congress while in jail. With the exception of James Thomson Callender, who later turned against his former protector, Jefferson, and the scientist, lawyer, and publicist Dr. Thomas Cooper who accused John Adams of incompetence, the other prosecutions concerned lesser-known figures: Thomas Adams, Anthony Haswell, William Durell, Charles Holt, William Cobbett.[28]

Jefferson and Madison's counter-offensive during the summer of 1798 assumed the shape of a daring constitutional challenge, as befitted the ongoing drama of a usurpation of power by the national government. The two illustrious revolutionaries thus engaged in an attempt at "reclaiming the American Revolution," as William Watkins phrases it.[29] The Kentucky Resolves, passed by the state legislature on 16 November 1798 and 22 November and 3 December 1799, were initially drafted secretly by Thomas Jefferson himself, his authorship only coming to light confusedly some twenty-five years later; they constituted a condemnation of the Alien and Sedition Acts and a severe attack on the Federalists' broad interpretation of the Constitution, which aimed at extending the powers of the national government over the states. The first set of resolutions, introduced by John Breckinridge, declared that the Constitution merely established a compact between the states and that the federal government had no right to exercise powers that were not specifically delegated to it under the terms of the compact. It followed that, if the

---

[27]   Mott, *American Journalism*, 147-152; Dunn, *Jefferson's Second Revolution*, 112-116.

[28]   Mott, *American Journalism*, 149-152; Dunn, *Jefferson's Second Revolution*, 168-174. On the press of the new nation, the Federalist-Republican rivalry, the Sedition Act and the prosecutions under it, see also Michael Emery and Edwin Emery, with Nancy L. Roberts, *The Press and America: An Interpretive History of the Mass Media*, 8th ed. (1954; repr., Boston: Allyn and Bacon, 1996), 61-74.

[29]   William J. Watkins, Jr., *Reclaiming the American Revolution: The Kentucky and Virginia Resolutions and Their Legacy* (New York: Palgrave, 2004).

federal government were to assume such powers in violation of the Constitution, its acts under them would be unauthorized and therefore void. It was the right of the states and not of the federal government to determine the constitutionality of such acts. In the second set of resolutions the Kentucky legislature went one step further; it affirmed:

> That the several states who formed that instrument, being sovereign and independent, have the unquestionable right to judge of its infraction; and that a *nullification*, by those sovereignties, of all unauthorized acts done under color of that instrument, is the rightful remedy.[30]

Madison wrote the more moderate Virginia Resolutions of 24 December 1798, which did not contain the objectionable word "nullification," but "peremptorily" declared

> that in case of a deliberate, palpable, and dangerous exercise [by the federal government] of other powers, not granted by the said compact, the states who are parties thereto, have the right, and are in duty bound, to *interpose* for arresting the progress of the evil, and for maintaining within their respective limits, the authorities, rights and liberties appertaining to them.[31]

Much has been written on the subsequent use of the Jeffersonian concept and term "nullification" by later generations, notably the southern "nullifiers" and states' righters who claimed Jefferson as their progenitor in 1828. Recent scholarship does not rule out his hope of "overthrow[ing]" "the constitutional government of 1787-88" thanks to his "doctrine of state nullification," which accounts for his having "cloaked his authorship under a mantle of secrecy."[32] Yet, neither Jefferson nor Madison intended to offer a theory of nullification and interposition; rather, they wanted to protect the integrity of the First Amendment. Besides, the Kentuckians described themselves as "Faithful to the true principles of the federal union" and "unconscious of any designs to disturb the harmony of that Union" and the Virginians "most solemnly [declared] a warm attachment to the Union of the States."[33] Jefferson may have toyed with the idea of secession should the worse come to the worst, but he did not advocate it publicly. Still, what was at stake was the distribution and balance of powers between the federal government and the

---

[30]   My emphasis. Cf. Draft of the Kentucky Resolutions, October 1798; Final text of the Kentucky Resolutions: "Resolutions in General Assembly," 3 December 1799, at http://www.yale.edu/lawweb/avalon/alsedact.htm.

[31]   My emphasis. David B. Mattern et al., *The Papers of James Madison*, vol. 17 (31 March 1797-3 March 1801, with a Supplement, 22 January 1778-9 August 1795) (Charlottesville: University Press of Virginia, 1991), 185.

[32]   Ferling, *Adams vs. Jefferson*, 115.

[33]   Cf. Draft of the Kentucky Resolutions, October 1798; Final text of the Kentucky Resolutions: "Resolutions in General Assembly," 3 December 1799; and the Virginia Resolution, 1798, Agreed to by the Senate, 24 December 1798, at http://www.yale.edu/lawweb/avalon/alsedact.htm.

states. Understandably since the Sedition Act had "broken and changed the rules of the game," the Kentucky and Virginia Resolutions smacked of southern sectionalism and harked back to the Articles of Confederation and the alleged blessings of a weak national government.[34]

By the fall of 1798, as John Adams prepared to go back to Philadelphia, he had made up his mind not to declare war on France. He did not believe in a French invasion and did not wish to see Hamilton assume command of the army and be given an opportunity to indulge in martial histrionics, for example against Spanish Florida or against alleged conspirators below the Potomac, as was persistently rumored and as the general's secret correspondence showed. Adams's State of the Union address revealed a changed man, which did not escape Jefferson. The president knew both that Talleyrand had been throwing out feelers here and there with a view to resuming negotiations[35] and that the war fever had abated in the United States; he was also convinced that evil forces lurked within his own party. He decided to send an envoy to Paris forthwith without consulting his cabinet, which departed from his usual practice. His message to Congress on 18 February 1799, was a political bombshell that astounded and infuriated the Federalists, especially the Ultras who vented their "disgust." He announced he was sending William Vans Murray to France as a minister plenipotentiary. He eventually compromised slightly after a stormy meeting with his cabinet and prominent leaders of his party in Congress: he would add two more envoys—Chief Justice Oliver Ellsworth and North Carolina Governor William R. Davie—and wait for further assurance from Paris. He ordered them to sail in early August after hearing from Talleyrand and knowing in addition that a "parliamentary" coup d'état on 18 June 1799, had profoundly modified the Second Directory. They would not embark for Paris until 3 November, owing to the treacherous Pickering's dilatory tactics. Six days later (9 November or 18 Brumaire 1799), unbeknown to Adams, General Bonaparte staged a full-scale coup d'état and established a military dictatorship in France. The French Revolution was over.[36]

Napoleon's coup d'état, together with George Washington's death (14 December 1799), naturally fueled the political debate between Federalists and Republicans. Jefferson was labeled the "Jacobin First Consul" by the Federalist

---

[34]   Dunn, *Jefferson's Second Revolution*, 111-112.

[35]   One of his informants was Dr. George Logan, a Philadelphia Quaker, a prominent Republican, and a friend of Jefferson's, who had traveled privately to Paris in mid-June 1798 and had been received by Talleyrand. His visit to France (June-November 1798) and his diplomatic meddling precipitated the passing of the Logan Act of 30 January 1799 (originally enacted as 1 Stat. 613, now codified as 18 U.S.C. § 953), which made it a high misdemeanor subject to fine and imprisonment for any unauthorized citizen to carry on any correspondence or intercourse with a foreign government in any controversy in which the United States was engaged. Last amended in 1994, the Act is still on the statute books but there appears to have been no prosecutions under it in over two hundred years. I am indebted to Melvyn Stokes for drawing my attention to this subsequent "addition" to the Sedition Act.

[36]   Albert Soboul, *La Révolution française*, new rev. and enl. ed. (Paris: Gallimard, 1984), 502-504.

press while the vice president warned his followers against General Hamilton, the American "Buonaparte." Napoleon had become a bogey for both sides. Reaction to the political situation in France continued to be the telltale sign of ideologies. As a matter of fact, Federalists and Brumairians had a lot in common, their love of order and their intolerance for opposition. Jefferson, who was disappointed with the fate of revolution and republicanism in France and found nothing in Bonaparte to redeem his despotism, clearly distanced himself from his old French allies and friends.[37] The fact that the presidential election was only a year away both intensified electoral maneuvering and made politicking more strident. The Federalists and Republicans went to battle with diverging opinions on the legitimacy of "the voice of the people," the latter being more in tune with the democratic aspirations of the turn-of-the-century Americans, as the election of 1800 would show with the accession to the presidency of "the Friend of the People," Thomas Jefferson. By that time many "Republicans," as Jefferson liked to call his followers, "were already adding the adjective democratic and moving toward the later appellation Democrats."[38]

"The War of Words" was on.[39] The Sedition Act failed to hurt the Republican press significantly. New grass-roots papers sprang up all over the country, an estimated sixty-percent increase. Partisan newspaper networks thrived and derived part of their effectiveness from their decentralization.[40] They campaigned actively and vigorously and their zeal and energy in raising every issue imaginable was in stark contrast with Federalist passivity. Jefferson and his party appealed to small farmers and planters in the North and South, to northern workers, such as unskilled laborers, skilled tradesmen and small business owners, and to immigrants. The vice president did not really campaign, nor did he respond to Federalist attacks. He chose to rely on his friends for editorializing and pamphleteering. The Federalist papers tried to play by the new rules, as the Republicans were doing, by republishing from each other so as to make every issue or attack resonate throughout the country. They focused on Jefferson, the most potent enemy of their party, with an avalanche of accusations and aspersions of all kinds, like reviving the Mazzei letter controversy[41] or hinting that he lived with one of his female slaves at Monticello.[42] They resorted to unrelenting character assassination: he was a dangerous government theorist, a Jacobin bent on destroying American institutions and society, a hypocrite on

---

[37]   Dunn, *Jefferson's Second Revolution*, 127-129.

[38]   Ibid., 134-135, 141; Pasley, "1800 as a Revolution in Political Culture," 126.

[39]   Dunn, *Jefferson's Second Revolution*, 137-152.

[40]   Ibid., 140; Pasley, "1800 as a Revolution in Political Culture," 139, 142.

[41]   In a letter of 24 April 1796, to his old Italian friend Philip Mazzei, Jefferson had made disparaging comments about George Washington, a statement picked up in the American press a year later. See for example Bernstein, *Thomas Jefferson*, 120-121; Joseph J. Ellis, *American Sphinx: The Character of Thomas Jefferson* (1997; repr., New York: Vintage, 1998), 190-191.

[42]   Before the political journalist James T. Callender turned against his former hero and underwriter, and spread the story widely in September 1802, there had been rumors of a sexual relationship between Jefferson and one of his female slaves, Sally Hemings. Cf. Bernstein, *Thomas Jefferson*, 154-155; Ellis, *American Sphinx*, 259-262, see also 363-367 ("A Note on the Sally Hemings Scandal").

slavery, a deist, an atheist. Paradoxically and ironically, prosecutions under the Sedition Act were stepped up to hinder the Republicans' publication of their political opinions at a time when High Federalists like Pickering were showering abuse on their leader, John Adams. Actually, most notorious sedition cases took place in 1800, which gave the measure of the Federalists' vindictiveness and state of panic at the prospect of being ousted from power: James Callender's indictment for his articles in the Richmond *Examiner* and his trial, presided over by Associate Supreme Court Justice Samuel Chase; Charles Holt, editor of the New London *Bee*; William Duane, the editor of the *Aurora*, already prosecuted in 1798 and 1799 and by far the most persecuted of all newspaper editors.[43]

The Federalists defended their own record and conception of government but in doing so they unwittingly depicted an elitist, stratified society that they wished to perpetuate and revealed their aristocratic contempt for the lower classes, thus widening the gap between their party and the voting public to whom they increasingly appeared as "monocrats" and Anglophiles, hierarchy-prone royalists in the colonial mould. The Federalist Party, however, was on the brink of implosion; there was increasing evidence of a split between the Ultras that Adams had antagonized with his peace policy and those Federalists who supported him and shared his dislike and fear of Hamilton. After the party caucus that nominated Adams and Charles Cotesworth Pinckney as presidential and vice-presidential candidate in the spring of 1800, the president fired Secretary of War James McHenry and Secretary of State Timothy Pickering. Irate Federalists turned against him and made him a convenient scapegoat, even accusing him of collusion with Jefferson. Hamilton was out to draw blood: "My mind is made up. I will never more be responsible for [Adams] by my direct support, even though the consequences should be the election of Jefferson. If we must have an enemy at the head of the government, let it be one whom we can oppose, and for whom we are not responsible."[44] His fifty-four page *Letter from Alexander Hamilton Concerning the Public Conduct and Character of John Adams*, published in October, should logically have triggered against him a prosecution under the Sedition Act for attacking the president, as Thomas Cooper, who had just served a jail sentence for criticizing Adams, publicly underlined in an attempt to demonstrate that only Republicans were punishable under that law.[45]

The Republican caucus nominated Thomas Jefferson and Aaron Burr as their standard-bearers but, unlike the Federalists, indicated the party's choice as president (Jefferson) and vice-president (Burr) for the benefit of the electors. The campaign was to show how efficient and deft the Republicans had become at using the press to their advantage and at communicating with the voting public within a more democratic context that paid greater heed to the rank and file. Committees of correspondence, societies, and clubs were created to disseminate their literature. Only eighteen Republican newspapers existed in 1795, which amounted to about 14 percent of the nation's total number of papers; in 1798 they constituted almost 30

---

43   Dunn, *Jefferson's Second Revolution*, 164-174.
44   Ibid., 161-162; Ferling, *Adams vs. Jefferson*, 141.
45   Dunn, *Jefferson's Second Revolution*, 163-164.

percent of the country's print media. The Sedition Act interestingly turned out to be a counter-productive measure in that it achieved the reverse of the intended result: paradoxically, it boosted the opposition press instead of blocking its growth, so much so that by 1800 Republican papers represented about 40 percent of the partisan organs in the United States. Contrary to what many Federalists thought, there was no centralized coordination of the campaign. The Alien and Sedition laws became a powerful anti-Federalist argument and plotting Hamilton a favorite target, on account notably of his economic policies. Another major issue was the increase of direct taxes that resulted from the heavy defense expenditures.[46]

On Election Day (3 November) the presidential electors were to meet "in their respective States, and vote by Ballot for two Persons, of whom one at least shall not be an Inhabitant of the same State with themselves." The Electoral College ballots were not to be officially counted until 11 February, but rumors about the outcome quickly spread and on 12 December the *National Intelligencer* in Washington, basing its scoop on reports from thirteen of the sixteen states, announced: "Mr. Jefferson may, therefore, be considered our future president."[47] The final count was given by several newspapers before Christmas: Jefferson and Burr tied at 73 votes each; 65 for Adams; 64 for Pinckney; 1 for John Jay. The election would therefore be thrown into the Federalist-dominated House of Representatives.

The House of Representatives convened for a momentous session on 11 February 1801, which would last seven days on end; but the previous weeks, after the returns were unofficially printed, had been most eventful, replete with behind-the-scene negotiations in and between both camps. The suspense ended on 17 February. On the thirty-sixth ballot Jefferson was chosen president by ten states, each having one vote, and Burr was elected vice-president.[48] The third president ever after denied having struck a deal with the Federalists but several scholars believe that the once unreliable evidence "suggests otherwise" today.[49] As Joanne B. Freeman convincingly puts it, when approached by the go-between Samuel Smith, a friend of his, "Jefferson took advantage of the blurred bounds between politicking and socializing to make an official statement by unofficial means."[50] The Federalists had decided reluctantly to turn over power peacefully to their opponents instead of prolonging the deadlock. During the interregnum they never thought of extending the Alien and Sedition Acts, and the controversial measures that had partly caused their downfall were left to expire on 4 March 1801. They did, however, enact the Judiciary Act of 13 February 1801.

Some twenty years later, in a letter of September 1819 to the Virginia jurist and essayist Spencer Roane, Jefferson would refer to his election as "the Revolution of 1800." He claimed that it was "as real a revolution in the principles of our

---

[46]   Ferling, *Adams vs. Jefferson*, 144-147.
[47]   Ibid., 163.
[48]   Ibid., 175-193; Dunn, *Jefferson's Second Revolution*, 191-217.
[49]   Cf. Richard B. Morris, ed., *Encyclopedia of American History*, 6th ed. (1953; repr., New York: Harper, 1982), 157; Ferling, *Adams vs. Jefferson*, 193-196; Joanne B. Freeman, "Corruption and Compromise in the Election of 1800: The Process of Politics on the National Stage," in Horn, Lewis, and Onuf, *The Revolution of 1800*, 109-111.
[50]   Freeman, "Corruption and Compromise in the Election of 1800," 111.

government as that of 1776 was in its form,"[51] which many of his contemporaries failed to see in that light. Beyond its exaggeration and immodesty, Jefferson's statement is far from absurd. The election of 1800 to a great extent heralded a democratic revolution that worried such conservatives as Gouverneur Morris or Fisher Ames.[52] The transfer of power had taken place in perfect conformity with the constitutional procedures. But the preliminaries had not been that peaceful. Admittedly, on neither side was there a plunge into extremism. Indeed the Federalists were the first political incumbents in modern history to hand over power to their political adversaries. Yet even if verbal attacks did not translate into physical aggression, there was a lot of pent-up violence, and menacing rumors of a resort to arms were rife from mid-December 1800 to mid-February 1801.[53]

In the end, despite the turbulences, the Americans of 1800 witnessed the triumph of orderly government. The Constitution had survived a major crisis. Both sides had agreed to abide by the constitutional rules; neither had tried to crush the other. The election had not taken a revolutionary turn because enough men in both parties had been committed to the Constitution and the Union.[54] Many during those weeks of uncertainty had deplored the failure of the Framers of the Constitution to foresee and prevent the potential problem in their system for choosing the president and vice-president. The Twelfth Amendment of 1804 would aim at avoiding the difficulty that had appeared in 1796 and 1800 by providing for separate ballots for president and vice-president.[55] The so-called "Revolution of 1800" also had a rich and enduring legacy. Its aftermath includes notably the spread of popular voting in presidential elections—i.e., the choice of electors by popular vote—which ushered in the age of the Common Man in the 1820s, as well as the advent and development of newspaper politics. Ironically this trend led the former proponents of sedition laws to champion freedom of the press, and a "ferociously partisan" Republican president to recommend "a few prosecutions" in state courts in order to suppress "the overwhelming torrent of slander."[56] Thus the Republican revolution had come full circle.

---

[51] Jefferson to Spencer Roane, 6 September 1819, Jefferson Papers, *op. cit.* Cf. Ferling, *Adams vs. Jefferson*, 208; Dunn, *Jefferson's Second Revolution*, 273-274.
[52] Ferling, *Adams vs. Jefferson*, 209-210; Dunn, *Jefferson's Second Revolution*, 231.
[53] Dunn, *Jefferson's Second Revolution*, 206-207, 209-210, 212, 214-215; Ferling, *Adams vs. Jefferson*, 181, 188-189.
[54] Lewis, Jr., "What Is to Become of Our Government?" 10, 16, 20, 23-24; Michael A. Bellesiles, "'The Soil Will Be Soaked with Blood': Taking the Revolution of 1800 Seriously," in Horn, Lewis, and Onuf, *The Revolution of 1800*, 79-80; Pasley, "1800 as a Revolution in Political Culture," 123-124.
[55] Lewis, Jr., "What Is to Become of Our Government?" 22.
[56] Pasley, "1800 as a Revolution in Political Culture," 127, 136, 138; Freeman, "Corruption and Compromise in the Election of 1800," 111-114; Dunn, *Jefferson's Second Revolution*, 234-235.

REPRESSION AND EXCLUSION
AS KEYS TO LIBERTY AND DEMOCRACY:
THE POLITICAL THOUGHT OF JAMES FENIMORE COOPER

Thomas Clark

Introduction

Behind every discussion of democracy and political repression in American history there looms a question both eminently political and absolutely fundamental to one's understanding of the United States: is political repression an unfortunate, corrigible aberration from American democracy, or is it its systemically inherent product? A case study of a single nineteenth-century mind can certainly not pretend to furnish an exhaustive answer. However, James Fenimore Cooper's socio-political thought is particularly suitable for exploring the connections between what I have expanded into a conceptual foursome: liberty and repression, democracy and exclusion.[1] The title of this essay summarizes my conclusion on where he stands. It remains to present the evidence, explain the apparent paradox and consider the implications of Cooper's thought for a broader view of American democracy.

There are two sides to Cooper. There is the novelist, America's "first maker of its myths," the "dreamer of its national dream," chronicler of the frontier as the cauldron from whose virtue, heroism, and violence American identity was wrought.[2] Cooper's stories were inevitably and indeed explicitly bound up with questions of power and repression that form the history of American colonial and national expansion.[3] So deeply embedded are they in his narratives, that scholars cannot agree on where Cooper actually stood on them. Thus Leslie Fiedler concludes that his attitudes were "racist, sexist and anti-democratic; based on an ethnocentric, culturally imperialist and hierarchal view of society,"[4] a fanfare, in other words, of a starkly repressive American regime. In contrast Allan M. Axelrad and others argue that Cooper's work is anti-racist and multi-culturalist, i.e. non-repressive, critically reflecting rather than endorsing the deficiencies of American liberty.[5]

---

[1] I find this division useful as a means of differentiating between two key American forms of repression on which I will be focusing in my discussion of Cooper: slavery as the ultimate form of depriving a person of liberty, and exclusion from political power, which in the context of a participatory democracy constitutes a severe form of repression, as it deprives its victims of the central means of defending or asserting their other civil liberties and interests in society.

[2] Leslie A. Fiedler, *Love and Death in the American Novel*, rev. ed. (New York: Stein and Day, 1966), 190, 87.

[3] See John P. McWilliams, *Political Justice in a Republic: James Fenimore Cooper's America* (Berkeley: University of California Press, 1972).

[4] Leslie A. Fiedler, "James Fenimore Cooper: The Problem of the Good Bad Writer," James Fenimore Cooper Society, at http://external.oneonta.edu/cooper/articles/suny/1979suny-fiedler.html.

[5] Allan M. Axelrad, "The Last of the Mohicans and the Holocaust," in Hugh C. MacDougall, ed., *James Fenimore Cooper: His Country and His Art*, Cooper Seminar

Either way Cooper's fiction confirms the narrow limits and the deeply problematic nature of nineteenth-century U.S. democracy, but its ambiguity precludes a clear identification of his own ideas, which interest us here. For this purpose we must look at Cooper the public intellectual and author of political tracts, from whence his positions emanate quite clearly. At first he may not seem a representative choice through which to study the issue of democracy and repression in antebellum America: as a social conservative who hated the Whig Party, a nativist who avidly supported Jackson, a classical republican in the age of white mass democracy he resists easy ideological compartmentalization. But the elements that make up his idiosyncratic mental map actually provide an ideal case study of how repression and exclusion could coexist with liberty and democracy in one mind. Cooper was a dedicated civil libertarian, who, from his personal experience of being hounded by the Whig press,[6] strenuously insisted on the protection of minorities against majority tyranny. He was also an ardent supporter of a Jeffersonian-style democracy. At the same time Cooper combined a Whig dislike of immigrants with a Jacksonian callousness about the oppression of African Americans. The first led him to argue for a partial disfranchisement of what he considered unqualified citizens, the second to downplaying, against his own better judgment, the discrimination of free blacks, and to defending the institution of slavery. Moreover, Cooper held these positions on what he considered an entirely pragmatic, realistic and constitutionally sound basis. Rejecting notions of American exceptionalism and patriotic cant, he considered himself a cosmopolitan voice of reason among provincial demagogues, explaining the simple facts of life to American citizens.

Attempting to explain what appears to be a set of glaring contradictions takes us back to the initial question of whether exclusion and repression are accidental or essential properties of American democracy. The former position has most prominently been taken by the liberal school of political science and historiography beginning with Tocqueville, epitomized by Louis Hartz's *The Liberal Tradition in America* and shaping the social sciences to this day.[7] Arguing that the United States

---

Papers (Oneonta: State University of New York College at Oneonta, 2001), 7-16. For other views of Cooper as a racist, see Therman B. O'Daniel, "Cooper's Treatment of the Negro," *Phylon* 8.2 (1947): 164-176 and Robert D. Madison, "'Gib a Nigger Fair Play': Cooper, Slavery, and the Spirit of the Fair," in George A. Test, ed., *James Fenimore Cooper: His Country and His Art* (Oneonta and Cooperstown: State University of New York College, 1991), 37-47; Nadesan Permaul, "James Fenimore Cooper and the American National Myth," *James Fenimore Cooper Society Miscellaneous Papers* 23 (2006): 7-16. For Cooper as a keen observer of the complexities of race, an anti-racist, or early multiculturalist, see Kay Seymour House, *Cooper's Americans* (Columbus: Ohio State University Press, 1966); James D. Wallace, "Cooper and Slavery," at http://external.oneonta.edu/cooper/articles/ala/1992ala-wallace.html; J. Gregory Harding, "'Without Distinction of Sex, Rank, or Color': Cora Munro as Cooper's Ideal and the Moral Center in *The Last of the Mohicans*," in MacDougall, *James Fenimore Cooper*, 36-40.

[6]   See Dorothy Waples, *The Whig Myth of James Fenimore Cooper* (London: Yale University Press, 1938).

[7]   See Rogers M. Smith, "Beyond Tocqueville, Myrdal, and Hartz: The Multiple Traditions in America," *American Political Science Review* 87.3 (1993): 549 and "The

is and always has been an embodiment of a liberal democratic paradigm based on principles of liberty, equal rights and universal suffrage required deviations from this political monoculture to be sidelined as temporary aberrations. This endearing and enduring myth has been challenged from numerous perspectives and I would like to name three of them here which are central to understanding Cooper.

The first follows Rogers Smith in arguing that there has always been a considerable plurality of political ideologies in America rather than liberal hegemony; that among these have been several ascriptive theories of inequality and exclusion, such as coherent theories of racism and gender or class inequality. These ideologies theoretically argued for and legitimized in practice the political exclusion and oppression of large segments of the population, not from an anti- or undemocratic perspective, but, strangely blended with liberal principles, in the name of white, male or virtuous democracy.[8] As a classical republican, Cooper deeply believed both in human inequality and in the need to inscribe it into a democratic political order.

The second, closely related argument, picks up on Edmund Morgan's great study *American Slavery, American Freedom: The Ordeal of Colonial Virginia*. In this 1975 classic, Morgan argued that what enabled southern gentlemen to become fervent democrats in the first place, was that their laboring underclass was securely bondaged and racially branded and thus safely and permanently excluded from the political sphere.[9] The conviction that democracy required exclusion was shared by New England elites, which had great difficulties, however, in circumscribing their unqualified underclass, mainly resorting to property qualifications. This logic has consistently resurfaced in American society, as during the Progressive Era, where demands for democratic reform went hand in hand with attempts to eliminate unsuitable subjects, particularly recent immigrants, from the citizenry.[10] Interestingly, the liberal Gunnar Myrdal himself had already pointed out that democratic egalitarianism could lead to a reinforcement of racism as a necessary means of justifying exclusion and oppression while maintaining democratic ideals, just as easily as to the questioning of evident inequalities.[11] Cooper fits this mold, as he excused both slavery and the repression of free blacks by emphasizing African Americans' inferiority.

The third argument concerns the paradox in American political thought of locating the essence of the American nation in its democratic and constitutional character and then compromising democracy and constitutional rights in the name of preserving the nation's integrity. Throughout its history real or imagined threats to American security, identity and interests have been answered by curtailing civil

---

'American Creed' and American Identity: The Limits of Liberal Citizenship in the United States," *Western Political Quarterly* 41.2 (1988): 225-240.

8   Smith, "Beyond Tocqueville, Myrdal, and Hartz," 549-550.

9   Edmund Sears Morgan, *American Slavery, American Freedom: The Ordeal of Colonial Virginia* (New York: Norton, 1975), 380-381.

10   Thomas Goebel, *A Government by the People: Direct Democracy in America, 1890-1940* (Chapel Hill: University of North Carolina Press, 2002), 59.

11   Colin Wayne Leach, "Democracy's Dilemma: Explaining Racial Inequality in Egalitarian Societies," *Sociological Forum* 17.4 (2002): 681-696.

rights: beginning with the constitutional founding which its supporters considered essential to the nation's survival, but which could only be achieved through the compromise on slavery; and continued with the Alien and Sedition Acts; the removal of unassimilated native Americans whose land was required to maintain an agrarian republic, the persecutions of World War I, the post-World War I and World War II Red Scares, the internment of Japanese Americans in World War II, and the Patriot Act of recent date, just to name the well-known examples. To put it provocatively: no one with a knowledge of U.S. history should be surprised at blatant violations of civil rights and the repression—sometimes subtle, sometimes brutal—of certain population groups identified more or less directly as a political threat to American security or a cultural threat to American identity, as they are part of how U.S. society has worked since 1776.[12] Cooper is part of this tradition in two ways: as a paranoid nativist who considered immigrants to be dangerous subversives, and by believing that tolerating slavery was essential to preserving the union. The paradox is explained, then, by the fact that Cooper felt empowered to conveniently designate in- and outgroups and was willing to sacrifice the liberty and rights of the latter for the security and freedom of the former. This is precisely the logic that has governed the Bush administration's post-9/11 policy, which thus turns out to have a notable pedigree.

I will begin my survey of how these strands contribute to the formation of Cooper's democratic ideology by discussing his emphasis on individual rights. I will then contrast this with his views on degraded citizens and his view of free and enslaved African Americans. My conclusion from this examination will be that what made it possible for Cooper to see repression and exclusion as keys to liberty and democracy was the combined belief in the inequality of humans and a paranoid fear of America's corruption by sinister forces, convictions deeply rooted in the American mainstream.

Liberty, Inequality and the Dangerous Citizen

Cooper viewed individual rights as the key legacy of the American Revolution. "The end of liberty," he declaimed "is the happiness of man, and its means, that of leaving the greatest possible personal freedom of action, that comports with the general good."[13] Government provided a framework, essentially to protect the weak from the strong, within which individuals equipped with equal rights were free to pursue their

---

[12]   "Rather than being an exception, war-era violations of civil liberties in the United States are the accepted norm of government." Michael Linfield, *Freedom under Fire: U.S. Civil Liberties in Times of War* (Boston: South End Press, 1990), 2. On civil liberties in wartime, see Geoffrey R. Stone, *Perilous Times: Free Speech in Wartime from the Sedition Act of 1798 to the War on Terrorism* (New York: W.W. Norton & Co., 2004). On western expansion as driven by republican anxieties, see Thomas R. Hietala, *Manifest Design: Anxious Aggrandizement in Late Jacksonian America* (Ithaca, NY: Cornell University Press, 1985).

[13]   James Fenimore Cooper, *The American Democrat: Or, Hints on the Social and Civic Relations of the United States of America* (New York: Vintage Books, 1956), 147.

self-interest in agreement with the laws of nature. In stark contrast to Tocqueville's thesis of American equality Cooper viewed inequality as the necessary result of this process:

> By possessing the same rights to exercise their respective faculties, the active and frugal become more wealthy than the idle and dissolute; the wise and gifted more trusted than the silly and ignorant; the polished and refined more respected and sought, than the rude and vulgar.[14]

Contrary to the artificial inequality of European feudalism American inequality was the natural result of virtue and talent asserting themselves under conditions of equal opportunity: "In order not to interfere with the inequality of nature, her laws must be left to their own operations, which is just what is done in democracies."[15]

Now, where Cooper wholeheartedly agreed with Tocqueville, was in the major threat to this form of liberty: the tyranny of a majority striving to create a false, unnatural conformity and depriving minorities of their rights.[16] Cooper rejected the majoritarian ideology of Jacksonians such as George Bancroft, who argued that *vox populi* was *vox dei* and he warned of the effects of public opinion in democracies: It caused men to conceal unpopular beliefs, because of its power to effectively ostracize dissidents, sentencing them to what amounted to social death. From this perspective Cooper came to see constitutions and institutions such as the judiciary not as products of the popular will, but rather as bulwarks against the tyranny of the majority:

> It ought to be impressed on every man's mind, in letters of brass, *"That in a democracy, the publick has no power that is not expressly conceded by the institutions, and that this power, moreover, is only to be used under the forms prescribed by the constitution. All beyond this, is oppression...."*[17]

Cooper sounds very much the libertarian in defending the rights of the individual or minority groups against overbearing majorities, and he sees government as strictly limited except where it functions as a protector and enforcer of fundamental rights superior to positive law. But the very distrust of the people that fueled his argument, together with his classical republican belief in different levels of virtue and talent is what led him to argue for the disfranchisement of citizens whose votes might corrode the edifice of American government. Admittedly, this was a difficult argument for Cooper to make, because as a good Jeffersonian he rejected the stake-in-society argument, whereby political virtue was simply equated with a certain amount of property which gave a voter a genuine interest in the government protecting it, while excluding idle ne'er-do-wells.[18] Nevertheless Cooper viewed the

---

[14]   Ibid., 78.
[15]   Ibid.
[16]   Ibid., 49.
[17]   Ibid., 145.
[18]   Ibid., 139.

suffrage not so much as a right than as a privilege to be earned. In *Notions of the Americans* he approvingly cited the example of the Connecticut citizen, who

> understands that all who have reached a certain standard of qualification, shall be equal in power and that all others shall be equal in protection. He does not give political power to the pauper, nor to females, nor to minors, nor to idiots, nor even to his priests. All he aims at is justice; and in order to do justice, he gives political rights to all those who, he thinks, can use them without abuse.[19]

In his 1838 tract on U.S. government and society, *The American Democrat*, Cooper confirmed his classical republican conviction that "[t]he elector who gives his vote, on any grounds, party or personal, to an unworthy candidate violates a sacred publick duty, and is unfit to be a freeman."[20] The right to vote, in other words, was contingent upon voting right. On this basis Cooper proposed disfranchising "the dissolute, unsettled, vicious and disorganizing," as he labeled them, on the municipal level. Vagrants or transient laborers had no business in the affairs of towns they drifted through, but could exert a dangerous influence as voters, such as tipping the balance in favor of electing a tavern keeper rather than the local gentleman into office.[21]

The most dangerous and easily identifiable unreliable citizens were the increasing numbers of non-English immigrants, whom Cooper considered aliens to democratic principles. Thomas Gladsky has shown that while immigration was never a prominent theme in Cooper's writings, they are suffused with a nativist subtext associating the foreign-born with crime, ignorance and the disorders of mass democracy.[22] One of his most explicit comments on the danger of immigrants is a passage from *The American Democrat* discussing universal suffrage, which Cooper claimed was made "doubly oppressive" to established citizens of those cities where immigrants were concentrated and thus exercised considerable political clout. Marked by the "prejudices of another and an antagonist state of society" they were men "who have few convictions of liberty beyond those which arise from a love of licentiousness, who are totally ignorant of its governing principles, and who, in their hearts and language, are hostile to the very people whose hospitality they enjoy."[23] Cooper disapproved that "principal places" in America were already under the control of such ignorant antidemocratic forces and he concluded that "[w]hatever may be said, on general principles, of the necessity of giving to a government the broadest possible base, few will contend that circumstances like these, ought not to qualify the regulation in practice."[24] In other words, he was arguing for the necessity

---

[19]   James Fenimore Cooper, *Notions of the Americans: Picked Up by a Travelling Bachelor*, 2 vols. (New York: Ungar, 1963), 2:265-266.

[20]   Cooper, *American Democrat*, 85.

[21]   Ibid., 140-141.

[22]   Thomas S. Gladsky, "Cooper's Other Americans: Cultural Diversity and American Homogeneity," James Fenimore Cooper Society, at http://external.oneonta.edu/cooper/articles/ala/1992ala-gladsky.html.

[23]   Cooper, *American Democrat*, 141.

[24]   Ibid.

of disfranchising citizens insufficiently Americanized by ascribing to them an inability to understand and a marked hostility towards democratic government.

But there was an even more sinister dimension to the immigrant threat: in an unpublished fragment, written while he was living in France,[25] Cooper described a conspiracy of European powers that was trying to destabilize the United States by virtue of systematically infecting it with antidemocratic ideologies such as Roman Catholicism. Democratic America and aristocratic Europe were involved in what amounted to a Cold War to which Americans were not paying sufficient attention. "The American who has had any circulation in the higher classes of European society, and who has not detected the strong desire to see our institutions overturned, and our growing power checked, must have travelled morally blindfolded," Cooper asserted. "[C]onverting us all to the Romish church, was the favourite project of the day," as this would undermine America's moral independence. Cooper was so convinced of the threat of fifth-column activity that "whenever I shall find a wide-spread tendency to rioting and disorder in America, I shall not be able to avoid the suspicion, that it proceeds, in reality, from the acts of those who wish to bring popular government into disrepute."[26] The Catholic immigrant was thus promoted to the level of a major national security risk, a pawn in an epochal struggle between powers and ideologies, which made his mere disfranchisement seem almost benevolent.

To summarize: The greatest risk to liberty and democratic government was the people at large in the shape of a tyrannical and ignorant majority. One way of defusing that danger was to increase the people's reliability by excluding hazardous elements from the body politic, especially where they were functioning as the agents of hostile foreign powers. Threats to American national security and to democracy as Cooper understood it required political repression in the form of excluding potentially dangerous citizens from the key power of the suffrage. Cooper's predisposition towards exclusionary measures was, however, checked by his belief in the necessity of equal rights, which is why he limited himself to calling for disfranchising unsuitable voters at the municipal level and never elaborated on how the principally legitimate exclusion of "citizen-immigrants" was to be practically addressed. Such reservations disappeared when Cooper discussed the situation of free blacks and slaves.

The Exclusion and Repression of African Americans

Whiggish as his attitudes about mass democracy and immigrants appear (though Cooper supported Jackson and actually considered the Whigs a dangerous commercial aristocracy), he did not share their relative compassion for the fate of

---

[25]   Nothing is known about this document, seemingly a letter, but the fact that in it he refers to Europe as "here" and bases his remarks on a conversation with a M. Cuvier and European dignitaries suggests it was written in France.

[26]   James F. Cooper, "[European Conspiracy]," in *James Fenimore Cooper Papers at the American Antiquarian Society* (Worcester, MA: n.d.).

blacks.[27] However, he also refused to follow the trend towards an ever more elaborated biological racism, which southern slaveholders in particular developed as a means of justifying and ultimately celebrating their "Herrenvolk democracy."[28] Cooper considered slavery "an evil,"[29] but rather than extending his libertarian views on majority tyranny into a call for abolition, or at least for black enfranchisement in the North, what led him to legitimize the political repression of free blacks and the total oppression of slaveswas a combination of factors:

- his classical republican belief in the inevitability of inequalities and hierarchies, among which black inequality was just one of many.
- his conservative fear of majorities threatening property rights, which extended to supporting the property rights of slaveholders over the natural rights of slaves.
- the fact that it was the national consensus on tolerating slavery which alone preserved the union and its constitutional order and thereby safeguarded the United States against its foreign and domestic enemies.
- the ability, shared with many whites, of lying to himself and to others about the actual conditions of African Americans both free and enslaved.

As in the case of immigrants, the ascription of inequality and inferiority combined with the deep-seated fear of a threat to American democracy and national security provided the rationale for exclusion and repression, only on a far more sinister scale.

---

[27] The—comparatively—sympathetic Whig attitude towards African Americans was grounded both in the anti-slavery stance of Whigs, as in the fact that blacks in the North traditionally voted Federalist/Whig, as they (rightly) viewed Republicans/Democrats as the party of slavery. However Whigs were split on the issue of how vocally to fend for free blacks and slaves between idealist "conscience" and pragmatic "cotton" Whigs. See Michael F. Holt, *The Rise and Fall of the American Whig Party: Jacksonian Politics and the Onset of the Civil War* (New York: Oxford University Press, 1999). Marvin Meyers first made the point that Jacksonianism contained a nostalgically anxious component reflecting a deep concern over preserving old republican values. Cooper is virtually the ideal type of a classical republican Jacksonian, a "venturous conservative," whose social conservatism and static social theory is deeply entangled with the shifting fortunes of his family and his own literary entrepreneurship. Cf. Marvin Meyers, "The Jacksonian Persuasion," *American Quarterly* 5.1 (1953): 3-15, Harry L. Watson, "The Venturous Conservative Reconsidered: Social History and Political Culture in the Market Revolution," *Reviews in American History* 22.4 (1994): 732-740.

[28] George M. Fredrickson in particular has argued that full-blown biological racism in the United States emerged in the antebellum era, though there is by no means a consensus on the issue. See Michael Tadman, "Class and the Construction of 'Race': White Racism in the American South," in Melvyn Stokes, ed., *The State of U.S. History* (Oxford, UK and New York: Berg, 2002), 328-31. For the southern United States as a "Herrenvolk democracy," see Kenneth P. Vickery, "'Herrenvolk' Democracy and Egalitarianism in South Africa and the U.S. South," *Comparative Studies in Society and History* 16.3 (1974): 309-328.

[29] Cooper, *American Democrat*, 173.

Contrary to egalitarian democrats, Cooper did not require biological racism as an ideological crutch to justify the exclusion and oppression of blacks. As a classical republican, he was comfortable with the idea that various forms of inequality, including slavery, pervaded even a democracy. Yet while his comments on African Americans emphasized the contextual causes of their supposed depravity, he framed the hierarchy between white and black as static and nearly unbridgeable. Of free blacks he said: "Without doubt most of them are ignorant and stupid, but it is the chance of their condition, as poor men and brought up in unfortunate circumstances."[30] Explaining the decrease in New York state's black population he argued:

> One must remember how few marriages take place among these people; their moral condition, their vagrant habits, their exposure, their dirt, and all the accumulated misfortunes of their race.

> I think it is quite fair to infer, from these statements, that freedom is not favourable to the continuation of the blacks while society exists under the influence of its present prejudices."[31]

A few sentences further he concluded that "[t]here is no doubt that the free blacks, like the aborigines, gradually disappear before the superior moral and physical influence of the whites,"[32] a superiority which, as he himself suggested, was not natural, but the product of white prejudice and power. Yet this state of affairs did not appear to him to constitute a scandalous oppression of a helpless minority by an unchecked majority tyranny. In fact, when defending the United States against the Swiss economist Sismondi's accusations of racism, he claimed: "In the free states the black is emphatically a free man. He enjoys all the rights of the white, with some slight exemptions...."[33] Cooper, writing in 1827, failed to mention that free blacks were being systematically excluded from the most fundamental civil right in a democracy: the suffrage. New Jersey, Maryland and Connecticut had disfranchised them before 1820 and all free states admitted to the Union after 1818 restricted the vote to white males.[34] In 1821, Cooper's own state of New York gave itself a constitution containing a $250 property requirement exclusively for African Americans, which in the 1825 election kept 29,403 out of 29,701 free blacks from the polls.[35]

---

[30]   James Fenimore Cooper and Robert E. Spiller, "Fenimore Cooper's Defense of Slave-Owning America," *American Historical Review* 35.3 (1930): 577.

[31]   Cooper, *Notions*, 1:285.

[32]   Ibid., 1:286.

[33]   Cooper and Spiller, "Fenimore Cooper's Defense," 579-580.

[34]   Alexander Keyssar, *The Right to Vote: The Contested History of Democracy in the United States* (New York: Basic Books, 2000), 55.

[35]   Phyllis F. Field, *The Politics of Race in New York : The Struggle for Black Suffrage in the Civil War Era* (Ithaca, NY: Cornell University Press, 1982), 37; Horst Dippel, ed., "Constitution of New York (1821)" in *The Rise of Modern Constitutionalism, 1776-1849* (München: K.G. Saur Verlag, 2007), at http://www.modern-constitutions.de/nbu

In Cooper's 1823 novel *The Pioneers*, the free black character Brom utters the words "Gib a nigger fair play" four times, "making that appeal to the justice of his auditors, which the degraded condition of his caste so naturally suggested."[36] Though the novelist was at times able to capture the structural racism of Northern society and its effects on blacks with a keen eye, the political thinker turned a deaf ear to free blacks' demands for "fair play."[37] He was equally unmoved by the coexistence of slavery and democracy.

Concerned as Cooper was in most of his work with the question of how natural justice and natural rights could be converted into man-made civil laws that ordered society,[38] one might have expected him to follow his Enlightenment precepts to the point of problematizing the existence of slavery in a political order based on the divine and natural right to life, liberty and property (including ownership of one's self). Since he was not willing to resolve the paradox by declaring blacks to be non- or subhuman, it is not surprising that Cooper skirted the issue, instead piling up numerous explanations for why American slavery was tolerable, inevitable, and even necessary. In *The American Democrat* he resorted to history, claiming that slavery had always existed and would in all likelihood continue to do so, and to the argument that it was entirely compatible with Christian doctrine.[39] Echoing John Winthrop's explanation for the unequal distribution of wealth, Cooper opined that the master-slave relationship provided the opportunity "of exhibiting some of the mildest graces of the character."[40] Indeed, Cooper did not view slavery as detrimental to blacks. In conventional Eurocentric fashion he argued that slavery was a benefit, "there being little doubt that the African is, in nearly all respects, better off in servitude in this country, than when living in a state of barbarism at home."[41] Slavery thus did not violate the democratic state's obligation to protect the weak, but, in Cooper's view, actually fulfilled this maxim. While American slavery was "mild" and "physical suffering cannot properly be enumerated among its evils," slavery was, however, detrimental to whites inasmuch as the slaveholder's absolute dominance was morally corrupting. Cooper even conceded that the "abject submission" of slavery and the need to keep slaves ignorant to ensure their

---

[36] .php?page_id=02a1b5a86ff139471c0b1c57f23ac196&viewmode=pages&show_doc =US-NY-1821-11-10-en&position=9.

James Fenimore Cooper, "The Pioneers: Or, the Sources of the Susquehanna," ed. James D. Wallace (1823; repr., Oxford: Oxford University Press, 1999), 193-197.

[37] While Cooper was "the first major American novelist to make use of Negro characters" they were usually cardboard characters embodying racist clichés. Cf. O'Daniel, "Cooper's Treatment of the Negro," 164, 168-169. On the other hand, Cooper could have a black character chastise his white protagonist for the use of the word "nigger." Cf. Wayne Franklin, *James Fenimore Cooper: The Early Years* (New Haven: Yale University Press, 2007), 151. Wallace, "Cooper and Slavery" emphasizes Cooper's literary sensitivity to the violence inherent in slavery.

[38] Cf. McWilliams, *Political Justice in a Republic*, 1-31.

[39] Cooper, *American Democrat*, 171.

[40] John Winthrop, "A Model of Christian Charity," in Perry Miller, ed., *The American Puritans: Their Prose and Poetry* (Garden City, NY: Doubleday, 1956), 74; Cooper, *American Democrat*, 171.

[41] Cooper, *American Democrat*, 172.

subjection limited their "moral existence" and concluded that in practice, slavery was an "impolitic and vicious institution."[42] Yet the outrageous act of repression committed in denying human beings their liberty did not particularly phase the libertarian Cooper, who believed the evils of slavery were generally exaggerated. Not only did he consistently argue that European subjects suffered far more under the heels of their oligarchs,[43] but the supposed ignorance of slaves itself qualified their oppression, because "it is a question whether men feel very keenly, if at all, privations of the amount of which they know nothing."[44] In other words, the defense of one's liberty is only an issue to the extent that one is aware of and can appreciate liberty. This kind of reasoning is crucial to understanding Cooper, as it reveals an elitist particularism at the heart of his libertarian ideology. His primary concern was not the defense of universal liberties, but of the liberties of gentlemen-individualists such as himself, which he felt were threatened by the unthinking many and their misguided majoritarianism. When Cooper insisted that "individuality is the aim of political liberty,"[45] he was not so much defending the fundamental right to be different but merely asserting the status of cultural aristocrats vis-à-vis democratic levelers: "The pursuit of happiness is inseparable from the claims of individuality. To compel all to follow this object in the same manner, is to oppress all above the average tastes and information."[46] Those marked as different due to their ascribed *inferiority* had no choice but to grin and bear their oppression—though Cooper trod out the cliché that being "a light-hearted and laughing race" blacks could not possibly be suffering too harshly under slavery.[47]

Cooper also did his best to dissociate slavery from American democracy. In his reply to Sismondi he argued that slavery was the legacy of the European colonial powers who had introduced it to America, which was now stuck with it. He pointed to the abolition of slavery in the Northern states as part of a process that would end in the disappearance of the institution. While this last point may have been a credible argument in the 1780s, it was sheer self-delusion in 1827 and even more so in 1838, when slavery was rapidly expanding westward and determining sectional controversies accordingly.[48] But rather than anticipating a war over slavery between North and South, Cooper envisioned a future where, once emancipated, blacks would clash with whites in a "war of extermination" fueled by unquenchable racial hatred. Though he said nothing of the outcome of that war, one may reasonably assume he believed it would resolve the race question in favor of a white America, if only at the cost of an apocalyptic conflict.[49]

---

[42]   Ibid.

[43]   Ibid., 173, Cooper, *Notions*, 2:260; Cooper and Spiller, "Fenimore Cooper's Defense," 580.

[44]   Cooper, *American Democrat*, 173.

[45]   Ibid., 182.

[46]   Ibid., 183.

[47]   Cooper, *Notions*, 2:260. Cf. Cooper and Spiller, "Fenimore Cooper's Defense," 580.

[48]   Cf. Michael A. Morrison, *Slavery and the American West: The Eclipse of Manifest Destiny and the Coming of the Civil War* (Chapel Hill: University of North Carolina Press, 1997).

[49]   Cooper, *American Democrat*, 173.

While Cooper held out the promise of an end to slavery in some indefinite future, he was quick to point out the impossibility of immediate emancipation. The logic of excluding incompetent immigrants or depraved free blacks from the polity in order to protect democracy applied to slaves also:

> The profession of the southern man is unquestionably that of equal rights; and it is undeniable that he holds the black in slavery; but this does not involve quite so great an absurdity as one would at first imagine. ... is it not possible to assert a principle under acknowledged limitations? The black man in the southern States of the Union is not considered a citizen at all. It would not be safe to consider him a citizen, in a country of equal political rights, since he is far too ignorant, and must, for a generation at least, remain too ignorant, to exercise, with sufficient discretion, the privileges of a citizen in a free government. It would, if any thing, be more prudent for the Virginian and Carolinian to admit boys of twelve years of age to vote and legislate, than to admit their blacks, in their present moral condition, without having any reference to the danger of a personal dissension. Equal rights do not, in any part of America, imply a broad, general, and unequivocal equality.[50]

A further difficulty of quick emancipation was that slavery was an issue of the states over which the federal government had no control. Moreover, not even a state government had the right to deprive a slaveholder of his legal property and thus "[t]here is not now, nor has there ever been since the separation of the colonies from the mother country, any power to emancipate the slaves, except that which belongs to their masters."[51] Cooper thus indirectly acknowledged that white property rights took precedence over the natural liberty of African Americans, just as the individual liberty of gentlemen weighed heavier than the collective freedom of an ignorant minority. Difference, in Cooper's world view, as in that of most of his contemporaries, was radically stratified.[52]

The belief in inequality furnished the rationale for defending slavery, but the reason that the peculiar institution mattered to the non-slaveholding New Yorker Cooper was an unacknowledged fear: that disagreement over the slavery issue would divide the union and thus endanger America and its democracy. As Northern Founding Fathers such as Gouverneur Morris had already argued during the constitutional convention, the union of the states guaranteed liberty for whites at the

---

[50]   Cooper, *Notions*, 2:265-266. It is not self-evident that Cooper's positions are always reflected in the observations of his fictional European observer, but this view on the limits of equality corresponds perfectly to *The American Democrat*. Interestingly, while Cooper was silent on the obligations of Northern society to overcome the prejudices that caused the depravity of free blacks, he did note the slaveholders' obligation to qualify their slaves for eventual citizenship, in order to remain ideologically consistent democrats.

[51]   Ibid., 2:259-260.

[52]   On the racialization of natural rights doctrines in Cooper, see Ezra F. Tawil, "Romancing History: The Pioneers and the Problem of Slavery," James Fenimore Cooper Society, at http://www.oneonta.edu/~cooper/articles/suny/1997suny-tawil.html.

cost of liberty for blacks. The right to keep slaves was the one non-negotiable demand of the southern states for joining the Union and endorsing a federal constitution, without which the states would have fallen victim to domestic anarchy and ultimately foreign interventions, both of which would eventually have led to the restoration of tyranny.[53] Robert Spiller observed of Cooper: "At the root of all his ideas lay his belief in the permanence of the union, and he refused, almost until the last, to consider slavery as a threat of secession."[54] This belief forced him to explain and defend slavery against European critics and domestic abolitionists so as to disprove its paradoxical and divisive nature. When conceding that Congress could theoretically attempt to abolish slavery by proposing an amendment to the constitution (which would require a two thirds majority in both houses) he called the idea "madness …, as it would infallibly fail and raise an irritating question without an object."[55] Cooper's 'pragmatic' approach to the question of slavery was intended precisely to avoid any such irritations. Though Cooper, understandably, never explicitly argued that black slavery constituted a pillar of white liberty, he did express the idea in an image. The coat of arms assigned to his fictional alter ego Cadwallader by the European friend introducing him into his bachelor's club consisted of "a constellation of twenty-four stars, surrounded by a cloud of *nebulae* with a liberty cap for a crest, and two young negroes as supporters."[56]

Conclusion

At the core of Cooper's thought we find a definition of liberty as a privilege to be earned or a right to be maintained at the cost of the freedom of those who have no true appreciation of it or are liable to abuse it; qualities Cooper felt competent to ascribe to specific groups that were thus delegitimized within his hierarchy of virtue and talent. The exclusivist ideologies of culturalist racism and virtue-oriented hierarchical republicanism, together with his paranoid fear that the United States was simultaneously threatened externally by foreign powers and immigrants and domestically by overzealous democrats and corrupt oligarchies convinced him of the need to support whatever guaranteed the power of the union and the restraining authority of the constitution and government, including slavery.

Of course, Cooper's elitism is only representative of one segment of American thought in the 1820s and 1830s. It is significant, however, that an independent thinker who never hesitated to speak his mind, unbound by party loyalties or any concern for public opinion, a Yankee who considered slavery an evil, an American who had studied his homeland from the outside for seven years, could conclude that the oppression of "un-American" citizens and African Americans was necessary for the survival of American democracy. While there were other, dissenting voices as

---

[53] A. Leon Higginbotham, *Shades of Freedom: Racial Politics and Presumptions of the American Legal Process* (New York: Oxford University Press, 1996), 71.
[54] Cooper and Spiller, "Fenimore Cooper's Defense," 575.
[55] Cooper, *American Democrat*, 174.
[56] Cooper, *Notions*, 1:xiii.

well, particularly of blacks themselves, Cooper's views testify to the nature of Jacksonian society as an era of uncertainty and vocal competition between various elements in society that did not hesitate to disqualify each other, verbally and in practice, in the name of preserving liberty and good government.[57] Furthermore, the extent to which Cooper's illiberal thinking was driven by deep anxieties over the possible failure or subversion of American democracy is unsettling, given how deeply ingrained this fear is in numerous strands of American thought—from Puritanism through the American Enlightenment and classical republicanism to Cooper's age with its anxiety-driven expansionism and fearful nativism. The list could easily be continued all the way to the current war on terrorism, which has once again exemplified how fear can lead to the willing suspension of civil liberties for the purpose of protecting democracy.[58] If Cooper gives any indication, democracy and repression are not merely entwined in the minds of fanatics, but in cool, collected realists. It is unsettling how well, across time, Martin Luther King's words apply to Cooper's "pragmatic" position on questions of black rights and slavery:

> I have come to the regrettable conclusion that the Negroes' great stumbling block in the stride toward freedom is not the White Citizens' "Councilor" or the Ku Klux Klaner, but the white moderate who is more devoted to "order" than to justice; who prefers a negative peace which is the absence of tension to a positive peace which is the presence of justice.[59]

Indeed, Cooper's ideology is hardly a dead letter. Scholars such as Robert Spiller wrote admiringly of his political thought and his version of democracy is still popular today among conservatives, who should be well aware of the implications of his ideas.[60] Far more unsettling is the reappearance of Cooper's logic in the security policy of the Bush II administration, which has traded off the liberty of vulnerable minorities—non-citizens, as well as Arab and Islamic Americans—for a supposedly

---

[57]   Field, *The Politics of Race in New York*.

[58]   See e.g. Robert A. Ferguson, *The American Enlightenment, 1750-1820* (Cambridge, MA: Harvard University Press, 1997), x, 38; Bernard Bailyn, *The Ideological Origins of the American Revolution* (Cambridge, MA: Belknap Press of Harvard University Press, 1967); Hietala, *Manifest Design*; Meyers, "The Jacksonian Persuasion"; David Harry Bennett, *The Party of Fear: From Nativist Movements to the New Right in American History* (Chapel Hill: University of North Carolina Press, 1988), x; Stone, *Perilous Times*, 550-557. For the importance of fear in contemporary America, see Peter N. Stearns, *American Fear: The Causes and Consequences of High Anxiety* (New York: Routledge, 2006).

[59]   "Letter from Birmingham Jail," in Peter B. Levy, ed., *Let Freedom Ring: A Documentary History of the Modern Civil Rights Movement* (Westport, CT: Praeger, 1992), 113.

[60]   See Cooper, *American Democrat*, xvi; xxv. The most recent edition of Cooper's political writings was published by the openly ultraconservative publishing house of Regnery: James Fenimore Cooper, *The American Democrat and Other Political Writings*, ed. Bradley J. Birzer and John Willson (Washington, DC: Regnery Publishing, 2000).

increased security of the majority.[61] As a political thinker, James Fenimore Cooper provides a telling case study not of an idiosyncrasy, but of an American intellectual tradition in which repression and exclusion repeatedly become the keys to liberty and democracy. For those uncomfortable with this vision of the American polity, there is perhaps some consolation in the fact that his best novels clearly transcended the limitations of their author.

---

[61]   See David Cole, "Enemy Aliens," *Stanford Law Review* 54.5 (2002), at http://www.questia.com/PM.qst?a=o&d=5000819175 and "Enemy Aliens and American Freedoms," *The Nation* (23 September 2002), at http://www.thenation.com/doc/20020923/cole. The extended argument is presented in David Cole and Jules Lobel, *Less Safe, Less Free: Why America Is Losing the War on Terror* (New York: New Press, 2007).

POLITICAL REPRESSION DURING RECONSTRUCTION: A LOUISIANA CASE STUDY. NATCHITOCHES, 1866-1878

Adam Fairclough

The suppression of the Republican Party in the southern states during and after Reconstruction may well be the most sweeping instance of political repression in American history. Other political parties and movements, of course, have been victims of repression. Government-led repression severely damaged the Socialist Party during World War I and virtually destroyed the Communist Party after World War II. However, the Democratic-led attack upon the southern Republicans dwarfed these other examples when judged in terms of scale, intensity and effect. The Democrats' campaign to dislodge the Republican Party was systematic and widespread; its effects were profound and long-lasting. In every former Confederate state, white Democrats engaged in guerrilla warfare—terrorism—of a kind never seen in America before or since, certainly not in peacetime. That campaign entailed the assassination of Republican Party leaders and the forcible suppression of the black vote by means of intimidation, violence and fraud.

The Democrats' terrorist campaign—symbolized by the Ku Klux Klan but actually much larger in scope—not only ensured the electoral defeat of the Republican Party in the South but also paved the way for the total destruction of that party. When the Democrat-controlled southern states disfranchised black voters en masse, the electoral base of the Republican Party disappeared. The suppression of the southern Republican Party not only underpinned the system of white supremacy that oppressed the black population but also had far-reaching national effects. By 1910 the South had become a one-party state, an enormous "rotten borough" that degraded the political system as a whole by grotesquely magnifying the power—especially in the U.S. Senate—of a relatively small number of white southerners. This repressive system endured well into the 1960s.

The suppression of the Republican Party was remarkable for its scale and duration. Moreover, the Democrats conducted their campaign of intimidation, violence, and vote-rigging in defiance of the federal government and under the noses of federal troops. Perhaps the most astonishing aspect of this episode—the crowning irony—was the fact that the Democrats persuaded the nation as a whole, and even the national Republican Party, that they, the southern white Democrats, had been the real victims of political repression. According to the Democratic analysis of Reconstruction, which became the dominant historical narrative and the dominant popular memory, the suppression of so-called Radical Reconstruction had been a necessary act, and had been carried out in a restrained, and even chivalrous, manner. Reconstruction thus presents a fascinating exception to the rule that history is written by the winners.

This essay presents an analysis of the political struggle between Democrats and Republicans in one southern community: the town of Natchitoches, Louisiana, and the surrounding parish (county) of the same name. It is not, however, another Reconstruction "horror story." Although Democrats elsewhere in Louisiana employed violence on a widespread scale, in Natchitoches they followed a deliberate policy of abstaining from violence. That fact in itself makes Natchitoches an interesting case study. Moreover, although the Democrats in Natchitoches succeeded in suppressing the black vote, thereby gaining political control, they permitted a skeleton Republican Party to continue to operate, and even allowed Republican leaders whom they had forcibly expelled to return to the community. This, too, requires explanation. Finally, the essay examines the way in which the victorious Democrats, in their effort to control the popular memory of Reconstruction, struggled to reconcile the reality of Reconstruction-era black militancy with their desire to portray blacks as docile and loyal servants.

On Saturday, 21 September 1878, the Democratic Party of Natchitoches—about a hundred white men—met in a state of high excitement. They convinced themselves that the local Republicans, who had the temerity to hold a meeting on the same day, were planning some kind of provocation, perhaps even an armed attack on the town. The Democrats appointed a committee, under the leadership of attorney Joseph Cunningham, to secure Natchitoches against this alleged threat. Cunningham told his fellow Democrats to go home and get their guns. The Democrats also distributed a hastily printed handbill that summoned all white men capable of bearing arms to assemble downtown. "Our wives and families must be protected at all costs." That evening, several hundred armed white men, many on horseback, patrolled the streets of Natchitoches military-fashion. The leaders of the Republican Party, who had occupied most of the public offices over the past ten years, quit the parish. Some were arrested and expelled; others fled before they could be caught. All knew that to remain in Natchitoches was no longer an option. "Mr. Cunningham said that he had never killed anyone," recalled Henry Raby, a Republican Congressman, and an African American, "but if I returned to the parish he would kill me himself."[1]

According to Cunningham's testimony to a U.S. Senate Committee, the Democrats had responded to a threat by Republican leaders to burn down the town. He related how an armed mob of blacks had already reached the outskirts of Natchitoches, and how prompt action by the whites—entirely unpremeditated— thwarted a black insurrection. Republican witnesses, however, told how Democrats had mounted a carefully planned coup d'état, executed by a paramilitary organization. The Democrats took over the town, expelled the leaders of the Republican Party, and so intimidated black voters that in the November elections the Republican vote, normally 1,800 strong, vanished.[2]

On one aspect of this day's events, however, both the Republicans and Democrats agreed. During the course of 21 September, Joseph Cunningham led a large party of whites to the home of Alfred Raford Blunt, the most influential black politician in the parish. The Democrats broke down the door and discovered Blunt hiding in the attic, a rifle and two pistols at his side. After a tense stand-off, Blunt

---

[1]   45th Congress, 3rd Session, Senate Reports, *Louisiana in 1878* (Washington, DC: Government Printing Office, 1879), 115-156, 485-514; *People's Vindicator* (Natchitoches), 22 March 1879, microfilm, Cammie G. Henry Research Center, Northwestern Louisiana State University, Natchitoches.

[2]   *Louisiana in 1878*, 114-158, 485-514; "Blunt's Mistakes," *People's Vindicator*, 23 November 1878.

laid down his arms and surrendered, having received a promise of safe conduct. The Democrats marched him to the court house, where Cunningham told him to leave Natchitoches forthwith. Before allowing Blunt to leave, however, Cunningham ordered his prisoner to disperse a group of blacks who were marching on the court house. Blunt sent his wife to calm the angry black crowd. At about one in the morning a group of armed men took Blunt out of town and left him on the road. One of the whites gave him some parting advice: "Leave the country and advise the negroes to let politics alone." Blunt started riding and made his way to New Orleans.[3]

According to the *Natchitoches People's Vindicator*, the local Democratic newspaper edited by James H. Cosgrove, the causes of the "disturbance" of 21 September 1878, could be summarized in one word: "Blunt." Blunt was the Republican leader whom the Democrats most wanted to silence. He was their bête noire. "Whenever a Negro assumes or acquires an unbounded influence over his race, it is ... in most instances for bad," Cosgrove editorialized. "Blunt had that influence and he was bad."[4]

Raford Blunt was typical of the black preacher-teacher-politicians of the Reconstruction era. Born into slavery in Georgia in 1838, and taken to Louisiana as a teenager, he enjoyed a spectacular rise after the Civil War. "When I was freed," Blunt recalled, "I went out as a woodchopper and sold wood to steamboats." He then began to "exhort," or preach, and quickly became the most influential black minister in the area. In 1869 he founded First Baptist Church in Natchitoches, with a five hundred-strong congregation. The following year he became president of the Twelfth District Baptist Association, which embraced twenty-eight black churches.

These black churches, a white Democrat observed, "mix up ... religion, school, and politics." As well as being a minister, Blunt served on the Natchitoches school board and taught occasionally. In 1870 he was elected to the state legislature, in 1872 to the state senate. In 1878 Blunt estimated his personal wealth at $7,000. He lived in a substantial two-story house and was proprietor of the local Republican newspaper. Democratic legend notwithstanding—a falsehood repeated by generations of historians—Blunt was not illiterate. An articulate, intelligent and ambitious man, Blunt personified the freedmen's desire to form their own religious communities and follow leaders of their own race.[5]

---

[3]   *New Orleans Republican*, 5 October 1878; "The Riot Saturday," *People's Vindicator*, 28 September 1878; *People's Vindicator*, 23 November 1878, 1 February 1879, and 22 March 1879.

[4]   "Blunt in Effect," *People's Vindicator*, 28 September 1878.

[5]   Eric Foner, *Freedom's Lawmakers: A Directory of Black Officeholders during Reconstruction* (Baton Rouge: Louisiana State University Press, 1996), xviii; 43rd Congress, 2nd Session, House of Representatives, Report 261, part 2, *Condition of the South* (Washington, DC: Government Printing Office, 1875), 214; William Hicks, *History of Louisiana Negro Baptists from 1804 to 1914* (Nashville, TN: National Baptist Publishing Board, 1915), electronic edition, Documenting the American South, University of North Carolina at Chapel Hill, http://docsouth.unc.edu/church/hicks/hicks .html; testimony of Albert Voorhies, 44th Congress, 2nd Session, House of Representatives, Miscellaneous Document 34, part 2, *Recent Election in Louisiana*

Reflecting upon these events in old age, Cosgrove depicted himself, together with a small band of fellow newspaper editors, as lonely crusaders against political oppression. He likened Louisiana's Reconstruction regime to the Southern Pacific Railroad of California. Like the *Octopus* of Frank Norris's novel, Louisiana's Republican government had been a corrupt machine that used its power to silence political opponents by bribing them or ruining them. "In business, in farming, where they could influence the negro labor; in transportation, then largely by steamboat, where they could control the licensing of the officers; in the tax departments, where they sold out without mercy; in the courts of law, where an attorney had the choice of silence or starvation ... did these [Republicans] hold us over their power. ... They bribed friends, armed foes, assaulted and shot at us, [and] rode us down with Merrill's Cavalry." Finally, their efforts to woo black voters having failed, the oppressed whites, groaning under oppressive taxation, formed the White League, which became the instrument of the state's "redemption" from Republican misrule.[6]

The Dunning school of Reconstruction history, the dominant interpretive paradigm until the 1960s, endorsed every one of Cosgrove's charges. Virtually every study of Reconstruction written between 1900 and 1950—other than those written by black historians like W.E.B. Du Bois—contended that enfranchising the former slaves had enabled a small class of white political adventurers to gain power in order to enrich themselves at the taxpayer's expense. Through extravagant appeals to black voters, and through appeals to the formers slaves' fear and hatred of the southern whites, these "carpetbaggers" and "scalawags" had arrayed the black electorate against their former masters. Once in power, an unholy alliance of ignorant black politicians, and wily white ones, proceeded to ruin the state through extravagance, misgovernment, and outright corruption. By excluding the people of intelligence and property—the native southern whites—these governments lacked political legitimacy. They clung on to power by rigging elections and, if necessary, summoning federal bayonets. Conditions became so oppressive that an outraged white citizenry took matters into their own hands—resorting to extreme but justified measures—in order to redeem the South and re-establish honest government.[7]

Nowadays, it is difficult to take this narrative of oppressed whites, gullible blacks, and thieving carpetbaggers seriously. The revisionism that swept the field in the 1960s, and which still holds sway, inverted the way we look at Reconstruction. The victims have become the oppressors; the oppressors, the victims. Blacks are no longer depicted as gullible sheep, but rather as a rational people who possessed unity, leadership, and a clear sense of their own self-interest. The mass

---

(Washington, DC: Government Printing Office, 1877), 1:144; "Rafael Blunt," Ward 12, Natchitoches Parish, 1870 U.S. Census, 30; "Raford Blunt," Freedman's Savings Bank Records, No. 8375, 14 March 1874; "Alice Louise Johnson," New Orleans, Louisiana Marriage Records Index, 13 July 1878, 829; "A.L. Blunt," Natchitoches Town Ward, 1880 U.S. Census, 25, all accessed through www.ancestry.com.

[6]   "Recollections and Reminiscences," *Cosgrove's Weekly*, 27 August 1910.

[7]   See, for example, Ella Lonn, *Reconstruction in Louisiana after 1868* (1918; repr., Gloucester, MA: Peter Smith, 1967); Garnie W. McGinty, *Louisiana Redeemed: The Overthrow of Carpet-Bag Rule, 1876-1880* (New Orleans: Pelican Publishing Company, 1941).

enfranchisement of black men—the very policy that so outraged the Dunning school—is now seen as self-evidently correct. It was not so much Republican corruption that alienated southern whites from Radical Reconstruction but their own intense racism, wedded to a desire to preserve the economic privileges that racial oppression had secured them. Nothing the Republicans did justified their white opponents' resort to violence.[8]

There is something intellectually troubling about such a stark reversal of heroes and villains. It underlines in an uncomfortable way the transitory nature of historical interpretations and the extent to which historians depend upon normative judgements. It is not surprising, therefore, that there have been glimmerings of what might be called a "post-revisionist" interpretation of Reconstruction. In 1979 William Gillette published a harshly critical appraisal of the national Republican Party, criticizing its use of the army to prop up fraudulent state governments (especially the one in Louisiana) and its deep hypocrisy over the question of race. J. Mills Thornton III analyzed the pattern of taxation in Republican-controlled Alabama and concluded that smaller white landowners had good reason for opposing Republican financial policies. They were not simply driven by racism. In his study of Mississippi, William Harris suggested that the extent of Klan violence against black schools has been greatly exaggerated. Focusing entirely on Louisiana, Lawrence Powell has provided a detailed analysis of how Republicans manipulated the electoral system to their advantage, including large-scale use of appointive offices and electoral gerrymandering. The most widely criticized feature of the Republican regime was its use of a "returning board" to certify election results. The state returning board assumed that any substantial shortfall between the black registration and the actual Republican vote resulted from Democratic intimidation. Thus it routinely refused to certify Democratic winners and awarded the victory to the defeated Republican. Yet according to John Rodrigue, Democratic complaints that black Republicans practised their own form of intimidation—subjecting Democrat-leaning blacks to social ostracism and even physical coercion—were valid.[9]

None of this, however, can explain the character of the Democratic assault on Reconstruction. Although post-revisionist criticisms of the Republican Party have merit, they run up against the fact that while the Republicans indulged in the kind of

---

[8]   The standard revisionist account is Joe Gray Taylor, *Retreat from Reconstruction, 1863-1877* (Baton Rouge: Louisiana State University Press, 1974).

[9]   William Gillette, *Retreat from Reconstruction, 1869-1879* (Baton Rouge: Louisiana State University Press, 1979), 104-135; William C. Harris, *The Day of the Carpetbagger: Republican Reconstruction in Mississippi* (Baton Rouge: Louisiana State University Press, 1979); J. Mills Thornton III, "Fiscal Policy and the Failure of Radical Reconstruction in the Lower South," in J. Morgan Kousser and James McPherson, eds., *Region, Race, and Reconstruction: Essays in Honor of C. Vann Woodward* (New York: Oxford University Press, 1982): 349-394; Lawrence Powell, "Centralization and its Discontents in Reconstruction Louisiana," *Studies in American Political Development* 20 (Fall 2006): 105-131; John C. Rodrigue, *Reconstruction in the Cane Fields: From Slavery to Free Labor in Louisiana's Sugar Parishes 1862-1880* (Baton Rouge: Louisiana State University Press, 2001), 170-172.

electoral shenanigans typical of nineteenth-century politics, the Democrats practiced intimidation and violence on a massive scale. Hence, like James Cosgrove's effort to liken the fight against the Natchitoches Republican Party to a Progressive Era reform movement, they fail to explain why the Democrats rejected normal political conventions in favor of physical coercion.

White southerners employed violence against the Republican Party on a massive scale. The New Orleans riot of 1866 left more than fifty black and white Republicans dead. During the presidential election of 1868, Democratic opposition was so violent—the U.S. Army estimated that at least a thousand blacks were killed—that Republican governor Henry Clay Warmoth advised blacks not to vote. The Colfax affair of 1873, when Democrats assaulted the court house in Grant Parish, resulted in about a hundred fatalities, almost all of them blacks. A year later, six white Republican officials from Coushatta in Red River Parish were murdered after Democrats had forced them to resign. General Philip H. Sheridan estimated that Louisiana saw about two thousand political murders between 1866 and 1875. Democrats scoffed at such figures, arguing that the Republican propaganda machine was a veritable "outrage mill." Yet Sheridan was not far wrong. Gilles Vandal has recently completed the monumental task of cataloguing and analyzing homicides in post-Civil War Louisiana. According to Vandal, whites killed at least 1,479 blacks during Reconstruction (1866-1877) whereas blacks killed only 117 whites. Moreover, of the 1,680 people who fell victim to *collective* violence during Reconstruction and its aftermath (1866-1884)—violence that was nearly always politically motivated—two-thirds were blacks killed by whites, whereas only 15 percent were whites killed by blacks. A quarter of all the blacks killed by whites were Republican officeholders or party activists.[10]

Democratic leaders excused and even applauded political violence. "We fully, cordially approve of what the white men ... did at Colfax," exulted Albert Leonard, editor of the *Shreveport Times*. Cosgrove's *Natchitoches Vindicator* likewise celebrated the murder of the six Republicans from Red River Parish. "The men who were killed met a just and fearful doom, and their deaths should serve as a warning." These newspapers openly called for the assassination of Republican leaders, sometimes naming the prospective victims.[11]

By 1876 the Democrats had undermined Republican rule in every southern state. Although the Republicans disputed Democratic claims to victory in Louisiana, South Carolina and Florida, the party's national leaders agreed to concede defeat in

---

[10]   Ted Tunnell, *Crucible of Reconstruction: War, Radicalism, and Race in Louisiana 1862-1877* (Baton Rouge: Louisiana State University Press, 1984), 106, 154-157, 192, 201; 41st Congress, 2nd Session, House Miscellaneous Document 154, *Louisiana Contested Elections* (Washington, DC: Government Printing Office, 1870), 32; 44th Congress, 2nd Session, Executive Document 30, *Use of the Army in Certain Southern States* (Washington, DC: Government Printing Office, 1879), 65, 156-158; Gilles Vandal, *Rethinking Southern Violence: Homicides in Post-Civil War Louisiana, 1866-1884* (Columbus: Ohio State University Press, 2000), 67-89.

[11]   43rd Congress, 2nd Session, House of Representatives, Report 261, part 2, *Condition of the South* (Washington, DC: Government Printing Office, 1875), 755, 765; *People's Vindicator*, 12 September 1874.

those states in return for a resolution of the contested presidential election in their favor. The Compromise of 1877 saw Republican Rutherford B. Hayes sworn in as president and the Democrats assume power in Louisiana.

The Compromise of 1877 did not, however, eliminate the Republican Party in the South. Although they had lost control of state government, Republicans still enjoyed substantial representation. President Hayes, in abandoning the use of military force in the South, believed that Democratic leaders would respond to his policy of "conciliation" by abandoning intimidation and violence against Republican voters. Indeed, the Democratic governor of Louisiana, Francis T. Nicholls, had explicitly promised to protect blacks' right to vote. Democratic leaders had repeated that pledge during the Compromise negotiations.[12]

The elections of 1878, therefore, were a decisive test of Democratic intentions. Natchitoches Parish was a strong Republican enclave. Despite Democratic threats, blacks still voted in large numbers, enabling the Republicans to retain power. Moreover, Natchitoches Parish provided the key to Republican control of Louisiana's Fourth Congressional District. One of four majority-black parishes, it contained the only town of any consequence, providing local Republicans with a strong and relatively safe base.[13]

The Democrats in Natchitoches, however, were not interested in conciliation: they moved in for the kill. "The best citizens of this parish," warned Cosgrove in the *People's Vindicator*, "are determined to wipe out the whole gang of Radical plunders ... [and] the colored people had better come with us or stand aside. No more Blunts . . . will strut officially through this parish. ... [T]heir efforts only serve to irritate and retard society—possibly to so outrage it as to invoke summary justice to rid the community of their evil presence." Two weeks before the September coup, Cosgrove insisted that "Blunt and his lieutenants must be put down. ... He is a standing menace to our peace, and must be swept away."[14]

Joseph Cunningham explained the Democratic sweep by arguing that the removal of Raford Blunt had relieved blacks of the pressure to vote Republican. [T]they felt free to vote the Democratic ticket, as they were not socially ostracized for doing so." In reality, black voters had been ordered to cast Democratic ballots after the Republican organization had been destroyed. "I consider the white people are bound to stand together," Cunningham explained, "because if they do not, the government will pass into the hands of the worst class of people. ... On the other

---

12   Taylor, *Louisiana Reconstructed*, 483-484, 494; Lonn, *Reconstruction in Louisiana*, 502-503.

13   The best study of Reconstruction in the Red River valley, which focuses on Red River Parish, is Ted Tunnell, *Edge of the Sword: The Ordeal of Carpetbagger Marshall H. Twitchell in the Civil War and Reconstruction* (Baton Rouge: Louisiana State University Press, 2001).

14   *Louisiana in 1878*, 485; "Candid Talk," *People's Vindicator*, 31 August 1878; "White Men. To Your Posts!" *People's Vindicator*, 31 August 1878; "Spirit of 1876," *People's Vindicator*, 7 September 1878; David Bruce Maxwell, "James Hugh Cosgrove: Louisiana Newspaper Editor, 1842-1914," (master's thesis, Northwestern State University of Louisiana, 1973), 48-49.

hand, I don't think it necessary for the colored people to combine together against the whites, as no good can come of it. Their objects are . . . to be secured by acting with us." Cosgrove, as usual, put it more frankly, "We are fully determined that no man shall mass the negroes against the material citizens." In short, the Democrats refused to recognize the legitimacy of the Republican Party because, in Cosgrove's words, it rested upon "a voting population, totally ignorant of their duties, full of bitter prejudice and of a lower race." In Natchitoches, he admitted, the Democrats aimed not only to defeat the Republican Party "but to kill that party in such a manner as to forever preclude the possibility of its resurrection."[15]

The Republican defeats in Natchitoches and elsewhere exposed Democratic pledges to protect black rights as worthless. "The Southern wing of the [Republican] party virtually disappeared," writes one historian. Recognizing the gravity of the 1878 results, a committee of the U.S. Senate amassed evidence of Democratic intimidation and violence. In 1879 the federal government prosecuted forty-eight Natchitoches Democrats in the case of *United States v. Cunningham*. After a New Orleans jury acquitted the first twelve defendants, however, the presiding judge halted the trials. The collapse of this case rendered futile any further attempt by the federal government to enforce fair elections in the South. The prosecution case was as strong as it could possibly be, yet, noted the *New York Times*, the government "has spent $40,000 to discover that it cannot vindicate a statute."[16]

James Cosgrove congratulated his fellow Democrats upon their chivalrous conduct; they had "stabbed the enemy to death ... with a smile on his lips." It was indeed true that Democratic leaders in Natchitoches had deliberately eschewed violence, and on more than one occasion quashed specific proposals to kill Blunt and other Republican officials. Observing the Senate investigation, a reporter for the *New York Times* was struck by the contrast between Democratic methods in Natchitoches and the violence Democrats employed elsewhere.

> In Natchitoches ... the leader of the Democracy is a gentleman of fine physical appearance and a pleasant address. He is a lawyer. In that place the Republican leaders, both black and white, were driven into exile—"charitably exiled," was the polite term selected to describe their expulsion; but no more physical force was used than was absolutely necessary to insure that result. There were no assassinations of negroes, nor whippings, nor any other violent methods of electioneering.

The location of Natchitoches made it all the more remarkable that Democrats there refrained from violence. It lay in the middle of the Red River valley, a region that

---

15   *Louisiana in 1878*, 524; *People's Vindicator*, 19 October 1878 and 16 November 1878. For evidence of blacks being compelled to vote Democratic in 1878, see testimony of Valcour Merritty, John Baptiste Vienne, John Hutson, Joe Reid, Ambrose Wallace, and Shedrick Brown, all in "The Natchitoches Prisoners," *People's Vindicator*, 15 March 1879.

16   Stanley P. Hirshon, *Farewell to the Bloody Shirt: Northern Republicans and the Southern Negro, 1877-1893* (Chicago: Quadrangle, 1962), 47-48; *Louisiana in 1878*, 114, 517, and *passim*; *New York Times*, 6 February, 9 and 17 March 1879.

saw more anti-black violence than any other area of Louisiana, possibly the entire South. Moreover, it adjoined both Grant Parish, site of the Colfax massacre, and Red River Parish, scene of the Coushatta murders.[17]

Several factors may explain the contrast. Whereas the Red River valley as a whole was settled in the nineteenth century, and still had a raw, frontier character that encouraged violence, the town of Natchitoches dated back to the eighteenth century. It was, in fact, the oldest town in Louisiana, dating back to 1714, four years before the establishment of New Orleans. In the second place, while the surrounding region was settled by Anglo-Saxon Protestants, many Natchitoches residents were French by birth or descent, and Catholic in religion. Also in contrast to the surrounding region, Natchitoches boasted a substantial population of free-born blacks, most of whom formed a tightly-knit community of French-speaking Creoles. These colored Creoles owned land and also, before the Civil War, slaves. They were well-educated and attended their own Catholic church. The Republican Party in Natchitoches was also distinctive. The white Republican leaders were native southerners, most of them born and raised in Natchitoches. They included lawyers, doctors, and planters. Some had served in the Confederate army. These were not northern interlopers; there was hardly a "carpetbagger" among them. The fact that they were native sons, whose family ties cut across party lines, may have afforded them some protection from physical violence.

Raford Blunt, the black leader, may also have inhibited Democratic violence. The Democrats hated Blunt but they also feared him. They recognized his influence over the black population—upon whose labor they completely depended—and worried that killing him would unleash some form of black retaliation. That retaliation might be in the form of arson, a violent uprising or, more likely, a withdrawal of labor from white landlords. Blunt made no overt threats, but he did not need to. Everyone seemed to understand that if he were physically harmed, blacks could ruin the white planters and merchants by letting their cotton crop rot in the fields.

Yet political repression in the United States has not relied primarily upon widespread violence. Indeed, the *New York Times* reporter who drew attention to the relative restraint exercised by the Democrats of Natchitoches concluded that "the clean-shirted and kid-gloved variety" achieved the same results through intimidation that Democrats elsewhere gained through violence. Be they "gentlemen" or "bandits," Democrats "were equally inflexible in their purpose to carry the election."[18]

---

[17] "Home Rule under Nicholls," *New York Times*, 20 January 1879. The *Times* reporter was describing Joseph Cunningham. Natchitoches Parish did see one murder that was indisputably political: the killing, during the 1868 election, of Alfred Hazen, a black Republican activist. Responsibility for the murder was never established, but the perpetrators were probably members of the Knights of the White Camellia from an adjoining parish. The Natchitoches branch of the KWC discussed violence but in the end dissolved without committing any violent acts.

[18] A.P. Breda, J.E. Breda, Natchitoches Town, 1880 U.S. Census, 29; Republican Parish Executive Committee, minutes, 12 August and 11 October 1883; 7 January, 18 February, 19 March, 5 April, 2 May, 12 July and 11 September 1884; 9 January 1888;

Political repression does not have to be total to be effective. The South was not, Gunnar Myrdal noted, a fascist or totalitarian regime. The Democrats employed only as much repression as was necessary to render the Republican Party impotent. They even permitted most of the exiled Republican leaders, including Blunt, to return to Natchitoches, and to reorganize the Republican Party. As long as the Democrats controlled the ballot boxes, they could come up with the result they desired. During Reconstruction the Republicans had polled 1,800 votes; after 1876 they struggled to poll 500. When, in 1890s, the rise of the Populist Party made the small Republican vote tactically significant, the Democrats adopted a new state constitution that eliminated the black electorate altogether.

Seeking to justify the events of 1878 and to shape the historical memory of Reconstruction, local Democrats related how the September coup had nipped a black uprising in the bud, thereby saving Natchitoches from an orgy of rapine and destruction.[19] Such insurrection scares were the stuff of Democratic propaganda, and Republican leaders dismissed them as such. White Republicans pointed out that blacks had neither the inclination nor the means to organize aggressive actions against the white population. The freed people were "naturally timorous," observed one, for they had been "raised under the whip." Indeed, lacking modern weapons and devoid of any military experience, they were incapable even of defending themselves. "Whenever they attempt to organize for self-defense," wrote another Republican leader, "the cry of 'negroes arming,' 'war of the races' is raised ... with the usual result of ten, twenty of fifty negroes killed, and perhaps one white man wounded."[20]

Yet the insurrection scares reflected real fear. It was the same kind of fear that, before emancipation, underpinned the ever-present anxiety of slave rebellion. In the aftermath of emancipation, and especially after black enfranchisement, many whites feared the worst. "We often had painful rumors of large bodies of negroes coming into the town to burn it up and murder the people," testified Natchitoches Democrat David Pierson. One of the more sober Democratic leaders, Pierson acknowledged that the rumors were unfounded. Yet the Democrats, in constantly warning of another St. Domingue, came to believe their own propaganda. It is the logic of every repressive system, be it a slave-owning society or a modern dictatorship, to perceive

---

25 September 1889; 15 April 1996, all in reel 3, J.P. Breda Family Papers, Hill Memorial Library, Louisiana State University, Baton Rouge.

[19] *Louisiana in 1878*, 158-159, 485-509; "The Riot," *Natchitoches Vindicator*, 28 September 1878; *Natchitoches Vindicator*, 5 October and 19 October 1878; history of Natchitoches, fragment, folder 17, box 1-G-4, Judge Jones Collection, Special Collections, Northwestern Louisiana State University, 157; H. Oscar Lestage, "The White League in Louisiana and its Participation in Reconstruction Riots," *Louisiana Historical Quarterly* 18 (July 1935): 617-695.

[20] Richard Talbot to S.B. Packard, 15 October 1974, *Use of the Army in Certain Southern States*, 87-288; William P. Kellogg to George H. Williams, 26 August 1874, roll 2, Letters Received by the Attorney General: Louisiana, RG60, M940, National Archives and Records Administration, College Park, MD.

any expression of defiance as a potential rebellion. Acts of defiance, however small, had to be quashed.[21]

By the end of the nineteenth century, as white southerners romanticized slavery and memorialized the Confederacy, their vision of black leaders like Blunt became troubling. The image of Blunt as an incendiary and insurrectionist could be used to justify white supremacy. But it did not accord with the idea of happy and docile blacks. One solution to this cognitive dissonance was to blame black assertiveness during Reconstruction on outside agitators, the "carpetbaggers." But if there were no carpetbaggers in Natchitoches—nearly all the Republican leaders, black and white, were home-grown—how did you account for the influence of a Blunt? One answer was simply to forget him. When he died in 1905 whites acknowledged his passing with scarcely a mention of his role in Reconstruction. There are no monuments to Blunt in Natchitoches.[22]

Whites did, however, erect a monument to the "Good Darkies of Louisiana." Paid for by a local businessman, it celebrated, in a paternalistic way, "the arduous and faithful service" of the black mammies and house servants who had raised generations of white children. Unveiled in 1927, this statue, as described by *Time* magazine, "depicts a Negro, old and stoop-shouldered, with shabby clothes, humbly and faithfully tipping his dusty hat." As a local white man explained, "Relations between the races have always been pleasant in this town and the country roundabout—not only in slavery times but down to the present." *Time* speculated that the "modern Negro" would see it as insulting. Yet local whites were none too enthusiastic either. "The majority of sentiment in the South is to damn the negro and consider him worthless," wrote a friend of the statue's white sponsor. "There will probably be some comments like this, 'Well, it's damn funny that the only statue we have in town is erected to a nigger; we have enough trouble keeping them in their place, and trying to get work out of them. I don't think this statue will help any.'" Regardless, the statue stood in downtown Natchitoches for nearly forty years, becoming something of a tourist attraction. The city eventually removed it in 1968 after blacks threatened to demolish it. The only public trace of Raford Blunt is a street of about one hundred yards of dilapidated houses, dead-ended by a railroad track.[23]

---

21   *Condition of Affairs in the South*, 217, 548; testimony of David Pierson, *Recent Election in Louisiana*, 4.127.

22   Moreover, after Blunt died in 1905 his church burned down. It had been situated on one of the town's most attractive downtown streets, surrounded by white property-owners. The land was sold and houses built on the site. Blunt's house also disappeared. Today there are still two First Baptist Churches, each claiming to be the legitimate descendant of Blunt's church. See First Baptist Church (Colored) Records, Natchitoches Genealogical Society.

23   *Time*, 3 January 1927, 1; S.M. Byrd, "An Old-Time Negro Honored," 29 August 1927 and G.A. Bryan to J.L. Bryan, 15 June 1926, Documents Relating to "The Good Darkie" Statue, both in J.A. Ducourneau Collection, Special Collections, Northwestern Louisiana State University. "Blount Street" owes its name to the fact that the land had been developed by Blunt's church, not to an official gesture by the city fathers.

SOUTHERN WHITE REACTION
AGAINST INTERRACIAL COOPERATION, 1900-1930

Mark Ellis

The maintenance of southern white supremacy in the early decades of the twentieth century took various well-known forms—denial of political rights, economic injustice, discriminatory law enforcement and impoverished education—all of which amounted to the systematic destruction of African American ambition. However, this mentality impacted coercively on the white population as well, because of the racial loyalty it demanded. The chief argument of this study is that some white southerners were deterred from promoting black opportunity and progress in the first quarter of the twentieth century by the intensely critical response that reform agendas provoked in the surrounding culture, and that would-be reformers experienced the racist orthodoxy as a form of repression. While they may not have endured hardship or physical pain, their social and mental discomfort was real, and stemmed from accusations that, in questioning the permanency of black subordination, they had revealed themselves to be deviant, irresponsible and, above all, disloyal.

Although the emergence of a substantial literature on interracial cooperation after 1880 demonstrates a high level of interest in the subject, little was done of a tangible nature to promote it. Why did a liberal southern approach to race evolve so slowly? The answer is partly that a longstanding supremacist tendency deterred many white dissenters from challenging the status quo until the New Deal or later, and even then they did so only on a small scale. Another reason is the power of loyalty as an ideal and the boost that this was given by American entry into World War I. During the war and the subsequent red scare, the suppression of dissent became a general reaction of government, law enforcement agencies, patriotic organisations and the press. Freedom of speech was curtailed and unorthodox views discouraged. This manifested itself nationally in attacks on German Americans and opponents of the draft and regionally in the resurgence of the Ku Klux Klan, which made a fetish out of loyalty in response to anxieties stemming from modernization and change. As W.J. Cash later observed about white southerners' experience of World War I,

> these men were superlatively ripe for hating. The organized propaganda of the war had drilled them in a habit of hate with a thoroughness and an intensity entirely without parallel in human history…. The very passion for "Americanism" in the South was at least in great part the passion that the South should remain fundamentally unchanged.[1]

---

[1]   W.J. Cash, *The Mind of the South* (1941; repr., New York: Vintage, 1960), 301, 303. On the war's effects, see also Carol Jensen, "Loyalty as a Political Weapon: The 1918 Campaign in Minnesota," *Minnesota History* 43 (1972): 43-57; Robert K. Murray, *Red Scare: A Study in National Hysteria, 1919-1920* (Minneapolis: University of Minnesota

Thus, an instinctive repressive reaction against racial reform, originating in slave-holding, was heightened in the 1920s.

During the 1890s, leading southerners of all stripes had agreed that the South was in crisis—economically, socially and culturally—and that one of the chief threats to peaceful progress was the race problem. Lynching was condemned, not as a particular wickedness toward black people (who were generally regarded as inherent criminals), but for the damage that vigilantism did to respect for the legal system and southern probity. To some commentators, a race war seemed probable, and the margins within which debate was allowed on race narrowed markedly. There was overwhelming intellectual and popular endorsement of the southern race settlement of the 1890s, in which segregation was promoted as a device for preserving both peace and racial integrity. By 1900, racist politicians and writers had begun to impose strict limits on what subsequent reformers could legitimately advocate and a pattern of denunciation of white liberals had begun to emerge.[2]

The notorious "Bassett Affair" of 1903 was a warning to southern liberals. John Spencer Bassett was a historian at Trinity College, in North Carolina, who claimed in the *South Atlantic Quarterly* (which he founded and edited) that an exaggerated fear on the part of whites about interracial sex lay behind the racial crisis and that if whites could only overcome their prejudices, blacks would make steady progress towards equality. Booker T. Washington, he added, was "the greatest man, save General Lee, born in the South in a hundred years." Bassett was mercilessly attacked in the white press, led by Josephus Daniels's *Raleigh News & Courier*. He survived this test of academic freedom, but left for Smith College in 1906, preferring "a peaceful atmosphere."[3] When North Carolina educationist Charles Lee Coon attacked unequal schooling for blacks in 1909, he was similarly denounced.[4] The crime of Bassett and Coon was to suggest that the flaws that had caused the southern crisis lay partly in white people's racial attitudes. There were other cases: the historian Samuel Chiles Mitchell, a racial moderate who took an interest in African American progress and expression found himself compelled to resign in 1913 by the attacks of race-baiters such as Governor Coleman Blease. When Robert T. Kerlin, professor of English at Virginia Military Institute, produced

---

Press, 264-265; Clemens P. Work, *Darkest before Dawn: Sedition and Free Speech in the American West* (Albuquerque: University of New Mexico Press, 2005).

[2] Jack Temple Kirby, *Darkness at the Dawning: Race and Reform in the Progressive South* (Philadelphia: Lippincott, 1972), 179. It took outsiders, like northern journalist Ray Stannard Baker and British colonial administrator Sir Harry Johnston, to reveal certain truths about race in the South. See Baker, *Following the Color Line: An Account of Negro Citizenship in the American Democracy* (New York: Doubleday Page, 1908), and Harry Johnston, *The Negro in the New World* (New York: Macmillan, 1910).

[3] Robert H. Woody, cv "John Spencer Bassett, 1867-1928," *Documenting the American South*, at http://docsouth.unc.edu/nc/bassettnc/bio.html. John Spencer Bassett, "Stirring Up the Fires of Race Antipathy," *South Atlantic Quarterly* 2 (October 1903): 297-305.

[4] William A. Link, *The Paradox of Southern Progressivism, 1880-1930* (Chapel Hill: University of North Carolina Press, 1992), 64-65.

a collage of vivid black expression from the riot-torn year 1919, *The Voice of the Negro*, he was fired.[5]

Democrat politicians were rarely controversial on race, knowing the likely reaction. (A notable exception was Governor Hugh Dorsey of Georgia, who listed examples of brutality against blacks in 1921 and was immediately denounced by the Dixie Defense Committee and accused by a future governor (and leading Klansman) of having issued an "infamous slander."[6]) In any case, racial deviance was always a useful stick with which to beat Republicans, who were routinely taunted in language redolent of the post-Reconstruction era. In 1921, Senator John Sharp Williams of Mississippi, a patrician Democrat, dismissed southern Republicans as "generally radicals and fanatics upon political questions without the ordinary common hard sense that leads a man to know the difference between a nigger and a white man."[7] Williams was responding to President Warren Harding, who, in a speech to a segregated audience in Birmingham, Alabama, had acknowledged racial difference, but also called for equality of educational and economic opportunity in the South. The *Birmingham Post* denounced Harding's "tactless" speech as a "violation of the proprieties" and the *Montgomery Journal* called it a "serious, if not fatal mistake."[8] During the 1928 presidential election campaign, Herbert Hoover's supporters were alleged to favor "making young white girls use the same water closets as negro men."[9]

Although most of the suspicion and anger was directed at northern whites, particularly those in the NAACP, its tone left reform-minded white southerners in no doubt as to the vilification they could expect if they tried to engage the racists in open debate. Implicitly, and sometimes openly, reformers had to contend with being told they lacked realism and did not understand certain basic laws about human nature. It was declared that black people lagged thousands of years behind Caucasians in intellectual and moral development, that this gap could not be closed

---

[5]   Michael Dennis, "The Skillful Use of Higher Education to Protect White Supremacy," *Journal of Blacks in Higher Education* 32 (Summer 2001): 115-123. Mitchell moved to become president of the University of Delaware until 1920. In 1919, unusually, force was used against whites who intervened on behalf of blacks: an assault on NAACP secretary John Shillady in Austin, Texas, by white men, including a judge; and the harassment of the Brattons—father and son attorneys—who assisted black defendants in the Elaine, Arkansas, race riot cases. Charles Flint Kellogg, *NAACP: A History of the National Association for the Advancement of Colored People* (Baltimore: Johns Hopkins University Press), 239-243; Richard C. Cortner, *A Mob Intent on Death: The NAACP and the Arkansas Riot Cases* (Middletown, CT: Wesleyan University Press, 1988), 40-42, 79-80; Gif Stockley, *Blood in Their Eyes: The Elaine Race Massacres of 1919* (Fayetteville: University of Arkansas Press, 2001), 101-105.

[6]   Julia A. McDonough, "Men and Women of Good Will: A History of the Commission on Interracial Cooperation and the Southern Regional Council, 1919-1954" (PhD diss., University of Virginia, 1993), 80.

[7]   I.A. Newby, *Jim Crow's Defense: Anti-Negro Thought in America, 1900-1930* (Baton Rouge: Louisiana State University, 1965), 164.

[8]   "The Negro's Status Declared by the President," *Literary Digest* (19 November 1921): lxxi, 8-9.

[9]   Newby, *Jim Crow's Defense*, 166.

artificially and that an education system that did not recognize certain innate inferiorities was pointless and potentially dangerous. Racial theorists maintained that black criminality increased as literacy rose and that educated individuals would forget their place in the social order.[10] The vehemence of such disapproval was enough to silence almost all dissenters.

A small minority of middle-class white professionals and businessmen in the South did call for better black schools and welcomed outside support for the Hampton-Tuskegee model of industrial training. Northern philanthropist William Baldwin called them "new leaders of southern thought," but, as James D. Anderson has demonstrated, they were heavily criticized in the New South by conservatives who feared any enhancement of black education might generate economic and political unrest. Advocates of investment in black schools who argued that citizenship training and expansion of industrial education could achieve progress without turmoil, were warned that a better-educated black population would soon demand the restoration of the vote, reject menial work and compete with white labor.[11] Thus, white southerners who saw racial discrimination as inhumane or a cause of economic backwardness risked ostracism in a regional culture in which reputation and social standing were paramount. And those who questioned the need for disfranchisement and other inequalities were accused of being undemocratic and disloyal. After all, argued Senator Tom Heflin of Alabama, the right to pursue happiness was a basic principle in a democracy and this was all the white majority sought in imposing segregation and supremacy. Racists attacked those suspected of planning to reform the system in intensely hostile language in the first quarter of the twentieth century: the various epithets noted by the Georgian historian Idus Newby included,

> "lunatics and visionaries," "howlers," "malignant agitators [for] office, or notoriety, or bribes," "seasonal agitators and philo-negrists," … "aspiring Mulattoes," … and "a few long-haired negrophilists … and a lot of short-haired white women who disgrace both their race and their sex."[12]

Unsurprisingly, then, very few white people argued openly before 1930 that African Americans were worthy of fuller rights of citizenship, or that southern racial attitudes were contributing to the region's economic backwardness and dependency, despite plenty of evidence that this was the case. As John Egerton has observed, "it

---

[10]   Ibid., 171-178.
[11]   James D. Anderson, *The Education of Blacks in the South, 1860-1935* (Chapel Hill: University of North Carolina Press, 1988), 94-102. Anderson cites a Virginian journal, the *Farmville Herald*: "When they learn to spell dog and cat they throw away the hoe." Ibid., 97. On the political economy of education reform and race, see also Anderson, "On the Meaning of Reform: African-American Education in the Twentieth Century South," in Craig S. Pascoe, Karen Trahan Leathem and Andy Ambrose, eds., *The American South in the Twentieth Century* (Athens: University of Georgia Press, 2005), 263-284.
[12]   Newby, *Jim Crow's Defense*, 155-156, 171.

took a special kind of courage—or madness—to speak and act against such overwhelming force."[13]

One group that possessed the necessary courage was the Commission on Interracial Cooperation (CIC), founded by white liberals in Atlanta in 1919 in an attempt to improve race relations in the South through the promotion of local dialogue. It hired some remarkable individuals who did important work between the wars, but its leadership was always afraid of infringing boundaries of racial separateness and hierarchy, because of the ease with which hostility and suspicion were aroused. As Dewey Grantham has put it, the CIC "pointed to a concrete and realistic mode of action. But at the same time the commission was carefully restricted by the bounds of white orthodoxy."[14]

The eminent black intellectual, W.E.B. Du Bois, editor of the NAACP's monthly journal, the *Crisis*, provided an acute insight into the way in which white supremacy repressed white dissent. In 1923, Ernest Gruening, the editor of the *Nation* magazine, initiated a series entitled, "These United States," and hired Du Bois for the article on Georgia. Published in January 1925, it is one of his most perceptive, and yet ambiguous, writings. Du Bois had lived in Atlanta from 1897 to 1910, when some of the most depraved events in Georgia's violent history had occurred, including hundreds of lynchings and a major race riot in Atlanta itself. In the *Nation* piece, he considered the ways in which a toxic concoction of race, sex, labor and voting had entrapped black and white Georgians in a monotonous cycle of hatred: "There must be living and breathing in Georgia today at least ten thousand men who have taken human life, and ten times that number who have connived at it." (The white adult male population of Georgia in 1925 numbered about 500,000.)[15]

Du Bois reflected that it was "fairly easy to be a reformer in New York or Boston or Chicago. ... But in Atlanta? ... [T]he politico-economic alliance stands like a rock in the path of real reform." Without naming the Commission on Interracial Cooperation, he dismissed it as a well-meaning irrelevance; it was nice of these liberals to campaign against lynching and for better wages, but such campaigns were useless in the context of disfranchisement and segregation. Du Bois read the mind of the type of white southerner who was drawn to the CIC:

> Of the spiritual dilemmas that face men today I know of none more baffling than that which faces the conscientious, educated, forward-looking white man

---

[13]   John Egerton, *Speak Now against the Day: The Generation before the Civil Rights Movement in the South* (Chapel Hill: University of North Carolina Press, 1994), 77. The new Ku Klux Klan and the growth of a powerful eugenics movement, which sponsored legislation such as Virginia's Racial Integrity Law (1924) regarding marriage, can both be seen as white supremacy's responses to those who questioned it from within.

[14]   Dewey W. Grantham, "The Contours of Southern Progressivism," *American Historical Review* 86 (December 1981): 1055. For full-length studies of the CIC, see Ann Wells Ellis, "The Commission on Interracial Cooperation, 1919-1944: Its Activities and Results" (PhD diss., Georgia State University, 1975), and McDonough, "Men and Women of Good Will."

[15]   W.E.B. Du Bois, "Georgia: Invisible Empire State," *Nation* 102 (21 January 1925): 63.

of Georgia. On the one hand is natural loyalty to what his fathers believed, to what his friends never question; then his own difficulty in knowing or understanding the black world and his inbred distrust of its ability and real wish; there is his natural faith in his own ability and the ability of his race; there is the subtle and continuous propaganda—gossip, newspapers, books, sermons, and "science'; there is his eager desire to see his section take a proud place in the civilized world. There is his job, his one party, his white primary—his social status[,] so easily lost if he is dubbed a "nigger lover." Facing all of this is lynching, mob murder, ignorance, silly self-praise of people degenerate in so many cases, exploitation of the poor and weak, and insult, insult, insult heaped on the blacks.[16]

In other words, intelligent, educated whites, well aware that the racial equation was immoral and vicious, were not radical enough to break with the past and or brave enough to risk everything by speaking openly. This led Du Bois to the view he basically held throughout the interwar period: southern white liberals were not worth knowing. Du Bois was not being completely fair, for the stance and methods of the CIC were certainly radical in the southern context, but he was right about the immense pressure to conform.

An embodiment of the social gospel idea, the CIC encouraged middle class white southerners to discover areas of mutual understanding with their black counterparts in order to lessen tension. Its members frequently engaged in acts of bravery and were prepared to risk ostracism and intimidation, up to a point. The chairman of the CIC, Ashby Jones, the son of Robert E. Lee's chaplain, was threatened for standing up to the Klan and confessed to the CIC annual conference in 1925, "I never know when the white caps will come to my door."[17]

Significantly, there was no comparable organization across the South with a key interest in the race problem. The interactions of southern universities on social issues had diminished during the war years, and religious bodies, such as the YMCA, usually approached racial questions with extreme caution. The NAACP, which, as a prime example of northern interference, was anathema to whites across the South, could not have attempted the work undertaken by the CIC. This was acknowledged by the NAACP's assistant secretary, Walter White, in 1923 in

---

[16]   Ibid., 64-65. Georgia's Jim Crow record included:
       1870, 1891 and 1899—segregation statutes regarding all transport;
       1872, 1877, 1895, 1926, 1933—laws providing racial segregation in education;
       1865, 1926, 1927, 1928, 1935—race classification laws banning interracial marriage;
       1908—disfranchisement of African Americans;
       1880-1920—more than 450 lynchings.

[17]   *Chicago Daily News*, 26 April 1925, clipping, frame 1649, reel 28, file 39, series IV, Commission on Interracial Cooperation (CIC) Papers, 1919-1944, Robert Woodruff Library, Atlanta University Center (AUC), Atlanta, GA.

correspondence about cases of Klan-type violence and peonage that the CIC was actively investigating.[18]

The CIC began its long and difficult battle against lynching long before it became fashionable to denounce such events. W. Fitzhugh Brundage has argued that the central CIC office in Atlanta and its local committees contributed to the decline in lynching and other racial violence after World War I. Even then, he does not see the urban middle class and local business elites that changed their views on lynching as having "sentiments of racial liberalism that were far in advance of the existing racial order."[19] They deplored lynching, not because of what it did to blacks, but because it was an embarrassment; it exposed Dixie to ridicule and disgust.

Although the CIC ultimately formed a bridge on which black and white southerners, and a few interested northerners, could meet to discuss racial issues, it never challenged segregation. It took a paternalistic view of black progress and retained only a small number of committed, long-term supporters, most of them white men. Nevertheless, Ann Wells Ellis has argued that "it played a vital role in preparing the middle and upper-class whites to accept the later civil rights movement [and] made it socially unacceptable to use violence and intimidation against blacks seeking to improve their status.... Without this change in attitude the civil rights movement would have been stifled at the outset."[20] The Swedish sociologist, Gunnar Myrdal, in *An American Dilemma*, credited the CIC with having made "interracial work socially respectable in the conservative South."[21] Eventually, this may have been true, and such claims can reasonably advanced for the New Deal era and World War II, but it was not true of the CIC's efforts in the 1920s.

The CIC had announced its presence in the South in August 1920 with an "Appeal to the Christian People of the South," following a conference of state and county delegates. The language of the "Appeal" was carefully chosen:

> We, a group of white Christian men and women of the South, absolutely loyal to the best traditions and convictions of the South, and especially the principle of racial integrity, voluntarily assembled upon the invitation of the Commission on Inter-Racial Cooperation, and after prayerful and careful consideration of prevailing inter-racial relations and conditions, do deliberately declare it to be our profound conviction that the real responsibilities for the solution of inter-racial problems in the South rest directly upon the hearts and consciences of the Christian forces of our land.

---

[18]   Walter F. White to James Weldon Johnson, 4 December 1923, CIC folder, box L13, group II, Papers of the National Association for the Advancement of Colored People (NAACP), Manuscript Division, Library of Congress (LC), Washington, DC.

[19]   W. Fitzhugh Brundage, *Lynching in the New South: Georgia and Virginia, 1880-1930* (Urbana: University of Illinois Press, 1993), 210-211.

[20]   Ellis, "Commission on Interracial Cooperation," preface. See also Wilma Dykeman, *Prophet of Plenty: The First Ninety Years of W.D. Weatherford* (Knoxville: University of Tennessee Press, 1966), 132-144.

[21]   Gunnar Myrdal, *An American Dilemma: The Negro Problem and Modern Democracy* (New York: Harper & Brothers, 1944), 847.

We are also persuaded that the best method by which to approach the
consideration and solution of such problems is through local organizations,
composed of the recognised Christian leaders of both races....

It is a matter of common knowledge that grave injustices are often suffered by
members of the Negro race in matters of legal procedure, travelling facilities,
educational facilities, and public press, domestic service, child welfare, and
other relations of life.[22]

Four key positions thus defined the CIC: the centrality of Christian duty and
leadership, the commitment to separateness (i.e., *"especially the principle of racial
integrity"*), the pledge to work locally and the admission that unwarranted ill-
treatment of African Americans was rife. Only the latter was in any way radical,
marking a break with the traditional southern insistence that black people were
basically content and that the South cared well for those who knew their place.

By the summer of 1921, the CIC was no longer just an aid to postwar
adjustment. Having depended heavily at first on the resources of the YMCA, it
secured substantial long-term financial backing from the Phelps-Stokes Fund and
later from the Laura Spelman Rockefeller Memorial (LSRM), the Carnegie
Corporation and the Rosenwald Fund.[23] It was quite clear that some of those who
helped set up the CIC in the first place were keen to minimize the African American
presence in the central organization and determined that it should be white-
dominated.[24] The state commissions were all chaired by white men, typically social
workers, ministers and college presidents. County interracial committees, consisting

---

[22] "An Appeal to the Christian People of the South," August 1920, cited in George
      Madden Martin, "Race Cooperation," reprinted from *McClure's* 54 (October 1922): no
      page numbers. On the early months of the CIC, see McDonough, "Men and Women of
      Good Will," 40-60.

[23] John J. Eagan to the Laura Spelman Rockefeller Memorial (LSRM), 1 October 1921,
      folder 974, box 96, Laura Spelman Rockefeller Memorial Collection (LSRMC),
      Rockefeller Archive Center (RAC), Sleepy Hollow, NY; Will W. Alexander to James
      H. Dillard, 1 October 1921, ibid.; Eagan to Raymond B. Fosdick, 31 December 1921,
      ibid. See also Ellis, "Commission on Interracial Cooperation," 1-38. For contemporary
      accounts of the CIC and other "racial cooperation" activities, see Jerome Dowd, *The
      Negro in American Society* (New York: Century, 1926), 547-565, and Paul E. Baker,
      *Negro-White Adjustment: An Investigation and Analysis of Methods in the Interracial
      Movement in the United States* (New York: Association Press, 1934), passim.

[24] See, for example, Thomas Jesse Jones to Robert R. Moton, 25 March 1920, enclosing
      Jones to R.H. King, 25 March 1920, folder 5, box 14, Moton Family Papers, Manuscript
      Division, LC. From the outset, the black membership of the general commission
      remained small and handpicked. Five "outstanding Negro leaders" were co-opted in
      February 1920, but by 1922, when the commission had grown to fifty-eight members,
      drawn from thirteen southern states, it still only included five blacks: Moton of
      Tuskegee Institute, John Hope of Morehouse College in Atlanta, Methodist Episcopal
      bishop R.E. Jones of New Orleans, Isaac Fisher of Fisk University and John M. Gandy
      of Petersburg Normal and Industrial Institute in Florida. The eight women on the
      general commission were all white. By 1924, the number of blacks on the commission
      had risen to twenty-two, all men.

of six to ten prominent whites and blacks, were always dominated by their white members, who determined local needs. Nevertheless, a CIC staff member recalled the state and local committees as "a social miracle" in the Klan-dominated atmosphere of the early 1920s.[25]

The CIC set itself a target of 759 local committees in counties in which the black population exceeded ten percent of the total and by June 1920 562 had been set up. They collaborated with chambers of commerce, parks commissions, farm bureaux and education departments to improve facilities and services for black citizens. The committees also persuaded newspapers to avoid sensationalizing news items concerning racial matters. However, the attrition rate of the local committees was high. Of those set up, only about half did anything tangible and most folded after a few years. By 1925, there were only eleven active local committees in Georgia, and eight of those were newly organized or consolidated.[26] It is not unreasonable to assume that widespread disapproval of the implications of interracial cooperation, particularly in rural settings, contributed to the failure of local committees to function much beyond their initial creation. Anti-black thought was so entrenched in Georgia that any deviation was likely to be denounced, as had been amply demonstrated by the careers of Tom Watson after 1904 and Hoke Smith.

A key member of the CIC staff was the research secretary, Thomas Jackson Woofter, Jr., who was central to campaigns for better black education provision and against lynching.[27] After graduating in 1912 from University of Georgia at Athens, where his father was dean of education, he worked for the Phelps-Stokes Fund in a series of southern field studies. Woofter's first project was a study of black life in his hometown. A sincere, if simplistic, attempt to promote reform and cooperation, it was in tune with the outlook of white participants in the interracial movement. It also gave Woofter what he called his "first taste of the feeling of isolation which came to a Southerner … who was a moderate on questions of race." By advocating cooperation and dialogue and calling for reform, Woofter had taken a radical stance. White people in Athens were polite to his face, but he sensed their disapproval: "A nonconformist on race was likely to be looked on as a renegade or "nigger lover" in the community."[28] What Woofter had written was "nonconformist" only insofar as it implied that whites ought to take more of an interest in uplifting African American communities, but the political economy of the New South did not openly admit such desires.

Part of the chill of disapproval felt by Woofter and others in the interracial cooperation movement flowed from the tendency in the South to regard attempts to draw attention to the region's problems as the perpetuation of northern lies. As

---

[25] Thomas Jackson Woofter, *Southern Race Progress: The Wavering Color Line* (Washington, DC: Public Affairs Press, 1957), 164-167.

[26] Martin, "Race Cooperation"; Charles Kirk Pilkington, "The Trials of Brotherhood: The Founding of the Commission on Interracial Cooperation," *Georgia Historical Quarterly* 69 (Spring 1985): 75; Report to Annual State Meeting, Atlanta, 28 October 1925, frames 46-52, reel 50, file 122, series VII, CIC Papers, AUC.

[27] "General Survey of the Work of the Commission on Interracial Cooperation for 1921-23," folder 975, box 96, LSRMC, RAC.

[28] Woofter, *Southern Race Progress*, 24.

David Carlton and Peter Coclanis have put it, "a persistent sense of grievance led most whites to identify any internal criticism with treason, and to force even the mildest dissenters into silence or exile."[29] Such hostility, or the prospect of it, could be so daunting, even in the 1930s, that southern liberals could apparently be driven to suicide. Journalism Professor Clarence Cason killed himself in 1935 in his office at the University of Alabama at Tuscaloosa on the eve of publication of *90° in the Shade*, a book described by his successor, H. Bailey Thomson, as a "frank but sympathetic analysis of southern politics, racism, and poverty." Cason was convinced that the book would provoke an adverse reaction, although this did not occur, perhaps because of his suicide.[30]

The Georgia Committee of the CIC was always the most active state committee, under the successive leadership of Woofter, Clark H. Foreman (later the New Deal's special adviser on racial matters) and the rural sociologist, Arthur F. Raper. Woofter worked hardest on education and lynching, two areas in which CIC Executive Director Will Alexander thought the organization could make a real difference. The Georgia committee complained that only four percent of the state's education expenditure was spent on black schools, although black citizens paid nine percent of the city taxes that supported education spending, and this disparity became a recurrent theme in CIC literature. Woofter stated in his annual report for 1922, "this means that Negroes are taxed to build white school buildings, which is unfair and undemocratic." He circulated further research that showed how poorly Georgia was funding education, generally, and campaigned for the strengthening of higher education in the state. He also called for better health care to tackle tuberculosis, venereal disease and infant deaths.[31]

The legal work of the CIC in Georgia concerned racially motivated assaults, peonage and the defrauding of black farmers out of their land and crops. The CIC monitored and denounced the Klan in several high-profile cases, protected black farmers who had been attacked by the Klan and sought redress through the courts. This led to various kinds of witness intimidation, so that Woofter was required to protect and transport witnesses during trials.[32] In 1922, he led the CIC's efforts in several cases, including that of a prosperous black farmer, Asbury McClusky, who

---

29   David L. Carlton and Peter A. Coclanis, eds., *Confronting Southern Poverty in the Great Depression: "The Report on Economic Conditions of the South"* (Boston: Bedford/St. Martin's, 1996), 3. Newby, *Jim Crow's Defense*, 142. See also Bruce Clayton, *The Savage Ideal: Intolerance and Intellectual Leadership in the South, 1890-1914* (Baltimore: Johns Hopkins University Press, 1972).

30   H. Bailey Thomson, "Clarence Cason: Journalist in Academe," *Alabama Review* 52 (July 2000): 177-198. See also Clarence Cason, *90° in the Shade* (Chapel Hill: University of North Carolina Press, 1935).

31   R.P. Brooks, "The University and the State," *Bulletin of the University of Georgia* 26.2a (February 1926): 3, 20. "Better Race Relations in Georgia," draft, 1922, CIC folder, box L13, series L, group II, NAACP Papers, LC.

32   T.J. Woofter, Jr., *Progress in Race Relations in Georgia: Report of the Secretary of the Georgia Committee on Race Relations for 1922* (Atlanta, GA: Commission on Interracial Cooperation, 1922), 4-10, 14-15; Wilma Dykeman and James Stokely, *Seeds of Southern Change: The Life of Will Alexander* (Chicago: University of Chicago Press, 1962), 100-109; Woofter, *Southern Race Progress*, 31-37.

had been attacked by a group of white men and forced to leave his land. Woofter sued on behalf of McClusky and kept both the NAACP and the American Civil Liberties Union confidentially informed about the case. He did not want national publicity, fearing that the CIC would be accused of encouraging outside interference, but he was aware that small legal advances in minor cases might contribute to wider gains. Two whites were eventually indicted in the McClusky case, but no convictions were secured due to the inability of the prosecution to secure any white witnesses.[33]

One of the CIC's main objectives was to curb violence and Woofter's writing and lobbying influenced the way in which lynching moved to the center of racial debate in during the 1920s. There had been other attempts by middle class white southerners to mobilize public opinion against lynching, notably by the University Commission on Southern Race Questions and by local groups such as the Committee on Church Cooperation in Atlanta, but these bodies were barely active after 1920. Woofter had been involved with the University Commission as a student at the University of Georgia, one of its strongholds, and in his migration studies for the government and in his doctoral research, he had drawn particular attention to lynching as a push factor in black mobility.[34]

His disgust at the persistent level of racial violence in the 1920s was central to his commitment to the CIC and showed in the tenor of its literature. He later played this down, commenting that CIC's work against violence was

> the most spectacular part of its program, [but one] that was negative and defensive. Its more basic objectives were to spread the philosophy of cooperation between the leaders of the races on the basis of frankness, man to man; to secure the participation of Negroes as full participants in constructive programs; and to create a climate of public opinion favorable to the operation of other organizations concerned for the progress of the South.[35]

Jack Woofter's promotion to research secretary reflected Will Alexander's fear that the new generation of middle class white southerners were as ill-informed and prejudiced about black people as their parents. A survey of white southern colleges revealed little teaching on race, outside of general sociology, and the only widely used books were three quaint contributions by Willis D. Weatherford. Woofter was

---

33 Woofter, *Southern Race Progress*, 35-37. T.J. Woofter, Jr. to Will W. Alexander, 11 August 1922, frame 1199-1206, reel 46, file 60, series VII, CIC Papers, AUC; Depositions of Odessa and Willie Peters, ? August 1922, frame 1627-1631, reel 45, file 36, ibid.; T.J. Woofter, Jr., to Roger N. Baldwin, 30 June 1922, CIC folder, box L13, series L, group II, NAACP Papers, LC; Walter F. White to Woofter, 11 July 1922, ibid.; Woofter to White, 14 July 1922, ibid.; White to Woofter, 17 July 1922, ibid.; Woofter to White, 16 December 1922, ibid.; White to Woofter, 19 December 1922, ibid.; White to Woofter, 4 December 1923, ibid.

34 Brundage, *Lynching in the New South*, 215-225; U.S. Department of Labor (Division of Negro Economics), Special Bulletin, *Negro Migration in 1916-17* (Washington, DC: U.S. Government Printing Office, 1919), 79.

35 Woofter, *Southern Race Progress*, 163.

given the task of writing a textbook, *The Basis of Racial Adjustment*, published in 1925 and subsequently adopted by courses on race relations in sixty colleges.[36] The concept of "racial adjustment" had meant various things since Reconstruction, such as the advancement of the freedmen through industrial education, and Woofter would certainly have encountered it as a student. In the 1920s, the terms "race adjustment" or "racial adjustment" or "adjustment of race relations" were used by both black and white commentators to indicate progressive reform, in general. It provided a way of implying a degree of reform and change, without suggesting anything drastic and avoided use of provocative words such as "rights," "social," "political," or "equality."[37]

At the time, *The Basis of Racial Adjustment* was a unique and prescient book, and it cemented Woofter as part of a new generation of white writers. It also showed the ways in which his experiences as a Phelps-Stokes researcher and CIC activist had sensitized him to things far beyond the experiences of most white southern men of his age. The book was a condensation of rational arguments for fairer treatment of blacks by southern states and recognition of their rights. Breaking fundamentally with the mentality of southern white orthodoxy, his analysis of the economic, legal, political and social circumstances of black Americans and his prescriptions for progress were radical, constructive and clear. In some of his other work on race and rural conditions in the 1920s and 1930s, Woofter was deliberately detached and politically neutral, but in *The Basis of Racial Adjustment* he tore into the fabric of white supremacy, its core beliefs and widespread injustices.

His one major concession to the South was his attempt to present some aspects of segregation in a positive light. In terms of education, health, work, religion, charity and local government, he saw no point in segregation. But "social intermingling" had to be prevented. This was not prejudice, he claimed, but "the fundamental sociological principle of consciousness of kind, of pleasurable association with similars." There were "forms of segregation which are cruel and others which are useless," but "the preservation of racial integrity" was paramount; thus, "protective taboos and restrictions against intermarriage and to some extent against intermingling," were normal, "especially if there is a wide ethnic difference."

> If, in the long run, the wisdom and justice of such a system is not recognized by the Negro himself, there will either be constant discontent and friction or

---

[36]   Thomas Jackson Woofter, Jr., *The Basis of Racial Adjustment* (New York: Ginn, 1925). The title may have been a deliberate variation on Edgar Gardner Murphy's *The Basis of Ascendancy* (1910). George B. Tindall, "Southern Negroes since Reconstruction: Dissolving the Static Image," in Arthur S. Link and Rembert W. Patrick, eds., *Writing Southern History: Essays in Historiography in Honor of Fletcher M. Green* (Baton Rouge: Louisiana State University Press, 1965), 341. Weatherford's books were *Negro Life in the South* (1910), *Present Forces in Negro Progress* (1918) and *The Negro from Africa to America* (1924).

[37]   See, for example, P.B. Young, "Contribution of the Press in the Adjustment of Race Relations," *Southern Workman* 57.4 (April 1928): 147-154.

amalgamation. There is no alternative to these two, except the systematic minimization of social contacts.[38]

W.E.B. Du Bois, reviewing Woofter's book in the *Crisis*, was agreeably shaken, considering Woofter's background:

> The Basis of Racial Adjustment ... is far and away the best thing on the relations of the races in the South that has come from a Southern white writer in our day. It is singularly fair and thoughtful; so eminently fair indeed, that after glancing at the first pages and noting the catholicity of treatment I was compelled to go through the rest of the book with a fine-tooth comb to find the lurking surrender to Southern race hate. I did not find it. ... I know of no book by a Southern white man with which I so thoroughly and heartily agree.[39]

Du Bois had obviously not read it especially carefully (he would dismiss Woofter's subsequent work on race as worthless), but these comments on the *Basis of Racial Adjustment* suggest that Woofter had, at least, made Du Bois reconsider the critical remarks he had made less than a year earlier in the *Nation* about white liberals in Georgia. Other African American readers were more cautious. A reviewer for the *Journal of Negro History*, possibly Carter G. Woodson, was disappointed by Woofter's failure to challenge segregation explicitly.[40] Another black reviewer, Eugene Kinckle Jones of the National Urban League, writing in *Opportunity*, called *The Basis of Racial Adjustment* "one of the most liberal books by a Southern white man…. But residing in Georgia, and in a professional way meeting almost daily the problems which he describes, one would naturally expect him to fail in his effort to treat the *whole* subject objectively." He thought Woofter seemed weak on black healthcare and unaware of organizations like the NAACP and the NUL, and he disliked Woofter's strictures against excessive social contact.[41]

Liberal white reviewers were generally enthusiastic and saw the book as a breakthrough. Praising Woofter's lack of prejudice, sensationalism and dogmatism, the *American Economic Review* called *The Basis of Racial Adjustment* "far and away the best balanced and sanest survey we have seen of the American race (negro) problem. As a text book it is all that could be asked." To the *American Political Science Review*, it was "informed and temperate," while the *Catholic World* called it a "very readable and fair-minded attempt to throw light on existing conditions among the Negroes, with some excellent suggestions regarding the solution of problems confronting both their race and ours." The *Survey* commented that "this book at once takes the front rank among textbooks available for study and discussion of this subject," although it was best suited to southern classrooms,

---

[38] Woofter, *Basis of Racial Adjustment*, 235-241. The "consciousness of kind" idea was taken from the work of sociologist Franklin H. Giddings, of Columbia University, where Woofter completed his PhD.

[39] *Crisis* 31 (November 1925): 31-32, reprinted in Herbert Aptheker, ed., *Book Reviews by W.E.B. Du Bois* (Millwood, NY: KTO Press, 1977), 77.

[40] Review in *Journal of Negro History* 10.3 (July 1925): 572-573.

[41] Review in *Opportunity* 3.35 (November 1925): 342-343.

because opinion in northern colleges was more advanced.[42] Clark Foreman, who had replaced Woofter as secretary of the Georgia Committee of the CIC, gave him an enthusiastic puff in the *Atlanta Constitution*, which Foreman's family owned. Calling Woofter "one of the best posted students of the race problem in the country," he described the book as much more than a textbook—it was "necessary for anyone making a study of the American negro"—and compared it to Murphy's *The Basis of Ascendancy*.[43]

By the end of the twentieth century, the general verdict on the CIC was that it was a false start on the road to civil rights; a body in which well-intentioned whites were shown to be ultimately irresolute and self-interested. The implication was that, had the CIC leadership been more outspoken and aggressive, more might have been achieved after World War I in terms of equal rights. Plainly, that view tends to ignore the enormous pressure to conform in the 1920s to existing white mores on race and it also ignores evidence that white people in the CIC wanted to go further, but dared not do so.

When the possibility of interracial meetings of young people of both sexes under the auspices of the YMCA and the YWCA in cities such as Richmond and Nashville arose in 1925, the CIC leadership handled it very warily. The *Chicago Daily News* reported that the annual conference was pleased that young southerners were interested in cooperation, but mixing young men and women of both races was thought too dangerous on several levels. It was agreed that "too much haste in this direction might result in misunderstanding and friction that would jeopardize all the good will generated by the commission in six years of patient effort." Chairman Ashby Jones stated, "There is still too much suspicion and there are too many immature minds in both races to permit our assuming a position whereby we might be held responsible for any trouble that might arise out of badly handled meetings of this character."[44] By the end of the 1920s, Jones was advocating granting the full rights of citizenship to blacks, including the vote, but he never abandoned his belief in the need for segregation.[45]

Will Alexander showed a greater willingness to relax the rules on segregation, but he hid his opinions as much as possible. He allowed the dining hall to be integrated at one of the CIC's interracial conferences for students in Missouri in 1922, but he kept the matter secret afterwards.[46] On the one occasion in the 1920s when he spoke out unambiguously, he was made to regret it. In an address to an Interdenominational Young People's Conference in Birmingham, Alabama, in 1926, Alexander was emboldened to state that Jim Crow laws were wrong: "I believe in the repeal of any unjust law, and it [segregation] is wrong." The conference turned on him and the next day white Methodist ministers in Birmingham jointly declared Alexander was "unsuited to take the lead in the discussion and direction of race

[42]   Extracts from *Book Review Digest* (1925), cf "Woofter, Thomas Jackson."
[43]   *Atlanta Constitution*, 7 June, 1925.
[44]   *Chicago Daily News*, 25 April 1925, clipping, frame 1649, reel 28, file 39, series IV, CIC Papers.
[45]   Brundage, *Lynching in the New South*, 220.
[46]   Link, *Paradox of Southern Progressivism*, 253.

relations." It almost caused him to be removed from the CIC leadership and was the last time he said it.[47]

One sympathetic black observer was Benjamin E. Mays, the president of Morehouse College for thirty years and the educator who most inspired Martin Luther King, Jr. Mays began teaching in Atlanta in 1921, in the midst of the tension between the CIC and the KKK. Looking back in the 1980s, he could see why some had criticized the CIC for being conservative, wedded to segregation and slow to push for a federal antilynching law, commenting, "The Commission never sought to abolish segregation; it worked to improve conditions between the races *within the segregated system*." He recalled that many whites nevertheless regarded the CIC as dangerous, requiring much of its work to be done in secret.

> If Alexander had set out in 1920 to abolish segregation, the Commission would never have been allowed to function, and Will Alexander would have been considered insane if he had insisted on it. If he had tried to abolish segregation, the Ku Klux Klan would have had the support of most white southerners [and] would have abolished the Commission.[48]

In March 1930, the *Southern Methodist* charged that the CIC was out to destroy segregation and that new chairman Robert Eleazer, had "Socialistic leanings." The following month, Eleazer issued a clarification designed to placate both white and black critics: "The Commission is definitely on record as being opposed to the stiffening of the segregation laws now prevailing. On the other hand, it has not deemed it wise or desirable to seek the abrogation of these laws at present."[49] As late as 1945, in debates within the Southern Regional Council, which replaced the CIC, Will Alexander was still hesitant about taking a stand against racial segregation.[50]

The CIC was very much a white initiative—it stood for interracial cooperation, but on terms laid down by white reformers, not black activists, and its limited impact was very much at the local level—county or town—rather than state. Its regional importance in the 1920s was questionable and its national profile was negligible. As Charles Pilkington has noted, "Compared to the specific demands of the NAACP, the Commission formulated remarkably imprecise policies."[51] This may have been a consequence of its reliance on localism, but it was primarily a response to the dangers of advocating radical ideas about race in the South in the repressive heyday of the new Klan.

Nevertheless, the CIC did achieve some things. During the 1920s, lynching became increasingly unacceptable behavior, condemned by politicians, pastors and the press, instead of being quietly ignored or subtly excused. This change was partly

---

[47]   Egerton, *Speak Now against the Day*, 48; McDonough, "Men and Women of Good Will," 85.

[48]   Benjamin E. Mays, *Born to Rebel: An Autobiography* (Athens: University of Georgia Press, 1987), 71-72.

[49]   McDonough, "Men and Women of Good Will," 85 n. 73, 88.

[50]   Egerton, *Speak Now against the Day*, 314-315.

[51]   Charles Clark Pilkington, "Trials of Brotherhood: The Founding of the Commission on Interracial Cooperation," *Georgia Historical Quarterly* 69 (Spring 1985): 78.

in response to the economic consequences of black migration, but the tone of disapproval stemmed also from the efforts of the CIC. When Jack Woofter gave his report to the annual conference of the Georgia state committee in 1925, he had only two lynchings (both gruesome) to report, whereas ten years earlier he could have reported twenty or more. Moreover, the Women's Committee of the CIC was the springboard from which Jessie Daniel Ames launched the Association of Southern Women for the Prevention of Lynching.[52]

John Kneebone has shown the connection between the CIC, white liberalism and the changing southern press. The CIC also helped to forge the South's New Deal generation. John Egerton, Patricia Sullivan and a host of other writers on southern liberalism and early civil rights activism all give the CIC a role in translating imprecise impulses in the southern mind to do the right thing into action, within certain limits. Did the CIC really challenge the system? Was Du Bois right about white liberals in the South? For so long as the CIC accepted second-class citizenship for blacks, it was a very one-sided "interracial cooperation," designed to make white southerners feel civilized and black people grateful. Not until after 1930, did a new generation of white southern reformers emerge, motivated by religion, prompted by black activists and encouraged by the assault of social scientists on the assumptions and malice underlying scientific racism. Finally, in the context of the New Deal, a few white people such as Howard Kester and others based in Tennessee, like H.L. Mitchell, and the Virginian journalist, Virginius Dabney—those Egerton calls the "new progressives"—were prepared to speak out and challenge Jim Crow.[53]

Prior to the New Deal, the creed of racial separatism was so severe that the most significant white southern engagement with the issue of race after World War I—the work of the CIC—was always inhibited in scope and style. The repressive effect of scorn and scepticism saw white liberals constantly censoring themselves to avoid reaction, while inching forward when they dared. As a consequence, the interracial movement in the South underachieved badly in the 1920s, at a time when black political consciousness and activism were rising fast and the southern economy and education system were ripe for modernization. Thus opportunities for collaboration and understanding were squandered.

When the New Deal administrator, Aubrey Williams, remarked, "In the South we have no liberals—only conservatives and radicals," he was being sardonic, but on the question of race he had a point.[54] Although southern white liberals were not actually absent, their status is perhaps best described as liminal. The very few individuals who questioned fundamentally the basis of white supremacy and

---

[52]   Report to Annual State Meeting, 28 October 1925, CIC Papers, AUC; Jacquelyn Dowd Hall, *Revolt against Chivalry: Jessie Daniel Ames and the Women's Campaign against Lynching*, rev.ed. (New York: Columbia University Press, 1993), 124-191.

[53]   Egerton, *Speak Now against the Day*, 74, 77-78. John T. Kneebone, *Southern Liberal Journalists and the Issue of Race, 1920-1944* (Chapel Hill: University of North Carolina Press, 1985). Patricia Sullivan, *Days of Hope: Race and Democracy in the New Deal Era* (Chapel Hill: University of North Carolina Press, 1996). Dabney published *Liberalism in the South* (Chapel Hill: University of North Carolina Press, 1932).

[54]   Cited in T. Harry Williams, "Huey, Lyndon, and Southern Radicalism," *Journal of American History* 60 (September 1973): 272.

enforced separateness, rarely spoke openly and, if they did, they chose their words carefully. A repressive consensus operated to minimize divergence by members of the more powerful race from the standard construction of the deficient Negro, permanently mired in lower standards of comfort, morality, civility, intelligence and vigor. In the interwar period, white people who held views that differed from the New South orthodoxy of African American subordination, or who sought dialogue with black leaders, were regarded by most southerners as extremists or dupes. From a later standpoint, the challenge posed to Jim Crow by southern white reformers may appear mild. They stressed the need for African American economic progress, better communication between the races and an end to brutality, but they also generally concurred with segregation. And yet, the swiftness with which white liberals were portrayed as disloyal to their race and region ensured that open criticism of the Jim Crow system was rare. Lynching declined after World War I, but emphatic segregationist positions were fortified by new laws, and diehard politicians went unchallenged, making the mountain that the civil rights movement would eventually have to conquer no less steep and the struggle no less bitter.[55]

---

[55]   Perhaps the one organization across the South that did encourage a full debate about race and changed the minds of whites who engaged with it was the YWCA, although it remained segregated until the 1940s. An important network of future civil rights activists emerged from the YWCA in the 1920s. See Brundage, *Lynching in the New South*, 221, and Hall, *Revolt against Chivalry*, 101-104.

REPRESSION AT HOME, LIBERATION ABROAD:
WILSONIANISM AND AMERICAN ANTICOMMUNISM, 1912-1920

Alex Goodall

In 1952, William E. Leuchtenberg wrote that, "No distinction is more revered by the American historian than that between domestic and foreign affairs and in few periods of our history has that distinction been more religiously observed than in the progressive era."[1] In the intervening decades, scholars have routinely broken down such barriers. But forty years later, Thomas J. McCormick was still able to complain with some justification that historians of American foreign relations tend to invest "more energy in debating the relative primacy of internal and external than in articulating their connectedness."[2]

This is certainly a valid criticism for the history of anticommunism in America, where the connection between the foreign and domestic spheres is problematic not least because it is so politically charged. The debate over communism's place in America centers upon the idea of foreignness, with anticommunists portraying American radicals as a product of subversive aggression by foreign agents, and anti-anticommunists depicting the Communist Party of the USA (CPUSA) as an indigenous vehicle for the expression of native radicalism. To use McCormick's schema, this debate remains about "primacy" rather than "connectedness."[3] But indigenousness and foreignness are not comfortable oppositions, as this debate would imply. As, most recently, Ellen Schrecker and Maurice Isserman pointed out, the un-American has been most threatening when domestic conspiracies were linked to foreign machinations.[4] Aliens are a problem when they live in America; foreignness is primarily a threat when it is domestic. In fact, the conception of a linear historical force proceeding in either direction can only satisfy the dogmatic.

After much lengthy debate, historians of communism have come some way toward highlighting the conflicted role American communists played in balancing

---

[1]   William E. Leuchtenberg, "Progressivism and Imperialism: The Progressive Movement and American Foreign Policy, 1898-1916," *Mississippi Valley Historical Review* 39.3 (December 1952): 483.

[2]   Thomas J. McCormick, "Roundtable: Explaining the History of American Foreign Relations-World Systems," *Journal of American History* 77.1 (June 1990): 125.

[3]   See, for instance, Preston's criticism of Murray for treating "the red scare of 1919-20 as largely, if not entirely, the result of World War I and of the Russian Revolution of 1917," and therefore underplaying deeper domestic currents of antiradicalism and nativism. William Preston, Jr., *Aliens and Dissenters: Federal Suppression of Radicals, 1903-1933* (Cambridge, MA: Harvard University Press, 1963), 2; Robert K. Murray, *Red Scare: A Study in National Hysteria, 1919-1920* (Minneapolis: University of Minnesota Press, 1955).

[4]   Most recently noted by Maurice Isserman and Ellen Schrecker in "'Papers of a Dangerous Tendency': From Major Andre's Boot to the VENONA files," in Ellen Schrecker, ed., *Cold War Triumphalism: The Misuse of History after the Fall of Communism* (New York: New Press, 2004), 149.

Cold War geopolitics with domestic activism.[5] But too often scholars still seek to rank the relative significance of foreign and domestic impulses, rather than examine their interrelationship. Even this progress has been absent in terms of the history of *anti*communism. Mary Dudziak and others have produced invaluable work on the way in which the prism of Cold War anticommunism affected the federal government's response to the civil rights movement.[6] Markku Ruotsila has helped to delineate a transatlantic community of anticommunist thinking before the Cold War.[7] But despite such honorable exceptions, the canon is still primarily populated by either domestic studies of American anticommunism or tightly-focused examinations of U.S. diplomacy toward rival communist states.

There is a rich seam untapped. It will have to suffice here to note that many of the major organizations involved in the development of anticommunism occupied a nether zone between foreign and domestic life. The counter-espionage apparatus of the U.S. Army and Justice Department, the Catholic church, congressional investigative committees, even whilst they draped themselves in the American flag, all operated with partially internationalised attitudes, agendas and organizational structures. Sometimes anticommunists extended their domestic fears to the international arena; sometimes they brought international politics home; most often, as in the case of the Wilson administration discussed here, ideas and policies emerged from a complicated, though not always intellectually consistent, interaction of both.

During the presidency of Woodrow Wilson, the United States transformed itself at home and abroad. The traditions of American foreign policy were abandoned for a campaign to establish political systems around the world modeled on the American system. Interventions in Mexico, Europe and finally Russia were undertaken with the stated aim of spreading democracy and freedom to oppressed peoples, plotting a middle way between imperialism and revolution. Efforts to engineer popular support for interventionism in Europe, however, led the administration to a less democratic approach toward domestic dissent. The political repression that followed helped shatter the old socialist left and collapse the progressive consensus in favor of a new pro-war alignment of center and right. Wilson's choices would ensure that for the next fifteen years, American politics would be dominated by a voluntarist conservatism that stressed the primacy of business over society, a conservatism that expected and enforced from its citizens a strict conformity to a narrowly defined conception of national loyalty.

---

[5]   Or, as Schrecker has put it, for viewing "US communism as a wildly contradictory movement that sought domestic reform while flacking for the Soviet Union." Ellen Schrecker, "The Spies Who Loved Us?" *The Nation* (6 May 1999), at http://www.thenation.com/doc/19990524/schrecker, accessed on 12 April 2007.

[6]   Mary Dudziak, *Cold War Civil Rights: Race and the Image of American Democracy* (Princeton: Princeton University Press, 2000); Thomas Borstelmann, *Cold War and the Color Line: American Race Relations in the Global Arena* (Cambridge, MA: Harvard University Press, 2001).

[7]   Markku Ruotsila, *British and American Anticommunism before the Cold War* (London: Frank Cass, 2001).

An anticommunist tradition was born that fused traditional forms of antiradicalism with Wilson's crusading idealism, rationalizing repressive practices within a democratic society as a necessary part of a wider project of universal human liberation. This anticommunist liberalism contrasts not only with contemporary anticommunists to Wilson's left and right, but also later forms of liberal anticommunism that stressed an aggressive anti-Soviet policy abroad, but tolerance for dissent as part of a commitment to reform at home. This article presents some tentative observations about the events between 1912 and 1920 that led to the evolution of this policy.

I

Woodrow Wilson's presidency is best remembered for its foreign policy. In the half century between the Gilded Age and the Cold War, the United States moved from continental expansion to a "neo-imperialism" based on the promotion of American ideology overseas and the selective use of military and economic power to ensure the establishment of favorable regimes and trading relations with client states. Whatever the impulses behind this transformation, President Wilson's critical contribution was to provide an intellectual framework in which the new foreign policy might operate: "grand strategy" *avant la lettre*. Progressive-era imperialism had lacked a *modus operandi*, struggling to explain itself beyond avowals of masculine vigor and the white man's burden. U.S. interventions between 1898 and 1912 were a muddle. As Americans struggled to find a foreign policy that suited its culture and traditions, they opted for, for instance: occupation and eventual annexation in the case of Hawaii; gunboat diplomacy and partial occupation in Panama; occupation without annexation in Puerto Rico; non-territorial control by legal amendment in Cuba; economic influence in China; intermittent military adventurism in Nicaragua; and "European-style" colonial imperialism in the Philippines. Wilson's achievement was to provide an intellectual framework that simplified the dizzying array of options available to diplomats and politicians. He provided a rationale for U.S. expansionism that could be sold to a voting public sincerely attached to America's anti-colonial heritage, yet vague enough to allow for the continuing protection and promotion of U.S. interests using whatever tool was most appropriate to each situation. Distilling and reframing the progressive rhetoric that underpinned U.S. foreign policy since the Spanish-American war, if not the Revolution of 1776, Wilson articulated America's foreign policy as a civilizing mission of spreading democracy throughout the world and repeatedly addressed his political pronouncements to abstracted "peoples," rather than their governments.

That this was his bequest to the nation was ironic, since Wilson had stated that his primary concern was domestic affairs. But the president's dominance of the progressive agenda after 1912 left little option for his opponents but to criticize his international policy. The president faced growing pressure to project power abroad. Wilson was forced to respond to this, but it would be unduly cynical to imply that the principles that Wilson articulated were mere gloss. For instance, Wilson sent the marines into Mexico to oust the government of a weaker nation, and he earned the eternal opprobrium of Mexican nationalists for doing so. But he sent his troops in to unseat the dictatorship of General Victoriano Huerta in the name of the constitutionalist forces of Venustiano Carranza, Emiliano Zapata and Francisco "Pancho" Villa. His predecessor, William Howard Taft, had by contrast looked to one side while his ambassadorial staff conspired to unseat the constitutionalists (then led by Francisco Madero) and install Huerta. Hindsight reveals that Wilson's intervention manifestly failed to promote democracy or liberty. But naïve as it may have been, the president genuinely believed that America's unique gifts made it possible to intervene in a way that would create a democratic space for subjected peoples to use. Wilson's liberal interventionism was both more restrained and more ambitious than that of his conservative critics. His "invasion" of Mexico comprised only the seizure of the customs house and city of Veracruz, but its declared aim was the liberation of the Mexican nation and the deliverance of its people.

Wilson's preferred method, especially towards powerful countries, was one of "watchful waiting"—the use of non-recognition, propaganda and economic policy as instruments of soft power. Indeed, the negative reaction Wilson witnessed in Mexico made him even more reluctant to resort to military force. The humanistic imperatives and preference for non-military action can also be seen in his three year refusal to intervene in Europe. In the end, traditional interest-based calculations made entry into the World War inevitable. Self-defence (the resumption of German submarine warfare) and security (the publication of the Zimmermann Telegram seemed to indicate that German was conspiring with Mexico to retake the former Mexican territories of the southwest United States) drove America to war. But war aims, especially following the March 1917 revolution in Russia that unseated the Tsarist regime, were still articulated within a conception of extending the sphere of American liberty and rejecting the old diplomacy. So strong was Wilson's aversion to traditional territorial and geopolitical war aims that the president insisted on joining the war as an "Associated" rather than "Allied" power of Britain, France and Russia.

In stark contrast, at home, the war saw the creation of agencies to coordinate and regulate private sector groups in explosive campaigns to root out disloyalty. Here, the Wilson administration acted as the enemy of liberty, locking up and deporting those who exercised their rights to free speech in ways that were deemed destabilizing to the government.

As Michael Heale has argued, since the late nineteenth century, antiradicalism had been growing rapidly as a force in American life, underpinned by the twin forces of industrialization and urbanization.[8] Intolerance was fuelled by the proximities of the city and the distances of class, along with the ethnic and racial tensions that accompanied the mass migration of peoples to the new centers of capital. Big business deployed anti-labor politics to keep the unions out of their factories and enterprises; the middle classes saw in the radical protestor a threat to their social order; and artisans saw in the industrial organizer a challenge to the privileged status of the craft union. Across all classes, white, English-speaking

---

[8]   Michael J. Heale, *American Anticommunism: Combating the Enemy Within* (Baltimore: Johns Hopkins University Press, 1990), 22.

Americans associated the radical with the mongrelization of the United States; while the religious mistrusted the supposedly atheistic proclamations of the revolutionary. At the same time, the power of the state was growing, and this stimulated the formation of lobby groups that sought to direct government policy and influence the state's choice of enemy. Lobbying highlighted internal disputes that had formerly lain dormant. When the Federal Council of Churches was formed in 1908 to lobby government as the supposed voice of Protestantism in America, tensions emerged within and among the Protestant denominations over what that particular voice should say. Soon, the council was being criticized by conservative and fundamentalist Protestant churches as a hotbed of radicalism.

Until the Wilson administration, the federal government had played no part in this phenomenon, and it had had little effect on U.S. foreign policy, which remained the preserve of the State Department elite. Antiradicalism was the preoccupation of private interests and the municipalities. Besides, when there was enthusiasm in government for the harassment of labor activists, there was no mandate for it.[9] Now, however, the federal government began to take a leading role in campaigns against radicalism, combining political repression with a virulent hostility to the German enemy and in the process merging traditional antiradicalism with Wilson's new globalising ideology of liberation. President Wilson used the growing power of the state to create a sophisticated governmental and para-governmental apparatus for enforcing loyalty and generating popular support for the war. Organizations like the Committee on Public Information (CPI) and the American Protective League were used to persuade and police the public will, and in turn these groups stimulated the anti-German activism of crusading organizations like the National Security League and American Defense Society.[10] He effectively aligned the conservative wing of progressivism with the right and away from social reformers and liberals. In a classic elision, the fact that left-wing anti-war agitation and German espionage produced similar consequences was used to demonstrate that they shared causes.

By the time of the October revolution in Russia then, the Wilson administration had already begun to demonstrate the contradictory tendencies that would come to characterise his response to Bolshevism between 1917 and 1919. The hypothesis was clear: resistance from within was engineered from without; to respond, America must control or expel dissenters in America whilst promoting development, multilateralism and democracy in Europe. Wilson directed the machinery of war toward emancipatory goals yet used the machinery of government on the home front to clamp down on dissent. By the end of the war, the administration was treating domestic radicals more violently than the Russian Bolsheviks it blamed them on. At the same time that foreign and domestic politics were coming together, the approach taken towards them appeared to be diverging.

---

[9]   Preston, *Aliens and Dissenters*, 5, 55-62.
[10]   Heale, *American Anticommunism*, 52.

II

The Wilson administration's attitude toward Bolshevism went through three main phases. During the first, between the summer of 1917 and the summer of 1918, Wilson was deliberately ambiguous about the possibility of conciliation with the Bolsheviks. However, he took little action to restrain his staff's persecution of dissent at home, except when he considered it to have a bearing on his policy in Russia. In the second phase, in the months following Russia's separate peace with Germany at Brest-Litovsk, the need to win the war led him to adopt a harder line both at home and abroad. However, even at this stage he continued to restrain himself in Russia, much to the annoyance of both the Allies and his staff. Finally, between the Armistice of November 1918 and the stroke that effectively incapacitated him ten months later, Wilson pushed for a liberal anti-Bolshevik strategy in Russia and withdrawal of all forces from Russian territory, whilst accelerating his antiradical rhetoric at home. The widening discrepancy between his approach to revolutionaries in Russia and America produced an embryonic containment doctrine on the one hand, and an incipient McCarthyism on the other.

After the first Russian revolution of March 1917, the president was optimistic for the new Russia. He believed that since the war was being fought to save democracy, the mass of the people in Russia would be eager to sustain the Eastern front. The Bolsheviks, the only group to argue consistently for an immediate peace, were irresponsible agitators. But despite such views, little was done in practice to support the Kerensky regime beyond dispatching Elihu Root on an ill-defined mission in June (and not even seeing him when he got back); sending an engineer who had helped build the Panama canal to advise on rebuilding Russia's railways; granting some modest credit to the government; and lavishing praise upon the regime from afar.[11] None of this helped avert the second revolution, and when, following the October seizure of power, the Bolsheviks declared their intention to conduct peace negotiations with the Germans, the president's anti-Bolshevik inclinations were hastily confirmed. Nevertheless, in the months leading up to the Russo-German peace of Brest-Litovsk, Wilson's position toward the new rulers of Russia remained moderate, especially if compared to most of those around him. Indeed, the president deliberately obscured his instinctive hostility to Bolshevism. He confined himself to making vague statements of faith in the patriotic spirit of the Russian people, hoping that it might be possible to sustain the Eastern front or that the Bolshevik regime would collapse once the depth of its abdication to German militarism became clear. It was a step too far to recognize the new regime, but Wilson resisted speaking out against the Bolsheviks until the ink upon the treaty of Brest-Litovsk was dry. He resisted, often by little more than fiat, the objections of Secretary of State Robert Lansing and his department, who were deeply hostile to the Bolsheviks.[12] He ignored moderates led by the Red Cross advisor in Petrograd,

---

11   Donald E. Davis and Eugene P. Trani, *The First Cold War: The Legacy of Woodrow Wilson in U.S.-Soviet Relations* (Columbia: University of Missouri Press, 2002), 30-52.

12   Wilson was considering asking for Lansing's resignation in September 1917. See Diary of Col. House, 9 September 1917, in Arthur S. Link, ed., *The Papers of Woodrow*

Raymond Robins, who called for immediate recognition and co-opting the Bolsheviks. Perhaps most significantly, he rejected the ministrations of his French and British allies, who, as early as December 1917, had come to the firm conclusion that full scale military intervention in Siberia and the ouster of the Bolsheviks was the only way to keep open the Eastern front. Wilson rebuffed these arguments in a classically liberal manner, noting that intervention was as likely to stimulate Bolshevism as undermine it, that the popular will of the Russian people was bound in the end to overcome the repressive rule of a minority, and that the principle of national self-determination meant that intervention was morally wrong.

The president's most hostile statement came in his December State of the Union address, in which he referred disparagingly to the Bolsheviks as "the masters of German intrigue" who had led "the people of Russia astray...."[13] But he significantly failed to refer to the communist revolutionaries by name. In his January "Fourteen Points" address, itself stimulated by the Bolsheviks' peace overtures, Wilson again avoided naming the Bolsheviks directly. He described them as sincere and earnest, and declared the Allies' treatment of Russia to be the acid test of their good will. In March, he even sent a message of friendship and good wishes to the Fourth All-Russia Congress of Soviets, although a scriptwriter's sympathetic reference to the ongoing "process of revolution" proved too much for Wilson, even behind gritted teeth (it was replaced with sympathy for the "struggle for freedom").[14] The Bolsheviks could have been forgiven for thinking that the United States was hinting that it might consider recognition. Raymond Robins, the only U.S. agent to have regular access to the Bolsheviks, believed that negotiation was possible, and the president failed to disabuse him of the notion: at the very least, in order to keep his options open.

Instead of attacking the Bolsheviks, the president focused on promoting the United States. The progressive faith in publicity as the solution to the world's problems was now made evident: the CPI was charged with selling America to the Russian masses. Dispatched in October, CPI representative Edgar Sisson arrived in Moscow just days after the fall of Kerensky. He set about a vigorous propaganda campaign on behalf of the United States. Before long, he was reporting to his superiors that American newsreels were running in virtually every cinema in Moscow and Petrograd, that he had printed material placed on 50,000 billboards, and aeroplanes were raining thousands of handbills down upon the soldiers at the front.[15] Ironically, the propaganda achieved very little to improve America's reputation in Russia, but it undoubtedly exacerbated the hostility to radicalism at home.

Wilson (Princeton, NJ: Princeton University Press, 1983), 44:176. Henceforth referred to as *WWP*.

[13] State of the Union Address, 4 December 1917, *WWP*, 45:199.

[14] Woodrow Wilson (hereafter WW) to Fourth All-Russia Congress of Soviets, 11 March 1918, *WWP*, 46:598.

[15] James R. Mock and Cedric Larson, *Words That Won the War: The Story of the Committee on Public Information, 1917-1919* (Princeton, NJ: Princeton University Press, 1939), 304.

Wilson's argument, that action taken to repress the Bolsheviks would only strengthen their appeal, could not have contrasted more clearly with his approach to domestic radicalism. In the pre-war years, Wilson had disapproved of the excesses of ultra-patriotism. As late as February 1917, the president had vetoed an Immigration Act which included strict controls on radicals seeking entry to the country. The president felt its wording would lead to the exclusion of "good" revolutionaries who had fought against tyrannical regimes abroad. In the words of William Preston, the president's "solicitude for foreign revolutionaries" seemed to stand in the way of Congress' desire to suppress the radical left.[16] But after the United States formally entered the war, Wilson began to move his concerns for political refugees to the back of his mind and focus instead upon a more aggressive attitude toward the regulation of dissent.

Believing that the workers would be the hardest class to get behind the war, the administration launched a campaign to crack down on radical labor groups. Anti-war activists were to be separated from the mainstream of the labor movement in order to reinforce the authority of the pro-war wing of the American Federation of Labor (AFL) under Samuel Gompers.[17] As early as 1915, Wilson had permitted investigations into radical activities in the Western states of California, Oregon, Washington and Utah.[18] By 1917, more or less open warfare between government and radicals had been declared. Congress ferried through new laws to increase federal power drastically. June saw the Espionage Act, which outlawed efforts to obstruct enlistment or interfere with war production. This was swiftly followed by the Trading With the Enemy Act, which included a clause giving the attorney general sweeping powers to ban foreign language publications. Using these new laws the Departments of Justice and Labor began pursuing radicals, particularly within the Socialist party and the Industrial Workers of the World (IWW), the Wobblies. Ironically, fearing just such a backlash, the IWW had not even formally adopted an anti-war plank in its program.

The administration was divided over the best method of prosecuting the Wobblies, with Secretary of Labor William B. Wilson more concerned for civil liberties than the staff of the Immigration Bureau, who wanted wholesale arrests and deportations for anyone who was even a member.[19] But despite a residue of civil liberties thinking, there was a general consensus over the need to try radicals during the war. The Attorney General Thomas Gregory with President Wilson's approval, led efforts to prosecute the leadership of the IWW and the publishers of the major socialist press, *The Masses,* the *American Socialist,* and *The Call*, for seditious conspiracy. Raids on sixty-four IWW offices in September 1917 were used to gather evidence. Then, in the first major mass loyalty trial of the war, in Chicago, 166

---

[16]   Preston, *Aliens and Dissenters*, 81.

[17]   Felix Frankfurter, Memorandum on IWW, 4 September 1917, *WWP*, 44:162. In instructions to the secretary of labor, he explained that investigations into conditions should take place as part of any anti-IWW prosecution, though no formal hearings would be established. WW to William Bauchop Wilson, 19 September 1917, *WWP*, 44:215.

[18]   Preston, *Aliens and Dissenters*, 60.

[19]   Ibid., 101-103.

Wobblies were indicted.[20] Since early 1917, the postmaster general had been restricting IWW publications from the mail. This damaged IWW efforts to contest their prosecution, appeal to public opinion, and raise contributions for defence. Even blank donation request forms were banned from the post.[21]

As well as the legislative approach, the government used the army to break strikes, especially after an IWW-led strike began in the lumber regions of the Northwest in June 1917. Since the administration had federalized the National Guard, it was left to the army to control radical industrial action. Between March and May, Wilson granted expansive new authority for local commanders to intervene against seditious or disloyal behavior.[22] From this point on, until the end of the war, the army was used intermittently to restrict IWW activities. On multiple occasions, various IWW headquarters were raided, with Wobblies arrested and held without trial for extended periods under a notional (but not constitutional) martial law. In the process of intervening in local employer-employee disputes, cooperation between local business and the army quickly became "close and customary."[23]

Wilson began to receive a trickle, then a steady flow of mail from public figures opposed to this reactionary turn. Many used the kinds of liberal arguments the president was deploying over Russia. Most assumed the president was an innocent party, failing to believe that their much-loved leader could have permitted his staff to introduce such draconian controls over freedoms of expression and assembly. Oswald Garrison Villard, Walter Lippmann, Upton Sinclair, Roger Baldwin, Amos Pinchot, Edward Prentiss Costigan and Herbert Croly were among those who wrote to express their fears.[24] Staunchly pro-war socialists were concerned by the attempted prosecution of the anti-war socialist press.[25] Even Wilson's closest and most loyal advisor, Col. Edward House, quietly expressed his concern over the president's tolerance of intolerance.

Wilson refused to bend to liberal opposition. He disarmed his critics with polite letters of acknowledgement that expressed his agreement with the spirit of their complaints without conceding any of their substance.[26] He did just enough to

---

20   Preston notes that "Once Attorney General Gregory had defined the Chicago IWW case as a war priority and described the Wobbly strikes and propaganda as antiwar, presidential intervention was not to be expected," ibid., 129.

21   Ibid., 146.

22   Ibid., 104-105.

23   Notably, military strike-breaking was limited to the Wobblies and other radicals. The AFL and "legitimate" groups were allowed to continue their stoppages throughout the war. It was not helped by the IWW's initial decision to respond with general strikes, which only polarised the issue still further. Ibid., 95, 112.

24   Osward Garrison Villard to Joseph Patrick Tumulty, 26 September 1917; Walter Lippman to Edward House, 17 October 1917; Herbert Croly to WW, 19 October 1917; Upton Sinclair to WW, 22 October 1917; Roger Nash Baldwin to WW, 27 February 1918; Amos Pinchot to WW, 24 May 1918; Edward Prentiss Costigan to WW, 29 May 1918, all in *WWP*, 44:272, 393-394, 420, 468-471; 46:481; 48:146, 150.

25   John Spargo to WW, 1 November 1917, *WWP*, 44:492.

26   For instance, Wilson responded to Herbert Croly that "the matter of censorship has given me as much concern as it has you and after frequent conversations with the Postmaster General I have become convinced that not only have his statements been

preserve his reputation as a guardian of American freedoms without acting in any meaningful way to restrain his staff, who were, after all, acting with his direct approval. Wilson made it clear that he would raise the occasional query when external parties complained about over-exuberance on the part of the postmaster general or the Justice Department. But he would only write once, telling Burleson, "I am willing to trust your judgment after I have once called your attention to a suggestion."[27] In this way, the president could put his concern for civil liberties on record, abdicate responsibility for the consequences of his appointees' actions, whilst benefiting from the pro-war militancy that was generated. Even in the most absurd instances of xenophobia, the president tried to avoid taking a stand. Faced with a letter asking his view on a proposed ban of teaching the German language in America, Wilson matched his disapproval of the idea with energetic effort to find "a proper and courteous way in which I could reply to questions of this sort without getting involved."[28]

The president's disarming replies and the faith that many still held in him ensured (both then and subsequently) that others in the administration were consistently blamed for excesses that should have been laid at his door.[29] The index to William Preston, Jr.'s classic work on federal repression of dissent, for instance, includes only seven references to the president.[30] Wilson's biographer, Arthur S. Link, painted a picture of a president sincerely and deeply concerned by, yet somehow apart from, the reactionary turn taken in public life. He largely failed to contrast this image with the president's ruthless control over policy elsewhere, and draw the inevitable conclusion that Wilson was deeply implicated in the suppression of liberty, notwithstanding his civilities.

The only times when the president acted meaningfully to protect civil liberties came when he felt it was directly affecting his policy toward Russia. Reports emanating from Petrograd and Moscow suggested that the Bolsheviks were using stories of American inquisitions as evidence that liberal democracy was a sham. Wilson was determined that they should be given no such opportunity. In this sense, the president's liberal approach to Bolshevism occasionally restrained his repressive habits at home. The best example was the Mooney case. Thomas J. Mooney, a Wobbly from California, had been prosecuted and sentenced to death on the basis of deeply suspicious evidence for his role in a bomb plot during a pro-war rally in July

---

misunderstood but that he is inclined to be most conservative in the exercise of these great and dangerous powers ...," 22 October 1917, *WWP*, 44:420. Or his reply to E.P. Costigan, "You may be sure that I sympathize with the spirit of your letter ... and I am going to look into the matter again." However, he refused even to meet Villard. WW to Joseph Patrick Tumulty, 28 September 1917, *WWP*, 44:273, 48:208.

[27] Cited in Preston, *Aliens and Dissenters*, 128. On Wilson's close co-operation with the postmaster general, see WW to Albert Sidney Burleson, 19 October 1917 and WW to Burleson, 30 October 1917, *WWP*, 44:397 and 473.

[28] WW to Joseph Patrick Tumulty, 10 April 1917, *WWP*, 47:311.

[29] A view explicitly rejected by the president himself. Upton Sinclair to WW, 22 October 1917; WW to Joseph Patrick Tumulty, 2 November 1917; John Spargo to WW, 1 November 1917, all in *WWP*, 44:468, 491-492.

[30] Preston, *Aliens and Dissenters*.

1916. When his staff in Petrograd and Moscow made it clear that the Mooney case was receiving wide circulation in Russia, Wilson became concerned. He wrote to the governor of California repeatedly during 1917 and 1918 to urge clemency, he organized a committee to investigate the affair, and allowed for his appeal to the governor to be published to ratchet up the pressure.[31] Undoubtedly, Wilson's interventions, and his emphasis on the international significance of the case, contributed to the governor's decision to commute Mooney's death sentence when the final verdict was handed down. Given Wilson's effect on a state-level decision (over which he had no constitutional power), one must conclude that the absence of action taken to restrain his own federal staff elsewhere was most revealing.[32]

After the treaty of Brest-Litovsk was signed in March 1918, Wilson lost the little faith he formerly had in the Bolsheviks' honor. After repeated requests from the Allied powers, in the summer of 1918 he finally agreed to two limited interventions in Russia. The first of these was a relief mission to Allied forces in the northern cities of Archangel and Murmansk. The second was an effort to assist the Czech Legion, which had begun to fight against the Bolsheviks in the East, and had captured large parts of the trans-Siberian railway. Unlike the period between October 1917 and March 1918, when foreign and domestic policies appeared to be running against each other, Wilson's policy towards radicalism at home and abroad now appeared to be consistent, reinforcing each other in a hard line approach to revolution and revolutionaries.

The president was informed that Edgar Sisson of the CPI had obtained conclusive proof that the Bolsheviks were German clients. Returning to America, Sisson brought him with him the now (in)famous, eponymous documents that appeared to prove the Bolsheviks were indeed paid agents of Germany. From this point on, any former distinction between prosecuting radicals for undermining the war effort, and attacking them as enemies of the state began to break down. In May 1918, Congress passed the Sedition Act, which went far beyond the laws of 1917, criminalizing language that expressed disloyalty to the United States or disrespect for the flag, the government or the constitution. In June, in conference with his attorney general, the president agreed to press for a retrial of the editorial board of *The Masses,* after the first trial had ended in a hung jury.[33] That same month, the administration arrested the most famous socialist leader in America, Eugene Victor Debs, for speaking out against the war. He refused to respond to appeals for clemency in the prosecution of the IWW leaders.[34] Most dramatically, in September, Wilson released the Sisson Documents to the press, admitting to Colonel House that

---

[31] WW to Thomas Watt Gregory, 24 September 1917; Creel to WW, 26 September 1917; WW to William Dennison Stephens, 22 January 1918, WW to William Dennison Stephens, 27 March 1918; WW to William Dennison Stephens, 4 June 1918, in which Wilson stressed "I would not venture again to call your attention to this case did I not know the international significance which attaches to it," all in *WWP*, 44:246, 267; 46:74; 47:160; 48:237.

[32] And even in the case of Thomas Mooney, the defendant was left to spend more than twenty years in prison.

[33] The second trial also produced a hung jury in October.

[34] Thomas Watt Gregory to WW, 11 May 1918, *WWP*, 47:467.

this amounted to a "virtual declaration of war upon the Bolsheviki Government."[35] The CPI produced a pamphlet, *The German-Bolshevik Conspiracy*, which alleged that the Bolsheviks were solely and simply agents of Germany. But since Wilson was not hearing appeals from either liberal or conservative sides on the conduct of his Russian policy, the only effect this dramatic publicity had was to heighten hostility toward radicals in America. Finally, in October, Wilson saw the passage into law of a new Immigration Act, which for the first time allowed for the deportation of alien radicals for membership in any organization that advocated the forcible overthrow of the American government. By the time of the armistice, the president had drifted so far from the liberal position in domestic affairs that even George Creel was warning that conservatives had hijacked Wilson's war for democracy. "All the radical, or liberal friends of your anti-imperialist war policy were either silenced or intimidated," by the Department of Justice and the Post Office, he wrote, thus grievously (and perhaps tactfully) underestimating the president's role in the affair.[36]

Wilson occasionally expressed his distaste for the extreme nationalism that came to characterize the war effort and famously gave a speech denouncing the "mob mentality," yet refused to entertain the notion that he bore any culpability for it. But as Lippmann had presciently written to Colonel House, the effort to engineer popular support for the war broke "down the liberal support of the war and ... [tended] to divide the country's articulate opinion into fanatical jingoism and fanatical pacifism."[37] In the longer term, this led directly to the conservative realignment of the 1920s and the destruction of American progressivism.

The left, already deeply divided over the war, was deeply damaged by this repression. In part this was from the direct consequence of arrests, police harassment and the refusal to mail socialist publications; but in itself, repression strengthened the hand of the radical left by implying that there was no accommodation with liberal capitalism. The left of the left, that is, began to look to the Bolshevik regime as a source of inspiration.[38] The Communist Party owed its origins to political divisions in the American left, the repressive atmosphere of the war years, *and* the inspiration of the Bolsheviks, but Wilson's illiberal attitude encouraged the public to see it as singularly a product of the latter. In short, driven by the war, a domestic understanding of radicalism as an exclusively foreign phenomenon began to emerge at exactly the time it found, in a new American communism, a perfect enemy to fight.

---

[35]   Even the State Department was concerned about the outlandish claims about the morality of the Bolsheviks that the Creel committee was putting forth, not least in terms of the impact it was likely to have on U.S. representatives in Russia, who could easily be arrested as a result. Robert Lansing to Edgar Sisson, 14 September 1918 and From the Diary of Colonel House, 24 September 1918, *WWP*, 51:4 and 104.

[36]   George Creel to WW, 8 November 1918, *WWP*, 51:645.

[37]   Walter Lippmann to Edward Mandell House, 17 October 1917, *WWP*, 44:393.

[38]   Indeed, in the face of anti-radical repression and deep internal divisions, it would be proved in the postwar years that only the guidance of Moscow could hold together the disparate elements that were to make up the Communist Party of America.

Even as domestic politics became more reactionary and polarized, Wilson resisted escalation in Russia. In September, responding to appeals from Secretary Lansing that the small fighting force in Archangel could not discharge its function and that the Siberian intervention was getting nowhere, Wilson brusquely stated that "we will not be a party to any attempt to form an Eastern front, deeming it absolutely impracticable from a military point of view and unwise as a matter of political action...."[39] The president repeatedly restated his belief that Americans should let the Russians "work out their own salvation, even though they wallow in anarchy for a while."[40] Indeed, after the end of the war removed the need for an Eastern front, Wilson's policy toward Russia rapidly became more liberal again. Intervention could now be nothing more than a conscious strategy to remove the Bolsheviks from power, and Wilson was unwilling to participate in such imperialistic ventures. As disturbing news from Europe spread across the ocean, of Eastern European nations falling to revolution and the menace of Bolshevism spreading ever westwards, Wilson focused on food aid, not military action, as the solution to the Bolshevik menace. The president repeatedly told those who would listen that the best way to beat Bolshevism was to remove its causes.[41]

No such liberalism could be found at home. Indeed, even Arthur Link concludes that by mid-August 1919, "Wilson was so set in his beliefs and his ways that he had become a veritable caricature of his former self."[42] In spite of appeals from across the political spectrum to curtail antiradicalism now that the war was won, the president refused to release Debs or take other steps to mollify the increasingly xenophobic public mood.[43] Moreover, frustrated by their inability to influence Wilson's policy in Russia, radical, liberal and conservative figures alike returned from Moscow and Petrograd to rehash their debates before the American public. Figures like Edgar Sisson, Raymond Robins, John Reed, Louise Bryant, and others who had witnessed the revolutionary impact of Bolshevism, now appeared before congressional investigative committees to tell their stories, and naturally the most lurid details gained front page headlines in the national press. In this manner, Wilson's firm hand on the tiller of international policy redirected the discussion over radicalism to the home front, his refusal to move away from his liberal understanding of Eastern European politics contributed to an increasingly conservative public attitude to dissent in America.

Executive branch action continued as well. The Sedition Act expired with the end of the war, and it would have seemed peculiar to prosecute aliens for espionage on behalf of a defeated enemy, so deportation under the 1918 Immigration Act

---

39   WW to Robert Lansing, 18 September 1918, *WWP*, 51:50.

40   Memorandum by Sir William Wiseman, c. 16 October 1918, *WWP*, 51:351.

41   See Memorandum by Franklin Knight Lane, 5 November 1918, *WWP*, 51:604.

42   *WWP*, 62:631.

43   Indeed, it was the thoroughly anticommunist socialist, John Spargo, who was left to voice the liberal view, declaring that a general amnesty was needed "as a bulwark against the mounting Bolshevist agitation." A. Mitchell Palmer to WW, 30 July 1919; WW to A. Mitchell Palmer, 1 August 1919; John Spargo Memorandum to WW, 25 August 1919, all in *WWP*, 62:557-558.

became the principle weapon for antiradicalism. This ultimately led to the Palmer raids of December 1919 and January 1920.

The most popular view of the Palmer raids again removes responsibility from the president. Wilson was seriously ill by the time the raids commenced in late 1919 and therefore unable to restrain his underlings. He had suffered a breakdown in April, a minor stroke in July and a far more serious one in October that, together, effectively put him out of action until the New Year. In this sense, the president was undoubtedly not on duty. This has led many to conclude that the Attorney General, A. Mitchell Palmer, was overstepping his authority, out of control, and—perhaps most dangerous of all—hoping for a run on the presidency. Palmer himself was struggling to control the ambitions of the head of the Radical Division, J. Edgar Hoover, but the combined recklessness of the two produced mass dragnet raids, the arrests of thousands, and eventual deportation of hundreds of radicals on trumped up charges of disloyalty and sedition.

Undoubtedly, Wilson's faculties were dimming, but to say that he had no impact on the Red Scare is unrealistic. Perhaps most importantly, Wilson consciously exploited fears of domestic insurrection to drum up support for the League of Nations in the tense summer of 1919. Time and again during his famous tour to promote the League, Wilson played up to antiradical suspicions, using hostility to Bolshevism to make the case for a new international order. At the Des Moines Coliseum, he declared the Bolsheviks to be "a little group of men just as selfish, just as ruthless, just as pitiless, as the agents of the Czar himself...."[44] At the Billings Auditorium a few days later he went further, declaring that Russia "came out of one tyranny to get into a worse [one]."[45] He called the Bolsheviks "the negation of everything that is America" and claimed that they planned "to brand the men under arms for them, so that they will be forever marked as their servants and slaves."[46] He associated Bolshevism with the German enemy.[47] He began by saying, "the only people who are dealing with the Bolshevist government are the Germans. … They are making all their plans that the finances of Russia and the commerce of Russia and the development of Russia shall be as soon as possible in the hands of Germans."[48] He implied that the secretive agents of Germany were afoot once more to undermine support for the League. "I know that all over the country German propaganda has lifted its hideous head again," he said, "and I hear the hiss of it on every side."[49] And, in apocalyptic language, he stressed the vulnerability of the United States to the threat of Bolshevism if it did not fulfil the war's democratic promise by supporting the League.

> [D]o you honestly think, my fellow citizens, that none of that poison has got in the veins of this free people? Do you not know that the world is all now one

---

[44] Address at the Des Moines Coliseum, 6 September 1919, *WWP*, 63:76.
[45] Address at the Billings Auditorium, 11 September 1919, *WWP*, 63:174.
[46] Des Moines address and Billings address, *WWP*, 63:77 and 174.
[47] The evasive language he used surely suggests that this was disingenuous.
[48] Address at Coeur d'Alene, 12 September 1919, *WWP*, 63:214.
[49] After-dinner speech in Los Angeles, 20 September 1919, *WWP*, 63:401. See also Address at Coeur d'Alene, 12 September 1919, *WWP*, 63:215.

single whispering gallery? Those antenna of the wireless telegraph are the symbols of our age. All the impulses of mankind are thrown out upon the air and reach to the ends of the earth. And quietly upon steamships, silently under the cover of the postal service, with the tongue of the wireless and the tongue of the telegraph, all the suggestions of disorder are spread through the world … it is spreading, and, so long as disorder continues, so long as the world is kept waiting for the answer to the question of the kind of peace we are going to have and what kind of guarantees are to be behind that peace, that poison will steadily spread, more and more rapidly, spread until it may be that even this beloved land of ours will be distracted and distorted by it.[50]

As well as generally conjuring the menace of Bolshevism to serve his political ends, Wilson also made statements that could be interpreted as a call to action. He stressed the theme that, as he put it, "Disordered society is dissolved society," and his hope that "the lesson of Russia … be burned into the consciousness of every man and woman in America. And that lesson is that nobody can be free when there is not public order and authority."[51] "There are disciples of Lenin in our own midst," he told the crowds in Billings. "To be a disciple of Lenin means to be a disciple of night, chaos and disorder. There must be no discord or disorganization. Our immediate duty, therefore, my fellow countrymen, is to see that no minority, no class, no special interest, no matter how respectable, how rich or how poor, shall get control of the affairs of the United States."[52]

Moreover, he explicitly condemned social unrest at home as disloyal in the same breath that he exaggerated the threat of Bolshevik insurrection. In particular, he denounced the Boston Police Strike, which had erupted in the midst of his tour, comparing the police to soldiers who had deserted their posts before a battle.[53] "When the police of a great city walk out and leave that city to be looted they have committed an intolerable crime against civilisation," he cried, to the sound of "long and loud" applause.[54] Wilson's physician wrote in his diary that when one such comment was "telegraphed back to Boston it had a very salutary effect in forcing the Governor of Massachusetts to act in aiding Mayor Peters and the Boston city authorities to control the mob and restore order."[55] For antiradicals across the country, Wilson's words must have seemed a powerful encouragement.

Wilson's behavior during the fall of 1919 parallels Truman's fateful decision of 1947 to "scare the hell out of the American people" when lobbying Congress to support the Marshall Plan. If historians have given Truman some of the blame for McCarthyism, then Wilson must take some of the blame for the Palmer Raids. Truman spoke several years before McCarthy's rise to national celebrity. Wilson was inflaming popular sentiment against radicals at the very moment that his own

---

[50]   Des Moines address, *WWP*, 63:76-77.
[51]   Address at St. Paul Auditorium, *WWP*, 63:145.
[52]   Billings Address, *WWP*, 63:174-175.
[53]   At the time, a crime punishable by execution after court martial.
[54]   Coeur d'Alene Address, *WWP*, 63:216.
[55]   Diary of Dr. Grayson, *WWP*, 63:169.

appointees were developing the plans for massive repression. In the end, the Palmer raids were conducted in a violent, excessive and sloppy manner that seems contrary to President Wilson's instincts for propriety and form. But this does not remove from him responsibility. Although the president was not around to disapprove of Palmer's actions, there is nothing to suggest that he was necessarily closer in spirit to Assistant Secretary of Labor Louis Post, who spoke out against the raids, than the attorney general or Hoover. And the conceptual framework—a conservative antiradical strategy at home buttressing a liberal antiradicalism abroad—was distinctively Wilsonian.

III

Wilson's antiradical legacy was enshrined in the Colby Note of August 1920. Named for the new secretary of state, Bainbridge Colby, but authored by the anticommunist socialist John Spargo, the Colby Note explicitly linked the United States' continuing refusal to recognize Soviet Russia with the presence of radicals in America. This note deployed domestic antiradicalism to justify an ongoing policy of "watchful waiting" towards Russia, and would provide the framework for U.S.-Russian relations until 1933. But arguably, the Colby Note was as important in justifying antiradical attacks on domestic radicals as in perpetuating non-recognition toward Russia. Whilst during the war, the foreign-domestic nexus had produced divergent consequences, even appearing to act against each other at times, and many liberal commentators had remarked on their inconsistency, by 1920 Wilson's policies had come to reinforce one another in a powerful and uncompromising manner. The United States, which had diligently resisted the blandishments of its more hostile wartime Allies, was ultimately to become the last major international power to recognise the Bolshevik regime.

   Taken altogether, Wilson's policies towards radicalism between 1917 and 1919 present a complex and rapidly shifting picture. But the approach to revolution abroad and revolutionaries at home were intimately linked through a common effort to make the world safe for democracy. Unlike the Cold War liberals who would argue that the way to defeat communism was ruthlessness abroad combined with relative liberalism at home, Wilson chose the opposite path. In so doing, he set a powerful precedent for his successors. To win the war, the president abandoned his liberal instincts in favor of an unprecedented campaign against domestic radicalism, but consistently resisted pressure to take a hard line against the Bolsheviks in Russia, preferring to emphasise national self-determination and development as the road to democracy. To win the peace, Wilson kept the antiradical fever alive at home, but nearly killed himself pushing for a new international order to guarantee freedom and liberty throughout the world. Radicalism became a foreign cancer within the body politic, and Bolshevism's chief sin lay in its machinations in America. Domestic political repression became a necessary component of the exceptional mission to promote human liberty around the world. In this way, the entanglement of foreign and the domestic antiradicalism under Wilson was one of his most profound, and certainly one of his most perplexing, legacies.

CENSORSHIP IN WORLD WAR I:
THE ACTION OF WILSON'S COMMITTEE ON PUBLIC INFORMATION

Daniela Rossini

Censorship and Propaganda in Wartime America

The Committee on Public Information (CPI) has been called "America's propaganda ministry" during World War I.[1] Created by President Wilson at the outset of the war, it rapidly became a gigantic organization, which effectively promoted propaganda both at home and abroad. According to its director George Creel, its influence spread "to every community in America and to every corner of the civilized world."[2] Domestically, its far ranging efforts helped to revolutionize American public opinion as the nation was transformed from an anti-militaristic and self-centered country into a global power. Abroad, it launched the first massive crusade to americanize the world.

Propaganda, though, was not the CPI's only duty. Censorship was also a prerogative of this novel institution. The union of those two crucial aspects of the conduct of war in the same organization reveals features of the management of public opinion in wartime America. It shows how much Wilson's administration was already at ease with the methods of leadership in a mass society. We can perceive that by contrasting them with the old-fashioned policies adopted in Europe, and particularly in Italy, during the same period.

Actually, stern repression existed in the United States, but was limited to marginal groups. It included imprisonment of anarchist, pacifist and socialist leaders and every kind of obstacle to the activity and public visibility of their organizations, such as meetings or circulation of the press. Between 1917 and 1918, several Acts greatly curtailed First Amendment rights, such as the freedom of speech, press and assembly: the Espionage Act of June 1917, the Trading-with-the-Enemy Act of the following October and the Sedition Act of May 1918.[3] This legislation gave not only

---

[1]   James R. Mock and Cedric Larson, *Words that Won the War: The Story of the Committee on Public Information 1917-1919* (Princeton, NJ: Princeton University Press, 1939), 4.

[2]   George Creel, *Complete Report of the Chairman of the Committee on Public Information, 1917, 1918, 1919* (Washington, DC: Government Printing Office, 1920), 10.

[3]   The First Amendment of the American Constitution says that Congress shall make no law "abridging the freedom of speech or of the press; or the right of the people peaceably to assemble and to petition the government for a redress of grievances." Minority critics asserted in 1918 that the Espionage Act, together with similar later legislation, violated the constitutional rights of free speech and free press, but in 1919 the Supreme Court denied the claim. As Mock and Larson observe, "So much of America's articulate opinion was thus friendly to the general idea of the espionage legislation ... that the new bill ... might easily have become enacted into law without protest if it had not been for newspaper alarm at indications of a coming press censorship"; Mock and Larson, *Words that Won the War*, 28.

to the CPI, but also to the Justice Department and to the postmaster general, to Military and Naval Intelligence and to a number of national and local authorities the power to act in open disregard of constitutional freedoms. Postmaster General Burelson suppressed antiwar publications, such as *The Masses* and the *International Socialist Review*, while Attorney General Gregory put behind bars the socialist party leader Eugene Debs and tried to criminalize the entire leadership of the *Industrial Workers of the World*. "All in all," Alan Dawley concludes, "it was the greatest campaign against free expression in the nation's history."[4] Censorship was officially abolished at the end of November 1918, but in practice was kept alive by the first serious wave of the *Red Scare*.[5]

The great majority of the population, however, were to be convinced, using the new techniques of mass communication. A lack of public enthusiasm for the war could become the administration's ultimate problem. To win public support, therefore, the CPI strived to obtain a self-imposed conformism by the media, so that the public could be hit by a massive dose of pro-war news. That was why censorship and propaganda should march hand in hand.

George Creel as a Censor

George Creel, the CPI chairman, always claimed that there was no real censorship in wartime America, but just "voluntary censorship" by the national press. In particular, the CPI was not an agency of censorship, but acted just as "a reference bureau in connection with voluntary censorship, advising and interpreting the Government's requests." Therefore, the CPI merely assisted the press in not giving the enemy useful information and the journalists' compliance rested entirely upon their honor and patriotism. For that reason, Creel devoted to censorship only five pages of his three-hundred-page final report:

> ... the Committee on Public Information was not an agency of censorship, nor was the press of the United States at any time under any compulsion of statute in the sense that the European press was curbed and supervised. Instead of being bound by prohibitive laws, backed by drastic penalties, the newspapers of the United States were put upon their honor, and made the partners of Government in guarding "military information of tangible benefit to the enemy." ... As it was realized that the requests of Government were concerned with human lives and national hopes, as it was driven home that the passing

---

[4] Alan Dawley, *Changing the World: American Progressives in War and Revolution* (Princeton, NJ and Oxford: Princeton University Press, 2003), 157.

[5] John Tebbel and Sarah M. Watts, *The Press and the Presidency: From George Washington to Ronald Reagan* (New York and Oxford: Oxford University Press, 1985), 384-385. "Sentences of five, ten and twenty years were imposed with a liberal hand, though only the shortest of these were served to completion, for President Harding freed many of the offenders and President Coolidge ordered release of the 'last political prisoner' on December 15, 1923," Mock and Larson, *Words that Won the War*, 43.

satisfaction of a news item might endanger a transport or a troop train, the voluntary censorship grew in strength and certainty.[6]

Creel, a well-known muckraker journalist, strongly believed in the role of "publicity" in a democratic regime. Like most Progressives, he thought that exposing the problems of industrial America to public opinion was the only way to combat political corruption, labor's exploitation and the excessive power of trusts. Therefore, since the days before intervention, he had opposed admirals, generals, and conservative politicians (like Secretary of State Robert Lansing) who asked for a strict control of all media of communication. Creel argued that the control of the press was not only impossible, but also dangerous: "*expression*, not *suppression*, was the real need."[7] He maintained this position throughout the war.

His behavior, however, was different from his declarations. He became, in fact, "much more of a censor than he was ever willing to admit."[8] While American involvement in the world war progressed, he came to have a higher regard for censorship in general, stretching his control from press to literature, from mail and cable communications to moving pictures. It was precisely his well-known association with censorship that made him *persona non grata* for the American correspondents at the Paris peace conference and forced Wilson to prefer Ray Stannard Baker for the position of press secretary of the American delegation at Paris.

Creel's familiarity with and reliance on the censors' action reached the point of asking Military Intelligence to undertake a "very definite" and "very confidential" "investigation of every person" working in the CPI, "with the view of ascertaining their fitness for employment by the Government during the present critical period."[9] Oddly enough, Creel thought that the best way to defend himself and his organization from the violent attacks made from various constituencies (such as Congress, the press, and the State Department), was to ask the military censors to control each one of the twenty-six CPI divisions and almost every individual among the CPI's 395 employees, from Creel himself down to the last messenger boy. The bulk of them passed the censors' examination: "suspicion of one sort or another" was cast only on fourteen people, most of whom were afterwards discharged. The charges were "extreme radical views" or "pro-German views or associations" or

---

6   Creel, *Complete Report*, 10, 12.

7   George Creel, *Rebel at Large: Recollections of Fifty Crowded Years* (New York: G.P. Putnam's Sons, 1947), 157 [Italics in the original].

8   Robert C. Hilderbrand, *Power and the People: Executive Management of Public Opinion in Foreign Affairs, 1897-1921* (Chapel Hill, NC: University of North Carolina Press, 1981), 146.

9   Letter from Creel to Colonel R.H. Van Deman, 10 April 1918, reproduced in the first page of the forty-five-page "Report on the Committee on Public information by M. I. 4-5, The Military Intelligence Branch, Executive Division, General Staff," May 1918, General Correspondence of George Creel, box 5, folder [after 145]: "Military Intelligence Report on the CPI," CPI 1-A1, Records of the Committee on Public Information, RG 63, National Archives, College Park, MD (hereafter cited as "CPI Papers").

"disloyalty." The most frequent charge was that of being "socialist," but, the censors argued,

> there are socialists and socialists.... Of the two divisions into which American socialism split, one has proclaimed Germany the enemy of humanity as well as of Socialism, and has given the war its most hearty support. ... A different feeling is suggested by the term "Bolsheviki," which has come to be a by-word of contempt and loathing.[10]

The forty-five-page report concluded that "the percentage of those against whom anybody has expressed a doubt is less than four percent. ... With these exceptions, the committee should be given a clean bill of health."[11] This document, though mild in its general attitude, shows the dark side of Creel himself. It might be seen as an anticipation of practices that would become frequent during the future waves of the *Red Scare*.[12]

During the war, the control of the press was one of Creel's main concerns. In the first days of belligerency, he hastily drew up a "Preliminary Statement to the Press," delivered to the Washington correspondents at the end of May 1917. Stating that "public opinion is a factor in victory no less than ships and guns," the document divided war news into three categories: dangerous, which should not be printed; doubtful, which needed CPI's approval; and routine, which did not influence the conduct of the war. Questionable news should be authorized by the CPI, which, if approved, would label them "passed by the Committee on Public Information." Compliance with those regulations should be voluntary: as the CPI statement observed, "reckless journalism, regrettable enough in times of peace, is a positive menace when the Nation is at war...."[13] So, censorship, the document emphasized, was essentially the responsibility of the journals' editors.

In fact, in the field of the domestic press, CPI's censorship was subtle. Magazine publishers had to submit articles weeks before publication deadlines, for CPI approval.[14] The main control, though, was at the source of news. For the first

---

10   In a chapter entitled "Socialism, Bolshevikism [*sic*] and the I.W.W.," the report argued that: "It will be noted ... it is hard to get two people to agree on what socialism is, ... pro-war socialists have been among the most ardent workers. ... A different feeling is suggested by the term 'Bolsheviki', ... Americans in general believe that but for them the war would have ended long ago, with Germany crushed instead of Russia," "Military Intelligence Report on the CPI," CPI Papers, 12.

11   Ibid., 45.

12   Analyzing the Division of News, for example, the military censors quoted a statement made by a visitor of the Department present in their files: "What sort of an outfit is this Creel Bureau anyhow? They have nothing but Denver Labor people and I.W.W.'s in the office.... The Division is evidently in need of a thorough house-cleaning," ibid., 14.

13   Hilderbrand, *Power and the People*, 146; Stephen L. Vaughn, *Holding Fast the Inner Lines: Democracy, Nationalism, and the Committee on Public Information* (Chapel Hill, NC: University of North Carolina Press, 1980), 218-219, Mock and Larson, *Words that Won the War*, 80-83.

14   Robert W. Rydell and Rob Kroes, *Buffalo Bill in Bologna: The Americanization of Europe, 1869-1922* (Chicago and London: University of Chicago Press, 2005), 137.

time there was a single agency charged with disseminating official information. CPI reporters were distributed in crucial points of the administration, such as the White House, the War, Navy and Labor Departments, besides national councils and boards. They "fabricated" the news and distributed it through a press-release bulletin, which reached thirteen thousand journals. In the year and a half of its operation, the CPI issued more than six thousand press releases. Beside that, several thousand rural weeklies and dailies were furnished with a weekly service of condensed war news. The overall task became of such proportions that it required the News Division to remain open twenty-four hours a day and seven days a week. If we couple this with the steady stream of propaganda material sent all over the country, we see how far the channels of communication were literally choked with official news and opinion. In future years, Creel could boast that even his detractors took "a daily diet of our material."[15] As Stephen Vaughn concludes, "the CPI engaged in a subtle censorship, ... when it filled the country with official news."[16]

Journalists were impatient with this situation and felt robbed of one of the pillars of their work: the gathering of news. In the decisive field of war information, they were shut out of access to the news sources and had to become mere distributors of CPI's press releases, which they had to accept at face value. Despite the pains taken to formulate them objectively, those official press releases always sounded laudatory of the administration's policies and of the Allies' war effort. As was often ironically pointed out, CPI reporters were "creeling" the news, and the national press, however reluctantly, should comply. This transition from the role of gatherers to that of mere disseminators of war news was difficult for American reporters, but nonetheless they generally accepted it. Only major newspapers—like the *Washington Post*—or national leaders—like former President Theodore Roosevelt or Senator Henry Cabot Lodge—could maintain a space of criticism.

In fields other than the press, Creel's attitude was more openly in favor of strict control of public expression. He was a member of the Censorship Board, an advisory body aimed at coordinating censorship and making recommendations on this matter. This position, together with his continuous cooperation with the Department of Justice, the postmaster general, the Military and Naval Intelligence, made him a key figure in the field of censorship at large.

Besides the press, mail and cable communications, books and movies were censored in various ways. Not only was "dangerous" information censored, but so were all attitudes that were not in line with the war spirit. A good example is the movie *The Spirit of '76*, which was finished just before American intervention. This movie about the American Revolution depicted British soldiers killing children, raping women and committing all sorts of vile offenses. The government's response was exceptionally severe and the producer was sentenced to ten years of imprisonment. The severity of this sentence was partly due to the fact that the

---

[15]   George Creel, *How We Advertised America: The First Telling of the Amazing Story of the Committee on Public Information that Carried the Gospel of Americanism to Every Corner of the Globe* (New York: Harper, 1920), 109. See also the "Military Intelligence Report on the CPI," 11.

[16]   Vaughn, *Holding Fast the Inner Lines*, 234.

producer had failed to comply with the censors' indication that the most questionable scenes should be eliminated. In any case, it shows the compulsion behind the CPI requests for screenplay alterations, the big stick that was hidden behind "voluntary" censorship.[17]

But the field in which Creel felt free to use extensively his power of censorship was that of the media products for distribution abroad. The attention Creel devoted to the CPI's Foreign Section is reflected by the large space reserved to it in his final report: two-thirds of it describe its bold worldwide campaign meant to conquer the mind of mankind and make the United States the new model society. The Committee became indeed a world organization aiming not only to explain the reasons of American intervention, but also to carry "the gospel of Americanism to every corner of the globe."[18]

This goal had to be achieved by the dissemination of "carefully produced information about the United States to a worldwide audience."[19] News, feature articles, photos for magazines, exhibits or window displays, posters, postcards and movies were carefully selected or crafted by CPI experts for foreign use. As Robert Rydell and Rob Kroes point out, "never before had the mass cultural resources of a nation been mobilized on such a scale."[20] Because of the importance and delicacy of this endeavor, Creel deemed that all these mass products should be strictly reviewed and any of them which reflected a bad image of the United States should be censored and stopped.

Three divisions within the CPI supplied the foreign posts with a constant flow of propaganda material: the *Telegraphic Service*, directed by Walter Rogers, sent every day, by air or cable, press releases suitable for distribution to the foreign press; the *Foreign Press Bureau*, directed by the novelist Ernest Poole, enrolled the best journalists and writers to write "color articles" on daily life in the United States and at the front and sent them through the diplomatic mail; and finally the *Foreign Film Division*, directed by Jules Brulatour, was in charge of distributing American movies abroad. Soon a *Pictorial Service* was added for the distribution of all kinds of images, like pictures for the press or for window displays and exhibits, posters, postcards, flags, etc.[21]

Special attention was paid to the new medium of the moving pictures. In those years, in fact, the American movie industry was ready to conquer the world. Precisely because the American censors were aware of the ideological power of

---

17   Hilderbrand, *Power and the People*, 160.
18   Creel, *How We Advertised America*, subtitle.
19   Rydell and Kroes, *Buffalo Bill in Bologna*, 135.
20   Ibid., 137.
21   "This daily news service by wire and radio was supplemented by a mail service of special articles and illustrations that went into foreign newspapers and magazines and technical journals and periodicals of special appeal. We aimed to give in this way a true picture of the American democracy, not only in its war activities but also in its devotion to the interests of peace. There were, too, series of illustrated articles on our education, our trade and industry, our finance, our labor conditions, our religions, our work in medicine, our agriculture, our women's work, our Government, and our ideals," Creel, *Complete Report*, 6.

motion pictures, they took great pains in ascertaining that their content was not dangerous in respect to the image of the United States that they wanted to project worldwide. Mass culture was one of the main weapons of the new world power: by the end of the war, all kinds of images depicting the United States as a rich and democratic society circumnavigated the globe and became not only a new kind of mass entertainment, but also cultural products invested with ideological meanings.

In cooperation with the Army, the Navy and the Customs Service, the CPI set up a department for export licenses with headquarters in New York City. All movies intended for export had to be approved. The censor team of around thirty people, mainly military officers, but also CPI representatives, established a set of guidelines for the export of films. Not only should movies not contain any information of military interest, but neither should they give a negative image of life in the United States. Therefore, images representing breadlines or immigrant exploitation or pacifist demonstrations or stories of political corruption had to be censored. Even scenes of fights between American soldiers and Indians could be used as evidence of race discrimination in the United States and were censored. Westerns such as *Jesse James* were denied a license for export because they portrayed a "false" image of America as a violent and unlawful country.[22] By the end of the war, over eight thousand movies had been reviewed: most of them passed the test for patriotism.[23] However, Rydell and Kroes estimate that, in the months of July and August 1918 alone, nearly one hundred thousand feet of film were cut by American producers in order to gain access to overseas markets.[24]

Therefore, various kinds of censorship existed in wartime America and their features shed light on the new techniques of executive management of public opinion in the United States, as well as abroad. Often censorship and propaganda were so intertwined that it was not always easy to see which aspect was prevalent. Creel, for example, attached the following condition for granting the export license to movies: each shipment had to contain "a certain amount of American propaganda film," as the official war pictures, to be shown in foreign countries together with Hollywood's films.[25]

However, it is important to remark that censorship in the United States was not only different, but also noticeably milder than in all the other warring nations, where it was mainly in the hands of military officials. In most European countries, in

---

[22]   Emily S. Rosenberg, *Spreading the American Dream: American Economic and Cultural Expansion, 1890-1945* (New York: Hill and Wang, 1981), 81.

[23]   "What we wanted to get into foreign countries were pictures that presented the wholesome life of America, giving fair ideas of our people and our institutions. What we wanted to keep out of world circulation were the 'thrillers' that gave entirely false impressions of American life and morals. Film dramas portraying the exploits of 'Gyp the Blood,' or reproducing the lawless life of the old western frontier, were bound to prejudice our fight for the good opinion of neutral countries. ... Oftentimes it was the case that a picture could be made helpful by a change in title, or the elimination of a scene, and in no instance did a producer fail to make the alterations suggested," Creel, *Complete Report*, 103-104.

[24]   Rydell and Kroes, *Buffalo Bill in Bologna*, 138-140.

[25]   Creel, *Complete Report*, 7.

particular, the press was censored daily, not to mention control of public speeches or movies. The brutal repression within the Army in France and Italy included court-martials and summary executions.[26]

The CPI developed new ways to control public opinion that were more suitable to a mass democratic society. Repression was linked with the fabrication of consent. The aim was a general conformism of the great majority of the population. This conformism should even prevail in private relationships as is shown in a number of CPI posters: in them it is suggested how to behave in friendship and family circles, how to write a good letter to a relative serving in the Army, or even how to celebrate Mother's day. These ads differ from the bulk of the other, more famous, war posters, because they rely not only on images or colors, but also on long, "old-fashioned" texts explaining in detail how to behave in the different circumstances.

The CPI was largely successful in this respect. Creel himself spent relatively little time in administering censorship, while he was mostly absorbed by the more important and innovative plans in the field of mass propaganda. These new means of control and management of public opinion show how far the CPI staff were aware of their role as agents of Americanization, both at home and abroad. Thanks to them, the Wilson administration obtained a general and self-imposed conformism of the media, together with the majority consent of articulate opinion. Minority critics were silenced. That was, indeed, what would be called the dictatorship of the majority.

Italian Censorship in American Eyes

James Mock and Cedric Larson, who in 1939 studied the activity of the CPI with an eye to the needs of "war information" for the approaching World War II, concluded that in the United States in 1918:

> … there was little expressed difference of opinion. It was illegal to express dissent of certain kinds, but for most people no law was necessary. The Committee on Public Information had done its work so well that there was a burning eagerness to believe, to conform, to feel the exaltation of joining in a great and selfless enterprise.[27]

To understand the salient features of public opinion control in wartime America, it is useful to contrast it with the situation in other belligerent countries. In Italy, for example, censorship was very strict. Ruled by a liberal, but not democratic political class, Italy was just at the beginning of the process of democratization. Iron discipline and repression were the main means to control public opinion both on the military and the domestic front.[28] Only during the last year of war, did the shock of the ruinous defeat of Caporetto, which spread the specter of a possible revolution,

---

[26]   Vaughn, *Holding Fast the Inner Lines*, 214-215.

[27]   Mock and Larson, *Words that Won the War*, 6.

[28]   See Enzo Forcella and Alberto Monticone, *Plotone di esecuzione: I processi della prima guerra mondiale* (Bari: Laterza, 1968), xvi-vii and 442-445.

push the ruling class to couple repression with persuasion and promote a number of initiatives in the field of mass propaganda.

In the difficult period following the rout of Caporetto, the effective American propaganda machine got involved in Italy. The country was flooded not only by every kind of propaganda material pervasively distributed by the Italian Branch of the CPI, but also by large amounts of relief items distributed by the American Red Cross and the YMCA. The American campaign confirmed in the eyes of the Italian populace the image of the United States as a rich, modern and democratic country, solicitous towards the needs and aspirations of common men, an image that was already present in the regions of emigration.[29]

Charles Merriam headed the CPI Commission to Italy. He was a professor from Chicago University and a political activist, who later became a key figure in the new academic discipline of political science. In Italy, Merriam strove to look far beyond the field of propaganda, gaining a good grasp of the political situation. Being a Progressive reformer, as were most CPI agents, he observed with contempt the shortsighted policy of straight repression that was prevalent in Italy. In particular, during the summer of 1918, Merriam sent to Washington a confidential report on "Italy's Censorship":

Italy's censorship is too stupid to be stupid. It exercises a political and often a steering control on local and foreign correspondence. It is a pistol loaded with the bullet of conservatism. It is apparently shifting aim toward the very heart of American idealism. The Italian censorship follows a political rather than a military design. The result is a subtle influence on the press rather than a reasonable liberty of it. … It keeps the Italian public in ignorance of the political and social evolution and revolution which the war is forcing in the outside world.[30]

Italian censorship indeed appeared to most Americans as a relict of another geological age. The sole use of repression, without any attempt at what they called "mass education,"[31] seemed not only useless, but also dangerous. The executive

---

29 On these aspects, see my book: *Il mito americano nell'Italia della Grande Guerra* (Roma and Bari: Laterza, 2000), chapters 1 and 5. English translation, *Woodrow Wilson and the American Myth in Italy. Culture, Diplomacy, and War Propaganda* (Cambridge, MA: Harvard University Press, 2008).

30 "Italy's Censorship," Press Report, Rome, Week Ending July 31, Propaganda Records of the Executive Division, File of G. Creel, Jan.-Nov. 1918, box 1, folder 11: "Italy," CPI 1-C4, CPI Papers, 1. Just before that, the report stated: "Italy's ruling classes show no real disposition to accept Wilsonian democracy. They have no sympathetic contact with the generally ignorant mass of the people, who are instinctively democratic. The American editors and the public … are colossally ignorant in matters of Italian politics. America's journalistic mirror does not reflect the imperative need for American propaganda of an educational and democratic nature in Italy. The Italian censor is at bottom to blame for this state of things."

31 J.H. Hearley, Director, Committee on Public Information, "Final Report—Rome Office Activities," n.d. [but January-February 1919], box 10, folder 5, Charles E. Merriam

control of the war conduct looked fragile and could easily be overridden by a wave of popular protest. Furthermore, it prevented the formation of a democratic public opinion, keeping the majority of population in ignorance of what was happening at home and abroad. In this way, it was indeed "a pistol loaded with the bullet of conservatism," as Merriam observed in the previous quotation.

Most American observers shared this opinion. John Hearley, an American journalist who served as the CPI deputy director, wrote in a confidential letter to Ray S. Baker at the end of 1918:

> ... the people are a wee bit bewildered and the Italian censor is one of the reasons for the bewilderment. He "cuts" and "cuts" to his heart's content and my discontent...."[32]

Like most Americans, he believed that something more than censorship was required for an effective leadership of public opinion in wartime. Even the American ambassador, who was not a Progressive activist at all, but a southern gentleman and novelist nostalgic of the way of life in the "Old South," often mentioned in his reports the "heavily censored" press.[33]

Moreover, censorship and propaganda were two sides of the same coin. Merriam not only organized in Italy the first mass propaganda campaign, but carried his influence on the Italian government to the point of suggesting a plan to reorganize more effectively Italian propaganda in the United States. This document shows how sophisticated his vision of propaganda was. In a four-page memorandum, he stressed the perils of remaining confined to the Italian communities, insisting that it was essential to reach the American public at large. That meant to supply the press with news suitable for "the enormous appetite of the American public for foreign news particularly at the present time," to be aware of the power of the press, given by the "huge circulation of newspapers, periodicals and books in America," and finally to get entrance into "clubs, societies and other groups where public opinion is formed," like the women's organizations. In a further document, Merriam described in detail both the different branches of this new

---

Papers, University of Chicago Library, Chicago, IL, 1, published with modifications in Creel, *Complete Report*, 191-194.

[32]   Handwritten letter of J.H. Hearley to R.S. Baker, 30 December 1918, reel no. 29, Ray Stannard Baker Papers, Library of Congress, Washington, DC.

[33]   Letter from T.N. Page to Colonel House, 14 April 1919, House Papers, Manuscripts and Archives, Yale University Library, New Haven, CT: He mentioned twice the "heavily censored" Italian press. In those days of the sharp Italian-American confrontation at Paris on the Adriatic Question, Page described the role of misinformation on the part of the Italian press: "The attitude of the press ... is certainly very exasperating, and I doubt not that it is having a very far reaching influence on the people, but I hope that it will be distinctly understood that the Italian people are neither responsible for this attitude nor should be made to suffer from it. They are indeed the victims of it. If they are misled it is because they are ignorant of all outside of Italy." As this document shows, censorship in Italy remained well after the war's end.

propaganda organization to be established in the United States and even the names of the Italian officers who could effectively work there.[34]

The Italian ruling class, on the contrary, ignored the advantages that could come from a clever influence on the Italian and foreign press and remained faithful to its repressive policies. In particular, it remained utterly suspicious of journalists. Lilian Mowrer, wife of Edgar Mowrer, the well-known American journalist who spent around a year in Italy during the war, observed that "until 1917 American correspondents were not welcome" at the front.[35] In general, American correspondents were puzzled by the apparent inability of Italians to grasp the importance of obtaining good press coverage. Alexander Powell, a reporter of the New York's *World*, which was at that time the major newspaper in the United States, wrote toward the end of the war:

> They [the Italians] are only just commencing to realize the political value of our national maxim: "It pays to advertise." ... Instead of welcoming neutral correspondents and publicists, they have, until very recently, met them with suspicion and hindrances. What little news is permitted to filter through is coldly official, and is altogether unsuited for American consumption. The Italians are staging one of the most remarkable and inspiring performances that I have seen on any front—a performance of which they have every reason to be proud—but diffidence and conservatism have deterred them from telling the world about it."[36]

American correspondents' bewilderment was understandable, but, even under pressure, the Italian conservative politicians were willing to change only slightly their traditional attitude, because they abhorred mass politics. America hardly existed for them: of the changes revolutionizing the world, Sonnino, Italy's minister of Foreign Affairs, only said "I shall not see them. I am too old."[37] Therefore, throughout the war, they relied mainly on repression, and censorship remained one of the pillars of the government's management of public opinion well after the end of the war.

The war, however, was also a "Great War of Words."[38] Victorious on the military front, Italy was a loser in the domain of international communication. The

---

[34]   "Memorandum on Italian Propaganda in America," n.d., box 10, folder 5, Merriam Papers, and "Italian Information for America," Office of the Commissioner at Rome, box 1, CPI 20-B3, CPI Papers.

[35]   Lilian T. Mowrer, *Journalist's Wife* (New York: William Morrow, 1937), 38. On page 30 she observed: "Centuries of rotten government had resulted in a complete lack of enlightened public opinion."

[36]   E. Alexander Powell, *Italy at War and the Allies in the West* (New York: C. Scribner's Son, 1917), 6.

[37]   Florence Colgate Speranza, *The Diary of Gino Speranza: Italy, 1915-1919* (New York: Columbia University Press, 1941), 2:126.

[38]   Peter Buitenhuis, *The Great War of Words: British, American, and Canadian Propaganda and Fiction, 1914-1933* (Vancouver: University of British Columbia Press, 1987).

Versailles setback can also be seen as a huge failure in "publicity." The Italian government, indeed, failed to realize how far in the emerging global world advertising was a primary need.

Conclusion

In a mass society, such as the United States during the first decades of the twentieth century, we can grasp the character and scope of censorship only by considering at the same time the new powerful tools at the disposal of the government to master public opinion. This capacity to use propaganda was lacking in the European warring nations, especially in Italy, where the era of mass politics was still to come.

Despite its accomplishments, or precisely because of them, George Creel and his "much-maligned" organization were frequently under attack by Congress, the press and the State Department.[39] They questioned various aspects of the CPI initiatives and succeeded in limiting its allotment of funds and the range of its activities at home and abroad. Initially, CPI censorship was the main target of their criticism, but soon the propaganda side of its work became more and more alarming.

Creel defended himself strenuously, and quite naively, pointing out his excellent management of funds, the outstanding results of the CPI's domestic and foreign campaigns and the very low number of ascertained "lies" in the CPI's huge production of official information.[40] He never seemed to realize that the crucial point was the very existence of this institution and its apparent success in molding public opinion.

In fact, a new specter was emerging in the political arena at that time: the fabrication of consent, which undermined the basic assumptions of the Progressive Era about the independence and rationality of the general public. This concept of an enlightened public opinion, informed and intelligent, able to sort out truth from falsehood and take considered decisions, was one of the main casualties of war. In the disillusioned Twenties, John Dewey expressed a widely shared opinion, when he stated that "sentiment can be manufactured by mass methods for almost any person or any cause."[41] As Lee Huebner put it, "publicity, the hope of the Progressive Era, became propaganda, the scourge of the Twenties…."[42]

In the dawning age of mass communication and expanding presidential power, both the concepts of "repression" and "democracy" needed a thorough reconsideration. Starting with the intellectuals that had worked for war propaganda,

---

[39] Henry F. May, *The End of American Innocence: A Study of the First Years of Our Own Time 1912-1917* (1959; repr., New York: Columbia University Press, 1992), 387.

[40] "Consider for a moment!" Creel urged the reader in his postwar writings. The CPI was charged with giving false information only four times out of an enormous amount of press releases, pamphlets, daily issues of the Official Bulletin, etc. Creel, *How We Advertised America*, 50.

[41] John Dewey, *Individualism Old and New* (New York: Minton, Balch & Company, 1930), 42-43.

[42] L.W. Huebner, "The Discovery of Propaganda: Changing Attitudes towards Public Communication in America 1900-1930" (PhD diss., Harvard University, 1968), 200.

like Walter Lippmann, Will Irwin and Edward L. Bernays, an animated debate developed immediately after the war and kept up momentum because of the more sinister uses of propaganda promoted by the emerging totalitarian regimes in Europe. Walter Lippmann's trilogy about public opinion—*Liberty and the News* (1920), *Public Opinion* (1922) and *The Phantom Public* (1925)—testifies his arduous search for new ways to keep democracy alive in modern societies. Coming back from the Paris Peace Conference in early 1919, after years of collaboration with the Wilson administration, Lippmann felt that "something had gone badly wrong, that his work had miscarried." People had been saturated with propaganda and now half believing everything, in fact they believed in nothing.[43]

In the interwar years, scholars of the new field of mass communication were keenly attracted by CPI techniques and stressed the outstanding results of this experiment in executive control of public opinion. In 1927, Harold Lasswell, one of the pioneers of this field of study, called Wilson "the great generalissimo on the propaganda front" and observed that his "matchless skill ... in propaganda has never been equalled in the world's history."[44] Ten years later, James Mock and Cedric Larson, in a chapter significantly entitled "Blueprint for Tomorrow's CPI," defined the CPI as "a social innovation brilliantly conceived and in many ways brilliantly executed," an impressive testimonial of Creel's ability as its creator.[45]

More recently, historians have arrived at a more sober appraisal of the activity of the Creel Committee. If they generally praise its originality and effectiveness as a nationalizing force at home and an Americanizing agent abroad, they are much more cautious when the functioning of democracy is concerned. In fact, by a crusading attitude and a skillful combination of selective repression, centralization of information, control of the media and propaganda, the CPI was able to mobilize public opinion in an unparalleled way. Also because of its novelty, it obtained a general conformism of American media and people, creating a social atmosphere which was not favorable to the expression of dissent.

Creel directed the CPI with the same crusading spirit that had characterized his activity as a muckraker journalist and a Wilsonian supporter in the pre-war years. For him and for most Progressive activists that flocked to Washington in 1917-1918, the war had transposed their urge for reform from American society to the world

---

[43] A well-known political analyst, Lippmann worked for the Wilson administration both within the *Inquiry*, a consultant body charged with the preparation of the American peace program, and within the military propaganda in Europe; see my book, *Woodrow Wilson and the American Myth in Italy*, chapters 6 and 7, and Huebner, "The Discovery of Propaganda," 238-239. For Will Irwin, who directed the CPI's Foreign Section, see "Age of Lies: How the Propagandist Attacks the Foundation of Public Opinion," *Sunset* (December 1919), and *Propaganda and the News, or What Makes You Think So* (New York and London: Whittlesey House and McGraw-Hill Book Company, Inc., 1936). For Edward L. Bernays, who worked for the CPI in Latin America and later became a leader in public relations, see *Crystallizing Public Opinion* (New York: Boni and Liveright, 1923), and *Propaganda* (New York: H. Liveright, 1928).

[44] Harold D. Lasswell, *Propaganda Technique in the World War* (1927; repr., New York: Peter Smith, 1938), 216 and 217.

[45] Mock and Larson, *Words that Won the War*, 51-52 and 338.

scene. Americanism became a secular religion and this new faith did not leave space for dissention or even criticism. The Progressive spirit of crusade acquired illiberal tones. If the war with its emotional appeals and bitter disillusionment prepared the reaction and hysteria of the postwar years, some aspects of these phenomena were rooted in the ante bellum politics. Thus, isolationism, illiberalism, and intolerance were the paradoxical legacy of a war waged for world democracy.

DOUBLE "V":
WALTER WHITE, THE NATIONAL ASSOCIATION
FOR THE ADVANCEMENT OF COLORED PEOPLE (NAACP)
AND WORLD WAR II, 1939-1945

Kevern Verney

At first sight the policies and actions of the NAACP during World War II may seem an unlikely topic for inclusion in a volume of essays on the theme of political repression. Neither the Association itself, nor the African American community in general, can be said to have suffered overt political oppression by the federal government during the war years. Indeed, despite their reputation for militancy not a single African American newspaper was suppressed during the war. Admittedly, NAACP Secretary Walter White did later claim that, in a December 1942 meeting with Franklin Roosevelt, the president had warned him that he was under pressure from officials to bring indictments for sedition against African American newspaper editors for publishing articles and editorials damaging to the war effort. Fortunately, the potential crisis was quickly defused. After listening to what he had to say, according to White, Roosevelt "called in his advisers and ordered them to abandon" such an "absurd and dangerous proposition."[1]

Repression can, however, take a variety of forms and can manifest itself in more subtle ways than direct government action. It can be argued that mainstream African American leaders, like White, engaged in voluntary self-censorship during the war years that rendered intervention by the Roosevelt administration unnecessary. There were clearly good reasons for such acts of self-denial. Statements that challenged the nation's record on race relations could appear unpatriotic. Moreover, whatever the evils of racial segregation and discrimination within the United States the extremes of pseudo-scientific racism that prevailed in Nazi Germany were worse, raising questions about the wisdom of any course of action that might damage the Allied war effort and, by implication, make an Axis victory more likely.

Such considerations notwithstanding, a central theme in civil rights historiography since the 1970s has been that rather than being marked by timidity the war years saw increased militancy in African American communities. Neglected as a field of research during the "King-centric" years of the 1960s, by the 1980s and 1990s it had become common practice for scholars to portray World War II as a time of heightened racial consciousness among African Americans that sowed the seeds for the postwar civil rights movement.

---

[1] This claim is made in Walter White, *A Man Called White* (Athens: University of Georgia Press, 1995), 208. The most detailed account of the controversy is Patrick Washburn, *A Question of Sedition: The Federal Government's Investigation of the Black Press during World War II* (Oxford: Oxford University Press, 1986), 93. Washburn suggests that White was mistaken in his recollection of events and that it was actually not Roosevelt but U.S. Attorney General Francis Biddle who deserves the credit for the withholding of indictments.

The policies and actions of the NAACP during World War II provide an appropriate case study for examining this thesis. Easily the largest and most important black civil rights organization of the period, the Association saw its national membership rise from just 50,000 in 1940 to around 500,000 by the end of 1945.[2] Returning to the NAACP in 1944, after a ten-year period of absence, the veteran scholar and civil rights campaigner W.E.B. Du Bois professed to be "astonished" at the transformation in the fortunes of the organization. In addition to the growth in membership, the number of staff employed by the Association had tripled and income quadrupled. In short, "it had become a big business, smoothly run and extraordinarily influential. The newspapers vied for its releases, courts listened to its attorneys, and men of prominence readily accepted places on its Board of Directors."[3]

Given such impressive credentials it is the more surprising that scholarly research on the NAACP remains a comparatively neglected field of study. Despite its considerable importance, the NAACP has for many years been "the stepchild of civil rights historiography." Although recent scholarly developments have begun to remedy this situation, published research on the work of the Association during World War II remains limited.[4] The period 1939-1945 may no longer constitute what historian Richard Dalfiume once described as "the forgotten years" of the civil rights struggle, but they continue to be a neglected era in the history of the NAACP.[5]

Preliminary analysis of NAACP initiatives during these years would appear to lend support to the wartime militancy interpretation. Belying the Association's reputation as an organization that sought advances in civil rights through a courtroom-based strategy, and lobbying influential social and political contacts, in April 1941 Walter White intervened in a labor dispute at the Ford car plant in Detroit to urge the more than 9,000 African American workers employed on the River Rouge production lines to support a strike called by the United Automobile Workers union. Similarly, in June 1941 the NAACP endorsed A. Philip Randolph's March on Washington Movement despite the Association's longstanding distrust of

---

[2]   Adam Fairclough, *Race and Democracy: The Civil Rights Struggle in Louisiana, 1915-1972* (Athens: University of Georgia Press, 1995), 48, 50; Statement of Walter White at 37th Annual Meeting of the NAACP, 7 January 1946, *Papers of the NAACP, Part 1, Minutes of the Board of Directors, Records of Annual Conferences, Major Speeches and Special Reports, 1909-1950* (microfilm, University Publications of America, 1982-), reel 14, frame 756-757; Roy Wilkins with Tom Mathews, *Standing Fast: The Autobiography of Roy Wilkins* (New York: Da Capo Press, 1994), 190.

[3]   W.E.B. Du Bois, *The Autobiography of W.E.B. Du Bois: A Soliloquy on Viewing My Life from the Last Decade of Its First Century* (New York: New World Paperbacks, 1979), 328.

[4]   Manfred Berg, *The Ticket to Freedom: The NAACP and the Struggle for Black Political Integration* (Gainesville: University Press of Florida, 2005), 1. In addition to Berg's impressive study other recent important works relating to the history of the NAACP include Kenneth Robert Janken, *White: The Biography of Walter White, Mr. NAACP* (New York: New Press, 2003) and Gilbert Jonas, *The NAACP and the Struggle against Racism in America, 1909-1969* (New York: Routledge, 2005).

[5]   Richard M. Dalfiume, "The 'Forgotten Years' of the Negro Revolution," *Journal of American History* 55.1 (June, 1968): 90-106.

entering into alliances with other civil rights organizations and its wariness of large-scale public protests.[6]

The reward for such solidarity, Roosevelt's Executive Order 8802, establishing the Fair Employment Practices Committee (FEPC) to counter racial discrimination in the wartime defense industries, had significant consequences for the Association. The Committee reaffirmed for the NAACP leadership the importance of a labor-based agenda at a time when its activity in this area was in danger of declining with the end of the Great Depression and the winding up of New Deal agencies. The vigorous campaigning by the Association to secure more equal opportunities in the defense industries was clearly an important factor in the rapid growth in NAACP membership during the war years. The attention of Association officials was focused on bread and butter employment issues that could command widespread appeal in African American communities in contrast to less inspiring, albeit important, courtroom initiatives and the longstanding NAACP objective of securing the passage of a federal anti-lynching law.

FEPC related activity benefited the NAACP in other ways. Traditionally the Association suffered from its image as a hierarchical, bureaucratic organization in which important decisions were made at NAACP headquarters in New York City, and the activities of grassroots members were restricted to little more than fund-raising and the organization of social events. The involvement of local chapters in monitoring levels of discrimination in defense plants and helping to gather evidence to be presented at FEPC hearings helped to counter such negative perceptions.[7]

In another departure the Association showed signs of beginning to overcome its traditional reluctance to support civil rights protests at the local level. On 26 January 1941 the National Office coordinated a day of nationwide protest against discrimination in defense hiring. A meeting in Los Angeles alone was attended by some 2,000 people and resulted in the formation of a local committee to organize the campaign on a permanent basis. Encouraged by such success the national NAACP leadership organized a follow-up protest on 26 April 1941 to picket industrial plants that held government contracts and discriminated against African American workers.[8]

There were other indications of a new mood of assertiveness by the Association's national leadership as well. In 1941 the Association opposed the creation of an army airbase for black pilots at Tuskegee, Alabama, because the segregated camp was contrary to the Association's commitment to integration. This stand represented a stiffening of resolve on the part of the NAACP in comparison to

---

[6]   Report of the Secretary, Minutes of the Meeting of the Board of Directors, 14 April 1941 and March on Washington, Minutes of the Meeting of the Board of Directors, 26 June 1941, both in *Papers of the NAACP, Part 1*, reel 3, frame 24-25, 52-53.

[7]   Merl E. Reed, *Seedtime for the Modern Civil Rights Movement: The President's Commission on Fair Employment Practice, 1941-1946* (Baton Rouge: Louisiana State University Press, 1991), 34-35, 46.

[8]   Report of the Secretary for the February Meeting of the Board, 1941; Report of the Department of Branches for the February Meeting of the Board, 1941; Report of the Secretary for the May Meeting of the Board, 1941, all in *Papers of the NAACP, Part 1*, reel 6, frame 524, 535, 565; Reed, *Seedtime*, 272, 315.

World War I when, in June 1917, the NAACP Board of Directors had compromised its principles in supporting the formation of a segregated officer training camp at Des Moines, Iowa, on the grounds that this was a lesser evil than having no African American officers trained at all.[9]

Another potentially controversial decision came in March 1943 when the Board of Directors refused to join a publicity campaign by the American Red Cross to encourage blood donors and also refused the Red Cross permission to site collection boxes and advertising posters in NAACP offices. This rebuttal was the culmination of mounting resentment by the NAACP leadership at the discriminatory practices employed by the charitable organization. In November 1941 the Red Cross had initially refused to accept any blood from African Americans. The ban was lifted in January 1942, but only on the understanding that blood supplies from white and black donors would be segregated. This continued to be Red Cross policy until the end of the war, despite the fact that as early as May 1942 the American Medical Association confirmed that there was no scientific justification for segregating blood supplies. Indeed, if supplies were not segregated at the point of collection it was impossible to determine the race of the donor. To add further insult, Red Cross recreational facilities for servicemen were also segregated.[10]

Perhaps the most notable departure in NAACP strategy during the war years was the unprecedented interest shown by Walter White in race relations outside the United States. In the period 1909-1939 the Association had shown limited concern at developments in the international arena and then this often reflected the particular interest of one or two leading individuals within the organization. The involvement of the NAACP in the Pan African congress movement after World War I was thus largely attributable to the enthusiasm of W.E.B. Du Bois but, as Du Bois's most recent and scholarly biographer has noted, the Congresses "never quite caught on with the NAACP Board of Directors."[11]

Similarly, James Weldon Johnson, NAACP secretary 1920-1930, took a personal interest in developments in Haiti. A former diplomat who had served as a consular official in Venezuela, 1906-1909, and Nicaragua, 1909-1912, Johnson undertook a fact-finding tour of Haiti on behalf of the NAACP in 1920, following

---

9   Press Release, "Negro Militancy Outstanding in 1941 Walter White Says," 3 January 1942 and Mr. William Pickens, Minutes of the Meeting of the Board of Directors, 9 February 1942, both in *Papers of the NAACP, Part 1*, reel 3, frame 112-113 and reel 14, frame 569; Walter White to Dr. Patterson, March 3, 1943, in *Papers of the NAACP, Part 9, Discrimination in the U.S. Armed Forces, 1918-1955, Series B: Armed Forces Legal Files, 1940-1950*, reel 25, frame 574.

10   The American Red Cross, Report of the Secretary for the February Meeting of the Board, 1942 and The American Red Cross, Minutes of the Meeting of the Board of Directors, 8 March 1943, both in *Papers of the NAACP, Part 1*, reel 3, frame 227 and reel 6, frame 662-663; American Red Cross Files, *Papers of the NAACP, Part 15, Segregation and Discrimination/Complaints and Responses, 1940-1955, Series B: Administrative Files*, reel 1, frame 39, 156-162, 915.

11   David Levering Lewis, *W.E.B. Du Bois: The Fight for Equality and the American Century, 1919-1963* (New York: Henry Holt and Company, 2000), 499; Berg, *Ticket to Freedom*, 139; Janken, *White*, 278.

the occupation of the island by the United States in 1915. Sharply critical of U.S. rule there, in the years that followed Johnson tried to publicize the plight of the Haitian people and to support their quest for independence.[12]

In 1935 the Italian invasion of Ethiopia predictably attracted much discussion and criticism in the pages of the NAACP journal *The Crisis*, but as with the Pan African Congress movement and Haiti, such interest in foreign affairs was the exception not the rule. The national NAACP leadership did not seek to develop a leading role for the Association in mobilizing U.S. opinion against Mussolini. Instead White and the NAACP Board of Directors concentrated their attention on issues closer to home, most notably the impact of the Great Depression and the New Deal on African American communities within the United States and the Association's longstanding campaign for a federal anti-lynching law.[13]

The outbreak of World War II dramatically changed this situation, particularly when it evolved into a truly global conflict following the Japanese attack on Pearl Harbor on 7 December 1941. The struggle against Nazi racial ideology in Europe, and the fate of European colonial empires in Africa and Asia in the postwar world, inevitably became key issues for the Association. White in particular attached increasing importance to international developments. In September 1941 he wrote to Winston Churchill highlighting instances of apparent British racial discrimination. The following year White sought to enlist Madame Chiang Kai-shek as a speaker on "national and global aspects of the color problem," an invitation that was declined on the grounds that Madame Chiang "did not want to appear for special organizations," preferring to devote herself to broader causes in support of the war effort, such as the Red Cross or War Bonds.[14]

Disappointed in his efforts to establish links with Madame Chiang, White concentrated his energies on India. In 1942 he became a member of the India League, the leading voice for the Indian National Congress in the United States, and was one of more than fifty well-known Americans to put their name to a full-page petition in the *New York Times* calling for the reopening of negotiations between the British Government and Indian Nationalist leaders. Reflecting his preference for quiet behind-the-scenes negotiation, White engineered a number of private meetings with Lord Halifax, the British ambassador to the United States, during 1942-1943, in an effort to secure a commitment by the United Kingdom to de-colonization.[15] At the same time he sought to persuade President Roosevelt to send a three-man commission to meet with Nationalist leaders in India and assure them of U.S.

---

[12]   James Weldon Johnson, *Along This Way: The Autobiography of James Weldon Johnson* (New York: Viking Penguin, 1990), 344-353.

[13]   Berg, *Ticket to Freedom*, 97; Janken, *White*, 279.

[14]   Report of the Secretary for the May Meeting of the Board, 1942, *Papers of the NAACP, Part 1*, reel 6, frame 715-716; File on Madame Chiang Kai-shek, 1942-1943, *Papers of the NAACP, Part 14, Race Relations in the International Arena, 1940-1955*, reel 6, frame 277-278, 291.

[15]   Penny M. Von Eschen, *Race against Empire: Black Americans and Anticolonialism, 1937-1957* (Ithaca, NY: Cornell University Press, 1997), 30; Brenda Gayle Plummer, *Rising Wind: Black Americans and U.S. Foreign Affairs, 1935-1960* (Chapel Hill: University of North Carolina Press, 1996), 92-93.

support for independence. Indeed, White became so enthused about the initiative that he even got so far as drawing up a list of his preferred choice of members for the commission; namely former Republican Party presidential candidate Wendell Wilkie, U.S. Supreme Court Justice Felix Frankfurter and "a distinguished American Negro," most probably W.E.B. Du Bois. Unfortunately, and not for the first or last time in his career, White overestimated his powers of persuasion. Although Halifax and Roosevelt both purported to welcome the venture the president concluded that such a step "right now" would be inappropriate, a situation that remained unchanged for the duration of the war. White was similarly disappointed in 1944 when the British government turned down a request by the NAACP secretary to travel to India to meet with interned Congress party leaders.[16]

Undeterred by these setbacks in 1944-1945 White embarked on two extended tours of American military bases overseas that served to reinforce his growing internationalism and his belief in the interconnectedness of race relations in the United States with racial problems around the world. Between January and April 1944 he undertook a 20,000 mile visit to the European Theater of Operations, United States Army (ETOUSA) that included an extended stay in the United Kingdom, to meet with African American servicemen stationed there in the build up to D-Day, as well as trips to Africa and the Middle East; the former being White's first visit to that continent. From December 1944 to April 1945 White followed this up with an even more exhausting thirty-six thousand-mile tour of the Pacific theater of war, taking in Hawaii, Guam, Saipan, the Philippines and Dutch New Guinea.

Predictably, both tours enabled White to better understand the catalogue of racial injustices experienced by African Americans in the military, ranging from certain towns and localities in the United Kingdom being declared "off limits" to off duty servicemen in order to segregate white and black troops, through to the discriminatory punishments meted out to African American servicemen by white military policemen and army court-martials. A less obvious outcome of the tours was that White became convinced that, like him, African American servicemen had a deep affinity with non-white peoples around the world. He believed they saw strong similarities between the evils of colonialism overseas and the discrimination and segregation that they experienced in the United States. "World War II has given to the Negro a sense of kinship with other colored—and also oppressed—peoples of the world," he noted in his 1945 account of the two tours. African American servicemen may not have "thought through" or "informed" themselves about "the racial angles of colonial policy and master race theories", but they sensed "that the struggle of the Negro in the United States is part and parcel of the struggle against imperialism and exploitation in India, China, Burma, Africa, the Philippines, Malaya, the West Indies and South America."[17]

Inspired by such thoughts, in April 1945 White used his influence with Eleanor Roosevelt to secure a place for the NAACP as one of forty-two consulting organizations at the San Francisco Conference, convened to pave the way for the

---

[16]   File on India, General, March-May 1942-1945, *Papers of the NAACP, Part 14*, reel 9, frame 10, 17-18, 24-31, 34-35, 46, 50-52, 154; Plummer, *Rising Wind*, 97.

[17]   Walter White, *A Rising Wind* (Westport, CT: Negro Universities Press, 1971), 144.

founding of the United Nations organization. The conference was central to White's belief that any lasting postwar settlement had to be committed to de-colonization and racial equality. "The United States, Great Britain, France and other Allied nations must choose without delay one of two courses," he prophetically noted. They must either "revolutionize their racial concepts and practices, to abolish imperialism and grant full equality to all of its peoples, or else prepare for World War III. Another Versailles Treaty providing for 'mandates,' 'protectorates,' and other devices for white domination will make such a war inevitable."[18] In the heady political atmosphere of the day, when for a time it seemed possible to shape a new, enlightened postwar world order, White appears to have genuinely believed that it was his destiny to ensure that it was the former option that was pursued. Given the responsibility for articulating the thoughts and aspirations of all African Americans, and convinced of his personal ability to charm the great and the powerful, White's contribution at the conference could, as NAACP Assistant Secretary Roy Wilkins flatteringly pointed out to him, "represent the peak of your distinguished career as the guiding genius of the NAACP."[19]

Such lofty ambitions on the international stage combined with the NAACP's actions on the home front would, at first sight, seem to belie any suggestion that the Association engaged in self-censorship or repression during the war years. Appearances can, however, be deceptive. To begin with it should be noted that many of the Association's bolder domestic initiatives, such as its support for the March on Washington Movement, occurred between 1939-1941 when the United States enjoyed the status of a neutral power. During this period, as Harvard Sitkoff has noted, it was easier for an organization like the NAACP to be critical of the pattern of U.S. race relations and demand changes in the status quo without suffering the opprobrium of seeming to be unpatriotic.[20] From this perspective the Japanese attack on Pearl Harbor on 7 December 1941 can be seen as constituting a Rooseveltian equivalent of the terrorist attacks of 9/11 sixty years later. After "12/7" it became more difficult to campaign against racial injustice at home without appearing to be disloyal or compromising the nation's war effort.

An indication of the changed political climate is reflected in the fact that in September 1940 the NAACP Board of Directors voted that the Association's Legal and Defense Committee "give aid to any American citizen desiring to enlist in the Army or Navy, who is refused the privilege of enlisting on account of race or color."[21] However, when in June 1942 Winfred Lynn, an African American serviceman, initiated a legal challenge against being drafted into a segregated regiment the NAACP declined to come to his aid. Indeed the Association did the opposite, urging him to drop the case. When Lynn decided not to accept this advice

---

[18]   Janken, *White*, 430-431 n. 9; White, *A Rising Wind*, 154-155.

[19]   Roy Wilkins to Walter White, 20 April 1945, *Papers of the NAACP, Part 14*, reel 18, frame 130-131.

[20]   Harvard Sitkoff, "African American Militancy in the World War II South: Another Perspective," in Neil R. McMillen, ed., *Remaking Dixie: The Impact of World War II on the American South* (Jackson: University Press of Mississippi, 1997), 71.

[21]   Negroes and the Armed Forces, Minutes of the Meeting of the Board of Directors, 9 September 1940, *Papers of the NAACP, Part 1*, reel 2, frame 1076-1077.

the national NAACP leadership retaliated by expelling his lawyer brother Conrad from the NAACP branch in Jamaica, Long Island, on the grounds that the determination of the two men to pursue the issue was unpatriotic in time of war. Moreover, Thurgood Marshall, NAACP Special Legal Counsel, lobbied the American Civil Liberties Union to dissuade it from taking up the case.[22] The fact that the FBI engaged in a campaign to label the Lynn brothers as communist "fellow travelers" doubtless provides some explanation for Marshall's actions. However, perhaps the best insight into the Association's heavy-handed response to the Lynn family is provided by an apparent pledge made by Walter White to President Roosevelt in 1940 that the NAACP would not support any legal challenge to the draft in the event that the United States became a combatant in the war.[23]

In fairness to White and the NAACP Board of Directors, it should be noted that, if true, the adoption of such a self-denying ordinance was motivated by more than just moral cowardice at the thought of appearing unpatriotic. In retrospect, it is easy to see the entry of the United States as the decisive turning point of World War II, after which it was only a matter of when, rather than if, the Allies were to emerge victorious. This was not so apparent at the time, when for many months the outcome appeared to be genuinely in doubt. The apprehension generated by such uncertainty was reflected in an NAACP press release, "Fight for Liberties Here While Fighting Dictators Abroad" in which White noted that "we Negroes are faced with a Hobson's choice." However, there was a choice. "If Hitler wins every single right we now possess and for which we have struggled here in America for more than three centuries will be instantaneously wiped out.... If the allies win, we shall at least have the right to continue fighting for a share of democracy for ourselves."[24] In another small, but telling, indication of the mood of public anxiety, four months later in 1942 the Board of Directors passed a resolution requiring White to "make enquiries as to photo-stating or microfilming the Association's important records and storing them in a secure place in the event of bombing of the city of New York."[25]

The following month, at the suggestion of Thurgood Marshall, the Board endorsed the "Double-V" campaign launched by the African American newspaper the *Pittsburgh Courier* to encourage black Americans to fight against Nazi racism abroad as well as segregation and discrimination at home.[26] Civil rights scholars continue to debate the meaning and significance of the *Courier's* initiative. Viewed

---

[22]   Lee Finkle, *Forum for Protest: The Black Press during World War II* (London: Associated University Presses, 1975), 151.

[23]   George Q. Flynn, "Selective Service and American Blacks during World War II," *Journal of Negro History* 69.1 (Winter 1984): 22-23; Finkle, *Forum for Protest*, 151.

[24]   Press Release, "Fight for Liberties Here While Fighting Dictators Abroad Says NAACP," 12 December 1941, *Papers of the NAACP, Part 1*, reel 14, frame 563.

[25]   Preservation of NAACP Records, Minutes of the Meeting of the Board of Directors, 13 April 1942, *Papers of the NAACP, Part 1*, reel 3, frame 133.

[26]   Double "V" Campaign, Minutes of the Meeting of the Board of Directors, 11 May 1942, *Papers of the NAACP, Part 1*, reel 3, frame 140; Double "V" Campaign, Minutes of NAACP Staff Conference, Thursday April 9, 1942, *Papers of the NAACP, Part 17, National Staff Files, 1940-1955*, reel 4, frame 561.

from one perspective the "Double-V" campaign can be seen as a sign of militancy on the part of opinion formers in the African American community, particularly compared to the experience of World War I, when mainstream black spokespersons like W.E.B. Du Bois generally urged African American communities to "close ranks" in support of the nation's war effort, and to put off voicing their grievances about racial injustice at home until the end of the conflict.

An alternative point of view, most notably expressed by the historian Lee Finkle, has been to argue that, behind the bold rhetoric, the "Double-V" campaign can be more accurately viewed as an attempt by conservative African American leaders to win over the support of skeptical rank and file black communities for the war.[27] If this interpretation is accepted as being at least partially valid it may put Walter White's burgeoning internationalism in the years 1941-1945 in a different light. Rather than being viewed simply as a sign of growing radicalism, such a strategy can also be seen as embodying strands of accommodationism. Simply put, an inevitable consequence of the emphasis placed by White on global issues in race relations was that it would make African Americans more likely to support the war effort.

Moreover, focusing on the evils of racism and colonialism abroad had the effect of externalizing evil, deflecting at least some attention away from the problems of segregation and discrimination at home. In this context it is noticeable that White's efforts on behalf of imprisoned Congress Party leaders in India were not matched by a similar level of concern for interned Japanese Americans within the United States. Roosevelt's 1942 imprisonment of more than one hundred thousand Americans of Japanese descent in specially created camps constituted arguably the most flagrant act of racial injustice by the Roosevelt administration during the entire course of the war. Rather than being of suspect loyalty and potential fifth columnists for the Japanese war machine, as was alleged, the overwhelming majority of those interned were industrious, law-abiding and patriotic. Their incarceration had more to do with pandering to longstanding ethnic prejudices against the Japanese in California than in countering any threat to national security. In these circumstances it might be supposed that the NAACP would have been at the forefront of a campaign to protest against such action. This was not the case. The internment issue was marginalized at monthly meetings of the Board of Directors and the initial public response of the NAACP was confined to an expression of concern that the detainees be humanely treated. In California the Association even attempted to take advantage of the situation by trying to persuade fruit growers to hire African Americans as replacement labor for their incarcerated Japanese workers. It was only in 1944 that the NAACP seriously challenged the principle of internment and questioned the racial motivation behind it. By this time, however, public criticism of the measure had already become widespread.[28]

---

[27] Lee Finkle, "The Conservative Aims of Militant Rhetoric: Black Protest during World War II," *Journal of American History* 60.3 (December 1973): 692-713; Finkle, *Forum for Protest*, 114, 221-223.

[28] Berg, *Ticket to Freedom*, 102; Plummer, *Rising Wind*, 75.

The tardy response of the NAACP to the internment issue reflected a recurring tendency by Walter White to defer difficult and controversial issues until the end of the war, or at least until such time as final victory was in sight. A further example of this came in December 1944 during his Pacific tour. Acting in his capacity as a war correspondent White penned an article for the *New York Post* expressing his concern at an incident in Guam in which a court martial convicted forty-four African American servicemen following an affray with white soldiers. Intended for publication in January 1945, the release of the story was delayed by the United States Navy for six months, until 11 July 1945. Rather than voicing immediate public protest at such an act of censorship, White did not reveal details of the case until a radio broadcast on 7 July.[29]

Perhaps the most notable example of White's procrastination was in respect to his policy on imperialism. In 1942-1943 he worked to secure an immediate pledge from European powers like the United Kingdom to give independence to their colonies. By 1944-1945 this objective had shifted to securing a commitment to de-colonization through the auspices of the new postwar international peace keeping organization that was to take shape in the form of the United Nations. White, as has been indicated earlier, became genuinely convinced that he would be a key player in establishing the framework for the United Nations at the 1945 San Francisco conference. This was not the case. The consulting organizations invited to the conference were never intended to be co-creators of the United Nations Charter in the way that White believed. Their presence was rather an attempt by the Roosevelt administration to ensure the support of U.S. public opinion for a new postwar order at an early stage, thereby avoiding the mistake of Woodrow Wilson who realized too late the need for such a consensus to secure U.S. membership of the League of Nations after World War I.[30]

Moreover, whatever the president's intentions it was inevitable that the views of an organization like the NAACP would be of little note in comparison to the influence wielded by wartime allies of the United States like Britain and France. "The doughty NAACP delegation" at San Francisco, as David Levering Lewis has cruelly but accurately observed, "amounted to little more than a gnat among the superpower pachyderms." Even the United States military had a vested interest in opposing a de-colonizing agenda because of the desire of army chiefs to retain control of Pacific islands seized from Japan during the course of the war.[31]

White's high-minded, yet unrealistic expectations at San Francisco were typical of the NAACP secretary's strategy of securing change through quiet diplomacy as opposed to public protest. In part, as Kenneth Janken has noted, this seems to have derived from White conflating access to powerful people and the

[29]. Finkle, *Forum For Protest*, 178.

[30]. Janken, *White*, 300; Carol Anderson, *Eyes Off the Prize: The United Nations and the African American Struggle for Human Rights, 1944-1955* (Cambridge: Cambridge University Press, 2003), 40.

[31]. Lewis, *W.E.B. Du Bois*, 507; Anderson, *Eyes Off the Prize*, 43; James H. Meriwether, *Proudly We Can Be Africans: Black Americans and Africa, 1935-1961* (Chapel Hill: University of North Carolina Press, 2002), 71.

centers of power with power itself.[32] It was also an indication of White's unshakeable belief in his ability to win over the hearts and minds of the good and the great through the irresistible combination of his personal charm and intellectual acumen. In holding fast to this conviction White not only overestimated his own abilities but also arguably underestimated the extent to which such powerful and shrewdly calculating individuals might influence him. In his high level diplomatic discussions on India, White hoped to impress on President Roosevelt and Lord Halifax the need for immediate action, but instead seems to have been more persuaded by them of the efficacy of delay.

Keeping such discussions behind closed doors doubtless also seemed a more attractive option than public protest, which might risk the NAACP appearing to be unpatriotic by fomenting divisions between the United States and one of its most important wartime allies. Ironically, perhaps the most significant concession by the Roosevelt administration on race relations during the war years, the creation of the FEPC, was only realized precisely because of the threat of public protest. That however, was before the "day of infamy" at Pearl Harbor on 7 December 1941 transformed the political climate and made a repeat of any such strategy infinitely more problematic.

Wars, by their nature give rise to complex and difficult situations for the individuals, groups and societies that become involved in them. Such was the case for the NAACP between 1939 and 1945. In some respects the emergency conditions of the period, and the revulsion of Americans at the extremes of Nazi racism, provided new opportunities for the Association. At the same time, the need to avoid action that might seem disloyal or that might assist the Nazi war effort imposed limitations. Walter White and the NAACP Board of Directors responded to the challenges arising from wartime conditions in a variety of ways.

In the period 1939-1941 there were a number of indications that the NAACP was becoming more assertive and innovative in its actions. After 7 December 1941 through to the end of the war the Association's national leadership was inclined to be more cautious. On some occasions this could result in White consciously subordinating the objectives of the NAACP to the needs of the war effort, as in his commitment not to support a legal challenge to the draft when the United States became a combatant in the conflict. More generally, he sought to channel the energies of the NAACP into initiatives where the interests of the Association and the American war effort could both be served at the same time. White's growing internationalism in these years could thus be justified as a logical extension of the Association's stand against racial injustice, but also had the tendency to divert attention away from discrimination and segregation at home and to make African American communities more likely to support the war effort.

On one level an ideal solution to the dilemmas confronting the Association during a time of national emergency, the adoption of this duel strategy came at a price. There was the risk of a blinkered approach in the development of NAACP policy, a lack of imagination in failing to give full consideration to other possible initiatives, such as organized public protests, that may, or may not, have been more

---

[32]   Janken, *White*, 226, 300.

effective courses of action but would clearly have been more controversial in nature. Similarly, in the emotive political climate of the day White appeared either unable or unwilling to think through the potential shortcomings of initiatives that he did pursue. The NAACP secretary's anti-imperialist agenda may have reconciled the ideals of the Association with the needs of the American war effort but did not include any realistic appraisal of its chances of success. The predictable desire of European powers to hold on to their colonies, and the probability that the Roosevelt administration would give greater weight to the wishes of wartime allies than the counsel of the NAACP, were factors that White failed to recognize until compelled to do so in 1945.

If repression in this broader sense, of a narrowness of outlook, was a shortcoming of Walter White and the NAACP in the years 1939-1945 it has been no less of a problem for civil rights historians in their interpretations of World War II. Aware of the impending civil rights protests of the 1950s and 1960s it is, as Neil McMillen has noted, easy for scholars to succumb to "teleological error." In short, to engage in a form of historical determinism and see every development in wartime race relations as a portent of the storm to come.[33] An examination of the role of the NAACP during the war years suggests the need for a more cautious assessment. If some of the policies of the Association can be viewed as signs of increased assertiveness other actions can be cited as indicators of conservatism. Moreover, it would also be wrong to assume the existence of a simple binary divide between militancy and accommodationism. Depending on the perspective that is taken, some initiatives, such as White's internationalism, can be seen as incorporating elements of both. The dilemma for historians is to take account of the diverse nature of this evidence without being blinkered by preconceived notions as to what they should find. Political repression, as was noted earlier, can take a variety of subtle forms, and can be an issue not just for the participants in historical events but also for the scholars that interpret them.

---

[33]   Neil R. McMillen, "Fighting For What We Didn't Have: How Mississippi Black Veterans Remember World War II," in McMillen, *Remaking Dixie*, 95.

THE LONG SILENCING OF THE SPANISH MEMOIRS OF U.S. AMBASSADOR CLAUDE G. BOWERS: A CASE OF FORBEARANCE OR POLITICAL REPRESSION?

María Luz Arroyo

Introduction

This article aims to examine the relationship between voluntary censorship and the repression of freedom of expression in the United States, focusing attention on the book written by Claude G. Bowers, *My Mission to Spain: Watching the Rehearsal for World War II*.[1]

Claude G. Bowers was the American ambassador in Spain, from 1933 to 1939. He therefore witnessed the crises of the Second Spanish Republic and the Civil War. During that period, he wrote a book manuscript that was not published until 1954, a year after his retirement and fourteen years after it was finished. The manuscript was based upon his diary, personal contacts, and dispatches.

Bowers was very sympathetic toward the Spanish republicans and their attempt to establish a more democratic form of government. He criticized the "narrow course" policy, which the United States and the European powers adopted towards the Spanish Civil War and considered that it was an error to sacrifice democracy in Spain in order to seek peace elsewhere.

The paper will examine diplomatic and other sources to document and highlight the reasons why there was such an enormous interest in stopping the publication of Claude Bowers's text in the United States and in Spain, and how the manuscript was withheld from publication during World War II and later in the United States. In summary, the essay suggests a possible case of one individual's "historical memory" that powerful governments strove to silence.

Bowers's Biographical and Diplomatic Profile

After his six years in Spain, Claude G. Bowers (Westfield, Indiana 1878-New York 1958) was American ambassador to Chile for fourteen years. Before becoming a diplomat, Bowers had a distinguished career as a journalist, writer, historian, and Democratic politician.[2] He was appointed to the post in Spain in 1933 and remained

---

[1]   The author gratefully acknowledges financial aid awarded by the Spanish Ministry of Education and Science for research project HUM2006-11365/HIST, of which this essay is a part.

[2]   Some of Bowers's historical publications are: *Pierre Verniaud: Voice of the French Revolution* (New York: Macmillan, 1950); *The Young Jefferson, 1743-1789* (Boston: Houghton Mifflin, 1945); *Jefferson in Power: The Death Struggle of the Federalists* (Boston: Houghton Mifflin, 1936); *The Tragic Era: The Revolution after Lincoln* (Boston: Houghton Mifflin, 1929); *Jefferson and Hamilton: The Struggle for Democracy in America* (Boston: Houghton Mifflin, 1925); *The Party Battles of the Jackson Period* (Boston: Houghton Mifflin, 1922).

there until the end of the Spanish Civil War in 1939.[3] When he was summoned home for "consultation," he resigned, considering that "it would be out of the question … to continue as ambassador after the Franco government was recognized by Washington."[4] On Franklin D. Roosevelt's request he accepted an ambassadorship in Chile in 1939 and remained there until 1953. While he was in that country, Bowers wrote a book, *Chile through Embassy Windows, 1939-1953*, based on his diary, correspondence and memories, which was finished in New York in 1956 and published a year later.[5]

As far as his diplomatic career in Spain is concerned, he sympathized "with the Spanish Republicans and their democratic ideology."[6] In his opinion, the Spanish Civil War was not one between monarchy and republic, which he could have viewed objectively. Once the participation of the Axis powers in the Spanish struggle became clear, Bowers felt that it had become a war for and against democracy, and as a Jeffersonian democrat, he could not do otherwise than side with democracy.[7] Thus, he supported the defenders of the Republic, such as Manuel Azaña and Diego Martínez Barrio.[8] For instance, he described Manuel Azaña as having great intellectual power, showing an admiration that we can also see in the letters that he wrote to Roosevelt, in

---

[3]   The historiography of the Spanish Civil War is immense. See for example, Anthony Beevor, *The Battle for Spain: The Spanish Civil War 1936-1939* (London: Weidenfeld & Nicolson, 2006); Helen Graham, *The Spanish Republic at War, 1936-1939* (Cambridge: Cambridge University Press, 2002); Raymond Carr and Juan Pablo Fusi, *Historia de España. La República y la Guerra Civil. La crisis de la España Contemporánea (1931-1939)* (Madrid: Espasa Calpe, S.A., 1999); Paul Preston, *A Concise History of the Spanish Civil War* (London: Fontana, 1996); Gerald Brenan, *The Spanish Labyrinth: An Account of the Social and Political Background of the Civil War.* (Cambridge: Cambridge University Press, 1990); Manuel Tuñón de Lara, *Historia de España. La crisis del estado: La dictadura, república y guerra, 1923-1939* (Barcelona: Editorial Labor, S.A., 1981); Paul Preston, *The Coming of the Spanish Civil War* (London: Macmillan 1978); Hugh Thomas, *The Spanish Civil War* (New York: Harper & Row, 1977); Raymond Carr, ed., *Estudios sobre la República y la Guerra Civil española* (Barcelona: Ariel, 1973); Gabriel Jackson, *The Spanish Republic and the Civil War, 1931-1939* (Princeton, NJ: Princeton University Press, 1965).

[4]   Claude G. Bowers, *My Life: The Memoirs of Claude Bowers* (New York: Simon & Schuster, 1962), 291.

[5]   Claude G. Bowers, *Chile through Embassy Windows, 1939-1953* (New York: Simon & Schuster, 1958).

[6]   Claude G. Bowers, *My Mission to Spain: Watching the Rehearsal for World War II* (New York: Simon & Schuster, 1954), vi.

[7]   Ibid., vi and 272.

[8]   Manuel Azaña was president of the Second Spanish Republic (May 1936-April 1939) and Diego Martínez Barrio was president of the Second Spanish Republic in exile (1945-1962). See Manuel Azaña Díaz, *Memorias políticas y de guerra* (Barcelona: Grijalbo, 1996); Manuel Azaña Díaz, *Diarios, 1932-1933 (los cuadernos robados)* (Barcelona: Crítica, 1997); Luis Arias Argüelles-Meres, *Azaña o el sueño de la razón* Madrid: Nerea, 1990); Diego Martínez Barrio, *Memorias* (Barcelona: Planeta, 1983).

which he affirmed that Manuel Azaña was "the bulwark of the Republic," "the ablest man of Spain."[9]

In summary, the main message that Bowers wanted to transmit in his book was that democratic nations ought to defend their political ideals abroad as well as at home, and not be indifferent in cases such as the Spanish one. Bowers felt this was essential to preserve the political and cultural values of the West. He felt the loyalists were doing all they could by sacrificing their lives for democracy, but in the end this was not enough as they needed the support of other democratic nations. For him, the Spanish Civil War was the start of World War II.[10]

Bowers on the International Response to the Spanish Civil War: The Appeasement Policy

In his Spanish memoirs, Bowers criticized the international response to the Spanish Civil War.[11] He affirmed that "in September 1936, the war in Spain was not a 'civil war'… Arrangements had been made long before for the participation of Hitler and Mussolini."[12] In fact, Bowers's unequivocal, wholehearted, and repeated conviction was that it was "a war of aggression openly waged by Hitler and Mussolini,"[13] and "a war of Fascism against democracy, and the beginning of a World War by the Axis powers to exterminate democracy throughout Europe."[14]

---

[9]   Letter from Claude G. Bowers to Roosevelt, 21 November 1934, *Franklin Delano Roosevelt's Office Files, part 2: Diplomatic Correspondence File 1933-1945*, reel 32 (microfilm edition, Roosevelt Study Center, Middelburg, The Netherlands).

[10]   Bowers, *My Mission*, vi.

[11]   On the international context of the Spanish Civil War, see for example J.F. Berdah, *La democracia asesinada. La República española y las grandes potencias, 1931-1939* (Barcelona: Crítica, 2002); Sebastian Balfour, and Paul Preston, eds., *Spain and the Great Powers in the Twentieth Century* (New York: Routledge, 1999); David F. Schmitz and Richard D. Challener, *Appeasement in Europe: A Reassessment of U.S. Policies* (Westport, CT: Greenwood Press, 1990); Juan José Carreras, "El marco internacional de la II República," *Arbor* 109.426 (June 1981): 37-50; F. Schwartz, *La internacionalización de la Guerra Civil española* (Madrid: Editora Nacional, 1971); Dante A. Puzzo, *Spain and the Great Powers, 1936-1941* (New York: Columbia University Press, 1962).

[12]   Bowers, *My Mission*, 272.

[13]   Ibid., 354

[14]   Ibid., 336. There is a general historiographical consensus on the importance of the intervention of Hitler and Mussolini in the Spanish Civil War. See for example, Rodrigo Botero, *Ambivalent Embrace: America's Troubled Relations with Spain from the Revolutionary War to the Cold War* (Westport, CT: Greenwood Press, 2001) 107-108; Christian Leitz, "Nazi Germany and Francoist Spain, 1936-1945," in Balfour and Preston, *Spain and the Great Powers*, 127-148, and *Economic Relations between Nazi Germany and Franco's Spain, 1936-1945* (Oxford: Oxford University Press, 1996); R. García Pérez, *Franquismo y el Tercer Reich* (Madrid: Centro de Estudios Constitucionales, 1994); Robert H. Whealy, *Hitler and Spain: The Nazi Role in the Spanish Civil War, 1936-1938* (Lexington: University Press of Kentucky, 1989); Raymond L. Proctor, *Hitler's Luftwaffe in the Spanish Civil War* (Westport, CT:

Bowers was especially unhappy about the attitude of European democratic countries and particularly the Non-intervention Committee, an international body created in September 1936 to seek a collective response to the Spanish conflict in order to prevent its spread abroad. This had been proposed in early August 1936 in a joint diplomatic initiative by the governments of Léon Blum in France and Neville Chamberlain in Great Britain. The first meeting of the Non-Intervention Committee was in London on 9 September 1936. Eventually twenty-seven countries, including Great Britain, France, Russia, Germany, Italy, Portugal, and Belgium, decided to prohibit the sale of war material to the two sides in the Spanish Civil War.[15]

However, the Non-intervention Agreement was a complete failure in Bowers's opinion. It theoretically prevented all signers from selling arms and ammunition to either side in Spain, and this was enforced against the legal government, even though they, under international law, had a right to buy arms. In contrast, with the full knowledge of the Committee, which did not protest, Germany and Italy were supplying Franco with arms, ammunition and soldiers. Focusing his attention on the passive attitude of the Non-intervention Committee, Bowers criticized its "blindness" towards the activities of the Axis.[16]

On 23 August 1937, the Spanish president, Manuel Azaña, expressed his grave concern regarding the intervention of the Axis, and its toleration by the Committee.[17] A year later, in August 1938, the foreign volunteers who supported the republicans withdrew.[18] Bowers regretted the abandonment by the Western democracies of the Spanish republic, which prevented the government that they

---

Greenwood, 1983); John F. Coverdale, *Italian Intervention in the Spanish Civil War* (Princeton, NJ: Princeton University Press, 1975); Peter Elstob, *Condor Legion* (New York: Ballantine, 1973).

[15]   On the Non-intervention Committee, see Douglas Little, *Malevolent Neutrality: The United States, Great Britain, and the Origins of the Spanish Civil War* (New York: Cornell University Press, 1985); William E. Watters, *An International Affair: Non-Intervention in the Spanish Civil War, 1936-1939* (New York: Exposition Press, 1971). For a strong critique of its impact on the Spanish Civil War, see Francisco Olaya Morales, *La comedia de la no intervención en la guerra civil española* (Madrid: G. del Toro, 1976).

[16]   Bowers, *My Mission*, 315.

[17]   See Manuel Azaña, *Memorias de guerra* (Barcelona: Grijalbo Mondadori, 1978), 229.

[18]   There are many works on foreign combattants in the Spanish Civil War. See for example, Antonio R. Celada, Manuel González de la Aleja, and Daniel Pastor García, eds., *Los brigadistas de habla inglesa y la Guerra Civil española* (Salamanca: Editorial Ambos Mundos, 2006); Arthur H. Landis, *Death in the Olive Groves: American Volunteers in the Spanish Civil War, 1936-1939* (New York: Paragon, 1989); John Gerassi, *The Premature Antifascists: North American Volunteers in the Spanish Civil War 1936-39. An Oral History* (New York: Praeger, 1986); Bill Alexander, *British Volunteers for Liberty: Spain, 1936-1939* (London: Lawrence and Wishart, 1982); Dan R. Richardson, *Comintern Army: The International Brigades and the Spanish Civil War* (Lexington: University Press of Kentucky, 1982); Robert A. Rosenstone, *Crusade of the Left: The Lincoln Battalion in the Spanish Civil War* (Lanham, MD: University Press of America, 1980).

recognized as the legal constitutional regime from obtaining arms. Azaña and others could see no possibility of victory. It was evident that the Non-intervention Committee had tightened its control of sales to the Spanish government.[19]

Eventually, when, in Bowers's opinion, the Agreement had become a loathsome farce, Maxim Litvinov, the Russian on the Committee, openly gave notice that "unless the one-sided intervention ceased on a stipulated date, Russia would not consider herself bound to any greater extent than any other signatory of the pact." Since nothing was done, the Russian government began selling tanks and planes to the Spanish loyalists.[20] However, on the Soviet help to the republican government, it should be understood that, according to Sumner Welles, the U.S. undersecretary of state, "it was only a token" compared to the assistance obtained by Franco from Germany and Italy.[21]

Bowers was especially critical of Neville Chamberlain's attitudes. He felt that it was impossible to believe in the good faith of the British government, and stated in a document that he sent on 12 January 1937 that he perceived a lack of sincerity in his frequent conversations with the British ambassador, Sir Henry Chilton, accusing the British of creating "obstacles to the legal government" in Spain. He was particularly unhappy about Chamberlain's policy of appeasement towards Germany and Mussolini.[22] That policy, which the United States supported, was in his opinion "the narrow and not the broader course." He felt it was absurd to hope that peace would be maintained elsewhere through the appeasement of Hitler and Mussolini.[23]

The ambassador felt that the abandonment of Czechoslovakia to Hitler at Munich in 1938 was crucial too. He had no faith in Chamberlain as a mediator between fascism and democracy, and deplored Chamberlain's visit to Germany as a surrender to Hitler. He thought that the Munich bargain gave democracy a brutal blow, and that it was the greatest British tragedy since Austerlitz. Bowers was not surprised, but he was bitterly disappointed, when Chamberlain announced there would be a speedy "settlement in Spain—in the spirit of the settlement at Munich."[24]

---

[19]   Bowers, *My Mission*, 381.

[20]   Ibid., 315. On Soviet involvement, see Daniel Kowalsky, *La Unión Soviética y la Guerra Civil Española: Una Revisión Crítica* (Barcelona: Editorial Crítica, 2003); Daniel Kowalsky, *Stalin and the Spanish Civil War* (New York: Columbia University Press, 2004).

[21]   Sumner Welles, *The Time for Decision* (New York: Harper & Brothers, 1944), 58.

[22]   On this British prime minister, see Keith Feiling, *The Life of Neville Chamberlain* (London: Macmillan and Co., Ltd., 1946) and on his policy of appeasement, see for example Richard A. Harrison "The United States and Great Britain: Presidential Diplomacy and Alternatives to Appeasement in the 1930s," and Douglas Little, "Antibolshevism and Appeasement: Great Britain, the United States, and the Spanish Civil War," both in Schmitz and Challener, *Appeasement in Europe*, 103-144, and 21-50; and Martin Gilbert, *The Roots of Appeasement* (London: New American Library, 1966).

[23]   Bowers, *My Mission*, 417.

[24]   Ibid., 390-391, and 393.

Bowers also criticized Lady Austen Chamberlain who he said was "notoriously partial to Mussolini" and who in the late autumn of 1938 made "a good-will tour through Fascist territory." She was "hailed as a political figure, with her strangely timed visit interpreted as further proof of the adherence of the Chamberlain government to the Fascist cause in Spain."[25] Bowers directly accused Great Britain of supporting Franco, and showed his contempt for the impressive number of foreigners who toured Spain "under the ciceronage of the Fascists," purportedly "to get the truth" about the country and the civil war.[26]

Moreover, the ambassador complained that Mr. Chamberlain closed his eyes to Axis' aid to Franco. For instance, noting the arrival of Italian soldiers, and in an ironical tone, Bowers added that Chamberlain believed in the word of Mussolini who assured him that he had not sent any arms since he signed the Agreement. France asked for greater control, and a patrol system was adopted, but according to Bowers "the patrol system was a farce from the beginning, and the Italian and German ships continued to pour men, arms and ammunition" into Spain.[27]

Anthony Eden, the British minister of Foreign Affairs, admitted that infractions were committed and that no measures were taken to counteract them. Bowers blamed Chamberlain for the fact that Mr. Eden had to leave the British government because he had become an obstacle to the program of "appeasement."[28] In the summer of 1937, Spanish President Manuel Azaña expressed his own opinion that the Italian and German thesis of combating communism was a mere pretext.[29] In any case, according to Bowers, the Spanish temperament was not compatible with communism.[30]

Moreover, Bowers observed that many diplomats from totalitarian states were aggressively Fascist, while those from democratic nations by contrast seemed either indifferent to democracy or actually antidemocratic, as revealed in their conversation. For instance, he criticized diplomats such as Jean Herbette, who "misrepresenting France, had gone over bag and baggage to Franco and the generals within three weeks," and his British colleague, Sir Henry Chilton, who "was violently against the loyalists from the first day, and he habitually called them 'reds.'"[31]

---

[25]   Ibid., 390-391.
[26]   Ibid. See also Sandie Holguin, "National Spain Invites You: Battlefield Tourism during the Spanish Civil War," *American Historical Review* 10.5 (December 2005): 1399-1426.
[27]   Bowers, *My Mission*, 328.
[28]   Ibid., 374. See Anthony Eden's autobiography, *The Memoirs of the Rt. Hon. Sir Anthony Eden KG, PC, MC: Full Circle*, 3 vols. (London: Cassell, 1960-1965) and a biography written by the historian D. Richard Thorpe, *Eden: The Life and Times of Anthony Eden. First Earl of Avon, 1897-1977* (London: Chatto and Windus, 2003).
[29]   See Azaña, *Memorias de guerra*, 170. Manuel Azaña made this statement on 26 July 1937.
[30]   Bowers, *My Mission*, 319.
[31]   Ibid., 290-291.

U.S. Policy

The Roosevelt administration supported the non-interventionist policies of France and Great Britain to the advantage of the Fascist forces of General Franco in Spain.[32] Closely following the Anglo-French initiative, Cordell Hull, the American secretary of state, supported a neutrality and non-interference policy. However, the Neutrality Act of February 1936 did not cover civil wars, so "a moral embargo" was proclaimed on 7 August 1936 that affected Spain, since Americans were asked not to sell arms to either side.[33] Nonetheless, at the end of 1936, an American arms dealer, Robert Cuse, prepared weapons to be sent to Spanish loyalists in Madrid, disregarding the administration's appeal. Thus, new legislation was urged and approved by Congress on 8 January 1937. In May 1937, Roosevelt signed the new Neutrality Act, which made it unlawful to export any weapons from the United States to Spain.[34]

Cordell Hull defended the U.S. neutrality policy in terms of both domestic interests and the international situation: "Our policy had nothing to do with our views on the right or wrong in the Spanish Civil War. We were not judging

---

[32] Useful general works on Spanish-U.S. relations are Lorenzo Delgado and María Dolores Elizalde, eds., *España y Estados Unidos en el siglo XX* (Madrid: Consejo Superior de Investigaciones Científicas, 2005); Rosa Pardo, "La política norteamericana," *Ayer. Revista de Historia Contemporánea* 49 *La política exterior de España en el siglo XX* (2003): 13-53; Carlos Elordi, *El amigo americano: de Franco a Aznar. una adhesión inquebrantable* (Madrid: Temas de Hoy, 2003); Antonio Niño Rodríguez, "50 años de relaciones entre España y los Estados Unidos," *Cuadernos de Historia Contemporánea* 25 (2003): 9-33; Botero, *Ambivalent Embrace*; José Manuel Allendesalazar, "España y EE.UU. en el siglo XX," *Política Exterior* 15.81 (May/June 2001): 136-150; Boris N. Liedtke, "Spain and the United States, 1945-1975," in Balfour and Preston, *Spain and the Great Powers*, 229-244; Juan Durá Domenech, *U.S. Policy toward Dictatorship and Democracy in Spain, 1931-1953* (Sevilla: Arrayán Ediciones, 1985).

[33] On Anglo-French influence on U.S. policies regarding Spain, see for example Botero, *Ambivalent Embrace*, 108-109; Enrique Moradiellos "The Allies and the Spanish Civil War," in Sebastian Balfour and Paul Preston, eds., *Spain and the Great Powers*, 96-126; Richard P. Traina, *American Diplomacy and the Spanish Civil War* (Bloomington: Indiana University Press, 1968), 73; Wayne S. Cole, *An Interpretative History of American Foreign Relations* (Homewood, IL: Dorsey Press, 1968), 445; Welles, *The Time for Decision*, 58.

[34] On American policy regarding the Spanish Civil War useful sources are: Joan María Thomas, *Roosevelt y Franco. De la Guerra Civil española a Pearl Harbour* (Barcelona, Edhasa, 2007); Dominic Tierney, "FDR and the Spanish Civil War," *The Volunteer* 2 (June 2005): 6-8; Marta Rey García, *Stars for Spain. La guerra civil española en los Estados Unidos* (A Coruña: Ediciós do Castro, 1997); Traina, *American Diplomacy and the Spanish Civil War*; F. Jay Taylor, *The United States and the Spanish Civil War* (Princeton, NJ: Princeton University Press, 1965); Dominic Tierney, *FDR and the Spanish Civil War: Neutrality and Commitment in the Struggle that Divided America* (Durham, NC: Duke University Press, 2007).

between the two sides ... to keep aloof from the Spanish conflict was in the best interest of the United States."[35]

In the beginning, Senator Key Pittman, chairman of the Foreign Relations Committee and author of the embargo, according to Bowers, also thought the embargo was "good in that it would keep other nations out, and localize the war."[36] The only kind of American aid that was allowed to be sent to Spain was humanitarian, in the form of clothes and food. Although Bowers was unwilling to admit that he had initially supported the embargo of the United States, this was indeed the case.[37]

Nevertheless, Spanish Republican politicians expected the United States to change their attitude. This did not happen in spite of the fact that, as Manuel Azaña mentioned in his memoirs on 9 October 1937, Roosevelt had announced that he would take an active part for the sake of peace.[38]

Meanwhile, the Axis powers continued to send arms, ammunition and even troops to Franco. This, he felt, was reason enough to lift the embargo, which in Bowers's opinion, was too rigidly and unfairly enforced. With this action, the Spanish government, which had the right under international law to buy arms and defend itself, was unable to do so. This, in effect, meant that the United States collaborated with the Axis powers.[39]

On 1 March 1939, Bowers was summoned to Washington "for consultation" with the State Department and, since he had not received a summons home for consultation until that moment, he commented: "It may not have seemed worthwhile to the Department, since it knew precisely my interpretation of the significance of the Spanish war."[40] It seems likely that Bowers was not called to Washington for actual consultation but to give him an easy way to resign. He would not want to serve as ambassador to Franco's Spain and neither would it be in the United States' interest.

Bowers firmly declares in his Spanish memoirs that in his dispatches he had clearly informed and warned the Roosevelt administration of his well-founded fears regarding the following facts:

---

[35] Cordell Hull, *The Memoirs of Cordell Hull* (New York: Macmillan, 1948), 1:481-492.

[36] Bowers, *My Mission*, 419.

[37] Peter J. Sehlinger and Holman Hamilton, *Spokesman for Democracy: Claude G. Bowers 1878-1958* (Indianapolis: Indiana Historical Society, 2000), 200.

[38] Azaña, *Memorias de guerra*, 314. "Los Estados Unidos son poderosos y su Presidente habla el lenguaje de la justicia. ¡Gran fortuna! Los imbéciles y los miedosos que dirigen las 'grandes democracias' europeas sentirán algún alivio ... Roosevelt alude claramente al Mediterráneo y sus piratas, y a la intromisión en la guerra civil. Y anuncia una participación activa con el propósito de salvar la paz". "The United States is powerful and its president speaks the language of justice. Great fortune! The stupid and fearful who run the 'great European Democracies' will feel some relief ... Roosevelt is clearly referring to the Mediterranean and its pirates and to their interference in the Civil War, and he has announced an active participation with the purpose of preserving the peace." All translations by the author unless otherwise noted.

[39] Bowers, *My Mission*, 419, and Bowers, *My Life*, 283.

[40] Bowers, *My Mission*, 411. On the tensions between Bowers and the U.S. State Department, see Thomas, *Roosevelt y Franco*, 56-62.

1. That after the first days of considerable confusion, it was plainly shown to be a war of the Fascists and the Axis powers against the democratic institutions of Spain.
2. That the Spanish war was the beginning of a perfectly thought-out plan for a Second World War with that as the intent.
3. That the Non-intervention Committee was a shameless sham, cynically dishonest, in that Germany and Italy were constantly sending soldiers, planes, tanks, artillery, and ammunition into Spain without any interference or real protest from the signatories of the pact.
4. That Germany and Italy were using Spanish towns and people for experimental purposes in trying out their new methods of destruction and their new techniques of terrorism.
5. That the Axis, in preparation for the continental struggle, was using Spain to see how far it could go with the silent acquiescence of the great democracies and to test their spirit, courage, and will to fight in defense of their ideals.
6. That the Axis powers believed that with the conversion of Spain into a Fascist state, it could, and would, be used as an entering wedge in South and Central America. I informed Washington of the open boasting of the Franco press of the determination to "liberate" South America from "Yankee bondage and atheism."
7. That the purpose was manifest in a book prepared for use in schools bitterly attacking democracy in general and that of the United States and Britain in particular.
8. That the attacks, ridicule, and insults aimed at the United States and England by the Franco press left no possible doubt as to its position.
9. That while the Axis powers poured in armies, planes, tanks, artillery, technicians, and engineers for Franco, the Non-intervention Committee of the European democracies and our own embargo were making a powerful contribution to the triumph of the Axis over democracy in Spain; ... that the first country to be attacked by the Axis—Germany and Italy together—was Spain.
10. That ... the next attack would be on Czechoslovakia.
11. I had informed Washington that our interests, ideologically, commercially, and industrially, were bound up with those of democracy in Spain, whose government we recognized as the legal constitutional government, and that the victory of Franco would be a danger to the United States, especially in South America.[41]

In spite of Bowers's efforts and warnings, the embargo continued because the United States wanted to remain neutral and was determined not to get involved in this matter. As his biographers have recently stated: "One ambassador's advocacy

---

[41]   Bowers, *My Mission*, 411-412.

proved no match for the neutrality sentiment at home and the State Department's determination to avoid involvement."[42]

In fact, Roosevelt himself was not happy about the course the United States had followed. Bowers blamed Hull, maintaining: "Of course there was a wide divergence of views within the Department even during the struggle in Spain. Roosevelt was in sympathy with the loyalists throughout, but Hull, the secretary of state followed the Chamberlain line and it would have been politically dangerous to have broken with his Secretary."[43] The president wrote to Bowers in a letter on 31 August 1938: "Perhaps a little later on … I can make some kind of a move for the purpose of at least aiding the Spanish War."[44] In 1939, he told Bowers: "We have made a mistake; you have been right all along."[45] The same opinion was shared by Senator Key Pittman who, according to Bowers, also admitted: "I am afraid we have made a mistake in Spain."[46]

In response to Bowers's accusation that events had proved that the U.S. government had actually collaborated with the Fascists, Roosevelt also confessed to his friend that "while our intent was originally good, the effect had been to align ourselves with the aggressor nations."[47] On 14 July 1939, he had asked the Congress to change the Neutrality Act, and in a speech made on 21 September 1939, the president insisted that the Neutrality Act of 1 May 1937 had been a serious blunder. He said: "I regret that the Congress passed that act. I regret equally that I signed that act."[48] However, Roosevelt failed to win revision of the Neutrality Act in 1939 because of stiff opposition from isolationists in Congress.

Although Bowers maintained that Roosevelt sympathized with the Spanish loyalists from the beginning,[49] according to Frank Freidel, Roosevelt's sympathies with the loyalists were not so defined until February 1937.[50] For his part, Dominic Tierney argues that there was an evolution in Roosevelt's stance, from an initial position of indifference regarding which side won the Spanish Civil War to a

---

[42]   Sehlinger and Hamilton, *Spokesman for Democracy*, 274.

[43]   Letter from Claude G. Bowers to Fernando Valera Aparicio, 8 December 1954, file Fernando Valera Aparicio, box 32, dossier 9, Archives of the Spanish Republic in Exile, Fundación Universitaria Española, Madrid (hereafter cited as ASRE, FUE). At that time, Valera was the minister of state and international relations of the government of the Spanish republic in exile, of which he served as president from 1971 to 1977.

[44]   Letter from Franklin Delano Roosevelt to Claude G. Bowers, 31 August 1938, Bowers Mss. II, Manuscript Department, Lilly Library, Indiana University, Bloomington.

[45]   Bowers, *My Mission*, 418. On Roosevelt's admission of his mistake in supporting the embargo in a meeting with his cabinet, see Douglas Little, "Antibolshevism and Appeasement: Great Britain, the United States, and the Spanish Civil War," in Schmitz and Challener, *Appeasement in Europe*, 41.

[46]   Quoted by Bowers, *My Mission*, 419.

[47]   Quoted by Bowers, *My Life*, 283-284.

[48]   Franklin Delano Roosevelt's Message to Congress Urging Repeal of the Embargo Provisions of Neutrality Act, 21 September 1939, reprinted in John Gabriel Hunt, *The Essential Franklin Delano Roosevelt* (New York: Gramercy Books, 1995), 176.

[49]   Claude G. Bowers to Fernando Valera Aparicio, 8 December 1954.

[50]   Frank Freidel, *Franklin Delano Roosevelt: A Rendezvous with Destiny* (Boston: Little, Brown and Company, 1990), 270

"position as a partisan for the leftist government," since Spain came to matter a great deal to him.[51] It seems clear that Franklin Delano Roosevelt's attitudes did indeed evolve, although not necessarily from an initial attitude of indifference, after the tardy realization that he had made a mistaken choice of policy.

Sumner Welles stated that Roosevelt regretted having signed the neutrality legislation in 1937 to some extent because of the issues involved in the Spanish Civil War, but also because the real character of Hitlerism was becoming increasingly obvious. The president decided to make an earnest effort to convince public opinion that in its own interest the United States should suggest some constructive plan for international action "to check forces of aggression before they succeeded in engulfing the world."[52] On 5 October 1937, in an address delivered in Chicago, Roosevelt expressed his grave concern and anxiety regarding the political situation in the world. Clearly referring to Spain, Roosevelt deplored international interventions in the internal affairs of foreign countries. The bombing of Guernica on 26 April 1937, was particularly hateful in his view:

> Nations are fomenting and taking sides in civil warfare in nations that have never done them any harm. Nations claiming freedom for themselves deny it to others.... If those things come to pass in other parts of the world, let no one imagine that America will escape, that it may expect mercy, that this Western Hemisphere will not be attacked....[53]

In spite of Roosevelt's efforts to get support to take action in foreign policy, according to Sumner Welles, "the public, stimulated by isolationist leaders and the pacifist organizations, clamored against his proposals."[54] In May 1938, due to increasing popular sympathy for the Republic, an attempt to repeal the embargo was presented by senator Gerald Nye, but it failed since it lacked support in the State Department. To some, it seemed that, in approving the Neutrality Act in the first place, "Roosevelt may have acted partly to appease the largely urban Catholic voters in the United States."[55] Consequently, there may also have been some concern that a move to change U.S. policy would alienate Catholic voters.[56]

In a message to Congress on 4 January 1939, Roosevelt brought U.S. neutrality laws into question:

> But the mere fact that we rightly decline to intervene with arms to prevent acts of aggression does not mean that we must act as if there were no aggression at

---

[51] Tierney, "FDR and the Spanish Civil War."

[52] Ibid.

[53] See Franklin Delano Roosevelt's Speech at Chicago, Illinois, 5 October 1937, reprinted in Hunt, *The Essential Franklin Delano Roosevelt*, 141-144.

[54] Welles, *The Time for Decision*, 63. A wide-ranging study that deals with public attitudes is Allen Guttmann, *The Wound in the Heart: America and the Spanish Civil War* (New York: Free Press-Macmillan Co., 1962).

[55] Cole, *An Interpretative History*, 445. See also for example, Thomas, *Roosevelt y Franco*, 25.

[56] Botero, *Ambivalent Embrace*, 133.

all.... There are many methods short of war, but stronger and more effective than mere words, of bringing home to aggressor governments the aggregate sentiments of our own people.... At the very least, we can and should avoid any action, or any lack of action, which will encourage, assist or build up an aggressor. We have learned that when we deliberately try to legislate neutrality, our neutrality laws may operate unevenly and unfairly—may actually give aid to an aggressor and deny it to the victim. The instinct of self-preservation should warn us that we ought not to let that happen any more.[57]

In that same vein, Sumner Welles, the U.S. undersecretary of state, in his 1944 book also ascribed some of the misfortunes of the world to the appeasement policy in Spain. Welles wrote that, in his own personal opinion, Spanish policy was a black blot on the U.S. record as a democracy, concluding that "in the long history of the foreign policy of the Roosevelt administration, there has been, I think, no more cardinal error than the policy adopted during the Spanish Civil War."[58]

For his part, Harry S. Truman explained in his memoirs, published in the middle of the Cold War:

I voted in favor of the much-disputed Neutrality Act of 1937, because I thought it would help to keep us out of involvement in the civil war then going on in Spain. However, I saw the need for its revision in 1939 and again in 1941 as global warfare made the original measure unworkable. I believe it was a mistake for me to support the Neutrality Act in the first place. I was misled by the report of the munitions investigation, which was headed by Gerald Nye, a demagogue senator from North Dakota.[59]

In effect, under the chairmanship of Gerald Nye a misdirected inquiry was conducted by the Special Committee Investigating the Munitions Industry, that made it appear that the munitions manufacturers had caused World War I, resulting in the U.S. Neutrality Act. Truman declared that this law, by placing an embargo on arms shipments to the democratic forces in Spain, "was partly responsible for our losing that country as a potential ally in World War II."[60] Truman apologized for having voted in the Senate in favor of the embargo and admitted that U.S. policy contributed to the overthrow of the Spanish Republic. He explained that in 1939 he voted "against continuing the mandatory arms embargo, because there never should have been one in the first place. Republican Spain was lost on account of the embargo."[61] Claude Bowers thus felt vindicated and expressed his satisfaction to Fernando Valera Aparicio: "Truman has seen the light and in his Memoirs says he

---

[57]   See Franklin Delano Roosevelt's Sixth Annual Message to Congress, 4 January 1939, reprinted in Hunt, *The Essential Franklin Delano Roosevelt*, 147.
[58]   Welles, *The Time for Decision*, 61.
[59]   Harry S. Truman, *Memoirs*, vol. 1, *1945 Year of Decisions* (New York: Doubleday and Company, Inc., 1955), 153.
[60]   Ibid., 214.
[61]   Ibid., 178.

made a mistake in voting for the embargo."[62] Nonetheless, Truman's tardy recognition of his mistake, in 1948 and 1955, might also reflect his need to persuade U.S. public opinion that the United States must oppose Communism in the world and not make the same mistake made when lack of opposition to Fascism led to even worse consequences.

The narrow course policy followed by the United States was also opposed by Henry L. Stimson, former American secretary of state. He argued for the enforcement of the well-established rule of international law that we "should furnish arms to the government that had been recognized as legal, and to no other." In the case of Spain this was the loyalist government. This is a statement Mr. Stimson was sorry he had not made sooner. He had made no secret of his sympathy with the loyalists (thus taking sides) but he had held back from direct opposition to the policy of the administration. By January 1939, it was too late for any statement to be of any use, for the Republican government was finally being overcome by the superior force of Fascist intervention. Stimson was not a left-winger, but he believed, and repeatedly argued, that "the Fascists were incomparably more dangerous to us; more active in their proselytizing; and more dangerous and intolerant of international law and methods." And, of course, in the case of Spain, it remained a clear and simple fact that the Republic was the legal and elected government, recognized as such by the United States.[63]

By the time Bowers returned to Washington in the spring of 1939, he found a powerful public sentiment favorable to the Spanish loyalists, but the realization that the embargo had been a key factor in giving victory to the Fascists came too late to save Spain's republican regime.[64]

Bowers's Fourteen-Year Wait to Publish His Memoirs

In November 1953, Bowers stated in the foreword of his book:

> The manuscript was withheld from publication during the World War because its caustic treatment of Mr. Chamberlain might have been misinterpreted as an attack upon the English people; and later because I doubted the propriety of its publication while active in the foreign service in the United States. Now that I have retired it can be published after fourteen years.[65]

---

[62]   Bowers, *My Life*, 283-284. See also Letter from Claude G. Bowers to Fernando Valera Aparicio, 15 July 1956, file Fernando Valera Aparicio and Claude G. Bowers, box 32, dossier 9, ASRE, FUE.

[63]   McGeorge Bundy and Henry L. Stimson, *On Active Service in Peace and War* (New York: Harper & Brothers, 1948), 313-317.

[64]   Bowers, *My Mission*, 414. On antifascist opinion and popular sentiment regarding Spain in the United States, see for example Peter N. Carroll and James D. Fernández, eds., *Contra el fascismo. Nueva York y la guerra civil española* (New York: Museum of the City of New York, New York University Press, [2007]; Guttman, *The Wound in the Heart*, cit.

[65]   Bowers, *My Mission*, v.

Although Bowers had, in fact, planned to publish his memoirs immediately after the Spanish Civil War, Roosevelt asked him not to publish his memoirs at that time, and Bowers acquiesced. By saying that his book "was withheld," he carefully avoided clarifying whether he did this voluntarily as an exercise in temporary self-censorship or under orders.

To some degree, one might argue that Bowers's self-censorship is a form of political repression. His conduct was certainly conditioned by the constraints of different loyalties, to his party, to his government, to his professional code as a diplomat in the national service, and above all perhaps to Franklin Delano Roosevelt, who was his friend. These loyalties together with Roosevelt's arguments regarding the greater issues connected with World War II, effectively countered, for the moment, Bowers's desire to publish his views and information about Spain. This situation raises interesting questions about the forms and definition of political repression, in this case regarding freedom of expression. There is no doubt that Bowers wanted to publish his book in 1939, and at this point, it is difficult to evaluate with certainty the relative weight of Bowers's forbearance in the light of his own understanding of the special circumstances, of Franklin Delano Roosevelt's powers of persuasion, and of the pressures brought to bear by different government agencies. What is clear, however, is that Bowers yielded in the belief that his silence would be temporary.

After the Allied victory in 1945, Bowers believed it was the "appropriate moment" to publish his manuscript, and President Harry S. Truman not only offered no objection to the publication of the book at that time, but even seemed to think it was a good idea. There are two letters, one from Bowers to Truman and one from Truman to Bowers, which address the matter explicitly. The former letter is a request to Truman for permission to publish. In it, Bowers provided a description of the situation in Spain during his mission, adding that "for four years my memoirs of these six years have been ready for a publisher, but because of the war I had thought it improper to give it publication." He went on to describe the book succinctly, and urged that now might be the right moment to publish, although he was also careful to express his respect for government opinions. "Of course, it will not be published against the desire of Washington, but now that our Government makes no secret of its contempt for Franco's regime, I am sure the book would more than justify that attitude. I think it should be published next spring."[66]

In his reply, Truman who seemed to be perfectly amenable to Bowers'ss suggestion, stated that he saw no reason why he should withhold permission to publish. The president even added that the book would be a useful contribution to a better understanding of Spain in the United States.[67]

However, the State Department insisted on approving the manuscript. Bowers refused: "I cannot afford to have my impressions and story censored by anyone in

---

[66]   Letter from Claude G. Bowers to Harry S. Truman, 9 November 1945, Bowers Mss. II, Manuscript Department, Lilly Library.
[67]   Letter from Harry S. Truman to Claude G. Bowers, 30 November 1945, ibid.

or out of the State Department."[68] Clearly Bowers believed that the State Department would not allow the publication of the manuscript or would impose restrictions that he could not tolerate. Bowers had criticized the State Department on different occasions and therefore felt that it would not judge the book impartially. For instance, he affirmed that he had sent dispatches from Spain for more than two years, and that he had never received any comment whatsoever from the Department.[69] He also stated that when he returned home in 1939 he found that: "There was a sharp division in the State Department on our policy in Spain, though the pro-Franco element was more numerous and strategically placed."[70] Bowers's biographers, Peter J. Sehlinger and Holman Hamilton, point out that other "political considerations also contributed to postponing the publication," noting in particular that "the book might embarrass friends in the Senate by stirring up Catholic hostility."[71]

The relationships between Franco and the Roosevelt and Truman administrations had been very tense. In December 1946, the United Nations had subjected Spain to a harsh policy of diplomatic isolation. However, by 1948 a tentative rapprochement was beginning between the governments of Spain and the United States. Two formidable forces were working to that end: on the one hand, a pro-Spanish Catholic lobby in Congress was working to relieve Spain's isolation and offer some economic help; on the other hand, U.S. military leaders began pushing the government to see the importance of taking advantage of the strategic geographic position of Spain, in the context of Cold War diplomacy and defense. Military concerns moved the State Department to report on the need to improve relations with Spain in October 1947, although it recognized that change could not be effected too quickly. These factors may have greatly increased apprehension in U.S. government circles that the publication of Bowers's book would alienate Franco and spoil any chance of securing Spanish military cooperation in the dangerous diplomacy and defense issues of the Cold War.[72]

Gradually, responding to pressure from the State Department, the Pentagon and the Spanish lobby, the executive began to establish a closer relationship between the United States and Spain. Consequently, between 1951 and 1953, there were

---

68   Quoted by Bowers's biographers, Sehlinger and Hamilton, *Spokesman for Democracy*, 205-206.

69   Bowers, *My Mission*, 413.

70   Ibid., 414. Sehlinger and Hamilton, *Spokesman for Democracy*, 413, comment on Bowers's reference to internal divisions in the State Department.

71   Sehlinger and Hamilton, *Spokesman for Democracy*, 206.

72   On the importance of U.S. propaganda in Spain during World War II, see for example Alejandro Pizarroso Quintero, "La propaganda norteamericana en España en la segunda guerra mundial," in Carmen Espejo Cala, ed., *Propaganda impresa y construcción del estado moderno y contemporáneo* (Sevilla: Ediciones Alfar, 2000), 73-101; "Diplomáticos, espías y propagandistas: norteamericanos en la España de Franco durante la Segunda Guerra Mundial," in *Travelling across Cultures/Viaxes Interculturais: The Twentieth-Century American Experience* (Santiago de Compostela: Publicacións da Universidade de Santiago, 2000), 415-446; and "Información y propaganda norteamericana en España durante la Segunda Guerra Mundial: la radio," *Revista Complutense de Historia de América* (Madrid) 24 (1998): 223-246.

negotiations between the two countries in an attempt to reach a bilateral agreement that offered the possibility of integrating Spain into the western defense system, since France and Great Britain had already rejected the admission of Spain into NATO. On 26 September 1953 three executive agreements were signed. The first agreement authorized the United States to build and use military bases in Spain and to establish troops and necessary equipment. However, it did not stipulate the commitment to mutual defense in the case of war. The second agreement concerned military help, by which the United States agreed to modernize Spanish military equipment. The third agreement dealt with economic aspects.[73] Thereafter, much to the disgust of Spanish democrats, the United States continued to support the Franco regime due to their interest in the bases. Bowers commented bitterly on this to Fernando Valera in 1957: "the position of the United States in the Spanish medley is largely responsible for sustaining the Franco regime and keeping the Fascist flag afloat financially, and this is dictated in great part by the army, which never before was permitted to exercise such power and authority, because they want bases."[74]

President Dwight David Eisenhower accepted Bowers's resignation as ambassador in Chile on 3 August 1953. The attainment of the coveted executive agreements with Spain meant that Bowers had to wait only a short while to be able, at long last, to publish his Memoirs. He signed a publishing agreement with Simon and Schuster on 11 November 1953, and the book came off the press in 1954.[75] A

---

[73]   On the agreements between Spain and the United States, see Oscar Calvo-González. "Neither a Carrot Nor a Stick: American Foreign Aid and Economic Policymaking in Spain during the 1950s," *Diplomatic History* 30.3 (June 2006): 409-438; Antonia Sagredo Santos, "Estados Unidos y el franquismo. De la neutralidad a la cooperación. El pacto de Madrid de 1953," in Juan Carlos Pereira, ed., *Del aislamiento a la apertura. La política exterior del de España durante el franquismo* (Burgos: Universidad de Burgos, 2006), 125-130; Fernando Termis Soto, *Renunciando a todo. El régimen franquista y los Estados Unidos desde 1945 a 1963* (Madrid: UNED, 2005); Carlos Escudé, "¿Cuánto valen esas bases? El tira y afloja entre Estados Unidos y España, 1951-1953" *Cuadernos de Historia Contemporánea* 25 (2003): 61-81; Oscar Calvo-González, "Bienvenido, Míster Marshall! La ayuda económica americana y la economía española en la década de 1950," *Revista de Historia Económica* 19 (extraordinario, 2001): 253-275; Angel Viñas, *En las garras del aguila. Los pactos con Estados Unidos, de Francisco Franco a Felipe González, 1945-1995* (Barcelona: Crítica Contrastes, 2003) and *Los pactos secretos de Franco con los EE.UU.. Bases, ayuda económica, recortes de soberanía* (Barcelona: Ediciones Grijalbo, 1981); Mark S. Byrnes, "'Overruled and Worn Down': Truman Sends an Ambassador to Spain" *Presidential Studies Quarterly* 29 (June 1999): 263-279; Arturo Jarque Iñiguez, *'Queremos esas bases!' el acercamiento de EE.UU. a la España de Franco* (Alcalá de Henares: Universidad de Alcalá, 1998); Antonio Marquina, *España y la política de seguridad occidental, 1939-1986* (Madrid: Ed. Ejército, 1986); R. Richard Rubottom and J. Carter Murphy, *Spain and the United States since World War II* (New York: Praeger, 1984).

[74]   Letter from Claude G. Bowers to Fernando Valera Aparicio, 4 December 1957, file Fernando Valera Aparicio, box 32, dossier 9, ASRE, FUE.

[75]   See Publishing agreement between Simon and Schuster, Inc. and Bowers in Bowers Mss. II, Manuscript Department, Lilly Library. The correspondence between Fernando Valera Aparicio and Claude G. Bowers on the publication of his book extends to 34 letters between 19 November 1954 and 4 December 1957, ASRE, FUE.

Spanish translation was published in 1955 in Mexico, which had become home to a very large number of Spanish Republican exiles, but the book did not appear in Spain until 1978, three years after Franco died, during the transition to the new democratic constitutional monarchy under King Juan Carlos I.[76]

Reaction in Spain

During Franco's dictatorship, Spanish diplomats serving in Washington naturally regarded Bowers with hostility and were on the alert to the possible publication of his book. In a brief biographical note about Bowers that was written in 1947 for the Spanish ministry of Foreign Affairs, government sentiment was clearly stated: "It is said that he is neither a friend of Spain nor of our regime and he has expressed this on several occasions in his country."[77]

In Spain, Bowers's opinions were considered to be a threat to the new regime, and consequently Franco tried to prevent the publication of his memoirs. This was made very clear in a letter from the director of the Spanish ministry of Foreign Affairs to the Spanish chargé d'affaires in Washington, Eduardo Propper de Callejón, written on 2 December 1953.[78]

> The book was regarded suspiciously by the American government to the point that his personal friend, President Roosevelt, asked him to postpone the publication. When he died, the State Department forbade him to do so while he occupied a diplomatic post. It now seems that Mr. Bowers intends to publish it shortly, and it would be very convenient that you try to prevent it, with the means at your disposal and the good friends that we have in that country (among them Mr. McCarthy), reminding them of the different postponements that it has suffered—precisely in periods in which our relations were not as cordial as now—and make them see, in addition, the leftist tendency of the author, his friendship with the Government of the Popular

---

[76] Claude G. Bowers, *Mi misión en España* (México: Editorial Grijalbo, 1955); Claude G. Bowers, *Misión en España: en el umbral de la Segunda Guerra Mundial 1933-1939*, translated by Juan López S. and revised by Agustín Barta (Barcelona: Edic. Éxito, 1978).

[77] Report of the Dirección Política de España "Asunto: Personalidades," 13 January 1947, file 3184, dossier 31, AMAE.

[78] The Spanish ambassador in Washington since 27 December 1950 was José Félix de Lequerica. He had been chosen by Franco to occupy the post of "Inspector of Embassies, Legations and Consulates" in April 1948. On this diplomat, see María Jesús Cava, *Los diplomáticos de Franco. José Félix de Lequerica, temple y tenacidad* (Bilbao: Universidad de Deusto, 1989). Eduardo Propper de Callejón was in charge in the absence of the ambassador.

Front and the lack of historical veracity that the whole text will probably contain.[79]

Propper was told to do everything in his power to make sure that Bowers's information and opinions on the evolution of the Second Spanish Republic and the Civil War stayed hidden, even to the point of emphasizing the former ambassador's left-leaning ideology, in the hope that that this would have an effect in the conservative McCarthy period. It is to be supposed that Propper de Castejón did try to put some pressure on Franco's American friends, but if they in turn attempted to act as a result of this pressure is not certain. In any case, they were evidently unsuccessful.

By contrast, the Basque government-in-exile had a very different opinion on Bowers and his memoirs:

> He saw a lot, he observed a lot, he understood the backstage of the Spanish tragedy and he knew of the close collaboration of Germany and Italy with the Franquist rebels.... But the sincere diary written by Bowers was contemplated with unease by the American government. First Roosevelt, his personal friend, begged him "not to publish it yet" and after Roosevelt's death, the State Department prohibited its publication as long as he held diplomatic posts for the United States. Now, Claude Bowers, with his hands free, is thinking of publishing shortly a book on Spain....[80]

Both the Spanish ministry and the Basque nationalists thus made almost identical affirmations that, in the absence of other evidence, must remain as suspicions since Bowers does not actually say that the State Department prohibited his publication. When the minister of Foreign Affairs received this text, he sent it to the ambassador in Washington. The minister's opinion was that it was a typical product of "the red propaganda of the Basque government," and he feared that the "publication of the book would favor their position and the ideals that they defend."[81]

---

[79] Dispatch of the Director of Foreign Affairs to the Spanish chargé d'affaires in Washington Eduardo Propper de Callejón, 2 December 1953, R. 47, dossier 373, AMAE.

[80] Reference taken from the Propaganda of the Basque Government, November 1953, R. 145, dossier 5, AMAE. "Vió mucho, observó mucho, conoció los bastidores de la tragedia española y comprobó la estrecha colaboración de Alemania e Italia con los rebeldes franquistas ... Pero el sincero diario de Bowers fue mirado con recelo por el Gobierno americano, primero Roosevelt, su amigo personal, le rogó que 'no lo publicara todavía' Después de la muerte del mandatario, el Departamento de Estado le prohibió su publicación mientras siguiera desempeñando puestos diplomáticos para USA. Ahora, Claude Bowers, con las manos libres, piensa editar en breve plazo un libro...."

[81] Dispatch of the Director of the Ministry of Foreign Affairs to the Spanish Ambassador in Washington, 30 December 1953, R. 49, dossier 408, AMAE.

Responses to the Publication

After the publication of his Spanish memoirs in 1954, Bowers confessed that he was being "flooded with letters from all over the world."[82] Spanish republicans were naturally enthusiastic over the book. Fernando Valera was given the task of collaborating with Bowers to promote its circulation, on the recommendation of the president of the Second Spanish Republic in exile, Diego Martínez Barrio.[83] Valera would help Bowers to get the book translated and published in as many languages as possible.[84] Understandably, they had a strong vested interest in the international diffusion of Bowers's version of events during the Second Spanish Republic and the Civil War, particularly at this time, in the mid-1950s, when it was necessary to counter a movement that seemed to be gaining ground to officially rehabilitate Franco's regime.[85] It is therefore somewhat surprising that the republican government acquired only sixty books to distribute to people who should read it, although Fernando Valera Aparicio did send a few copies of the book to some libraries in Spain. When the French edition came out, Francisco Valera wrote to Bowers and told him that the government of the Republic in exile would buy one hundred books to be sent to the most outstanding public figures, since that was their best argument.[86]

In celebration and appreciation of the book, the republican government in exile awarded him the Order of Liberation of Spain. However, Bowers felt that he could accept it only symbolically. In the letter that he wrote to Fernardo Valera Aparicio, he stated that

> it would be a great honor to receive the decoration of the Republic. Unhappily, under the rules of the State Department no one in the diplomatic service is permitted to receive decorations from foreign governments. Under certain conditions a decoration may be accepted when a refusal to accept would be misunderstood, but even then the decoration must be deposited in the State Department.... I conclude it would be less embarrassing to my friends in the State Department not to take a decoration. In place of that a personal letter including the citation that would have gone with the decoration and signed by

---

[82]   Letter from Claude G. Bowers to Fernando Valera Aparicio, 17 February 1955, file Fernando Valera Aparicio, box 32, dossier 9, ASRE, FUE.

[83]   Letter from Diego Martínez Barrio to Fernando Valera Aparicio, 17 December 1954, file Fernando Valera Aparicio, box 32, dossier 9, ASRE, FUE.

[84]   Bowers's book came out in French *Ma mission en Espagne, 1933-1939* (Paris: Flammarion, 1956) and in Italian *Missione in Spagna, 1933-1939. Prova generale della seconda guerra mondiale* (Milan: Feltrinelli Editore, 1957).

[85]   Letter from Fernando Valera Aparicio to Claude G. Bowers, 8 October 1955, file Fernando Valera Aparicio, box 32, dossier 9, ASRE, FUE.

[86]   On the circulation of the Spanish edition, see the letter from Fernando Valera Aparicio to Claude G. Bowers, 7 December 1955, and on the French edition the letter written in Paris, 6 July 1956, file Fernando Valera Aparicio, box 32, dossier 9, ASRE, FUE.

the President of the Republic—a letter that I would treasure—would do as well.[87]

Francisco V. Portela, a journalist working for *La Prensa*, a newspaper that was published in Spanish in New York, asserted that the book constituted a sincere contribution to contemporary history, and that it was an important and necessary document for the analysis of the Spanish Civil War. Summarizing the central thesis of the book, Portela concluded that Bowers blamed the British government of Neville Chamberlain and its policy of non-intervention for the fact that the government of the Republic was unable to suppress the rebellion.[88]

However, there were other more negatively critical views. The author was accused of omitting material that did not support his views, such as the weaknesses of the Spanish Republic and Communist pressures on Spanish Republicans.[89] The Spanish Republican writer in exile, Ramón Sender thought that, although Bowers was an honest man, his views were biased and he was unable to see Moscow's influence in Spanish affairs.[90]

As far as the Spanish monarchists were concerned, a good few were enthusiastic about Bowers's publication, as is manifested in the letters that were sent to him. According to Bowers, these monarchical supporters actually meant that they liked his "crucifixion of Franco," confirming, in his view, that Franco's supporters were "confined to the Fascist group."[91]

Truman asserted that Bowers's book was something that had needed to be said for a long time.[92] Bowers mentioned in a letter that Truman had confessed to him that the Spanish Memoirs had cured him of wishful thinking.[93]

In general, American and European liberals lauded Bowers. In a review that appeared in *Newsweek*, another author pointed out that Bowers presented the Spanish war as it seemed to many Americans at the beginning: "As the rebellion of a mixed group of military officials and ultra right wing politicians against the legal Republic of Spain ... its reading produces an effect of going back to the past, revealing what many Americans thought of the world situation."[94]

The liberal American historian Gordon A. Craig, a professor of History at Princeton University, commented in the *Herald Tribune* on 13 June 1954, that the book reflected Bowers's unconditional support of the Spanish Republic, underscoring that in the 1930s there had been a great deal of confusion in the public

---

[87]   Letter from Claude G. Bowers to Fernando Valera Aparicio, 8 December 1954, file Fernando Valera Aparicio, box 32, dossier 9, ASRE, FUE.

[88]   Francisco V. Portela, "Mi Misión en España," *La Prensa New York*, 13 June 1954.

[89]   Sehlinger and Hamilton, *Spokesman for Democracy*, 206-207.

[90]   See commentary of the news agency EFE on the article written by Ramón Sender that appeared in the liberal publication *New Leader*, 1954, file 3586, dossier 10, AMAE.

[91]   Letter from Claude G. Bowers to Fernando Valera Aparicio, 17 February 1955, file Fernando Valera Aparicio, box 32, dossier 9, ASRE, FUE.

[92]   Quoted by Sehlinger and Hamilton, *Spokesman for Democracy*, 267.

[93]   Letter from Claude G. Bowers to Fernando Valera Aparicio, 15 July 1956, file Fernando Valera Aparicio, box 32, dossier 9, ASRE, FUE.

[94]   Review of Bowers's Memoirs, in *Newsweek*, 14 June 1954.

mind concerning Spain: "The Franco Insurrection was sold to a large section of the Western public as a defensive action against communism; Axis intervention was defended as a war to prevent the Soviet Union from taking over Spain." Craig seemed to support Bowers's view when he stated that governments had misled public opinion, deliberately countering their sympathies with the Spanish Republic, by trying to portray it as a "red" regime, and so, justifying Fascist intervention.[95]

Herbert L. Matthews, a *New York Times* journalist and a member of the *Times* editorial board who had reported from Spain in 1936-1939, said that "The United States had few diplomats in those days who served the cause of democracy so well" and confessed that he had been "waiting impatiently" for Bowers's publication for fourteen years.[96] Nonetheless, he noted that the book had all the "weakness and freshness of an account written in the heat of the battle" and that it had to be read "in the frame of mind of 1939, not 1954. It is not judicious, unbiased, academic; it is passionate, biased and provocative." Mr. Matthews advised people to read the book with reservation since there was considerable distortion, but at the same time he said there was "a great mass of inside, first hand expert information that could only come from Mr. Bowers and that needed to be printed.... What we have is not history but some valuable material for history that experts will know how to use."[97] He pointed out that there were a number of mistakes in terms of certain exaggerations and bias. However, he felt that in spite of this, most of the information was valuable and sound. Mr. Mathews therefore recommended reading the book to those interested in the Spanish Civil War and in the preliminaries to World War II and added: "In these days of McCarran and Mc Carthy it should be read as an example of how a true American democrat interpreted one of the most misunderstood and at the same time one of the most important events in modern history."[98]

Hannen Swaffer in the London socialist newspaper *The Daily Herald* hailed Bowers as an independent witness, defending the leftist views on the Spanish case. He was especially impressed by a pointed warning that Bowers made in his foreword: "We should not return to the shoddy days just before the war, when it was popular in high circles to believe that to oppose Communism one must follow the Fascist line."[99]

An article that appeared in the newspaper *El Plata* of Montevideo written by Anna Lenah Elgstrom, president of the Swedish Women's Neutral Committee to Help Spanish Children, said that Bowers gave first hand information of what had happened in Spain, and expressed her admiration for a diplomat who defended democracy, since most of the diplomatic corps in Spain did not do so. In her

---

[95]   Gordon Craig, "Our Former Ambassador Sets the Spanish Story in Perspective," *Herald Tribune Book Review*, 13 June 1954.

[96]   Herbert L. Matthews, "As Bowers Saw the War in Spain," *New York Times Book Review*, 13 June 1954.

[97]   Ibid.

[98]   Ibid.

[99]   Bowers, *My Mission*, v.

opinion, Bowers's book was "a convincing human document."[100] The Swedish press had laudatory reviews of some length so that Bowers even thought that a Scandinavian edition of his book might be possible.[101]

On the reaction of the State Department to the publication, the author remarked with astonishment: "I had expected that it would be ignored or attacked, but the *Foreign Service Journal*, the organ of the Department, had a highly complimentary review of the book."[102]

In short, the publication of the book left nobody indifferent. It commanded a great deal of public attention. It was a bold, passionate, and biased book, which offered a first-hand account of a crucial moment not only in Spanish history but also in world history. Certainly, it was criticized as giving a personal, idealized and partial vision of reality, because Bowers tended to give a very positive image of the government of the Second Spanish Republic, he left out information concerning Russian intervention, and he failed to acknowledge any Communist influence on the republican government. Neither did he mention his early support of the United States policy of non-intervention in Spain, or describe the evolution of his opinions. Nevertheless, despite these distortions and a few errors, Bowers's memoirs remain a useful source of information for historians.

Conclusion

The publication of Claude G. Bowers's Spanish memoirs was delayed in the United States for a considerable period of time. Postponement during World War II was undoubtedly decided in order to avoid difficulties with the British government. Here the main factor for the silence was probably Bowers's own forbearance, despite his strong desire to publish. He agreed with his friend Roosevelt not to risk affecting relations with Great Britain. His attitude seems to have been at this point dictated mainly by his own sense of responsibility. Nevertheless, after the war, Bowers asked Harry S. Truman to give him the green light to publish his memoirs. Bowers thought that the time was right and Truman apparently agreed. However, the State Department insisted on approving the manuscript before allowing it to be published. Bowers absolutely rejected this prospect, and preferred to postpone publication rather than accept any official censorship of his manuscript.

In the early Cold War years, between 1947 and 1953, the predominant concern of U.S. governments revolved around strategic issues. They sought to establish military bases in Spain and could not afford to alienate General Franco. Negotiations were held between 1951 and 1953, and the pacts between Spain and the United States were safely signed in September 1953. Immediately afterwards, Bowers signed his publishing agreement with Simon and Schuster and his book was finally published in

---

[100]   Cited in "El Gigantesco Bluff de la Guerra Civil Española," *El Plata*, 24 September 1954. Leading article of the newspaper, probably written by the Basque refugee Vicente de Amézaga.

[101]   Letter from Claude G. Bowers to Fernando Valera Aparicio, 8 December 1954, file Fernando Valera Aparicio, box 32, dossier 9, ASRE, FUE.

[102]   Ibid.

1954. Political repression is an elastic concept that may take many forms. In sum, the available evidence suggests that the fourteen-year delay was a result of both initial forbearance on the part of Bowers himself, and varying degrees of personal and political pressure on the part of different U.S. government officials to curtail his freedom of expression.

POLITICAL REPRESSION AND THE RULE OF LAW:
THE COLD WAR CASE OF WILLIAM SENTNER

Ellen Schrecker

William Sentner was lying in bed completely naked at 7:25 a.m. on 17 September 1952, when two FBI agents burst into his hotel room in Rock Island, Illinois, with a warrant for his arrest. An open member of the Communist Party (CP) as well as the most important left-wing labor leader in the Midwest, Sentner was being charged with conspiracy along with four other St. Louis Communists under the 1940 Alien Registration Act, better known as the Smith Act. At the time of his arrest, he had been in the Rock Island area for several days, helping a United Electrical, Radio and Machine Workers of America (UE) local negotiate a contract.[1]

This was hardly Sentner's first brush with the law. During the labor unrest of the 1930s and 1940s, arrests were the standard occupational hazards of union organizers, especially when they became involved with strikes and demonstrations.[2] Arrested repeatedly in 1933 while trying to organize the African American women who shelled and sorted pecans at several plants around the city, Sentner was also detained for several days on charges of violating the National Recovery Act. And, in fact, it was a beating at the hands of the police the following year that led him, already a dedicated union activist, into the Communist Party.[3]

A few years later, Sentner, by then the UE's vice president in charge of Missouri and the neighboring parts of Illinois, Indiana, and Iowa, faced several prosecutions stemming from a sit-down strike in Newton, Iowa, in the summer of 1938. Not only was he charged with contempt for violating an injunction against the strike, but he was also indicted under a 1919 criminal syndicalism law that prescribed up to ten years in prison for teaching and advocating "crime, sabotage, violence, and other unlawful methods of terrorism" in order to achieve "industrial and political reform."[4] As so often happened during major work stoppages, the National Guard came to town. It imposed martial law, broke the strike, and hauled the union leaders before a secret military tribunal. During the course of his

---

[1]   Special Agent in Charge (SAC), Springfield to Director, FBI, 29 September 1952 and R.N. Hosteny, report, 27 September 1952, both in William Sentner FBI File, no. 181, William Sentner Papers, Washington University Library, St. Louis, Missouri (hereafter Sentner Papers). For a thorough and sympathetic portrayal of Sentner's organizing activities, see Rosemary Feurer, *Radical Unionism in the Midwest, 1900-1950* (Urbana and Chicago: University of Illinois Press, 2006).

[2]   For a good overview of the repression against union organizers in the 1930s, see Robert Justin Goldstein, *Political Repression in Modern America: From 1870 to 1976* (Urbana and Chicago: University of Illinois Press, 2001, 1978), 195-235.

[3]   Feurer, *Radical Unionism*, 42-43; undated memo, Trial Materials III, box 1, series 4, Sentner Papers.

[4]   Supplemental Prosecutive Report, St. Louis, 12 February 1952, no. 160, box 5, series 4, Sentner Papers; W.L. Bliss, Opinion, *State v. Sentner*, 298 N.W. 813 (Supreme Court of Iowa, 17 June 1941, no. 45227), Maytag Strike 1938-1940, box 3, series 1, Sentner Papers.

interrogation, Sentner admitted that he was a Communist, an admission that the prosecution later used during his criminal syndicalism trial as proof of his subversive intent. While that case was wending its way through the Iowa courts, Sentner was arrested again, this time in connection with an April 1939 strike in Evansville, Indiana. But, since he had been picked up in the middle of the night and incarcerated without a warrant in a blatant attempt to break the strike, he was soon released when a judge found the arrest completely "without cause."[5]

Sentner's criminal syndicalism case finally came to trial in October 1939 and, as expected, he was convicted. Let off with a $2,500 fine instead of a prison sentence, Sentner appealed nonetheless. A few days later, he was again arrested, this time at a strike in St. Louis.[6] By that point Sentner's open affiliation with the Communist Party had become such an embarrassment to his union that James Matles, the UE's director of organization (who was himself to be targeted for deportation as a Communist in the 1950s), asked him to resign from the CP, which he did.[7] Within a few years, however, Sentner again identified himself as a party member, admitting it first to a writer for *Fortune* magazine in 1943, and then to the FBI agents who were investigating him in connection with his recent appointment to the federal government's War Labor Board.[8] In the meantime, the Iowa Supreme Court overturned his criminal syndicalism conviction. Not only was Sentner's party membership completely legal, Chief Justice W.L. Bliss explained, but he had been seeking a wage increase for the striking workers and not "some radical change in industry."[9]

As Sentner's experiences reveal, the early 1940s was a period of flux with regard to the nation's attitude toward communism. While Iowa's judges were following a 1937 U.S. Supreme Court decision that threw out the criminal syndicalism conviction of the head of the Oregon Communist Party, Congress was rushing through a spate of anticommunist and anti-alien measures.[10] The Smith Act was one of those laws, as was the 1940 Hatch Act, which contained provisions for dismissing federal employees who belonged to "any political party or organization which advocates the overthrow of our constitutional form of government."[11] Although the White House was not eager to enforce the Hatch Act's proscription of Communists while the United States was allied with Stalin against Hitler, the threat of a partisan attack on the administration for employing a known party member led

---

[5]   Statement made in behalf of William Sentner by his attorney, Charles J. Eichel, 10 April 1939, Maytag and Sentner Trial 1938-1939, box 3, series 1, Sentner Papers.

[6]   Sentner to James Matles, 16 October 1939, folder 3, box 5, series 1, Sentner Papers.

[7]   Matles to Sentner, 18 October 1939 and Sentner to Matles, 13 December 1939, Reports to National Office, folder 2, box 5, series 1, Sentner Papers.

[8]   Feurer, *Radical Unionism*, 180; Transcript, 3 December 1943, Trial Materials III, box 1, series 4, Sentner Papers.

[9]   W.L. Bliss, Decision of Iowa Supreme Court, 17 June 1941, folder 2, box 3, series 1, Sentner Papers.

[10] *De Jonge v. State of Oregon*, 299 U.S. 353 (1937). U.S. Supreme Court opinions are found on this website: http://www.findlaw.com/casecode/supreme.html.

[11] Michal R. Belknap, *Cold War Political Justice: The Smith Act, the Communist Party, and American Civil Liberties* (Westport, CT: Greenwood Press, 1977), 22.

to Sentner's forced resignation from the War Labor Board in February 1944.[12] By this point, Sentner had already been under investigation by the FBI for five years and had "tentatively" been classified as one of the "[i]ndividuals believed to be the most dangerous and who in all probability should be interned in event of War."[13] Not surprisingly, the Bureau's interest in the UE leader continued into the postwar period. The local FBI office routinely monitored his activities and, at several points in the late 1940s and early 1950s, tapped his telephone.[14]

Meanwhile Sentner's foreign-born wife, Antonia, was also having problems with the law. Brought to the United States at the age of eight from what would later become Yugoslavia, Antonia Sentner was a radical in her own right. On 2 September 1942, a federal judge denied her application for citizenship on the grounds that she had failed "to prove attachment to principles of Constitution during statutory period required by law." She had admitted to an Immigration and Naturalization Service (INS) examiner that she had only recently left the CP, but, as he explained to his superiors, "she gave very vague and unsatisfactory reasons for the discontinuance of her membership in the Communist Party." When she reapplied in 1945, the same official intimated that she would be rejected again and, so, she withdrew her application. Then, on 1 September 1949, she was arrested for deportation and released on a $2,000 bail. The following year, after Congress passed the Internal Security Act of 1950, the so-called McCarran Act, with its beefed-up provisions for excluding, detaining, and deporting radical aliens, she was arrested again and held without bail for several days. She was then placed on supervisory parole and required to report monthly to the immigration authorities, submit to physical and mental examinations, and give up all her political activities and associates—including her spouse. Naturally, she appealed and, as her case ambled through the administrative machinery of the INS and the federal courts, her struggle to stay in the country paralleled that of her husband to remain out of jail.[15]

Sentner's Smith Act case was one of 126 so-called "second-string" prosecutions of the Communist Party's leaders that had been initiated after the

---

[12]   J. Edgar Hoover to SAC, St. Louis, 4 November 1943, no. 19; Hoover, Memorandum for the Attorney General, 10 January 1944, no. 21; Interdepartmental Committee on Employee Investigations to Dir., FBI, 17 February 1944, no. 26, all in William Sentner FBI File, Sentner Papers.

[13]   Bill Sentner's News Letter, 8 May 1954, 1954, folder 16, box 1, series 4, Sentner Papers; Hoover to SAC, St. Louis, 19 March 1942, no no., box 5, series 4, Sentner Papers, Series.

[14]   G.B. Norris, Report, 11 October 1945, no. 38; Hoover to Attorney General, 22 May 1947, no. 59; G.B. Norris, Report, 7 April 1950, no. 107; Memo, SAC, St. Louis to Hoover, 5 July 1951, no. 123; Teletype, Hostetter to Hoover, 21 December 1951, no. 155; Hoover to SAC, Atlanta, 28 April 1952, no no.; Memo, Baumgardner to Belmont, 29 August 1952, no. 172; Memo, Ladd to Hoover, 6 August 1951, no. 127, all in box 5, series 4, Sentner Papers.

[15]   Federal Works Agency, Investigative Report, 8 June 1943, 100-18332-14; William Sentner, Testimony before Commission on Immigration and Naturalization, 11 October 1952; Memo for the File, G.B. Norris, 13 June 1940, all in box 5, series 4, Sentner Papers; UE District 8 Sentner Defense Committee, Press Release, 17 December 1953, Smith Act Press Releases and Information, folder 17, box 1, series 4, Sentner Papers.

Supreme Court upheld the constitutionality of what was the first peacetime sedition act since the late eighteenth century. Passed during the tense period between the outbreak of World War II in Europe and Pearl Harbor, when hostility to foreigners was so fierce that, as one Congressman noted, "if you brought in the Ten Commandments today and asked for their repeal and attached to that request an alien law, you could get it," the Smith Act sailed through the Senate on a voice vote and the House by a 382-384 margin.[16] Besides calling for the annual registration of resident aliens, it also contained provisions against anyone who "advocates, abets, advises, or teaches the duty, necessity, desirability, or propriety of overthrowing or destroying the government of the United States ... by force and violence," provisions that certainly seemed to violate the First Amendment. Although the Smith Act had been invoked twice in the 1940s, its constitutionality had not been tested.

The Cold War created that opportunity. Despite the attorney general's reluctance to use the law, J. Edgar Hoover had long hoped to mount a criminal prosecution against the Communist Party and had been collecting evidence for such a case since the end of World War II.[17] By the spring of 1948, the Justice Department was under so much pressure to prosecute Communists that it decided to indict the party's top leaders for conspiracy under the Smith Act.[18] The trial, which took place in New York City, lasted from January to October 1949, the longest trial in American history to that date. Because the government could not prove that the CP's General Secretary Eugene Dennis and the other Smith Act defendants advocated "force and violence," it relied on undercover informers and ex-Communist witnesses who testified that the party's leaders had used the most incendiary passages in the Marxist-Leninist canon as the basis for their political and educational work. It was a strategy that strained credibility, but in the overwrought atmosphere of the early Cold War, with a judge who mercilessly hassled the defendants and their attorneys, a conviction was preordained. So, too, was the Supreme Court's decision to uphold that conviction, especially after the highly respected Learned Hand of the Second Circuit Court of Appeals did so in the immediate aftermath of the outbreak of the Korean War. In his June 1951 opinion in the *Dennis* case, Chief Justice Fred Vinson relied on Hand's invocation of a balancing act between security and liberty to insist that the CP constituted such a "clear and present danger" that the First Amendment did not apply.[19] It was, later

---

[16]   Belknap, *Cold War Political Justice*, 21-26, 152-56.

[17]   M.L. Ladd, Memorandum to Hoover, 22 January 1948, U.S. Congress, Senate, Select Committee to Study Governmental Operations with Respect to Intelligence Activities, *Final Report*, Book III, "Supplementary Detailed Staff Reports on Intelligence Activities and the Rights of Americans," 94th Cong., 2nd sess., 23 April 1976, 439; Hoover to SAC, New York, 7 July 1945, Smith Act Trials File, 100-3-74, no. X and Hoover, Memorandum to E.A. Tamm, Ladd, Clyde Tolson, 30 October 1947, Smith Act Trials File, 100-3-74, no. 1123, both in Sentner Papers.

[18]   Belknap, *Cold War Political Justice*, 47.

[19]   *Dennis et al. v. United States*, 341 U.S. 494 (1951).

commentators agree, a terrible decision.[20] Not only did it effectively criminalize the American Communist Party and thus justify the widespread repression directed against all the individuals and organizations associated with it, but, more immediately, it allowed the Justice Department to prosecute the party's lower-level officials.[21]

Even so, it was not until the beginning of 1954 that Sentner and his co-defendants found themselves in court. Like many of the people caught up in the political cases of the early Cold War, the St. Louis Communists faced considerable obstacles even before their trial began. To begin with, the government set their bail so high that three of the defendants remained in prison throughout the proceedings. That incarceration hampered their defense, for their jailer, insisting that he "wasn't going to permit communistic literature in the City jail as long as he was the Warden," refused to let them consult the publications that the government was planning to use against them.[22] In addition, like many other communist defendants, they had trouble finding attorneys. Sentner approached fifty-four lawyers and law firms with no success. Even though some seemed interested, they said that they could not afford to lose their other clients if they took the case.[23] Ultimately Sentner and his co-defendants ended up relying on a New York City lawyer and Sentner's former UE attorney.

The trial, which began in January 1954, was largely a replay of the original Smith Act case. Not only did the prosecutors rely on the same books and pamphlets to show the party's proclivity for "force and violence," but they used many of the same professional ex-Communists, along with some local men and women who had joined the CP at the FBI's behest.[24] Much of their testimony was vague, stale, or irrelevant. An undercover informant, for example, described a class he took with one of the defendants, but admitted that he had never talked about it with him "because I could not understand the substance of his teaching."[25] Since the Justice Department based its case almost entirely on showing that Sentner and the others were active

---

[20]   For a recent assessment of the decision, see Geoffrey R. Stone, *Perilous Times: Free Speech in Wartime from the Sedition Act of 1798 to the War on Terrorism* (New York: W.W. Norton, 2004), 407-411.

[21]   For a more fully developed discussion of the *Dennis* case, see Ellen Schrecker, *Many Are the Crimes: McCarthyism in America* (Boston and New York: Little, Brown and Company, 1998), 190-200.

[22]   Sentner to Judge Roy W. Harper, 6 January 1953, folder 9, box 1, series 4, Sentner Papers.

[23]   Memorandum, 28 November 1952, Trial Materials I, box 1, series 4, Sentner Papers.

[24]   Harry Richards et al. to Sydney L. Berger et al., 14 December 1953, folder 10, box 1, series 4, Sentner Papers.

[25]   Typescript, Testimony of Joe Schoemehl, 23 March 1954, and Testimony of Mrs. Ama Hanners, 11 February 1954, folder 10, box 1, series 4, Sentner Papers; Bill Sentner's News Letter, 6, 19, 27 February and 12, 26 March 1954, folder 16, box 1, series 4, Sentner Papers; John Lautner Testimony, Transcript, "In the United States Court of Appeals for the Eighth Circuit, *William Sentner vs. United States of America*—appeal from District Court for Eastern District of Missouri," 7-8, box 3, series 4, Sentner Papers; Obadiah Jones, Testimony, Narrative Statement, vol. 1, 634, box 3, series 4, Sentner Papers.

Communists, it never tried to establish that they had advocated force and violence. "It is the theory of the government's case," one of the prosecutors explained, "that the Communist Party is the organizational form which this conspiracy took."[26]

For some reason, the defendants borrowed some of the CP's less than successful legal tactics from the first Smith Act trial. Thus, for example, they challenged the make-up of the jury, charging that it had been chosen from a pool of potential jurors that deliberately underrepresented members of the working class. They also mounted a political, rather than a civil liberties, defense, maintaining that they were being prosecuted because they supported racial equality and opposed the Korean War.[27] The jury was unconvinced, deliberating only two hours and fifteen minutes before voting to convict the five defendants, a verdict Sentner called "part of the fascist conspiracy of big business seeking to destroy constitutional liberties and the Bill of Rights."[28] That kind of rhetoric proved self-defeating. Not only did it fail to win community support for the defendants, but the government was able to cite that language to justify its unprecedented decision to deny them bail as they prepared their appeal.[29]

Although that appeal dragged on for years, it ultimately succeeded. But the costs were high and money was a real problem. Sentner had lost his union job and, despite a serious heart condition, was working part-time for a construction company. Al Murphy, the only African American defendant, was in even more desperate straits. Not only did he have trouble finding a job, but, as he wrote Sentner in September 1954, "the Internal Revenue people are harassing hell out of me about the $38 I owe."[30] Since the other defendants were only marginally better off, they sought, and ultimately obtained, a financial dispensation from the Supreme Court that allowed them to file their appeal without having to pay for a printed brief. Their oral argument took place in May 1956, but no one expected a decision until after the Supreme Court disposed of the second-string California case that was already on its docket. Since that decision, *Yates v. U.S.*, effectively gutted the Smith Act by demanding that the government prove that the Communist defendants had actually advocated action to overthrow the state, rather than just supporting it in theory, it was clear the St. Louis defendants would prevail. By the time the appeals court finally reversed their conviction and remanded the case for a new trial in April 1958, Sentner had left the Communist Party. On 10 October the government officially

---

[26] U.S. Attorney Taylor, in Transcript, "In the United States Court of Appeals for the Eighth Circuit, *William Sentner vs. United States of America*—appeal from District Court for Eastern District of Missouri," 74, box 3, series 4, Sentner Papers.

[27] UE District 8 Sentner Defense Committee, Press Release, 15 January 1954, folder 12, box 1, series 4, Sentner Papers.

[28] Bill Sentner's News Letter, Memorial Day 1954, folder 16, box 1, series 4, Sentner Papers.

[29] SAC, St. Louis, Parole Report, 16 June 1954, in SAC, St. Louis Report, 16 June 1954, no. 208, box 5, series 4, Sentner Papers; Tonie Sentner to Dear Friend, 8 June 1954, folder 10, box 1, series 4, Sentner Papers.

[30] Al (Murphy?) to Sentner, 25 October 1954, folder 1, box 1, series 4, Sentner Papers.

dropped the charges. But Sentner had little time to enjoy his rehabilitation; he died of a heart attack two months later.[31]

*

That William Sentner was the victim of political repression is obvious. All his skirmishes with the repressive machinery of the state occurred because of his activities as a union organizer and an open Communist. By all accounts an extremely effective labor leader, Sentner was a skilled negotiator and tactician who was generally considered a moderating influence during strikes and other labor troubles. He had, in fact, earned so much respect within the larger community that, at least for a short time during World War II, he actually became part of the St. Louis political establishment.[32] Nonetheless, he *was* a Communist. Though it was not, either then or later, illegal to belong to the Communist Party, most members concealed their relationship. Thus, for example, while many UE and other left-wing labor leaders were in or near the CP, few, if any, identified openly with it. Sentner's public affiliation was unique. Even so, we must realize that the repression unleashed against him, while focusing on his relationship with the Communist Party, was part of a broader attack on his union. As the most powerful left-led labor organization in the United States, the UE and its leaders were relentlessly hounded during the early Cold War. From anticommunist legislation to congressional investigations to criminal prosecutions to deportation proceedings to FBI surveillance—the harassment continued until the union was essentially destroyed.[33] But, significantly, almost all the repression visited on the UE, as well as that Sentner experienced, was completely within the law—and, often, *was* the law. And, as I hope to show in the rest of this chapter, the legal harassment of William Sentner was completely in keeping with the American tradition of political repression.

Its unquestionable legality was, in fact, one of the key features of that repression. Notwithstanding a strong vigilante tradition and the contributions of the

---

[31] Report, SAC, St. Louis, 19 January 1955, no. 212; SAC, St. Louis, 18 July 1955, no. 219; Report, SAC, St. Louis, 30 July 1956, no. 223; Hoover to Assistant Attorney General William F. Tompkins, 11 February 1957, no. 226(?); Report, SAC, St. Louis, 26 August 1958, no. 234; Report, SAC, St. Louis, 28 October 1958, no. 236; Memo, SAC, St. Louis to Hoover, 15 December 1958, no. 238, all in box 5, series 4, Sentner Papers.

[32] Feurer, *Radical Unionism*, 137-176.

[33] On the McCarthy era repression against the UE, see Ronald L. Filippelli and Mark McColloch, *Cold War in the Working Class: The Rise and Decline of the United Electrical Workers* (Albany: State University of New York Press, 1995); Harvey A. Levenstein, *Communism, Anti-Communism, and the CIO* (Westport, CT: Greenwood Press, 1981); Steve Rosswurm, ed., *The CIO's Left-led Unions* (New Brunswick, NJ: Rutgers University Press, 1992); Ronald L. Filippelli, "The United Electrical, Radio and Machine Workers of America, 1933-1949: The Struggle for Control," (PhD diss., Pennsylvania State University, 1970); and Ronald W. Schatz, *The Electrical Workers: A History of Labor at General Electric and Westinghouse, 1923-60* (Urbana and Chicago: University of Illinois Press, 1983).

private sector, the most effective suppression of dissent usually occurred at the hands of the state as it enforced the law. Criminal prosecutions served many functions. No only did they threaten unpopular groups and individuals with prison terms and other sanctions, but they also forced them to drop their other work and concentrate on their own defense. More significantly, by criminalizing certain types of political activities, these legal proceedings delegitimized them and placed them beyond the pale of respectability. Once convicted, the defendants in such trials could then be viewed as outlaws by a law-abiding nation that did not have to treat them, their ideas, or activities as worthy of respect. Moreover, as J. Edgar Hoover well knew, political trials not only had the educational value of disseminating scenarios that criminalized dissenters, but they also rendered those individuals vulnerable to additional forms of repression.[34]

Sometimes, as with the Smith Act, the Iowa criminal syndicalism law, and the 1950 McCarran Act, the laws themselves were politically repressive. At other times, presumably neutral regulations, like those against disturbing the peace or disorderly conduct, were used to stamp out threats to the status quo. And, sometimes, the authorities simply manufactured criminal charges to rid their communities of supposed troublemakers. That kind of selective enforcement (and non-enforcement as well) of the law was, of course, most common in the South, where the white power structure used the legal system to keep African Americans in line. But it was also invoked against striking workers, left-wing radicals, and anti-war activists.

Every level of government participated. American federalism, the distribution of power between the states and the national government, is, at least in theory, supposed to protect the rights of ordinary citizens. Such a system, by ensuring against the central government's accumulation of power, would, so the founders hoped, prevent the development of a strong and tyrannical state. Unfortunately, at least with regard to political freedom, that has not been the case. Instead of limiting Washington's ability to crack down on dissent, state and local authorities have often joined the fray. The diffusion of power simply gave the agents of repression more opportunities for practicing their craft. We have only to look at William Sentner's two sedition cases—the first under Iowa's criminal syndicalism law and the second under the federal government's Smith Act—to understand how the existence of multiple jurisdictions intensified the repression he faced.

Nor have the American system's other checks and balances offered much protection to groups and individuals the establishment wanted to suppress. It is hard to think of any moment in the nation's history when judges or juries or state and federal legislators protected the rights of political undesirables from an intolerant public or authoritarian regime.

The judiciary, that institution which supposedly guards our civil liberties, has often shirked its responsibilities—especially during moments of stress. Sometimes its rulings legitimized the violations of individual rights perpetrated by the other branches the government. Sometimes, however, the nation's judges simply ducked the issue altogether, as the Supreme Court did during the Vietnam War when it refused to take up cases of antiwar activists on the grounds that they were "political"

---

[34]   Hoover to Tamm, Ladd, Tolson, 30 October 1947, Smith Act Trials File, no. 1123.

and thus outside its purview.[35] Similarly, during the antebellum period, Southern judges tried not to rule on cases of individual slaves, a strategy that would keep them from interfering with the power of masters and, thus, allow them to cordon off their region's peculiar institution from any broader considerations of justice.[36] But, whether its collaboration was direct or indirect, the American judiciary rarely, if ever, stood up against the forces of political repression.

The record of the legislative branch is equally dispiriting. As the speed and unanimity with which both the House and Senate rushed to pass the Smith Act in the summer of 1940 reveals, when Congress gets caught up in the furor of a crisis, it has all too often enacted some seriously repressive measures. Occasionally, it is true, these measures did meet with resistance. There was, for example, considerable opposition to the 1798 Sedition Act when the partisan nature of the Federalists' move to crack down on their political opponents became too blatant to conceal.[37] Similarly, because the American people were so deeply divided over the country's entry into World War I, both the House and Senate debated at length before passing the 1917 Espionage Act.[38] Usually, however, the invocation of national security, as well as the lawmakers' customary deference to the president, was enough to override most congressional hesitations. Rarely did Congress even debate the issue before authorizing whatever measures were deemed necessary for dealing with the dangers at hand.[39] Recall, for example, the ease with which the Roosevelt administration obtained unanimous congressional approval for its internment of the Japanese Americans during World War II.[40] Or the lopsided 391-1 tally by which the House of Representatives amended the Selective Service Act in 1965 to criminalize the burning of draft cards.[41] Or the near unanimity with which Congress passed the 342-page Patriot Act only a few weeks after 9/11.

Nor were the nation's lawmakers hesitant, if the White House displayed insufficient zeal, to take the initiative themselves. The Smith Act is only one example of a piece of legislation that Congress forced upon a reluctant administration.[42] And, sometimes, as with the 1950 McCarran Act as well as the

---

[35] John F. and Rosemary S. Bannan, *Law, Morality and Vietnam: The Peace Militants and the Courts* (Bloomington: Indiana University Press, 1974), 57, 65, 81, 200.

[36] Mark V. Tushnet, *The American Law of Slavery, 1810-1860: Considerations of Humanity and Interest* (Princeton, NJ: Princeton University Press, 1981), 57-73; Edward L. Ayers, *Vengeance and Justice: Crime and Punishment in the 19th-Century American South* (New York: Oxford University Press, 1984), 135; Michal R. Belknap, *Federal Law and Southern Order: Racial Violence and Constitutional Conflict in the Post-Brown South* (Athens: University of Georgia Press, 1987), 2.

[37] James Morton Smith, *Freedom's Fetters: The Alien and Sedition Laws and American Civil Liberties* (Ithaca, NY: Cornell University Press, 1956), 143.

[38] David M. Rabban, *Free Speech in Its Forgotten Years* (New York and Cambridge: Cambridge University Press, 1997), 249-254.

[39] Paul L. Murphy, *World War I and the Origin of Civil Liberties in the United States* (New York: Norton, 1979), 65-66.

[40] Peter Irons, *Justice at War* (New York: Oxford University Press, 1983), 66-68.

[41] Bannan and Bannan, *Law, Morality and Vietnam*, 40-41.

[42] Jason Epstein, *The Great Conspiracy Trial: An Essay on Law, Liberty and the Constitution* (New York: Random House, 1970), 44-45.

Immigration Act of 1917 with its literacy test and provisions for deporting aliens found to be "advocating or teaching" revolutionary doctrines, Congress overrode a presidential veto. [43]

State legislatures were no more solicitous about preserving freedom than the House and Senate. Because so much of the literature on political repression focuses on the federal government, we often overlook the seamless nature of that repression. After all, William Sentner's first major prosecution came under an Iowa, not a federal, anti-sedition statute; and it would have mattered little to him whether he served time in the Iowa State Penitentiary or a federal prison. By the 1950s, all but six states had some kind of anti-sedition, criminal anarchy, or criminal syndicalism law on the books. Sporadically enforced, they were usually invoked against those men and women whose activities seemed to threaten the status quo—Communists, union organizers, and, in the South, civil rights workers. [44] It was not until McCarthyism abated in the middle of the 1950s that the Supreme Court proscribed state sedition laws on the grounds that the Smith and McCarran Acts gave the federal government a monopoly in the area. [45] There was, it should be noted, an ironic synergy here: the Smith Act had been modeled directly on New York State's criminal anarchy law. [46]

In almost every case, these measures, both state and federal, made it a crime to criticize the government or call for its abolition. Just as the Federalists' Sedition Act of 1798 made it illegal to

> write, print, utter or publish ... any false, scandalous and malicious writing or writings against the government of the United States, or either house of the Congress of the United States, or the President of the United States, with intent to defame the said government, or either house of the said Congress, or the said President, or to bring them, or either of them, into contempt or disrepute. [47]

so, too, the Sedition Act of 1918 criminalized anyone who

> shall wilfully utter, print, write, or publish any disloyal, profane, scurrilous, or abusive language about the form of government of the United States, or the Constitution of the United States, or the military or naval forces of the United States, or the flag ... or the uniform of the Army or Navy of the United States,

---

[43]   William Preston, Jr., *Aliens and Dissenters: Federal Suppression of Radicals, 1903-1933* (Cambridge, MA: Harvard University Press, 1963), 83; William R. Tanner and Robert Griffith, "Legislative Politics and 'McCarthyism': The Internal Security Act of 1950," in Robert Griffith and Athan Theoharis, eds., *The Specter: Original Essays on the Cold War and the Origins of McCarthyism* (New York: Franklin Watts, 1974), 174-189.

[44]   Murphy, *World War I*, 86; Goldstein, *Political Repression*, 142, 203; David Brody, *Labor in Crisis: The Steel Strike of 1919* (Philadelphia and New York: J.B. Lippincott Company, 1965), 164; Belknap, *Federal Law and Southern Order*, 139.

[45]   *Pennsylvania v. Nelson*, 350 U.S. 497 (1956).

[46]   *Gitlow v. New York*, 268 U.S. 652 (1925).

[47]   Http://avalon.law.yale.edu/18th_century/sedact.asp.

or any language intended to bring the form of government ... or the Constitution ... or the military or naval forces ... or the flag ... of the United States into contempt, scorn, contumely, or disrepute.[48]

This kind of language, as well as the prohibitions against teaching and advocating revolutionary doctrines that graced the Smith Act and similar state criminal anarchy and syndicalism laws, raised serious First Amendment issues. But, in almost every case, neither judges nor juries nor politicians quibbled about the Bill of Rights when national security was at stake.

*

Prosecutions under these measures came in waves. Not surprisingly, they flourished during wars and at those moments when large numbers of men and women criticized the government or flocked to movements for social or political change. About a thousand dissenters were convicted under the Espionage and Sedition Acts of 1917 and 1918, while the post-World War I Red Scare produced some three hundred convictions under the various state sedition laws.[49] As left-wing activity and labor organizing picked up by the late 1920s and early 1930s, the powers that be again invoked those laws against political dissenters, although, as Sentner's experiences reveal, not always with success.

Rarely, of course, did juries fail to convict. Because such bodies were considered more solicitous of people's rights than magistrates, the authors of the 1798 Sedition Act had tried to placate its critics by requiring jury trials for the individuals accused of violating it. But the Federalist leanings of the early republic's juries ensured that they invariably convicted the dissenting newspaper editors and politicians who came before them.[50] Those compliant jurors set the pattern for those of later periods. There were few, very few, juries—or judges for that matter—who would acquit political defendants. This was well-known within the legal community. One of the federal attorneys who prosecuted the leaders of the Industrial Workers of the World under the 1917 Espionage Act admitted that "if these cases are presented to the grand jury, indictments will necessarily follow, and, if indictments should be returned, convictions will be secured as a matter of course."[51]

Even so, the authorities did have to go through the motions; and, in the process of constructing cases against dissenters that would stand up on appeal, prosecutors encountered some serious problems. The main one was that they had little evidence that the men and women they sought to convict had actually committed a crime. For

---

[48]   Http://www.gwpda.org/1918/usspy.html.

[49]   Regin Schmidt, *Red Scare: FBI and the Origins of Anticommunism in the United States* (Copenhagen: Museum Tusculanum Press, University of Copenhagen, 2000), 115-116; Goldstein, *Political Repression*, 113; Belknap, *Cold War Political Justice*, 10.

[50]   Smith, *Freedom's Fetters*, 144-145, 422; Michael Kent Curtis, *Free Speech, "The People's Darling Privilege": Struggles for Freedom of Expression in American History* (Durham: Duke University Press, 2000), 80-104.

[51]   Preston, *Aliens and Dissenters*, 122.

all his sectarian fervor, it was clear that William Sentner had never endangered the government of the United States, or even advocated its overthrow. His real offense was the espousal of an unpopular ideology. It was, therefore, quite a challenge for the authorities to turn his type of political dissent into a crime. As was often the case, they solved this problem by relying on conspiracy indictments.

Conspiracy has had a long and unsavory relationship with the suppression of dissent. For years, until the Supreme Court put a stop to the practice in the early nineteenth century, the authorities had treated labor unions as criminal conspiracies.[52] Described by Learned Hand as "the darling of the modern prosecutor's nursery," a conspiracy charge required little evidence. The government had merely to show that the individual defendants had some connection to each other. Then, once the existence of a conspiracy was established, everyone involved would be liable for whatever actions any other one of them had taken, even if they were unaware of what the particular person had done or even if—or especially because—that act, in and of itself, was not a crime.[53] Moreover, the conspiracy's success was irrelevant. As the U.S. attorney who prosecuted Emma Goldman for conspiring to violate the 1917 Conscription Act pointed out,

> in a conspiracy trial, it is not necessary to prove that the object of the conspiracy was accomplished.... It was only necessary to establish that certain overt acts were committed looking to the accomplishment of the object of the conspiracy.[54]

Anything at all could be a conspiracy, especially when the government could find no evidence that someone had committed a crime, as was the case with the Chicago anarchists, accused of fomenting the 1886 Haymarket massacre.[55] Conspiracy charges were the standard accoutrements of the labor wars of the late nineteenth and early twentieth centuries. From the bloody miners' battles in Coeur d'Alene, Idaho, to the Pullman strike of 1894 to the hat makers of Danbury, Connecticut, striking workers and their leaders often found themselves under indictment for conspiracy.[56] Similarly, many of the federal government's high-

---

[52] For a thorough study of the use of conspiracy charges against labor, see Christopher L. Tomlins, *Law, Labor, and Ideology in the Early American Republic* (New York: Cambridge University Press, 1993). See also Karen Orren, *Belated Feudalism: Labor, the Law, and Liberal Development in the United States* (Cambridge and New York: Cambridge University Press, 1991), 107.

[53] Jessica Mitford, *The Trial of Dr. Spock, The Reverend William Sloane Coffin, Jr., Michael Ferber, Mitchell Goodman, and Marcus Raskin* (New York: Vintage, 1970), 61-72; Epstein, *The Great Conspiracy Trial*, 87-93.

[54] Francis G. Caffey to John E. Kinnane (U.S. Attorney), Detroit, 4 August 1917, in *The Emma Goldman Papers: A Microfilm Edition* (Chadwyck-Healey, Inc., 1991), reel 57.

[55] Paul Avrich, *The Haymarket Tragedy* (Princeton, NJ: Princeton University Press, 1984), 272.

[56] J. Anthony Lukas, *Big Trouble: A Murder in a Small Western Town Sets Off a Struggle for the Soul of America* (New York: Simon & Schuster, 1997), 104, 149, 310-311; Goldstein, *Political Repression*, 56.

profile World War I prosecutions also involved conspiracy charges.[57] Perhaps the most notorious of these cases was that against 151 leaders and members of the IWW, arrested and indicted for conspiracy on a wide range of allegations after the government raided their homes and offices to find the evidence on which to base its 1917 prosecution.[58]

It was, therefore, hardly surprising that by the time William Sentner ended up in court the Justice Department was asserting that people who belonged to the Communist Party were, by definition, members of a criminal conspiracy. Though that scenario won convictions throughout the 1950s, by the end of the decade the nation's higher courts had begun to overturn those verdicts and question the evidence that the government produced to get them. Even so, conspiracy was too handy a tool for prosecutors to abjure. Accordingly, as the federal government moved against the antiwar and black power activists in the late 1960s, it turned again to conspiracy indictments. The Black Panthers were particularly vulnerable to such charges. So, too, were the leading opponents of the Vietnam War, although in some of the most high-profile prosecutions, the conspiracy turned out to be rather artificial. It was not, for example, until *after* they were arraigned, that the five "conspirators" in the case against Dr. Benjamin Spock finally met each other. "I don't know," one of their prosecutors admitted, "that I can say exactly the reason why these five" had been selected.[59] There was a similarly serendipitous quality to the conspiracy charges against the so-called Chicago Seven (or Eight if the Black Panther leader Bobby Seale is included), indicted in connection with the demonstrations against the 1968 Democratic Convention. Seale had not been involved in planning those demonstrations and had actually left Chicago before they began. But he was a Black Panther and for the nation's law enforcement agencies that was enough.[60]

The conspiracy that these individuals had supposedly organized was a violation of the federal government's Anti-Riot Act of 1968, the so-called Stokely Carmichael Act, that, in the aftermath of the ghetto uprisings of the 1960s, turned inciting a riot into a federal crime.[61] Until then, local officials had the monopoly on enforcing prohibitions against incitement. And they had used it, mainly to keep radicals and other undesirables off the streets and under control. Notorious individuals were especially vulnerable. Thus, for example, Southern sheriffs and police chiefs responded to the black power oratory of both Stokely Carmichael and Rap Brown, his successor as chair of the Student Nonviolent Coordinating Committee, with

---

[57]   Murphy, *World War I*, 213.

[58]   Preston, *Aliens and Dissenters*, 118-122.

[59]   Bannan and Bannan, *Law, Morality and Vietnam*, 90; Mitford, *The Trial of Dr. Spock*, xii-xiii, 5.

[60]   Epstein, *The Great Conspiracy Trial*, 75-101. See Paul Chevigny, *Cops and Rebels: A Study of Provocation* (New York: Pantheon, 1972) and Murray Kempton, *The Briar Patch: The People of the State of New York v. Lumumba Shakur et al.* (New York: E.P. Dutton, 1973) for detailed discussions of some Black Panther conspiracy cases.

[61]   Epstein, *The Great Conspiracy Trial*, 29-30.

repeated arrests for incitement.[62] The New York City police launched similar charges against Emma Goldman.[63]

Incitement to violence was only one of the many kinds of charges that the establishment used against political dissenters. Southern authorities, both before and after the Civil War, were particularly jittery about threats to the status quo, but, as William Sentner's experiences during the 1930s reveal, strikes, demonstrations, and public meetings could all lead to run-ins with the law. Disturbing the peace, parading without a permit, littering, violating local ordinances, "improper conduct": there were dozens of offenses that radicals or striking workers could be charged with—and were.[64] During the 1919 steel strike, the authorities arrested people on pretexts that included "cursing," "going out of his house before daylight," "laughing at the police," and "smiling at the state police."[65] The selective nature of such arrests makes it clear that they were used to suppress otherwise protected activities. Thus, for example, though the town fathers of Fresno and Spokane arrested every Wobbly who mounted a soapbox in the main commercial districts, they laid not a finger on President Taft, William Jennings Bryan, and the Salvation Army.[66]

As the civil rights movement spread throughout the South, arrests for minor charges proliferated. Even by-standers could find themselves on the wrong side of the law. When an argument ensued after an African American soldier refused to move to the rear of a New Orleans bus in 1943, the driver headed for the nearest police station and had all twenty-four black passengers arrested on charges of "disturbing the peace and reviling the police."[67] Demonstrators were routinely subjected to arrest, usually for parading without a permit. Antiwar activists during the Vietnam conflict faced similar charges. At one protest rally, Boston police picked up demonstrators for "sauntering and loitering in such a way as to engender a breach of the peace and likely to endanger passersby."[68]

Sometimes, the authorities did not even bother with a charge. "Make the raids first and look up the law afterward!" was the advice that the Cook County, Illinois, state attorney gave to the Chicago police in the aftermath of Haymarket.[69] In 1912, when the San Diego police chief arrested IWW agitators by the dozens, he explained, "I am going to charge some with disturbing the peace and others with

---

[62]   Taylor Branch, *At Canaan's Edge: America in the King Years, 1965-68* (New York: Simon & Schuster, 2006), 621, 634.

[63]   Candace Falk, ed., *Emma Goldman: A Documentary History of the American Years*, vol. 2, *Making Speech Free, 1902-1909* (Berkeley: University of California Press, 2005), 478.

[64]   Ayers, *Vengeance and Justice*, 103-104; Robert V. Bruce, *1877: Year of Violence* (1959; repr., Chicago: Quadrangle Books, 1970), 228; Rabban, *Free Speech in Its Forgotten Years*, 81, 110; Epstein, *The Great Conspiracy Trial*, 71; Paul Chevigny, *Police Power: Police Abuses in New York City* (New York: Pantheon, 1969), 129-130.

[65]   Goldstein, *Political Repression*, 153.

[66]   Rabban, *Free Speech in Its Forgotten Years*, 112.

[67]   Adam Fairclough, *Race and Democracy: The Civil Rights Struggle in Louisiana, 1915-1972* (Athens: University of Georgia Press, 1995), 82.

[68]   Michael S. Foley, *Confronting the War Machine: Draft Resistance during the Vietnam War* (Chapel Hill: University of North Carolina Press, 2003), 34.

[69]   Avrich, *Haymarket Tragedy*, 221.

offenses which I shall figure out tomorrow."[70] Similarly, when Emma Goldman wanted to know why she had been picked up by the police at a street meeting in Providence, Rhode Island, in September 1897, she was told, "You were arrested because you are Emma Goldman."[71] When a congressional committee asked Caesar J. Scarvada, the police chief of Flint, Michigan, why he had arrested the members of a Communist-led unemployment demonstration in the early 1930s, the following conversation took place:

> Mr. Scarvada: There was not any charge.
> Mr. Nelson: You just arrested them.
> Mr. Scarvada: That is all.
> Mr. Bachman: Why, you arrest them for disorderly conduct, do you not?
> Mr. Scarvada: Well, possibly that would be a good excuse. There is not any particular law we can act on.[72]

As late as the 1970s, that same vagueness still characterized the authorities' approach to the apprehension of radicals. "There is enough play at the joints of our existing criminal law—enough flexibility," Assistant Attorney General Richard Kleindienst boasted, "so that if we really felt that we had to pick up the leaders of a violent uprising we could. We would find some things to charge them with, and we would be able to hold them that way for a while."[73]

Vagrancy laws were another weapon in the repressive arsenal, used especially during the late nineteenth and early twentieth centuries to keep minorities and dissenters under control. As political scientist Karen Orren noted, these laws, which essentially punished able-bodied people who had no jobs, were unique in that they criminalized a status, not an act.[74] Their main function, therefore, was to coerce men and women into the workforce under unfavorable conditions. Not surprisingly, vagrancy arrests abounded in the post-Civil-War South, where they were used to force former slaves back onto the plantations.[75] White workers were also at risk, especially during periods of labor unrest and unemployment. During the hard times of the 1870s when jobless men rode the rails looking for work, over forty states passed so-called "tramp acts" that stigmatized "all vagrants living without labor or visible means of support, who stroll over the country without lawful occupation."[76] Throughout the late nineteenth and early twentieth century, state and local officials

---

[70]   Goldstein, *Political Repression*, 153, 87.

[71]   Falk, *Emma Goldman*, vol. 1, *Made for America, 1890-1901* (Berkeley: University of California Press, 2003), 303.

[72]   Goldstein, *Political Repression*, 204.

[73]   Ibid., 462.

[74]   Karen Orren, *Belated Feudalism: Labor, the Law, and Liberal Development in the United States* (Cambridge and New York: Cambridge University Press, 1991), 74-75.

[75]   Ayers, *Vengeance and Justice*, 151; David M. Oshinsky, *"Worse Than Slavery": Parchman Farm and the Ordeal of Jim Crow Justice* (New York: Free Press, 1996), 74-77.

[76]   Orren, *Belated Feudalism*, 76; Bruce, *1877*, 20-21.

routinely used vagrancy charges against union organizers, striking workers, and Wobblies.[77]

Besides these crimes of order, the authorities enforced ordinary laws in a politically discriminatory manner. Sometimes these prosecutions could be pretty far-fetched, as, for example, when the officials of Southburg, Connecticut, arrested members of the German American Bund in 1937 under the state's blue laws for clearing out their campsite on a Sunday or when the Colorado authorities cited the leaders of the Western Federation of Miners for desecrating the flag during a 1904 strike because a union leaflet contained a picture of the American flag with political statements on the stripes.[78] African Americans were particularly vulnerable, like the thirty-seven-year-old school teacher arrested on a "lunacy warrant" for trying to enroll at the University of Mississippi on the grounds that "any nigger who tried to enter Ole Miss *must* be crazy."[79] Similarly, minor crimes could receive exorbitant sentences if committed by racial minorities or political dissenters. Mississippi's so-called "Pig Law" of 1876, which targeted the kinds of offenses that the state's politicians believed were prevalent among African Americans, punished the theft of a farm animal or of any property valued at ten dollars or more with sentences of up to five years.[80] And then there was the two-to-five-year prison term imposed on Fred Hampton, the Chicago Black Panther leader, for supposedly stealing seventy-one dollars-worth of ice cream bars for ghetto children.[81] The Panthers, of course, were hassled mercilessly by the law enforcement community, charged with everything from murder to spitting on the sidewalk.[82]

Drug busts were common for sixties radicals of all persuasions.[83] One SNCC field worker in Texas got a thirty-year sentence for passing a joint to an undercover agent, while a white radical in Detroit got nine-and-a-half years for possessing two marijuana cigarettes.[84] Because the military authorities believed that the GI coffee houses run by antiwar activists near army bases were subversive, they encouraged the local police to harass them and their patrons. In a typical incident, local officials in Columbia, South Carolina, charged one coffee house proprietor with running an establishment where "marijuana and other narcotic drugs" were sold as well as

---

[77]   Vernon H. Jensen, *Heritage of Conflict: Labor Relations in the Nonferrous Metals Industry up to 1930* (Ithaca, NY: Cornell University Press, 1950), 139-141; Elizabeth Jameson, *All That Glitters: Class, Conflict, and Community in Cripple Creek* (Urbana and Chicago: University of Illinois Press, 1998), 214.

[78]   Goldstein, *Political Repression*, 72, 258; Lukas, *Big Trouble*, 202; Jensen, *Heritage of Conflict*, 144-145.

[79]   Oshinsky, *"Worse Than Slavery,"* 231.

[80]   Ibid., 40.

[81]   Epstein, *The Great Conspiracy Trial*, 125.

[82]   Chevigny, *Cops and Rebels*, passim.

[83]   James Kirkpatrick Davis, *Assault on the Left: The FBI and the Sixties Antiwar Movement* (Westport, CT: Praeger, 1997), 71.

[84]   Doug Rossinow, *The Politics of Authenticity: Liberalism, Christianity, and the New Left in America* (New York: Columbia University Press, 1998), 176; Epstein, *Great Conspiracy Trial*, 297.

displaying peace placards and obscene posters that corrupted minors.[85] In Killeen, Texas, the police arrested the manager of a Fort Hood coffee house for possession of marijuana after they found two-thousandths of an ounce in his car.[86]

Dissidents also went to prison for what have been called "offense artifacts," crimes like perjury and contempt that were the by-products of politically repressive congressional investigations and judicial injunctions.[87] During the early years of the Cold War, for example, perjury became the indictment of choice, wielded against suspected Communists when officials could find no other grounds for prosecution. Given the CP's proclivity for secrecy and clandestine activities, it was easy to prosecute party members for lying or using false names and forged passports. Contempt citations were equally useful. Though not criminal charges in the usual sense of the term, they did enable the authorities to prosecute political dissenters – and they posed no evidentiary problems. As a result, such cases became the common accoutrement of the anticommunist investigations of the 1940s and 1950s; by the time the inquisition wound down, Congress had cited more than one hundred people for contempt.[88] Political trials also produced contempt citations, especially in cases, like those of the Communist Party's Smith Act defendants and the Chicago Seven, where obstreperous defendants and argumentative attorneys faced obdurate judges.[89]

Injunctions provided still another tool for managing dissent. During the late nineteenth and early twentieth centuries, the judiciary routinely enjoined strikers from picketing, leafleting, or encouraging other workers to walk off the job. Between 1880 and 1930, American judges handed down 4,300 injunctions; by 1925 injunctions were so common that they figured in 25 percent of all strikes.[90] During particularly bitter walkouts, hundreds of strikers and union organizers defied injunctions and were rounded up and incarcerated, sometimes under primitive conditions.[91] Civil rights workers in the South were equally vulnerable to bans against demonstrations and—like the earlier union organizers—were sent to jail when they defied them. Eugene V. Debs and Martin Luther King, Jr., were only the most prominent victims of such judicial proceedings, both, it should be noted, imprisoned after the Supreme Court ruled that the injunctions against their activities were valid.[92]

Immigration proceedings, as the attempt to deport Antonia Sentner indicates, have also been used for repression. Although technically not criminal prosecutions, deportations have served much the same function and, for many years, constituted a

---

[85]   Robert Sherrill, *Military Justice Is to Justice as Military Music Is to Music* (New York: Harper & Row, 1970), 160-162.

[86]   Rossinow, *Politics of Authenticity*, 231-232.

[87]   Otto Kirchheimer, *Political Justice: The Use of Legal Procedure for Political Ends* (Princeton, NJ: Princeton University Press, 1961), 52.

[88]   Carl Beck, *Contempt of Congress* (New Orleans: Hauser Press, 1959), 15.

[89]   Epstein, *The Great Conspiracy Trial*, 269-274;

[90]   William E. Forbath, *Law and the Shaping of the American Labor Movement* (Cambridge, MA: Harvard University Press, 1991), 61.

[91]   Jensen, *Heritage of Conflict*, 32, 282-283,

[92]   Forbath, *Law and the Shaping of the American Labor Movement*, 75-76; Rabban, *Free Speech*, 170; Branch, *At Canaan's Edge*, 621.

major sanction imposed on political dissenters. Throughout American history, foreigners have rarely been liked and have often been viewed as a threat to the nation.[93] Moreover, since the idea that radicalism might stem from domestic inequities challenges some basic American myths, it was tempting to blame social unrest on alien agitators who injected their unhealthy notions into the nation's bloodstream. Woodrow Wilson was hardly alone when he castigated foreigners for "pouring the poison of disloyalty into the very arteries of our national life."[94]

It was, therefore, common for the powers-that-be to turn to immigration measures to maintain control. Even before the Federalists passed the 1798 Sedition Act, they cracked down on the French and Irish immigrants who, they feared, were supporting their political opponents. Not only did they extend the waiting period for naturalization to an unprecedented fourteen years, but they also authorized the deportation of any non-citizens considered "injurious to public peace and safety."[95] Though most of these anti-alien measures lapsed after 1800, efforts to restrict immigration and deport radicals revived during the industrial unrest of the late nineteenth and early twentieth centuries. Little by little, the nation's immigration laws became increasingly intolerant of political dissenters, until by the end of World War I, it became possible to deport foreigners who taught, advocated, or simply joined organizations espousing a revolutionary line.[96]

Because of a still-extant 1893 Supreme Court ruling that deportation is not a criminal punishment and thus not subject to the Constitution's constraints on criminal prosecutions, immigration proceedings are exempt from due process. Non-citizens facing deportation can be held without bail, deprived of a hearing, and subject to treatment that no citizen must endure. This is what happened during the notorious Palmer raids after World War I when thousands of supposedly radical aliens were rounded up, held incommunicado, and deprived of access to attorneys in the hope that they would confess to some kind of deportable offense or affiliation.[97] As the post-9/11 crackdown on Muslims and people from the Middle East and South Asia reveals, such violations of immigrants' rights are hardly a thing of the past.[98]

While the treatment of non-citizens is particularly egregious, political arrests and trials have frequently been characterized by abuses of due process, not to mention the use of informers, perjured witnesses, and illegal evidence. All too often, the authorities have believed themselves above the law when they seek to establish order and squelch dissent. As the state official charged with quelling an 1899 miners' strike in Idaho explained, "Absurd technicalities will not be allowed to stand

---

[93]   The standard work on American xenophobia is John Higham, *Strangers in the Land: Patterns of American Nativism, 1860-1925* (New Brunswick, NJ: Rutgers University Press, 1963; New York: Atheneum, 1981).

[94]   Murphy, *World War I*, 52.

[95]   Smith, *Freedom's Fetters*, 22-62.

[96]   Preston, *Aliens and Dissenters*, 63-87.

[97]   Ibid., 208-237.

[98]   For a good overview of the way in which immigration sanctions have been used to suppress dissent, see David Cole, *Enemy Aliens: Double Standards and Constitutional Freedoms in the War on Terrorism* (New York: New Press, 2003), 88-128.

in the path of justice."[99] Similarly, in supporting the Palmer raids on radical immigrants, the *Washington Post* expressed the commonly held disdain for "hairsplitting over infringement of liberty."[100]

Ultimately, it was exactly those split hairs and "absurd technicalities" that allowed some victims of political repression, like William Sentner, to be exonerated. Time and again, as the furor of the moment ebbed, the injustices that accompanied it declined as well and the nation's avowed respect for individual rights reasserted itself. Even so, we should not celebrate. While dissenters like Sentner may have avoided prison, their prosecutions usually suppressed their political activities. And that was, of course, their function.

---

[99]   Lukas, *Big Trouble*, 147.
[100] Murray, *Red Scare*, 217.

THE INQUISITION IN HOLLYWOOD:
REPRESSION ON/BEHIND THE SCREEN

Melvyn Stokes

Recent years have witnessed a considerable expansion in the number of books analysing how Hollywood has interpreted American history on film.[1] What few of these works bother to note is how small the number of such films actually is in comparison to the movie industry's total output. At its peak in the 1940s, the American film industry was turning out around 250-300 major productions a year.[2] The proportion of those dealing with "history," even in the broadest possible sense of that term (including, for example, "bio-pics" and westerns loosely based on real people and events), was very small. Conceding, moreover, that relatively few films were based on—or offered a view of—history in any meaningful sense, what strikes this historian is that the films that *were* actually produced ignored or structured out certain crucial aspects of the American experience.

Although it led to the creation of the United States as an independent nation, for example, very few films deal with—or are set against—the background of the American Revolution. In spite of its crucial role in American history, there are only a relatively small number of films about the American Civil War, and almost none that were hugely financially successful—apart from *The Birth of a Nation* (1915) and *Gone with the Wind* (1939).[3] With the exception of the same two films, almost

---

[1]   See, for example, Kenneth M. Cameron, *America on Film: Hollywood and American History* (New York: Continuum, 1997); Mark C. Carnes, ed., *Past Imperfect: History According to the Movies* (New York: Henry Holt, 1995); Robert Burgoyne, *Film Nation: Hollywood Looks at U.S. History* (Minneapolis: University of Minnesota Press, 1997); Trevor B. McCrisken and Andrew Pepper, *American History and Contemporary Hollywood Film* (Edinburgh: University of Edinburgh Press, 2005); Steven Mintz and Randy Roberts, eds., *Hollywood's America: United States History through Its Films*, 3rd ed. (New York: Brandywine Press, 2001); Peter C. Rollins, ed., *The Columbia Companion to American History on Film: How the Movies Have Portrayed the American Past* (New York: Columbia University Press, 2003); Peter Rollins, ed., *Hollywood as Historian: America Film in a Cultural Context*, 2nd ed. (Lexington: University Press of Kentucky, 1998); Robert A. Rosenstone, *Revisioning History: Film and the Construction of a New Past* (Princeton, NJ: Princeton University Press, 1995); Robert A. Rosenstone, *Visions of the Past: The Challenge of Film to Our Idea of History* (Cambridge, MA: Harvard University Press, 1995); Robert Brent Toplin, *History by Hollywood: The Use and Abuse of the American Past* (Urbana: University of Illinois Press, 1996).

[2]   The eight big studios released a total of 358 films in 1940, 379 in 1941, 358 in 1942, 289 in 1943, 262 in 1944, 234 in 1945, 252 in 1946, 249 in 1947, 248 in 1948 and 234 in 1949—an average of 286 a year. Thomas Schatz, *Boom and Bust: Hollywood in the 1940s* (New York: Charles Scribner's, 1997), 463.

[3]   See Bruce Chadwick, *The Reel Civil War: Mythmaking in American Film* (New York: Vintage, 2002); Melvyn Stokes, "The Civil War in the Movies," in Susan-Mary Grant and Peter J. Parish, eds., *Legacy of Disunion: The Enduring Significance of the Civil War* (Baton Rouge: Louisiana State University Press, 2003), 65-78.

no mention of the period of Reconstruction after the Civil War has ever made it on to American screens. The absence of movies about the civil rights movement is a glaring omission in the history of modern Hollywood (*Mississippi Burning* [1988] was much criticized for marginalizing the movement itself). Predictably, perhaps, with the exception of *On the Waterfront* (1954), *Blue Collar* (1978), *F.I.S.T.* (1978), *Matewan* (1987) and *Hoffa* (1992), there are few films dealing with the subjects of labour unionism, strikes, or industrial unrest. And, with the exception of *Reds* (1981)—largely made due to the persistence and commitment of Warren Beatty— and one other film that will be discussed shortly, there are almost no films that deal sympathetically with American communists.[4]

Can this extremely spotty coverage of American history be explained in terms of straightforward political repression? There are reasons for doubting it. The American film industry has operated under several apparently restrictive regimes: the National Board of Censorship set up in 1909, Will Hays's "Don'ts and Be Carefuls" of 1927, the Production Code of 1930, and the ratings system established in 1968. In each case, however, the restrictive regime was either welcomed or pioneered by the film industry itself to avoid more serious external scrutiny. The films approved for production and release were, on the whole, the ones the film companies *wanted* to produce. It usually came down in the end to the issue of what film projects were deemed the most likely to be financially profitable. By the late 1930s, for example, Civil War pictures were famous as loss-makers. "Forget it, Louis," Irving Thalberg allegedly advised Louis B. Mayer of M-G-M on one project, "no civil war picture ever made a dime."[5] Sadly for Thalberg and Mayer, the civil war film they passed on was *Gone with the Wind*.

One type of film in which Hollywood has shown continuous (and profitable) interest are movies about Hollywood itself.[6] But this enthusiastic self-reflexivity comes to a virtual full stop when the relations between Hollywood itself and the anti-communist "inquisition" of the late 1940s and early fifties are foregrounded. There are, indeed, only two modern mainstream Hollywood films—*The Way We Were* (1973) and *Guilty by Suspicion* (1991)—that deal with the direct effects of the investigations into the movie industry launched by the House Committee on Un-American Activities (popularly if inaccurately known as HUAC) during that period.[7]

---

4   As mentioned below, there were by contrast large numbers of anti-communist films.

5   Thalberg, quoted in Leslie Halliwell, *Halliwell's Screen Greats* (London: Grafton, 1988), 155.

6   Treatment of Hollywood itself in films has covered the whole spectrum from sentimental idealization, as in *Ella Cinders* (1926) and *Going Hollywood* (1933), through nostalgic reminiscences of the studio era, such as *Singin' in the Rain* (1952) and *The Eddie Cantor Story* (1953), to the sardonic and satirical, including *Sunset Boulevard* (1950) and *The Player* (1992). On this type of self-reflexivity in general, see Rudy Behlmer and Tony Thomas, *Hollywood's Hollywood: The Movies about the Movies* (Secaucus, NJ: Citadel Press, 1975).

7   There are, by contrast, several books on the impact of the HUAC "Inquisition" on Hollywood. See for instance Larry Ceplair and Steven Englund, *The Inquisition in Hollywood: Politics in the Film Community, 1930-1960* (Berkeley: University of California Press, 1983); Bernard F. Dick, *Radical Innocence: A Critical Study of the*

Of course, there have been other feature films that discuss the *impact* of HUAC and Senator Joseph R. McCarthy in general terms. In 1977, *The Front* dealt with the story of a man who allowed his name to be used by a blacklisted writer so that he could carry on working in television in New York. In 1989, *Fellow Traveller*, an Anglo-American production, also dealt with the travails of a blacklisted writer, in this case living in exile in London. *The Majestic*, released in 2001, was (again) about a blacklisted writer who overcomes depression, drunkenness and memory loss to challenge HUAC successfully on First Amendment grounds; a position, as Ernest Giglio notes, "that was never accepted either by Congress or the courts."[8] And *Good Night and Good Luck* (2005) did a reasonable job of looking at the circumstances, personal and institutional, that led broadcaster Edward R. Murrow to speak out against McCarthy and his methods on CBS television (though the film appeared to have *two* targets: not just McCarthy himself but the banality of much of 1950s American commercial television). But *The Way We Were* and *Guilty by Suspicion*, even after over half a century, still remain the only mainstream Hollywood films to look at the impact of the anti-communist inquisition on the film community itself.[9]

In chronological terms, the two films book-ended the serious involvement of HUAC with Hollywood. A relatively short section of *The Way We Were* had Katie Morosky (Barbra Streisand), once famed on campus as a communist activist ("Communist K-K-K-Katie"), joining in the initial attempt to fight HUAC at the start of its first serious investigation into Hollywood in 1947. Katie, married to glamorous but superficial movie screenwriter Hubbell Gardner (Robert Redford), leaves him behind to join the planeload of Hollywood celebrities organized by Philip Dunne and the Committee for the First Amendment that flew into Washington to support those who were about to become the "Hollywood Ten."[10] *Guilty by Suspicion* opens with HUAC taking secret testimony from friendly witnesses in Los Angeles in September 1951 and ends with the climactic scene of the December 1951 hearings in Washington.

Hollywood Ten (Lexington: University Press of Kentucky, 1989); John J. Gladchuk, *Hollywood and Anti-Communism: HUAC and the Evolution of the Red Menace, 1935-1950* (New York: Routledge, 2007); Robert Mayhew, *Ayn Rand and "Song of Russia": Communism and Anti-Communism in 1940s Hollywood* (Lanham, MD: Scarecrow Press, 2005); Victor S. Navasky, *Naming Names* (New York: Viking, 1980).

[8] Ernest Giglio, *Here's Looking at You: Hollywood, Film and Politics*, 2nd ed. (New York: Peter Lang, 2005), 96.

[9] There are, of course, a number of films (especially westerns) which critics have generally believed to offer indirect, metaphorical commentary on HUAC's investigations of Hollywood and the blacklist. These include *High Noon* (1952) and *Johnny Guitar* (1953).

[10] The "Hollywood Ten" were the first ten "unfriendly witnesses," all communists or former communists, who were subpoened to appear before HUAC in October 1947. Most were screenwriters (Alvah Bessie, Lester Cole, Ring Lardner, Jr., John Howard Lawson, Albert Maltz, Samuel Ornitz, Adrian Scott, and Dalton Trumbo), though Scott also worked as a producer. Herbert Biberman and Edward Dmytryk were both directors. All ten defied HUAC, were cited for "contempt of Congress," and eventually served terms in jail.

There are, of course, reasons why the American film industry would shy away
from making many films about HUAC and Hollywood. Many studio heads,
including Jack Warner and Walt Disney, supported the Committee's efforts.[11]
Hollywood's institutional collaboration with the anti-communist crusade led it to
produce a major cycle of anti-red films, including *The Red Menace* (1949), *I
Married a Communist* (1950), *I Was a Communist for the F.B.I.* (1951), *Big Jim
McClain* (1952), *My Son John* (1952) and *Pickup on South Street* (1953).[12] Members
of the Motion Picture Alliance for the preservation of American Ideals, led by its
president John Wayne (the star of *Big Jim McClain*), egged the committee on.[13]
Major stars, including Gary Cooper and Adolph Menjou, had acted as "friendly
witnesses" and named names before the Committee. Unions, including the Screen
Actors Guild, introduced a loyalty oath.[14] Hollywood would have many reasons, in
later years, to feel embarrassed by its relationship with HUAC. One symptom of that
embarrassment was the refusal, until very recently, to acknowledge the wrong done
to blacklisted directors and writers by restoring screen credits for their work done
under pseudonyms or "fronts."[15]

Given Hollywood's patent embarrassment, it may come as no surprise that the
idea for what became *Guilty by Suspicion* originated from someone outside the
American film industry: French film director Bertrand Tavernier. Tavernier's first
idea was to make a movie about blacklistees such as Joseph Losey, Jules Dassin and
Jack Berry, who had chosen the path of exile in Europe. Tavernier brought together
writer-director Abraham Polonsky, himself once on the blacklist, with veteran
producer Irwin Winkler.[16] Polonsky produced the first draft of a screenplay which
opened with a scene at the HUAC hearings. Both Winkler and Tavernier felt this
scene ought to be the climax of the film instead of the beginning. Polonsky decided
that in that case, as he expressed it, "it's no longer a survival-in-Europe story. It
should be a picture about Hollywood. And if it's a picture about Hollywood, it will
have to be a picture about the political controversy."[17] Subsequently, Tavernier
dropped out of the project and Winkler signed on to direct the movie. He also began

---

[11]   See Ceplair and Englund, *The Inquisition in Hollywood*, 157-58, 193, 210, 213, 258-
       259, 279-80, 281, 287, 299; Brian Neve, *Film and Politics in America: A Social
       Tradition* (London: Routledge, 1992), 108; Marc Eliot, *Walt Disney: Hollywood's Dark
       Prince* (London: Deutsch, 1994), passim.

[12]   Nicole Potter, "Tales of the Red Menace," *Films in Review* 47.9-10 (September 1996):
       33. Also see Dan Leab, "I Was a Communist for the FBI," *History Today* 46.12
       (December 1996): 42-47. James Naremore terms these films "anticommunist noir" and
       notes that they were "neither artistically nor commercially successful," although *I Was a
       Communist for the F.B.I.* spun off into a syndicated television series called *I Led Three
       Lives*. James Naremore, *More Than Night: Film Noir in Its Contexts* (Berkeley:
       University of California Press, 1998), 295 n. 29.

[13]   Potter, "Tales of the Red Menace," 30-31.

[14]   Giglio, *Here's Looking at You*, 104, 110; Ian Hamilton, *Writers in Hollywood, 1915-
       1951* (London: Heinemann, 1990), 285, 287; Potter, "Tales of the Red Menace," 31.

[15]   Giglio, *Here's Looking at You*, 100.

[16]   Victor Navasky, "Has 'Guilty by Suspicion' Missed the Point?" *New York Times*, 31
       March 1991, 9.

[17]   Ibid., 16.

to re-write the screenplay. The most crucial change involved changing the story's protagonist, David Merrill, from the communist he had been in Polonsky's original screenplay into a non-political naif who had attended a few Communist Party meetings in the thirties and had finally been thrown out for "arguing too much."

The film in its final form begins with the grilling of screenwriter Larry Nolan (Chris Cooper) by HUAC in secret session in Los Angeles. Nolan says to HUAC what actor Larry Parks really said, in almost exactly the same words: "I beg of you, please don't make me do this. Don't make me crawl through the mud. You *know* who they are. They're my friends."[18] That same evening, David Merrill (Robert De Niro), a film director, returns from France where he has been doing the groundwork for a film. In his absence, Merrill has been named as someone who had formerly attended Communist Party meetings. Darryl F. Zanuck (Ben Piazza), head of Twentieth-Century Fox, insists that he has to appear before the committee and clear himself before he can resume work on his film. When it is explained to Merrill by the lawyer to whom Zanuck sent him—ironically played by sometime blacklistee Sam Wanamaker—that he will have to "name names," he refuses.[19] The rest of the film is dominated by the choice between living up to his conscience or working at the job he adores. Merrill is barred from the studio lot, and finds it hard to hold down the most menial job even after moving to New York. But—when he does finally agree to testify—he changes his mind and defies the committee in words very similar to those by Army Counsel Joseph Welch in his denunciation of McCarthy during the Army-McCarthy hearings of 1954.[20]

In historical terms, *Guilty by Suspicion* got a lot right. As Larry Nolan says, the committee already knew who most of the communists in Hollywood were. Witnesses were asked to "purge" themselves by undergoing a ritual humiliation and providing the names of friends and colleagues. As Jeanne Hall notes, this transformed HUAC's supposed "investigations" into what Edward Herman and Noam Chomsky have termed "'flak'—actions meant to be punitive and threatening rather than fact-finding or truth-seeking."[21] The film also worked hard to show the reality of life on the "graylist," which was made up of men and women who had supported the Hollywood Ten or worked for liberal causes and were consequently victims of "guilt by association" (or, as the title of the film has it, "guilty by

---

[18] See Navasky, *Naming Names*, ix. Nolan is based on a combination of Parks and screenwriter Richard Collins, the husband of Dorothy Comingore. Nolan's naming of his wife, Dorothy, as a communist and his accusations that she was an alcoholic and an unfit mother to some extent echoed Collins' treatment of Comingore.

[19] The lawyer Felix Graff (Wanamaker) was based on a real lawyer, Martin Gang, who specialised in "clearing" individuals for the studios. Other victims of the blacklist associated with the film in addition to Wanamaker and Polonsky were Ileana Douglas, playing Zanuck's assistant (her grandparents were blacklisted) and Joan Scott, who appeared as a teacher (Scott was the widow of producer Adrian Scott, one of the original Hollywood Ten). Jeanne Hall, "The Benefits of Hindsight: Re-Visions of HUAC and the Film and Television Industries in *The Front* and *Guilty by Suspicion*," *Film Quarterly* 54.2 (2001): 18.

[20] Giglio, *Here's Looking at You*, 95.

[21] Hall, "The Benefits of Hindsight," 16.

suspicion"). The FBI surveillance of many graylistees is shown in the film (though not the extensive phone-tapping that took place). FBI men note down the registration numbers of the cars at the party given to welcome Merrill back from France and carry on harassing him in New York. He becomes so paranoid he thinks he is being followed by a stranger on Christmas Eve. Of course, as someone once said, just because you are paranoid does not mean that they are not out to get you. Merrill's final (unsuccessful) strategy before the committee is realistic: like Lillian Hellman, he tries to talk about his own actions but not those of others (the so-called "diminished Fifth"). Finally, HUAC's persecution of Merrill even though he is not and never has been a communist underlines the fact that the accusers and clearance committees *did* get things wrong: John Henry Faulk of CBS successfully sued the anti-communist organization *Aware* for wrongly suggesting that he had been a communist.[22]

At the same time, the fact that Merrill is not a communist is a major weakness of the film.[23] This plot change caused Polonsky to remove his own name from the movie's credits. It makes little sense in historical terms: Merrill had almost nothing to "purge." Someone like him would never have been subpoened by HUAC: he would have submitted a studio-drafted letter of apology to the committee, and that would have been that. Yet Winkler was convinced, as he declared in an interview, that if the movie was "about a communist, the end result would be perceived as a defense of Communism."[24] Winkler had a point: the immediate context of his film's production was the collapse of the communist regimes in Eastern Europe and the massacring of pro-democracy protestors in Tiananmen Square by an arthritic communist leadership intent on clinging to power in China. In 1991, the year of the film's release, the Soviet Union finally collapsed. At the beginning of the 1990s, seeing communism either as a threat or as a faith that had once appealed to many thousands of Americans had become quite literally incredible. On the other hand, as Victor Navasky observed, Winkler's decision not to focus on a communist also emphasised the result of seventy years of cultural and political repression: a deeply ingrained hostility to communism that demonstrated just "how far ... [Hollywood] and the political culture at large still have to go."[25]

Winkler's decision transformed *Guilty by Suspicion* into what was in effect a melodrama: the fall and (at least in terms of character) rise of David Merrill. In the entire film, there is only one avowed communist: director Joe Lesser, played in a cameo role by Martin Scorsese. In his only scene, Lesser arrives with a suitcase to see Merrill and two other directors at a secret 4 a.m. meeting. Lesser explains that he is one jump ahead of a subpoena and is leaving that night for London. Although based on the actual flight to Europe of Joseph Losey—the "film" Lesser is directing that he asks Merrill to finish for him is Losey's *The Boy with Green Hair* (1948)—

---

22   Faulk's story was recounted in the made-for-television film *Fear on Trial*, first broadcast by CBS in 1975.

23   Nicole Potter remarks of *Guilty by Suspicion* that "almost everybody seems to have been compromised by attending one meeting with a friend in the '30s." Potter, "Tales of the Red Menace," 32.

24   Polonsky quoted in Navasky, "Has 'Guilty by Suspicion' Missed the Point?" 16.

25   Ibid., 16.

this brief sequence gives little understanding of the difficulty and trauma that often accompanied expatriation. In actual fact, Losey's last memory of his homeland was hiding in a darkened house to avoid being served with his subpoena.[26]

Having Merrill as a non-communist and Lesser run away, the film consciously forecloses any possibility of covering the communist fight-back against HUAC. There can be no reference, for example, to the efforts of Herbert Biberman and the Blacklist Company to produce their own films, even if that initiative ended with the failure of *Salt of the Earth* (1954).[27] So far as Merrill is concerned, rather than the personal becoming the political, the political becomes the personal. "In the end," remarks Jeanne Hall, "David defies the Committee for a number of very personal reasons: it has kept him from working, injured his friends, frightened his son, implicated his wife, and generally pissed him off."[28]

The triviality (in historical terms) of Merrill's reasons for decisively opposing the committee—in the full knowledge that this will mean blacklisting and possible imprisonment—points up other weaknesses in the film's approach. The fact that Merrill is unaware of the activities and threat of HUAC when he returns from a two-month trip to France in 1951 is frankly unbelievable. As Dalton Trumbo later pointed out, the only innocents—in the sense of knowledge—were the original Hollywood Ten, including Trumbo himself. After 1947, everyone in Hollywood knew what the consequences of the Committee's actions would be. "All the people who took the First and Fifth Amendments after us," Trumbo declared, "knew something we had not known, namely, that they would not work for years. ... We didn't know how hot the water was."[29]

Another curious impression left by the film came from the fact that, when it begins, David Merrill and his wife are divorced and living apart. When the film ends, the couple are together, having been reunited in opposition to HUAC. The notion of HUAC as a catalyst for marital reconciliation is, to put it mildly, eccentric. As Jeanne Hall comments, "the blacklist was known for breaking up families, not bringing them back together."[30] The representation of the role of informers in the film is also rather limited and unconvincing. Larry Nolan is shown as caving in completely to the committee, not only giving them the names of his friends (including Merrill) but also his wife's name. "Bunny" Baxter (George Wendt) is a nice guy driven, in desperation, to ask his best friend Merrill if he can name him to the committee (on the grounds that Merrill is "already dead").[31] In the end, both

---

[26] Hall, "The Benefits of Hindsight," 25.

[27] For the story of the making and suppression of *Salt of the Earth*, a film produced by blacklistees and dealing with a strike of Mexican-American miners in New Mexico in 1951-1952, see Herbert Biberman, *Salt of the Earth: The Story of a Film* (Boston: Beacon Press, 1965) and James J. Lorence, *The Suppression of "Salt of the Earth": How Hollywood, Big Labor and Politicians Blacklisted a Movie in Cold War America* (Albuquerque: University of New Mexico Press, 1999).

[28] Hall, "The Benefits of Hindsight," 21.

[29] Trumbo, as quoted in Navasky, *Naming Names*, 393.

[30] Hall, "The Benefits of Hindsight," 26.

[31] This sequence, drawn from the original Polonsky script, was based on an incident in which David Raksin, who had written the score for Polonsky's *Force of Evil* (1948),

Baxter and Merrill defy the committee, but it seems apparent that in both cases this means reneging on earlier commitments to name names. The film creates the impression that informing was something done only by the weaker members of the film community in response to great pressure from HUAC. It ignores the actions of "friendly witnesses" who were ready, even eager, to name names within their own social circles.

What *Guilty by Suspicion* does not do, moreover, is to present the confrontation between HUAC and Hollywood in anything other than the simplest black and white terms. It offers what is in essence a broadly liberal perspective on the "inquisition" of the early 1950s. Yet the view of Hollywood and HUAC it puts across is doubly inadequate in terms of history. Not only is much of the context of the early fifties missing, but also the longer historical backcloth to the events of 1951-1952. We are not really informed of the fact that, in 1951 and 1952, anti-communism was a mainstream phenomenon with much institutional support. In fact, it is possible to regard the repression of the period as supported by a democratic consensus. Moreover, most scholars have interpreted the Hollywood inquisition as a stage in the repressive history of HUAC. But there may also be a case for perceiving HUAC itself as only a stage in the repressive history of Hollywood.

Political repression itself has tended to follow a different pathway in the United States to that in Europe. In many European countries between 1815 and 1914, as Robert J. Goldstein has argued, political repression was continuous enough—and strong enough—to destroy opposition groups or else drive them underground for many years. Such repression was based on suffrage restrictions, the systematic denial of civil liberties (freedom of press and speech, academic freedom, the right to assemble and form associations) and, ultimately, the use of violence and/or secret police techniques against reformers and dissidents.[32] In America, while the subordination of certain groups (African Americans, Native Americans, Asian Americans, Hispanics and women) was deep-seated and long-lived, continuous, institutionalised *political* repression of the European type was traditionally absent. "Political repression," Goldstein explains in his classic work on *Political Repression in Modern America*, "consists of government action which grossly discriminates against persons or organizations viewed as presenting a fundamental challenge to existing power relationships or key government policies, because of their perceived political beliefs."[33] It was only rarely that the ruling American elite decided that its self-interest was being seriously threatened and, giving up for a time its normally successful (supposedly) "pluralist" strategy, embraced repression and, often, an accompanying political hysteria as a means of protecting its power and status. Whereas repression and the constant struggle against it formed part of the European

---

asked the writer/director if he could name him before HUAC since Polonsky himself had already been blacklisted. Navasky, "Has 'Guilty by Suspicion' Missed the Point?" 16.

[32]   Robert J. Goldstein, *Political Repression in 19ᵗʰ Century Europe* (London: Croom Helm, 1983), xii-xiii, xv.

[33]   Robert J. Goldstein, *Political Repression in Modern America: 1870 to the Present* (Cambridge, MA: Schenkman, 1978), xvi.

process of modernization, therefore, American repression was on the whole considerably more episodic.[34]

Popular hysteria and repression have traditionally gone hand in hand in American history. According to Murray Levin, several elements have contributed to this pairing. Quite consciously, elites have from time to time deliberately fostered the idea that a conspiracy exists to undermine the American way of life. While they *may* sincerely believe this, it is also the case that alleging the existence of a conspiracy also has certain very tangible benefits. Among these, Levin observes, have been:

> strike-breaking, stereotyping opposition leaders as alien and radical, the justification of military expenditures and additional personnel for law enforcement agencies, expanding newspaper circulation, profits and fees for superpatriotic societies and speakers, and ... the creation of scapegoats so that failure of the economy and policy will be neither traced to the party in power nor to dominant American values.[35]

Levin identifies three situations that have encouraged American elites to abandon the normal techniques for exercising power and to engage in repression: firstly, the sudden, dramatic decline of a formerly dominant party (such as the Federalists facing the rising strength of Jeffersonianism in the late 1790s); secondly, in more modern times, the rising strength of organized labor (causing U.S. Steel and other business corporations to throw their support behind the "Red Scare" of 1919-1920); thirdly, the temptation facing political leaders (including A. Mitchell Palmer and Joseph McCarthy) to build a future power base by helping to create an anti-radical hysteria.[36]

Contrived leadership by an elite is only part of the explanation for the Federalist pursuit of sedition in the 1790s or the "Red Scares" of 1919-1920 and 1947-1954 (or, for that matter, the "national security" scare following 9/11). Historians such as Richard Hofstadter and David Brion Davis long ago drew attention to the tendency of ordinary Americans from time to time to become obsessed with the idea of a conspiratorial threat to the whole American way of life.[37] Political hysteria as a mode of repression is something manufactured by elites, but it could not succeed without mass popular acquiescence and approval. The roots of this popular acceptance may be found deep in the soil of American culture and, to an extent, also in the American psyche (Levin suggests that "the evil conspirator on the

---

34   See Murray Levin, *Political Hysteria in America: The Democratic Capacity for Repression* (New York: Basic Books, 1973), 4-5, 7; Goldstein, *Political Repression in 19th Century Europe*, xii.

35   Levin, *Political Hysteria in America*, 4-5, 6-7 (quotation from 6).

36   Ibid., 5.

37   Richard Hofstadter, *The Paranoid Style in American Politics, and Other Essays* (New York: Knopf, 1965); David Brion Davis, *The Fear of Conspiracy: Images of Un-American Subversion from the Revolution to the Present* (Ithaca, NY: Cornell University Press, 1971).

march" in reality reflected "the hated and feared secret self, finally out of control.")[38]

The difficulty with the linkage established between political repression, conspiracy and popular hysteria by scholars such as Levin is that it relies on an interpretation of history in which politicians in their own interest manufacture national panics without any real cause and many Americans, for reasons of their own, support crusades against spectral enemies. Yet there have also been organized groups in American society who—sometimes long in advance of politicians—have led campaigns to repress subversion and sedition. Some of these have been organisations in the public domain. Frank Donner, for example, has documented the history of police repression in American cities, from the "red squads" established to fight subversives in the Gilded Age to their modern equivalents in the late twentieth century.[39] Others have been private groups and organisations. Prominent among such groups were the bosses of the Hollywood studio system.

The conventional view of the events of 1947 and 1951-1952 in Hollywood suggests that, in Terry Christensen's words, "[t]he HUAC investigations provided an opportunity for pipsqueak politicians to bring mighty Hollywood to its knees." The movie industry "caved in, turned itself inside out, surrendered its workers to the committee's witch-hunters, and denied employment to talented people because of alleged past associations with communism."[40] Seen in this way, HUAC's interventions in Hollywood were straightforward examples of political repression by forces external to Hollywood itself. Research by Dorothy B. Jones seemed to confirm the success of HUAC's actions in terms of film content: the number of socially-conscious films produced by Hollywood declined by two-thirds between 1947 and 1954.[41] Yet this is to ignore Hollywood's troubled history of labor relations long before HUAC came on the scene.

The early days of the film industry on the West Coast had witnessed sometimes bitter struggles between the film companies and their employees. Attempts by the American Federation of Labor to unionize the studio construction crafts had led to three strikes in the period 1916-1921. Indeed, as Murray Ross argued, the formation in 1922 of the Motion Picture Producers' and Distributors' of America ("an open-shop organization of seventeen studios") was very largely an attempt to create "a unified labor policy among Hollywood's major film producers." In 1926, nine major film studios and five unions reached the Studio Basic Agreement; the first example of union recognition in Hollywood. Yet a combination of technical changes and, after 1929, economic depression worsened labor relations within the film industry.

[38]   Levin, *Political Hysteria in America*, 6 and 9 (quotations from 6).
[39]   Frank Donner, *Protectors of Privilege: Red Squads and Political Repression in Urban America* (Berkeley and Los Angeles: University of California Press, 1990).
[40]   Terry Christensen, *Reel Politics: American Political Movies from "Birth of a Nation" to "Platoon"* (New York: Blackwell, 1987), 87.
[41]   Jones found that what she termed "social theme movies" (defined as films with "social and psychological themes") declined from 28 percent of Hollywood's output in the second half of 1947 to 9.2 percent in 1954. Dorothy B. Jones, "Communism and the Movies: A Study of Film Content," in John Cogley, *Report on Blacklisting I: Movies* (New York: Fund for the Republic, 1956), 219, 221.

Technical changes created new occupations that were fought over by competing unions: a 1933 struggle over who should represent soundmen between the International Brotherhood of Electrical Workers and the International Alliance of Theatrical Stage Employees (IATSE) led to the comprehensive defeat of the latter. The depression led screenwriters, actors, and directors to fight for the recognition of unions of their own, organized in imitation of medieval guilds.[42]

Against a background of endemically poor industrial relations, studio bosses sought—sometimes with the help of organised crime—to control their unruly workforce. It was during this period that they adopted the strategy of labeling those who opposed them as "un-American" or "communists." Another tactic that first appeared in this period was the blacklist: labor organizer Irv Hentschel, who helped found the IA Progressives within IATSE in 1937, lost his job as a consequence of his union activities. He soon discovered that no-one else would hire him: his name had been placed on an invisible blacklist.[43] Both blacklist and anti-communism, therefore, were long-established tactics used to discipline the studio workforce and keep it tractable even before HUAC appeared on the scene.[44]

The years during World War II were essentially peaceful ones on the labor front. Labor unions remained committed to their "no strike" pledge (which was also supported by the American Communist Party). Yet immediately after the end of the war in Europe, a major dispute over who had jurisdiction over set decorators broke out between the revived IATSE and a new combination of craft unions, the Conference of Studio Unions (CSU). After an initial eight-month strike, the dispute rumbled on into 1946. Eventually, the CSU became victim of the studios' determination to break the influence of militant labor unions in Hollywood. In September 1946, studios locked out the carpenters, bought off the mob-dominated IATSE with a lucrative wage offer, and set out to break down the CSU through a combination of violence on the picket lines and mass arrests. By early 1947, the union was effectively destroyed.[45]

This conflict (which helped shape the Labor Management Act of 1947, better known as the Taft-Hartley Act, with its anti-union—and anti-communist— provisions),[46] also formed the immediate context for HUAC's investigation of Hollywood. It was no accident that those primarily targeted by HUAC were deeply involved in union and other off-screen activities. The studio bosses found an ally in HUAC, which helped destroy union militants through the same tactic as Hollywood: identifying them as communists. In November 1947, at their meeting at the Waldorf Hotel in New York, they also used the excuse of HUAC to give their pre-existing blacklist policy far wider application. Far from the usual image of HUAC repressing

---

[42]   Murray Ross, "Labor Relations in Hollywood," *Annals of the American Academy of Political and Social Science* 254, *The Motion Picture Industry* (November 1947): 58-62.

[43]   See Mike Nielsen and Gene Mailes, *Hollywood's Other Blacklist: Union Struggles in the Studio System* (London: BFI, 1995), 29-38.

[44]   Giglio, *Here's Looking at You*, 103.

[45]   Ross, "Labor Relations in Hollywood," 63-64: Gerald Horne, *Class Struggle in Hollywood, 1930-1950: Moguls, Mobsters, Stars, Reds, and Trade Unionists* (Austin: University of Texas Press, 2001), 3-4, 14-20, 153-222.

[46]   Horne, *Class Struggle in Hollywood*, 222.

the Hollywood community, it was acting in many ways as an instrument of one section of that community—the studio elite—in its own campaign to repress union militancy.

CLEAR AND PRESENT DANGER?
WHITE RACISTS AND THE RIGHT TO FREEDOM OF SPEECH[1]

Clive Webb

It lasted only a minute, but elicited a more impassioned public reaction than any other political broadcast aired in the South during the early 1970s. During the first days of August 1972, television and radio audiences across Georgia witnessed the sight of a man in dark suit and bow tie sitting at a desk with a large Confederate battle flag hanging behind him and a smaller version folded in the front pocket of his jacket. The heavy-lidded eyes that stared intently into the camera lens lent him a reptilian appearance and his heavily-accented voice was slow and deliberate. "I am J.B. Stoner," he announced. "I am the only candidate for U.S. Senator who is for the white people. I am the only candidate who is against integration. All of the other candidates are race mixers to one degree or another." Stoner identified the policies of moderate incumbent, Senator David H. Gambrell, as a particular threat to the racial purity of white voters. Then the aspirant for public office uttered the words that precipitated a political shockwave. "The main reason why niggers want integration is because the niggers want our white women. I am for law and order with the knowledge that you cannot have law and order and niggers too. Vote white."[2]

The commercial was the centerpiece of a radically racist campaign by Stoner, a man described by one scholar as "the patriarch of the White supremacist movement."[3] His manifesto pledged that if elected he would "STOP RACE MIXING INSANITY" through a series of measures including cutting off funds for busing and other federal initiatives to facilitate school desegregation, restricting the access of "lazy drunken Blacks" to public housing and welfare, campaigning for the repeal of civil rights legislation, and securing a federal law for the forcible repatriation of blacks to Africa.[4]

Stoner's campaign commercial posed liberals with an ethical dilemma. In order to protect the constitutional rights of all citizens, was it appropriate to defend the

---

[1]   I am very grateful to the following scholars for their helpful critical advice on this article: Mark K. Bauman, Robert J. Cook, Richard Follett, David J. Garrow, Kathleen Kendall, Kevin M. Kruse, Samuel Walker, and Stephen J. Whitfield.

[2]   *Atlanta Constitution*, 3 August 1972. A copy of the advertisement is available from the Julian P. Kanter Political Commercial Archive, Political Communications Center, University of Oklahoma, ID 45086.

[3]   Arthur E. Gerringer, *Terrorism: From One Millenium to the Next* (Lincoln, NE: Writers Club Press, 2002), 222.

[4]   "VOTE FOR the White People's Candidate J.B. Stoner the White Racist for United States Senator from Georgia STOP RACE MIXING INSANITY," campaign pamphlet, folder 15, box 29, Oscar Cohen Papers, Manuscript Collection No. 294, American Jewish Archives, Cincinnati, Ohio; "Stop Busing: Vote for J.B. Stoner for U.S. Senator," campaign pamphlet, American Jewish Committee Anti-Semitic and Extremist Collection, Jacob and Hilda Blaustein Human Relations Library, New York (hereafter cited as AJC Collection).

freedom of speech of every individual, even those who used that right to preach hatred and intolerance? Some concluded that it was. No matter how abhorrent the statements made by Stoner, in their opinion, he had as much right as any other citizen to freedom of speech under the First Amendment. The American Civil Liberties Union (ACLU), whose libertarian philosophy had led it to defend the constitutional rights of white racists throughout the civil rights struggle, issued a statement supporting Stoner's right to unrestricted freedom of speech.[5]

However, other civil rights activists reacted with indignation to the race-baiting language used in the commercial. Access to television and radio was of crucial strategic importance to an extremist candidate like Stoner. In contrast to mainstream political and civic leaders, he possessed limited resources and relied on the publicity provided by media coverage to reach out to the electorate. Civil rights organizations understood that restricting his access to the airwaves therefore promised to curtail his campaign. Accordingly, black and Jewish civil rights activists launched a collective campaign to silence Stoner. The National Association for the Advancement of Colored People (NAACP) and the Anti-Defamation League of B'nai B'rith (ADL) filed a joint complaint with the Federal Communications Commission (FCC). According to the signatories, Stoner's public address was not only offensive, but also intended to incite violence against African Americans. In the interests of public decency and safety, the FCC should therefore prohibit further broadcast.

Pressure on the FCC mounted as other civil rights groups added their voices to the chorus of protest against the commercial. The Georgia Council on Human Relations and the Atlanta Community Coalition on Broadcasting both issued statements in support of the petition. Hopes were high that the FCC would ban Stoner from the airwaves.[6]

This essay assesses the causes and impact of the protests against the Stoner campaign commercial. The repression of constitutional rights and liberties in the United States has historically served as a means by which conservative elites suppressed any challenge to their hegemony. The curtailment of free speech as a means to silence the dissenting voices of those seeking social and political change occurred consistently from the Alien and Sedition Acts of 1798, through the repressive policies of the plantation elite in the antebellum South, to the Palmer raids on the radical left following World War I. Traditionally, it is the politically less powerful who campaign for greater freedom of speech as a means to gaining equality. This essay nonetheless shows how, in the wake of the civil rights revolution, racial and ethnic minorities themselves attempted to use the power of the state to silence their political opponents.

The attempt to ban further broadcasts represented a dramatic shift in the policy of some civil rights groups on the constitutional rights of white racists to freedom of speech and assembly. At the height of the black freedom struggle, civil rights organizations had for a number of ideological and strategic reasons refrained from

---

[5]   *Atlanta Constitution*, 4 August 1972.
[6]   *Atlanta Journal*, 4 August 1972; *Charleston* (West Virginia) *Gazette*, 4 August 1972; *Billings* (Montana) *Gazette*, 3 August 1972.

legally campaigning for restrictions on hate speech. Black and Jewish activists certainly spoke out in strong condemnation of hate speech and hate symbols such as burning crosses and the Confederate battle flag.[7] There was, however, an important distinction between mobilizing public opposition to the words and actions of white racists and using the power of law to prohibit them. While the moral case was clear, legally and politically the situation was more complex. For a number of strategic reasons outlined below, civil rights groups had refrained from attempting to prohibit racist propaganda. In the autumn of 1972, black and Jewish activists abandoned their earlier circumspection and became embroiled in a very public controversy over the constitutional rights of hate speakers. The petition filed by the ADL and NAACP revealed a reversal of policy and philosophy, and espousal of the conviction that unrestricted civil liberties constituted a potential threat to civil rights.

*

Jesse Benjamin Stoner, Jr. had established a reputation as one of the most notorious anti-Semites and racists in the United States long before the public outcry created by his 1972 senatorial campaign. He was born on 13 April 1924, into a wealthy family in Walker County in northwestern Georgia. Stoner's childhood was marred by tragedy. At the age of only two-and-a-half, he suffered an attack of polio that crippled one of his legs. Shortly thereafter, his father died. These setbacks did not inhibit his ambition and he enthusiastically pursued a career in law, gaining admittance to the Georgia bar in 1951.[8]

By that time, Stoner had already embarked on a parallel career as a representative of the far right. In 1942, the eighteen-year-old Stoner became a member of the Association of Georgia Klans. From the outset, Stoner stood out even among his peers within the white supremacist movement for the rabidity of his racial and religious prejudices. During the 1930s and 1940s, white southern newspaper editors and political leaders saw no contradiction in denigrating Nazi racial ideology while defending Jim Crow. Stoner, by contrast, was a self-confessed fascist who considered the racial systems of Nazi Germany and the American South to be branches from the same tree.[9] His admiration for Hitler stemmed from a fanatical

---

[7]   See, for instance, Robert J. Cook, *Troubled Commemoration: The American Civil War Centennial, 1961-1965* (Baton Rouge: Louisiana State University Press, 2007), 167.

[8]   *White Extremist Organizations, Part II: National States Rights Party* (unpublished monograph, May 1970), 5, National States Rights Party, Federal Bureau of Investigation File, Federal Bureau of Investigation Electronic Reading Room, at http://foia.fbi.gov/national_states_rights_party/national_states_rights_party_part01.pdf, accessed on 13 March 2008; John George and Laird Wilcox, *American Extremists: Militias, Supremacists, Klansmen, Communists, & Others* (Amherst, NY: Prometheus Books, 1996), 354.

[9]   For further insight into the hypocritical attitude of southern segregationists toward Nazism, see Johnpeter Horst Grill and Robert L. Jenkins, "The Nazis and the American South in the 1930s: A Mirror Image?" *Journal of Southern History* 58 (November 1992): 667-694.

anti-Semitism. Stoner was at odds with most southern segregationists in having a greater animus toward Jews than African Americans. The authors of one study of political fanaticism go so far as to suggest that he was "Perhaps the most outspoken and obsessive anti-Semite in American history."[10] Convinced that Communist Jews had duped the United States into fighting on the wrong side in World War II, Stoner filed a petition with the U.S. House of Representatives, urging its members to approve a resolution that "Jews are the children of the devil" and should be expelled from the country. In 1945, he also established an independent organization, the Stoner Anti-Jewish Party.[11]

Stoner's political activities assumed a new intensity in reaction to the United States Supreme Court decision of *Brown v. Board of Education* outlawing segregation in public schools. Stoner believed that African Americans possessed neither the intelligence nor enterprise to coordinate a mass protest movement against white supremacy. He therefore concluded that a cabal of Communist Jews was responsible for the civil rights protests that shook the southern states in the years following the Supreme Court decision. According to Stoner, "the negro is not the enemy. The Jew is THE enemy of our White Race and the Jew is using the negro in an effort to destroy the White Race that he so passionately hates."[12]

Stoner attempted to defend white supremacy through the National States' Rights Party (NSRP), a militant segregationist organization that he helped found in 1958. During the next decade, the NSRP implemented numerous attacks on black and Jewish institutions, including a bombing campaign against southern synagogues. Stoner was personally responsible for the bombing in 1958 of the Bethel Baptist Church in Birmingham, Alabama, whose pastor was the fearless black civil rights activist Fred Shuttlesworth. It took more than two decades before the authorities finally brought Stoner to justice for that crime.[13]

In the intervening years, Stoner relentlessly pursued his hate campaign against racial and religious minorities. He helped lead the violent resistance to civil rights demonstrations in St. Augustine, Florida in 1964 and Bogalusa, Louisiana the following year.[14] He was also active as a lawyer representing numerous defendants

---

[10]   George and Wilcox, *American Extremists*, 354.

[11]   George Thayer, *The Farther Shores of Politics: The American Political Fringe Today* (London: Allen Lane, 1968), 35-36; "Activities of the Ku Klux Klan Organizations in the United States," Committee on Un-American Activities House of Representatives, 89th Congress, 2nd session (Washington, DC: U.S. Government Printing Office, 1966), part 5, 3806, 3807, 3809, 3810; Michael Newton, *The Invisible Empire: The Ku Klux Klan in Florida* (Gainesville: University Press of Florida, 2001), 116.

[12]   J.B. Stoner, "The Philosophy of 'White Racism,'" (n.d.), J.B. Stoner File, AJC Collection.

[13]   *New York Times*, 14 and 16 May 1980; *Washington Post*, 14 August 1982, 12 May and 3 June 1983.

[14]   For more on Stoner's role in directing white resistance to black demonstrators in these communities, see David R. Colburn, *Racial Change and Community Crisis: St. Augustine, 1877-1980* (New York: Columbia University Press, 1985), passim, and Adam Fairclough, *Race & Democracy: The Civil Rights Movement in Louisiana, 1915-1972* (Athens: University of Georgia Press, 1995), 344-380.

accused of racially-motivated crimes against African Americans. Most notoriously, in 1969 he served as a defense counsel for the murderer of Martin Luther King, James Earl Ray.[15] Throughout his political career, Stoner demonstrated a flair for the inflammatory rhetoric that aroused such controversy during his senatorial campaign. In the aftermath of the genocide committed during World War II, explicitly racist ideology, already on the wane, lost much of its intellectual and cultural legitimacy in the United States. Segregationist leaders increasingly refrained from defending Jim Crow in terms of white supremacy and black inferiority, emphasizing instead the more racially neutral language of states' rights. Stoner, by contrast, revelled in a more atavistic rhetoric that denied the essential humanity of African Americans and advocated the use of extralegal violence to enforce white hegemony. "The nigger is not a human being," he exclaimed at a white supremacist rally in 1965. "He is somewhere between the white man and the ape. We don't believe in tolerance. We don't believe in getting along with our enemy, and the nigger is our enemy."[16]

The attempt to suppress the Stoner campaign commercial represented a turning point in the attitude of civil rights activists who had previously advocated an expansive interpretation of the First Amendment right to freedom of speech. Civil rights organizations had on occasion challenged the right to freedom of expression when it resulted in racially derogatory representations of African Americans. The NAACP had, most notably, protested movie theater screenings of the D.W. Griffith film *The Birth of a Nation* because of its depiction of hypersexualized black males preying upon unsuspecting white women.[17]

However, during the era of mass black disobedience in the 1950s and 1960s, civil rights organizations for a number of strategic reasons retreated from the legal censorship of white racists. Civil rights activists understood that for the courts to impose limitations on the freedoms of speech and association would compromise their own cause. The civil rights revolution relied on the readiness of the federal judiciary to accord demonstrators the protections of the First Amendment. Black protest depended in part for its success on the safeguarding of speech interpreted by some as inflammatory and offensive. Southern law enforcement officers used the accusation of incitement to assault and arrest civil rights demonstrators. However, the courts continually ruled that these attempts to repress freedom of speech represented unconstitutional acts of censorship. The efforts of African Americans to gain the civil rights guaranteed by the Fourteenth and Fifteenth Amendments therefore relied on enforcement of the civil liberties granted by the First Amendment. As Ira Glasser observes, civil rights activists consequently "saw

[15]   *Los Angeles Times*, 24 and 30 March, 8 April, 27 May 1969.
[16]   "Activities of the Ku Klux Klan Organizations in the United States," 3821.
[17]   David W. Blight, *Race and Reunion: The Civil War in American Memory* (Cambridge, MA: Belknap Press of Harvard University, 2001), 395-396; Martha Biondi, *To Stand and Fight: The Struggle for Civil Rights in Postwar New York City* (Cambridge, MA: Harvard University Press, 2003), 95-97; Harry M. Benshoff and Sean Griffin, *America on Film: Representing Race, Class, Gender, and Sexuality at the Movies* (Malden, MA: Blackwell, 2004), 78.

equality and free speech as mutually reinforcing, twin pillars of a singular value system."[18]

One illustration of how an expansive interpretation of First Amendment rights facilitated civil rights protest is the student sit-ins of 1960. When violence broke out during the demonstrations, law enforcement officers arrested the students for provoking the disorder by intruding on private property. NAACP lawyers attempted to overturn the convictions by claiming that the sit-ins represented something more significant than a simple case of trespass or breach of the peace. The First Amendment, they insisted, permitted the students to protest publicly against racial segregation. While their acts were provocative, the use of violence to suppress the protests represented an infringement of their constitutional rights. The Supreme Court agreed. Between 1961 and 1965, it overturned the convictions of numerous student demonstrators. In the two most important of these cases, *Edwards v. South Carolina* (1963) and *Cox v. Louisiana* (1965), the Court established that even the threat of imminent violence from a hostile audience was insufficient grounds for the suppression of constitutionally protected speech.[19]

The commitment of the Supreme Court to facilitate civil rights protest also led to its decision in *New York Times v. Sullivan* that the First Amendment protection of free speech necessitated a higher criterion of proof in libel actions brought by public figures. On 29 March 1960, the *New York Times* ran a full-page advertisement with the headline "Heed Their Rising Voices." The authors of the advertisement were the Committee to Defend Martin Luther King and the Struggle for Freedom in the South. Their intention was to raise funds for the legal defense of the civil rights leader, who had been arrested by Alabama authorities on fallacious charges of tax evasion. "Heed Their Rising Voices" highlighted the brutal repression of black protesters engaged in non-violent protest. This "unprecedented wave of terror" included "truckloads of police armed with shotguns and tear-gas" ringing the Alabama State College in Montgomery and padlocking the doors of its dining hall in an effort to starve student demonstrators into surrender. Although the advertisement did not mention him by name, Montgomery police commissioner L.B. Sullivan filed a libel suit against the newspaper and four black ministers named in the advertisement. A Montgomery County jury awarded Sullivan $500,000, a decision upheld by the Alabama Supreme Court. The case then made its way to the United States Supreme Court. On 9 March 1964, Justice William Brennan delivered the opinion of the Court, which overturned the earlier ruling. Breaking with historical tradition, the Court ruled that the First Amendment protection of freedom of speech applied to libel cases. According to Brennan, the Constitution sanctioned "uninhibited, robust, and wide-open" speech, including "vehement, caustic and sometimes unpleasantly sharp attacks on government and public officials." The

---

[18]   Ira Glasser, "Introduction" in Henry Louis Gates, Jr. et al., *Speaking of Race, Speaking of Sex: Hate Speech, Civil Rights, and Civil Liberties* (New York and London: New York University Press, 1994), 2.

[19]   Samuel Walker, *In Defense of American Liberties: A History of the ACLU* (New York and Oxford: Oxford University Press, 1990), 263-264; *Edwards v. South Carolina*, 372 U.S. 229 (1963); *Cox v. Louisiana*, 379 U.S. 536 (1965).

application of the First Amendment led the Court to raise the burden of proof in libel cases through the introduction of the "actual malice" standard. This new standard made it necessary for a plaintiff to prove that the author of a statement knew that it was false or acted in "reckless disregard" of the truth. Although the court decision applied specifically to statements made about public officials, it demonstrated the commitment of the Warren Court to uphold the First Amendment protection of political debate.[20]

It was not only the lesson of history that warned black and Jewish activists that it was minorities that most stood to lose from any restriction on constitutional liberties. Only four years before the Stoner controversy, the conservative backlash to the radical black protest of the late 1960s had resulted in the federal government curtailing the rights of freedom of speech and assembly. In July 1967, police arrested H. Rap Brown of the Student Non-Violent Coordinating Committee (SNCC) for inciting a race riot that erupted on the streets of Cambridge, Maryland. Brown had, only hours before the outbreak of the disorder, declared at a civil rights rally that, "If Cambridge doesn't come around, Cambridge got to be burned down." The following year, Congress passed an amendment to the new Civil Rights Act which made it illegal to cross state lines and make speeches with the intent "to incite, organize, promote, encourage, participate in, and carry on a riot." In criminalizing militant black protest, the Rap Brown Amendment, as commentators labelled it, represented a clear warning even to more moderate civil rights activists that political dissenters were often the first victims of any restrictions on First Amendment rights.[21]

Civil rights activists therefore supported unrestricted freedom of speech because they saw it as essential to the success of their struggle against white racism. Ironically, their assertion that the Constitution allowed all citizens to express publicly ideas or opinions that others might find offensive forced them to defend the rights of their political enemies to the same freedoms. For the courts to impose restrictions on the First Amendment rights of white racists could create a dangerous precedent for the enforcement of similar limitations on black protesters. Civil rights activists who were tempted to use the judicial system as a weapon to fight hate speech were therefore conscious that it could prove a double-edged sword. The need to protect First Amendment rights led in at least one important instance to civil rights organizations publicly upholding the constitutional rights of their own bitterest adversaries. That this case occurred less than a decade before the storm of controversy broke over the Stoner campaign commercial demonstrates the sudden shift of policy on the hate speech issue that occurred in the early 1970s.

---

[20]   Michal R. Belknap, *The Supreme Court under Earl Warren, 1953-1969* (Columbia: University of South Carolina Press, 2005), 191-192; David J. Garrow, *Bearing the Cross: Martin Luther King, Jr. and the Southern Christian Leadership Conference* (New York: W. Morrow, 1986), 131, 135. The most extensive analysis of *New York Times v. Sullivan* is Anthony Lewis, *Make No Law: The Sullivan Case and the First Amendment* (New York: Random House, 1991).

[21]   For further information on the Amendment, see Bruce D'Arcus, "Protest, Scale, and Publicity: The FBI and the H. Rap Brown Act," *Antipode* 35 (2003): 718-741.

In 1961, two of Stoner's associates in the NSRP, Robert Lyons and Edward Fields, attempted to hold a rally in the small town of Fairfield, Alabama. A local court granted Mayor Claude Smithson an ex parte injunction—one issued without a hearing—against Lyons and Fields on the ground that they could incite a race riot. The two men nonetheless attempted to distribute copies of the NSRP newsletter, *The Thunderbolt*, to local townspeople. Arrested by the police, they appeared before the same judge who had issued the injunction against them. The court found them both guilty of violating the injunction and sentenced them to fines of $50 each and five days in prison.[22]

During the desegregation crisis, the ACLU had unfailingly attempted to uphold the First Amendment rights of white racists. Consistent with that policy, it launched an appeal to the Supreme Court on behalf of the two NSRP members, claiming that the injunction was an unconstitutional prior restraint on their rights of freedom of speech and assembly. ACLU Executive Director John de J. Pemberton, Jr. emphasized that the primary motivation for the appeal was less a concern for Lyons and Fields than the need to protect against courts issuing similar injunctions against civil rights demonstrations. In his opinion, "if the Supreme Court rules that such injunctions cannot be used to block free speech and association, one of the major obstacles to increased effectiveness of Negro and white opposition to racial discrimination will have been overcome."[23]

Although the actions of the ACLU were in accordance with established policy, what was more surprising was that the NAACP Legal Defense and Educational Fund should also file an amicus brief in the case of Fields and Lyons. Neither the prosecution nor the NSRP activists—no doubt embarrassed and repelled by the situation—assented to the NAACP acting as a friend of the court in the case. However, the court did grant permission. The brief filed by NAACP lawyer Jack Greenberg stated that, while his organization opposed the NSRP, it worried that should the Supreme Court uphold the convictions it would open the way to other restrictions on the freedoms of speech and assembly, including those of civil rights activists. According to Greenberg, some courts were already citing the case as precedent for the conviction of civil rights demonstrators who violated restraining orders issued without their having an opportunity to contest them. For the Supreme Court to uphold the original ruling could "seriously impede the movement for equal rights now current in the nation." In December 1963, the Supreme Court overturned the convictions of Fields and Lyons on the narrow ground that their handing out copies of *The Thunderbolt* did not constitute a violation of the injunction against an NSRP rally.[24] Although the case did not represent a complete victory for civil rights

---

[22]   George M. Snyder, Corporal, Intelligence Unit, Maryland State Police to Wesley McCune, 21 August 1964, box 246, Group Research Archives, Rare Book and Manuscript Library, Columbia University; *Denver Post*, 12 October 1961.

[23]   *Civil Liberties* 211 (November 1963); *Washington Evening Star*, 12 December 1963; *Washington Post*, 12 December 1963; *New York Times*, 12 December 1963; *Birmingham Post-Herald*, 12 December 1963.

[24]   *Fields v. City of Fairfield*, 375 U.S. 248 (1963) (per curiam); *Labor*, 28 December 1963.

activists, it did demonstrate how their desire to promote liberal interpretations of First Amendment rights paradoxically facilitated the cause of their political foes.

A further factor that curtailed an assault on hate speech was the fear that white racists would turn the situation to their political advantage by portraying themselves to the public as martyrs denied their constitutional rights. In reaction to the civil rights revolution, the postwar decades witnessed the emergence of a new racist discourse that emphasized the victimization of whites. Such rhetoric stressed that racial and religious minorities had improved their condition at the expense of a white majority that had seen its rights systematically eroded. Civil rights organizations worried that racists refused the right to freedom of speech would use the situation to dramatize their claim that whites were the real victims of oppression. "Every hatemonger alleges that attempts are being made to deny him freedom of speech," observed Dr. S. Andhil Fineberg of the American Jewish Committee. "When such a denial actually occurs, it brings to the bigot's support many conscientious citizens who detest his views—genuine liberals to whom freedom of speech is inviolate."[25]

*

Given their earlier caution about censorship of white racists, the confrontational attitude of some civil rights groups toward the Stoner campaign commercial represented a decisive policy shift on the hate speech issue. The effort to ban further broadcasts of the commercial demonstrated an alternative conviction that unrestricted freedom of speech posed a potential threat, rather than a measure to protect, equality.

The effort to silence Stoner raises some crucial issues. First, how do we account for the timing of the decision? Civil rights organizations had wrestled with the hate speech issue for years. Stoner himself had long used public addresses to make abusive statements about racial and religious minorities. There was therefore nothing new or surprising about the language used in the commercial. Nonetheless, it led some civil rights groups to abandon their strategic support of unrestricted freedom of speech and take a principled stand against public expressions of hate. Second, why did some black and Jewish organizations sign the petition to the FCC while others refrained from confronting Stoner? Unfortunately, neither the organizational records of the NAACP and ADL nor the published scholarship on the two civil rights groups provides much information.[26] In the absence of any explicit explanation for the shift in policy, it is necessary to rely on speculation.

[25]   S. Andhil Fineberg, "The Quarantine Treatment" in Edwin S. Newman, ed., *The Hate Reader* (Dobbs Ferry, NY: Oceana Publications, 1964), 114.

[26]   Neither of the most recent studies of the NAACP, for instance, discuss the issue of hate speech. See Gilbert Jonas, *Freedom's Sword: The NAACP and the Struggle against Racism in America, 1909-1969* (New York: Routledge, 2005) and Manfred Berg, *Ticket to Freedom: The NAACP and the Struggle for Black Political Integration* (Gainesville: University Press of Florida, 2005). No scholar has to date written an organizational history of the ADL.

It is probable that the change in policy reflected a broader redirection of civil rights activism. The purpose of the direct action protests of the 1960s was to expose the violent racism of white southerners to the rest of the nation, creating public pressure on an otherwise reluctant federal government to intervene in support of the demonstrators. When the police used dogs and fire hoses on black protesters during the Southern Christian Leadership Conference campaign in Birmingham, Alabama in 1963, it elicited angry condemnations from the press and politicians across the country.[27] By the early 1970s, there was less strategic need for the civil rights movement to publicize white racism. The movement had already demolished the legal foundations of Jim Crow and established many fundamental rights and protections for African Americans. With less immediate need to protect their own freedom of speech, civil rights organizations may therefore have worried less about the repercussions of censoring their political opponents.

A further factor that accounts for the abandonment of the formerly permissive policy on free speech is the increasing conservatism of the Jewish community. Events such as the Six-Day War led in the late 1960s to a reassertion by many American Jews of their distinct ethnic and religious identity. As historian Stuart Svonkin observes, for much of the twentieth century Jews had believed that the best means to protect and promote the interests of their community was by embracing the values of liberal universalism: justice, equality, and individual rights. The resurgence of ethnic and religious particularism, however, persuaded some Jews that the unlimited application of these ideals could endanger rather than strengthen their collective security. This resulted in a less tolerant attitude toward respecting the constitutional rights of those who publicly espoused anti-Semitic opinions.[28] In the words of Norman Podhoretz, "so long as we continue to honor the First Amendment, we will continue to be burdened as a political community with more freedom of speech than may well be good for us to live with, assuming that it is humanly possible."[29]

This shift toward support of political censorship occurred at the same time as the Nixon administration was also cracking down on political extremism. Federal repression of militants provided an opportune moment for Jewish defense agencies to push for restrictions on the First Amendment rights of their adversaries.[30]

---

[27]   See, for example, Adam Fairclough, *To Redeem the Soul of America: The Southern Christian Leadership Conference and Martin Luther King, Jr.* (Athens: University of Georgia Press, 1987), 137-139.

[28]   Stuart Svonkin, *Jews against Prejudice: American Jews and the Fight for Civil Liberties* (New York: Columbia University Press, 1997), 190-192.

[29]   Norman Podhoretz, "Living with Free Speech," *Commentary* 54 (November 1972): 7. Further attacks on unrestricted freedom of speech can be found in Walter Goodman, "The Question of Repression," *Commentary* 50 (August 1970): 23-28; and Joseph W. Bishop, Jr., "Politics and the ACLU," *Commentary* 52 (December 1971): 50-58.

[30]   For more information on the federal attack on political dissidents, see Dean J. Kotlowski, *Nixon's Civil Rights: Politics, Principle, and Policy* (Cambridge, MA and London: Harvard University Press, 2001) and David Cunningham, *There's Something Happening Here: The New Left, the Klan, and FBI Counterintelligence* (Berkeley: University of California Press, 2004).

The inclusion of the ADL in the coalition against Stoner also demonstrates how changing political circumstances encouraged Jewish defense agencies to take a more direct stand against hate speakers. Since the early 1960s, the agencies had steered clear of direct confrontation with political extremists such as Stoner. Instead, they had operated a policy of containment known as the quarantine strategy. The intention was to avoid public dialogue with the far right which, it was feared, would confer on the extremists a greater degree of political legitimacy. Jewish defense agencies successfully deployed the quarantine strategy during the 1960s, restricting the public impact of such prominent anti-Semites as American Nazi Party leader George Lincoln Rockwell and Alabama's John Crommelin, a former naval officer who frequently spilled his venom over the airwaves.[31] Jewish defense agencies also implemented a longer-term plan of promoting community education programs to foster racial and religious tolerance. "In the long run," concluded the American Jewish Committee, "the most effective defense against unsound ideas is more speech and more ideas, in the certain knowledge that ultimately truth will triumph."[32]

The quarantine strategy served Jews well during the school desegregation crisis when anti-Semitism reached unprecedented levels in the southern states. Jews were a small and marginal group in southern society—less than one percent of the population—and a more direct challenge to racial and religious bigots risked violent reprisal. The terrorist attacks on southern synagogues during the late 1950s were well within the living memory of most Jews in the region.[33]

However, by the early 1970s the civil rights movement and the rise to power of white racial moderates had eroded the political strength of militants such as Stoner. The election of Sam Massell, a Jew, as mayor of Atlanta in October 1969 symbolized a new era of social and political inclusion for Jews in the American South. This new political climate encouraged Jews to take a more public stand against the far right.[34]

The alliance between the ADL and the NAACP was also significant because it came at a time when the anti-Semitic public statements of some Black Power activists had undermined the political coalition between Jewish and African American civil rights groups. The cooperation between the NAACP and the ADL in attempting to suppress the Stoner campaign commercial therefore represented a

---

[31] Lawrence N. Powell, "When Hate Came to Town: New Orleans' Jews and George Lincoln Rockwell," *American Jewish History* 85 (1997): 393-419; Frederick J. Simonelli, *American Fuehrer: George Lincoln Rockwell and the American Nazi Party* (Urbana and Chicago: University of Illinois Press, 1999), 52-71.

[32] "Anti-Semitism and Problems in Dealing with it," Executive Board Meeting, 28-30 October 1960, Anti-Semitism/AJC file, AJC Subject Files Collection. Reports and memoranda on anti-Semitism in America and AJC's work to combat it, 1960-1962, American Jewish Committee Archives, at http://ajcarchives.org/AJCArchive/ DigitalArchive.aspx, accessed on 19 November 2007.

[33] The terrorist attacks on Jewish institutions are the subject of Melissa Fay Greene, *The Temple Bombing* (Reading, MA: Addison-Wesley, 1996).

[34] For more on the career of Mayor Massell, see Eli N. Evans, *The Provincials: A Personal History of Jews in the South* (New York: Atheneum, 1973), 225-254.

reaffirmation of the political alliance between moderate African Americans and Jews and the recognition that, despite the tensions that divided their communities, they must unite against their common enemies.[35]

Important as the alliance between the ADL and NAACP may have been, it is no less significant that other civil rights groups opted not to add their support to the petition against Stoner. That decision of organizations such as the American Jewish Congress and Southern Christian Leadership Conference to maintain their traditional policy of tolerance toward hate speech demonstrates a divergence of opinion emblematic of broader divisions within the civil rights coalition.

*

The ADL and NAACP faced a difficult task in attempting to censor Stoner for two reasons. First, the power of federal law appeared to protect Stoner from censorship. The Communications Act of 1934 not only compelled broadcasters to provide all political candidates with equal time on air, but also prohibited their imposing conditions on the content of campaign commercials. The provisions of the law were strengthened only a year before the senatorial race by the Federal Election Campaign Act, which required broadcasters to offer "reasonable access" to candidates for federal office.[36] Stoner further benefited from federal protection in the form of the Fairness Doctrine. Established by the Federal Communications Commission in 1949, the Fairness Doctrine obliged broadcast licensees to present contrasting points of view on controversial matters of public importance. As was true of the Communications Act of 1934, the federal government had fortified the legality of the Fairness Doctrine only shortly before the Stoner campaign commercial, in this case as a result of the Supreme Court decision in *Red Lion Broadcasting, Inc. v. Federal Communications Commission* (1969).[37]

The second reason for the difficulty, as previously discussed, was that the libertarian attitude of the courts toward freedom of speech benefited both proponents and opponents of civil rights reform. The enhancement of First Amendment protections by the Supreme Court bolstered the forces of racial liberalism. Conversely, the same expansionist interpretation of the First Amendment also protected hate speakers from prosecution.

The case with the most direct implications for the Stoner incident was *Brandenburg v. Ohio* (1969), in which the Supreme Court overturned the conviction of a Cincinnati Klansman in a case that in effect abolished the "clear and present danger" test for free speech established half a century earlier in *Schenck v. United States* (1919). Justice Oliver Wendell Holmes had attempted to impose a

---

[35]   Lewis Young, "American Blacks and the Arab-Israeli Conflict," *Journal of Palestine Studies* 2 (Autumn 1972): 72-73.

[36]   Peter B. Orlik, *Electronic Media Criticism: Applied Perspectives*, 2nd ed. (Mahwah, NJ: Lawrence Erlbaum Associates, 2001), 198-199.

[37]   *Red Lion Broadcasting Co., Inc. v. Federal Communications Commission*, 395 U.S. 367 (1969). For more on the Fairness Doctrine, see Thomas G. Krattenmaker and Lucas A. Powe, Jr., *Regulating Broadcast Programming* (Cambridge, MA: MIT Press, 1994).

constitutional barrier to the repression of free speech by stating that such action was only legally justified when the words used were "of such a nature as to create a clear and present danger that they will bring about the substantive evils that Congress has a right to prevent."[38] During the decades that followed, however, the broad interpretation of this standard resulted in significant governmental suppression of political dissent, especially during the McCarthyite witch-hunting of the 1940s and 1950s. However, a series of cases culminating in *Brandenburg* led to a substantial expansion of First Amendment protections. Brandenburg had a clear bearing on the Stoner case since it concerned a Klan leader who used the same racially derogatory language and publicly advocated similar policies, such as the forcible repatriation of African Americans and Jews. The Court overturned his conviction under the Ohio Criminal Syndicalism Law, concluding that the First Amendment protected the right to express racially or religiously inflammatory opinions so long as such language did not serve as a direct means to incite violence.[39]

The ADL and NAACP legal challenge asked the FCC to determine that the Stoner commercial represented a "clear and present danger" to the community, consistent with the criterion to restrict freedom of speech established in *Schenck*, but apparently abandoned in *Brandenburg*. Lonnie King of the NAACP evoked Justice Oliver Wendell Holmes' famous opinion in *Schenck* by claiming Stoner's efforts to create public disorder were comparable to "a man falsely shouting fire in a theater and causing a panic." The ADL and NAACP petition significantly emphasized that the language used by Stoner could not only incite white racists into violent acts against African Americans, but also cause blacks to take retributive measures against the stations that aired the commercial. According to the signatories, the Stoner campaign commercial posed "a serious and imminent threat to the safety and well being of the stations which air it and to the community at large." Indeed, the broadcast later resulted in anonymous threats to bomb both stations.[40]

The NAACP and ADL did not attempt to prove that Stoner's use of racial pejoratives and crude stereotyping of black male sexuality constituted an act of group slander. However, the two civil rights organizations did endeavor to show that the commercial could cause psychological harm. The petitioners included the expert testimony of Dr. Alex Robertson, a paediatrician at Georgia Medical College, who opined that exposure to the racial epithets that Stoner uttered would prove "detrimental to the normal psychological development of children."[41]

*

---

[38] *Schenck v. United States*, 249 U.S. 47 (1919).
[39] *Brandenburg v. Ohio*, 395 U.S. 444 (1969). For a fuller discussion of the liberalization of freedom of speech by the Supreme Court, see Samuel Walker, *Hate Speech: The History of an American Controversy* (Lincoln and London: University of Nebraska Press, 1994).
[40] *Billings* (Montana) *Gazette*, 3 August 1972.
[41] Lonnie King, Rev. Joe Boone and Stuart Lewengrub to William B. Ray, Chief, Division of Complaints and Compliance, Federal Communications Commission, 2 August 1972, folder 15, box 29, Cohen Papers.

On 3 August 1972, the FCC issued its decision on the Stoner commercial. It ruled that the ADL and NAACP had failed to offer sufficient evidence that the language used by Stoner would directly induce acts of violent lawlessness. In the absence of a "clear and present danger," the FCC concluded that the First Amendment protected Stoner from censorship.[42] The ADL and NAACP contemplated asking a federal court of appeal to overturn the decision, but concluded that this risked generating further publicity for Stoner.[43]

Stoner was understandably elated with the FCC ruling, interpreting it as a sign that his segregationist crusade had divine sanction. "I think that God has blessed me," he beamed to reporters. "God has protected me from the Jews and the niggers who were trying to take my constitutional rights of free speech away from me."[44] He seized on the FCC decision to reaffirm his opinion that, "Even for short pleasure with white women, niggers will risk life and limb."[45] These statements were characteristic of the way Stoner punctuated every remark about African Americans with use of the "N" word and references to their supposedly predatory sexual instincts.

The FCC ruling similarly emboldened Stoner to believe he could act with impunity in employing racial and religious slurs against his political opponents. When WSB-TV in Atlanta broadcast a debate between the candidates in the senatorial race, Stoner refused to shake hands with black activist Hosea Williams of the Southern Christian Leadership Conference and accused him on air of conspiring to deny jobs to white workers. He also retaliated against Mayor Massell by accusing him of being a "Christ-killing, race-mixing, Jew gangster."[46]

Despite his claims to the contrary, the outcome of the Democratic primary demonstrated that Stoner's election to public office was not part of the divine plan. Stoner came in fifth of thirteen candidates with 40,675 votes, 5.7 percent of the total. The overwhelming majority of his support, 27,821 votes, came from rural areas. While his election showing was less than spectacular, it represented a substantial improvement on Stoner's previous attempt to win public office, when he polled only 18,000 votes, 2.2 percent of the total, in the 1970 Georgia gubernatorial race.[47] Although electoral statistics do not provide an explanation for the motivations of

---

42   Ben F. Waple, Secretary, Federal Communications Commission, to Lonnie King, 3 August 1972 and Stuart Lewengrub, Memorandum to Arnold Forster, 8 August 1972, both in folder 15, box 29, Cohen Papers; *Atlanta Journal*, 3 August 1972; *Washington Post*, 4 August 1972.

43   *Atlanta Constitution*, 4 August 1972.

44   Ibid.

45   *Capital Times* (Madison, Wisconsin), 4 August 1972.

46   Stuart Lewengrub, "The Hate Campaign," *ADL Bulletin*, October 1972, 7-8; *Atlanta Journal*, 2 August 1972.

47   Numan V. Bartley and Hugh D. Graham, *Southern Elections: County and Precinct Data, 1950-1972* (Baton Rouge and London: Louisiana State University Press, 1978), 94, 112-115; Morris Fine and Milton Himmelfarb, eds., *American Jewish Year Book* (New York and Philadelphia: American Jewish Committee and Jewish Publication Society of America, 1971), 72:133; *Jet*, 24 August 1972; *Atlanta Constitution*, 11 August 1972 and 3 August 1978.

voters, it is difficult not to conclude that the upsurge in support for Stoner was due in part to the much-publicized controversy surrounding his campaign commercial. The ADL considered it "inconceivable" that, "in this day and age," Stoner should attract so many votes.[48] It is nonetheless an irony that the efforts of the ADL and NAACP to restrict Stoner's freedom of speech may have provided his campaign with greater media exposure than it would otherwise have received. The insistence of ADL officials that the commercial "was already a front-page and headline item" before they and the NAACP filed their petition is not entirely persuasive.[49]

The controversy surrounding the Stoner campaign is indeed replete with irony. First, the controversy found the two sides in the civil rights struggle reversing their relationship toward the federal government. During the desegregation crisis, southern whites pursued a policy of massive resistance against federal law. Segregationists claimed that the Supreme Court had usurped its constitutional authority in handing down the decision in *Brown*, which they saw as an attempt to impose desegregation in contravention of individual state control of the public school system. These reactionaries similarly resisted the liberalization of the law by the Warren Court in other areas such as school prayer. However, in responding to the protests against the Stoner campaign commercial, the white press and political leadership abandoned their strict constructionist interpretation of the Constitution and supported the unrestricted right to freedom of speech established by the Supreme Court during the preceding two decades. Opposition to the unconditional interpretation of freedom of speech came instead from civil rights activists. The NAACP and ADL wrote to a number of newspapers protesting their freedom of speech editorial line.[50]

Second, the controversy illustrates the argument made by historian Eckard Toy that hate groups paradoxically persecute racial and religious minorities while portraying themselves as victims.[51] During the course of the civil rights revolution, the more politically astute white southern racists started to understand that their best means to defend Jim Crow practices was to shift the terms of public debate away from race. Explicitly racist rhetoric had lost much of its cultural and intellectual legitimacy by the mid-twentieth century. For that reason, a growing number of segregationists abandoned their emphasis on the supposed inferiority of African Americans and instead attempted to rationalize their resistance to reform by claiming that they were merely protecting their own rights to freedom of choice about who shared classrooms with their children or bought homes in their neighborhood. According to this line of reasoning, the federal government increased

---

[48] Alexander F. Miller, Memorandum to Benjamin R. Epstein, 14 August 1972, folder 15, box 29, Cohen Papers.

[49] Stuart Lewengrub, Memorandum to ADL Southeastern Regional Board, ADL Supporters, B'nai B'rith Presidents, ADL Chairmen, Jewish Professionals, 9 August 1972, folder 15, box 29, Cohen Papers.

[50] See, for instance, *Atlanta Constitution*, 11 August 1972.

[51] Eckard V. Toy, Jr., "Right-Wing Extremism from the Ku Klux Klan to the Order, 1915 to 1988" in Ted Robert Gurr, ed., *Violence in America*, vol. 2, *Protest, Rebellion, Reform* (Newbury Park, CA: Sage Publications, 1989), 131.

opportunity for African Americans only by curtailing the citizenship rights of whites.[52]

While moderate segregationists recognized the need to choose between their emphasis on race on the one hand and the denial of their rights on the other, Stoner attempted to straddle these rhetorical strategies. He saw no contradiction between his incorporation of the language of white victimization and his stress on racist arguments to justify the denial of African Americans' constitutional rights. Stoner used the most offensive of words to demean African Americans, emphasizing through repetition his hatred of them and rejection of their humanity. He also drew on malicious stereotypes of black males as violent criminals and sexual predators to stress that African Americans posed a threat to supposedly civilized society. Although his language abused African Americans, his rhetoric represented whites as victims. The political establishment both at the federal and state level had, in Stoner's opinion, betrayed the electorate they were supposed to represent by implementing laws that undermined white privilege. This legislation, he claimed, rendered whites vulnerable to the predatory advances of African Americans.

Third, although Stoner claimed ordinary whites no longer possessed a representative voice in public life, he communicated his message through the medium of mass communications. While Stoner claimed he was the victim of a tyrannical political establishment, he used the protection of the state to address the electorate without restriction. Stoner ironically relied on the permissive policies of the FCC to make public his claim that the government in Washington was a dictatorship.

Fourth, what allowed Stoner to denounce racial equality in such inflammatory terms was an expansive interpretation of freedom of speech that owed much to the influence of the civil rights movement. During the 1950s and 1960s, the Warren Court facilitated black protest by including offensive and provocative language under the protection of the First Amendment. That protection now provided Stoner with the means to employ hate speech against African Americans. In a further twist, one of the members of the FCC board that ruled in favor of Stoner's right to freedom of speech was the future executive director of the NAACP, Benjamin L. Hooks. According to Hooks, African Americans must not let "the emotions of the moment blind them" to the broader importance of protecting First Amendment rights that had proved so important to the advance of racial egalitarianism. Banning the campaign commercial might offer temporary appeasement to African Americans, but in the longer term it was more likely to cause them harm.[53]

*

---

[52]   For a more thorough analysis of how segregationists reframed their arguments in terms of the threat to their own rights, see Kevin M. Kruse, *White Flight: Atlanta and the Making of Modern Conservatism* (Princeton, NJ and Oxford: Princeton University Press, 2005).

[53]   *Manitowoc* (Wisconsin) *Herald-Times* 9 August 1972; *The Bee* (Danville, VA.), 9 August 1972.

The efforts of civil rights organizations to restrict the hate speech of J.B. Stoner ended in failure. During the 1970s, the white supremacist ran for public office on several further occasions, using the protection of federal power to disparage racial and religious minorities in crudely offensive terms. In 1974, for instance, a federal judge ruled that public officials in Macon and Augusta could not prohibit the pasting of posters produced by Stoner, who was running for the lieutenant governorship of Georgia, on city buses. Stoner secured 73,000 votes, around nine percent of the total, in the election.[54] Four years later, Stoner ran against incumbent George Busbee for the Georgia governorship. That March, Busbee had signed the Georgia Fair Employment Practices Act into law. Stoner made the repeal of the new legislation the focus of his election bid. One of his television campaign commercials claimed that if Busbee was re-elected he would enact further laws that "take from the whites and give to the Niggers."[55] Despite a petition from the Atlanta NAACP, the FCC reaffirmed that Stoner's use of racially derogatory language did not constitute a "clear and present danger" to the community.[56] It is testimony to the residual power of white racism among rural and small town voters that he scored his most impressive result in the election of 1978, securing 71,000 votes or 10 percent of the total.[57]

In May 1980, Stoner once more entered the Democratic senatorial primary. However, Georgia party officials declared him ineligible to run because of his recent conviction for the attempted bombing of the Bethel Baptist Church in Birmingham twenty-two years earlier.[58] Stoner used the appeals process to escape incarceration for another three years. Even then, it needed a FBI manhunt to secure his arrest and imprisonment.[59] Released from prison in October 1986, Stoner renewed his assault on racial and religious minorities with what he called his "Crusade Against Corruption." The campaign focused on the AIDS epidemic which, Stoner claimed, was an act of divine vengeance against "jews and negroids."[60] Despite the inflammatory rhetoric used by Stoner, civil rights groups had learned from their earlier failures to restrict his right to freedom of speech and refused to respond

---

[54] *Kansas City Times*, 17 February 1977; *New York Times*, 29 April 2005.

[55] J.B. Stoner, "Opposed to Civil Rights Laws," Kanter Political Commercial Archive, ID 45088. For more information on the act signed into law by Governor Busbee, see Ginny Looney, "The Politics behind Georgia's Fair Employment Practices Law," *Southern Changes* 1 (1978): 21-23.

[56] Introduction to Collection Finding Aid, Series I: Topical, 1955-1996, box 305, Group Research Archives; Donald L. Grant, *The Way It Was in the South: The Black Experience in Georgia* (Athens: University of Georgia Press, 1993), 441; *Frederick News*, 29 July 1978; *Pacific Stars and Stripes*, 30 July 1978.

[57] *Atlanta Constitution*, 3 August 1978.

[58] *New York Times*, 2 May 1980; *Washington Star*, 4 June 1980; *Atlanta Constitution*, 31 July 1980.

[59] *Washington Post*, 12 February and 3 June 1983; *Atlanta Constitution*, 9 September 1983 and 6 October 1986.

[60] *Atlanta Constitution*, 13 November 1986; J.B. Stoner, "Praise God for AIDS" (August 1987), box 305, Group Research Archives.

publicly. Stoner continued to menace racial and religious minorities until debilitated by a stroke. He died on 23 April 2005.[61]

How serious a threat did Stoner really pose? His crude appeals to racial and religious prejudice had appeared anachronistic in the 1950s, when massive resistance leaders attempted to legitimate their opposition to desegregation by framing it in the context of states' rights, let alone the 1970s, when the civil rights revolution had demolished the legal foundations of Jim Crow.

Although the coarse language of Stoner did not attract a sizeable share of the white electorate, this did not mean that racism was not still an important element in southern politics. An opinion poll conducted a year before the election revealed that 53 percent of Georgia voters believed "public officials don't care what the people want."[62] Their resentment stemmed in substantial measure from federal enforcement of black civil rights. While other white candidates in the primary campaign strategically distanced themselves from the overt racism of Stoner, they espoused a similarly antiestablishment rhetoric rooted in opposition to racial reform. The outcome of the Democratic primary demonstrates that many whites who did not cast their ballots in support of Stoner still shared some of his convictions. Although David Gambrell won the first round with 34 percent of the vote, he lost the runoff election three weeks later to Sam Nunn. Nunn attained 54 percent of the vote by attracting the support of rural and small town voters who had cast their ballots in the first round for Stoner and another racial conservative, Ernest Vandiver. Even though Nunn eschewed the racist rhetoric of Stoner, his campaign shared a similar agenda. Nunn promised voters that he would "Get Tough in Washington" by restoring states' rights, strengthening law and order, and abolishing the use of busing to facilitate school desegregation. While there were crucial distinctions between Nunn and Stoner—one was a respectable politician, the other a racial extremist—both hoped to use white resentment of federal reforms to win public office.[63]

In an astute commentary on the Stoner incident, white moderate newspaperman Hodding Carter observed: "Hardly anyone preaches it [white supremacy] anymore—not because politicians' hearts are purer, but because that ploy no longer works."[64] What did work, as Sam Nunn demonstrated with his emphases on law and order and states' rights, was the use of racially encoded concepts to legitimize attacks on minorities. The hate speech of political mavericks such as Stoner was ultimately a distraction from this more insidious, and ultimately more successful, danger to civil rights reform. Ronald Reagan's references to "welfare queens" and George Bush's notorious Willie Horton campaign commercial would demonstrate

---

[61]   *Washington Post*, 28 April 2005.
[62]   *Atlanta Constitution*, 1 August 1972.
[63]   Bartley and Graham, *Southern Elections*, 94; Numan V. Bartley and Hugh D. Graham, *Southern Politics and the Second Reconstruction* (Baltimore and London: Johns Hopkins University Press, 1975), 171-172.
[64]   *Delta Democrat-Times*, 6 August 1972.

how, during the 1980s and beyond, mainstream politicians used implicitly racist messages to their electoral advantage.[65]

Beyond the confines of the primary campaign, the confrontational policy pursued by civil rights organizations can also be considered misjudged. The partnership between the ADL and the NAACP to silence Stoner did not resolve the broader problems that beset black-Jewish relations. Although the NAACP attempted to censor Stoner a second time in 1978, further failure led the organization to revert thereafter to its traditionally permissive policy on First Amendment rights. Moreover, the second challenge to Stoner significantly did not receive the support of the ADL. By that time, tensions between black and Jewish civil rights organizations had become increasingly acute as a result of such issues as affirmative action and the resignation of U.N. Ambassador Andrew Young.[66]

The reluctance of the ADL to renew its partnership with the NAACP suggests its recognition of failure in the Stoner incident. Five years later, when the National Socialist Party of America announced its intention to parade in the Chicago suburb of Skokie, the ADL and other Jewish defense organizations initially recommended a return to their traditional quarantine strategy. Although the protests of local Holocaust survivors eventually led them to petition for a banning order, the lesson they appeared to have learned, but then forgotten, from the Stoner episode was that the courts would protect the unlimited right to freedom of speech.[67]

---

[65]   For further discussion of coded racism, see Jean V. Hardisty, *Mobilizing Resentment: Conservative Resurgence from the John Birch Society to the Promise Keepers* (Boston: Beacon Press, 1999).

[66]   Young resigned following an unauthorized meeting with a representative of the Palestine Liberation Organization. Murray Friedman, *What Went Wrong? The Creation & Collapse of the Black-Jewish Alliance* (New York: Free Press, 1995), 312-313, 322-323; Cheryl Lynn Greenberg, *Troubling the Waters: Black-Jewish Relations in the American Century* (Princeton, NJ and Oxford: Princeton University Press, 2006), 242.

[67]   Philippa Strum, *When the Nazis Came to Skokie: Freedom for Speech We Hate* (Lawrence: University of Kansas Press, 1999), 17-18, 70-71, 88-92.

U.S. IMMIGRATION LEGISLATION SINCE 9/11: SOCIAL CONTROL AND/OR POLITICAL REPRESSION?

Catherine Lejeune

The U.S. government and Congress have long adopted measures aimed at silencing political dissent in the name of reinforcing national security, and by so doing have gone against certain Amendments to the U.S. Constitution. One may recall the Counter Intelligence Program (COINTELPRO) operations of the 1960s and 1970s[1] which often involved the infiltration of organizations "perceived" as subversive, and the illegal surveillance of such organizations as well as of individuals. The program which gave broad powers to the Federal Bureau of Investigation was ultimately judged unconstitutional. The case of COINTELPRO is not a random choice as the rationale behind such intrusive covert actions was to suppress movements for social change: a process, some legal and political analysts agree, which is, "still at work in the laws and policies that have been enacted in the name of countering terrorism."[2] The Patriot Act of 2001 with its surveillance provisions is reminiscent of the Counter Intelligence Program not just in the way it has affected American people's civil liberties but also in the Act's expansion of executive power.[3] Even before 9/11, the Anti-Terrorism and Effective Death Penalty Act (AEDPA) of 1996, not only gave a broader definition of national security (it now included the national defense, foreign relations and the economic interests of the United States), but also granted the secretary of state "broad authority to designate groups as 'engaging in terrorist activity' if they threatened the security of United States nationals or the national security of the United States"[4] (making just about anyone a potential terrorist). Non-citizens could thus be deported on the basis of "secret evidence," for belonging to organizations considered to be terrorist groups, without showing any proof of personal involvement in terrorist or criminal activity (in other words, for engaging in what would otherwise be associations protected by the First Amendment).[5]

---

[1]   The program started in 1956 and was officially terminated in 1971.

[2]   Natsu Taylor Saito, "Whose Liberty? Whose Security? The USA PATRIOT Act in the Context of COINTELPRO and the Unlawful Repression of Political Dissent," *Oregon Law Review* 81 (2002): 1080-1081. This aspect will be discussed further.

[3]   Ibid.

[4]   David Cole and James Dempsey, *Terrorism and the Constitution: Sacrificing Civil Liberties in the Name of National Security*, 2nd ed. (New York: New Press, 2002), 119.

[5]   William Banks and M.E. Bowman, "Executive Authority for National Security Surveillance," *American University Law Review 50* (2000): 110. According to David Cole, a renowned constitutional scholar, and James Dempsey, AEDPA was: "One of the worst assaults on the Constitution in decades. It resurrected guilt by association as a principle of criminal and immigration law. It created a special court to use secret evidence to deport foreigners labelled as "terrorists." It made support for the peaceful humanitarian and political activities of selected foreign groups a crime. And it repealed a short-lived law forbidding the FBI from investigating First Amendment activities, opening the door once again to politically focused FBI investigation." Cole and Dempsey, *Terrorism and the Constitution*, 2-3.

National security was invoked again after the terrorist attacks of 11 September 2001, to enact a law—the USA Patriot Act[6]—which, among other things, expanded the surveillance power of federal agencies, further limited the rights of immigrants, blurred the line between criminal and intelligence investigations and created a new and broadly defined crime of "domestic terrorism."[7] With this law, the so-called war on terror severely restricted the civil liberties of U.S. citizens and non-citizens alike by violating nothing less than the First, Fourth, Fifth and Sixth Amendments to the Constitution. Since 9/11, many immigration and counter-terror experts agree, the government has largely conflated national security and immigration enforcement, justifying most of its immigration restrictions on national security grounds.[8]

In its final report, the National Commission on Terrorist Attacks upon the United States (the 9/11 Commission) concluded that: "U.S. immigration authorities, prior to the terrorist attacks, were not focused on security. Instead, their primary concern was preventing people from entering the United States and seeking unauthorized employment."[9] As they did not appear to have any specific interest in working "illegally" in the United States, terrorists were not perceived by immigration officials to be a threat (and hence were allowed into the United States). The "illegal" entry of migrants into the territory, by contrast, was the major concern at the time of the attacks. They, unauthorized immigrants, represented a threat to national security. This fear of "uncontrolled" immigration to the United States is not a new phenomenon but the laws of 1996 represent a turning point in the history of immigration legislation. In the context of the *moral panic*[10] that developed in the 1990s, the U.S. Congress passed several extremely punitive laws, namely the Illegal Immigration Reform and Immigrant Responsibility Act, the Anti-Terrorism and Effective Death Penalty Act (previously mentioned) and the Personal Responsibility and Work Opportunity Reconciliation Act of 1996. Combined with local measures, these laws actually created a "national security regime" for immigrants, by considering immigrants as a problem of U.S. national security. In the context of 11

---

6   The USA Patriot Act was voted in October 2001. The acronym stands for "The Uniting and Strengthening America by Providing Appropriate Tools Required to Intercept and Obstruct Terrorism Act" (PATRIOT).

7   Saito, "Whose Liberty? Whose Security?" 1059.

8   Donald Kerwin and Margaret Stock, "National Security and Immigration Policy: Reclaiming Terms, Measuring Success, and Setting Priorities," *National Immigration Forum*, 18 July 2006. The *National Immigration Forum*, an immigrant rights organization, asked both authors for a report evaluating the national security implications of the immigration system.

9   Kerwin and Stock, "National Security and Immigration Policy," 3.

10   In the early 1990s—a period of economic recession—the perception that immigrants (Latinos in particular) endangered American society gained considerable acceptance among political commentators and created the emergence of *moral panic* (a notion developed by the British sociologist Stanley Cohen in *Folk Devils and Moral Panics: The Creation of the Mods and Rockers* (Oxford: Basil Blackwell, 1990). In a book entitled *Detained: Immigration Laws and the Expanding INS Jail Complex* (Philadelphia: Temple University Press, 2002), Michael Welch explains that the concept of *moral panic* can be applied to the immigration issue in that it helps understand turbulent societal reactions to immigration.

September, immigrants again became targets of increasingly repressive legislation and practices. The Patriot Act itself criminalizes immigrants. As for the long-awaited[11] immigration reform bill which collapsed in the U.S. Senate on 28 June 2007, it contained several disputable provisions.

A close examination of the various legislative proposals since 2005 will help to illustrate the fact that many of today's politicians still contemplate immigration as a function of national security. As I analyze the nature of recent immigration policies, I will attempt to show how they deny immigrants—whether "authorized" or not[12]—basic rights, thus undermining the very essence of democracy. Then, I will move the discussion onto the rationale behind these immigration laws (with a focus on detentions and deportations), suggesting that they constitute an instrument of the liberal state (here the United States) for repressing movements that oppose its domestic and foreign policies.

The 1996 Laws

A key moment in twentieth-century immigration legislation was the 1920s with its restrictive "racially-driven" quota laws. In the 1990s, immigration policy went from restrictive to punitive. The 1986 episode was already a sign of change compared with the "immigrant-friendly" law of 1965 which abolished national-origins quotas and instituted family reunification and desirable skills or knowledge as major criteria. Congress, which at that time was concerned with "illegal" immigration, passed the Immigration Reform and Control Act of 1986 (IRCA) which included a legalization program but also sanctions for employers who hired undocumented workers,[13] effectively criminalizing the latter.[14] The passage of Proposition 187 in California sought to deprive undocumented immigrants of health care, education and other public services, and to require social service providers to report to law-enforcement authorities any person they suspected of having undocumented status. Following this initiative, Congress passed three laws that went beyond Proposition 187.[15] The Illegal Immigration Reform and Immigrant Responsibility Act (IIRIRA) stripped immigrants and asylum seekers of several basic legal rights (including due

---

[11]   "Long-awaited" since the current immigration system is considered as broken. It is admitted by many commentators from a wide range of perspectives that "expanding the legal avenues to immigration—to reflect labor and family realities—would reduce illegal immigration and, as a result, would enhance security." Kerwin and Stock, "National Security and Immigration Policy," 44.

[12]   Since the term "illegal" is politically charged, I will use quotes each time it appears in the text and will otherwise use the more neutral terms of "undocumented" or "unauthorized." As for the notion of illegality, it will be discussed further.

[13]   Undocumented: a modern term, born under the modern regime of immigration restriction.

[14]   Suzanne Jonas and Catherine Tactaquin, "Latino Immigrant Rights in the Shadow of the National Security State: Responses to Domestic Preemptive Strikes," *Social Justice* 31.1/2 (2004): 2.

[15]   The 1994 state law has since been overturned.

process rights) and facilitated proceedings for exclusion and deportation by eliminating the right of appeal and judicial review[16] of decisions made by immigration agents. The Anti-Terrorism and Effective Death Penalty Act, adopted after the 1995 Oklahoma City bombing, contained seriously punitive anti-immigrant provisions stipulating, for example, mandatory detention of any immigrant—legal or not—who had ever committed a crime (including petty offences such as minor drug convictions or shoplifting) for which the penalty was one year in jail. Worse, the law was made retroactive: even if the offense had been committed fifteen or twenty years ago and the immigrant had obtained legal residency, he/she became deportable. Last, the Personal Responsibility and Work Opportunity Act (known as Welfare Reform), denied public services and benefits to all non-citizens, LPRs (lawful permanent residents) and undocumented alike. This law went far beyond Proposition 187 by denying benefits to all immigrants and not just the undocumented. Thus all non-citizens were now excluded. A new line of separation was being formed, not any longer between undocumented and legal immigrants but between citizens and non-citizens.

Other measures accompanied these laws, such as the militarization of the Border with Mexico, harsher attitudes towards legalization programs and even a proposal to repeal the Fourteenth Amendment which grants U.S. citizenship to anyone born in the United States. Taken together, as Jonas and Tactaquin posit, these measures created a "national security regime" for immigrants, stripping away their basic rights arbitrarily.[17]

The Patriot Act

The Patriot Act contains harsh provisions pertaining to the surveillance of U.S. citizens, namely a list of enhanced surveillance tools coupled with the right to use these tools with only minimal judicial and congressional oversight, as title II of the Act defines "foreign intelligence information" very broadly. Under this definition, any United States citizen's opinion on any matter of U.S. foreign policy is indeed "foreign intelligence information."[18]

The great majority of the Patriot Act's anti-civil liberties provisions were slated for congressional review under a 2005 "sunset" clause. As it turned out, the debate on re-authorization raised much controversy. It was expected by many (and not just civil libertarians) that the provisions would actually expire in December 2005. In fact, a majority of "ordinary" Americans felt that the surveillance to which they were subjected actually restricted their civil liberties (referring to the Fourth Amendment to the Constitution which protects people against "unreasonable searches"). Furthermore, six states and 370 cities adopted resolutions condemning

---

[16]   *Judicial Review* is the U.S. Supreme Court's power to invalidate the actions of other branches of government, such as declare an act of Congress unconstitutional for example.

[17]   Jonas and Tactaquin,"Latino Immigrant Rights," 2-3.

[18]   Nancy Chang, from the Center for Constitutional Rights, quoted by Kerwin and Stock, "National Security and Immigration Policy," 1115.

the abuses that such restrictions represented. Yet, in the context of the fight against terrorism and the war in Iraq, the Senate decided otherwise and voted in favor of re-authorization. In March 2006 the majority of the sixteen provisions became permanent (only a few concessions were made to limit the expansion of executive power).

Some of the Act's provisions—those concerning immigration—were not sunsetted from the start but were designed to be permanent. They did not generate the same concern as those pertaining to surveillance, yet they deserve some attention. Considered by many as the most troubling provisions, they authorize the government "to deny entry to foreigners because of speech rather than actions, to deport even permanent residents who innocently supported disfavored political groups and to lock up foreign nationals without charges."[19] More precisely, the 2001 Act broadens the definition of who is deportable under the Immigration and Nationality Act (INA) and gives the attorney general expanded powers to indefinitely detain non-citizens.[20] First, all persons—either undocumented or legal permanent residents—suspected of having terrorist ties could be detained for seven days without charges or access to a lawyer, much less to a court review (hence violating *habeas corpus*[21] and continuing the process of court-stripping begun in 1996). Additionally, once there was a deportation order against them, they could be held indefinitely if it was thought that their release and deportation to their home country might threaten U.S. national security. Second, according to a Justice Department regulation, undocumented immigrants and LPRs could be summarily subjected to preventive detentions and deportations without a judicial hearing or right to appeal, even in the absence of suspicions related to terrorism (for example, for solely immigration-related violations, such as over-staying visas or undocumented entry into the United States, effectively conflating immigrants with terrorists). Third, such detentions and deportations could include "guilt by association" as a rationale; deportation hearings could be held in secret and without access to a lawyer although several courts have challenged the Justice Department on this issue.[22] It should be specified that it is section 411 of the Act that makes "terrorist activity" a deportable offence, and under the INA new definition of terrorism (no longer only premeditated or politically motivated but now including any crime involving a weapon or other device "other than for mere personal monetary gain") a simple participation in a street fight could make a permanent resident deportable as a terrorist. There have already been numerous deportations (or attempted deportations) under the 1996 laws IIRIRA and AEDPA on the basis of such incidents.[23]

---

19   David Cole, "What We Don't Talk About When We Talk About the Patriot Act," *Nation*, 30 May 2005.

20   Saito, "Whose Liberty? Whose Security?" 1121.

21   The writ of *habeas corpus* is a civil proceeding in which a court inquires as to the legitimacy of a person's custody.

22   Jonas and Tactaquin,"Latino Immigrant Rights," 4-5.

23   Saito, "Whose Liberty? Whose Security?" 1121-1122.

The U.S.-Mexico Border

Part of the debate on immigration reform revolves around the securing of the U.S.-Mexico border. In September 2006, The Secure Fence Act was passed. It mandates the costly construction of seven hundred miles of barriers along the two thousand-mile border as an example of the border-enforcement-only approach to managing immigration, a costly approach which proves ineffective in stopping the flow of people going across. In fact, the wall has already been reinforced and, between 1990 and 2005, the United States tripled the size of its border patrol: not only is it estimated that the undocumented population (the majority of which is from Mexico and Central America) more than doubled during that period, but it currently shows no sign of abating. Since 1995, the number of such unauthorized immigrants has actually exceeded the number of legally admitted immigrants.[24] Finally, between 1993 and 2006, U.S. border patrol funding more than quadrupled (going from $362 million to $1.8 billion)[25] proving that border-enforcement policies have failed.

As immigrants now avoid the traditional points of entry and go across the desert of Arizona or California, the death rate at the border has dramatically increased.[26] Over the past few years, the number of casualties has raised concern among immigrant advocates and beyond. It might be the reason why immigration restrictionists have sought to relate their efforts to national security. Alarmist reports paint the picture of the presence of Mexican-based narco-traffickers at the border as posing a threat to the United States: not that of massive drug flows (which may exist to some extent) but the speculative threat that such traffickers could facilitate the access of terrorists to the United States. Although the "specter" of terrorists attempting to enter the country exists, it is not a primary national security threat faced by the United States, many experts admit, and, in any case, the Wall will not prevent any major terrorist plan.[27] So it seems that protecting the country requires a multifaceted approach at the very least, probably "combining border and workplace enforcement with mechanisms to regulate future flows of immigrants and allow the estimated 12 million undocumented workers in the U.S. to emerge from the shadows."[28] Today, the enforcement-only approach favored by conservatives is criticized, and not just by Democrats. Many moderate Republicans have joined in the fight for a "comprehensive" immigration reform, further blurring the divide between the two parties.

---

[24]   Jeffrey Passel, "Unauthorized Migrants: Numbers and Characteristics," *Pew Hispanic Center*, 14 June 2005.

[25]   Kerwin and Stock, "National Security and Immigration Policy," 40.

[26]   It is estimated that at least 460 migrants, "a record number," died trying to cross the U.S.-Mexico Border in 2005. B. Coyne, "US Immigration Policy Shift Causes Record Deaths," *New Standard* (4 October 2005).

[27]   Several surveys show that the best way to improve U.S. security at international borders and points of entry is to improve "port and cargo security." Dan Restrepo, *Center for American Progress*, 26 October 2006.

[28]   Jeffrey Passel, "Estimates of the Size and Characteristics of the Undocumented Population," *Pew Hispanic Center*, 21 March 2005.

The Race Factor

Of the undocumented immigrants present on the U.S. soil, more than half are Mexican. The fact that the preoccupation with national security has focused on the U.S.-Mexico border, and therefore on "illegal" immigration, is not neutral; it suggests that race and "illegal" status remain closely related.[29] In *Impossible Subjects and the Making of Modern America*, Mae Ngai explores the question of the emergence of "illegal" immigration as the central problem in U.S. immigration policy in the twentieth century. She postulates that the nation's restrictive immigration policy is also closely related to the development of twentieth century American ideas and practices about citizenship, race and the nation-state.

Indeed, the 1920s immigration laws did not assign numerical quotas to Mexicans, but the enforcement provisions of restriction—visa requirements and border-control policies notably—profoundly affected Mexicans, making them the single largest group of "illegal aliens." The actual and imagined association of Mexicans with "illegal" immigration was part of an emerging Mexican "race problem," which also witnessed the application of *Jim Crow* segregation laws to Mexicans in the Southwest and, as Ngai reminds us, at the federal level, the creation of *Mexican* as a separate racial category in the census. So unlike Euro-Americans, Asians' and Mexicans' ethnic and racial identities remained joined.[30] The legal racialization of these groups' national origin cast them as permanently foreign and unassimilable to the nation.[31] She argues that these racial formations produced "alien citizens," people born in the United States with formal citizenship but who remained alien in the eyes of the nation. This analysis is crucial in understanding the debate on immigration reform in recent years and months and the controversies over what policy should be implemented. The rhetoric used by ultra conservatives[32] is recurrently fuelled by such categorizations and beliefs, having made the path to citizenship a controversial provision of the proposed reform, hence the eligibility to citizenship for Latino immigrants very hypothetical.

Among the effects produced by immigration restriction in the 1920s was the fact that it meant much more than fewer people entering the country. It also generated unauthorized immigration and introduced that "problem" into the internal

---

29 Mae M. Ngai, *Impossible Subjects and the Making of Modern America* (Princeton, NJ: Princeton University Press, 2005), 2.

30 Ibid., 7-8.

31 Ibid., 8.

32 The politician Pat Buchanan is one of them. As for Samuel Huntington, a renowned scholar, author of *The Clash of Civilizations and the Remaking of World Order* (New York: Simon & Schuster, 1996), he has published a book with racist overtones: *Who Are We? The Challenges to America's National Identity* (New York: Simon & Schuster, 2004). In one paragraph of the book entitled "The Mexican/Hispanic Challenge," he postulates that Hispanics are unable to assimilate. *Hispanic* is a public-policy term initially coined by the U.S. administration to refer to people of Mexican origin (and from Central and Latin America) living in the United States. Though this umbrella term has become accepted by many and is now broadly used, some academics still favor the use of *Latino*).

spaces of the nation. As Ngai states, it produced the "illegal" alien as "a new legal and political subject, whose inclusion within the nation was simultaneously a social reality and a legal impossibility," in other words a subject barred from citizenship and without rights. Moreover, the need of state authorities to identify and distinguish between citizens, lawfully resident immigrants and "illegal" aliens posed enforcement, political and constitutional problems for the modern state. The "illegal alien" is thus, as Ngai coins it, an "impossible subject," a person who cannot be and a problem that cannot be solved.[33]

Immigration Reform

For a better understanding of the demise of the immigration reform bill of 2007 in the U.S. Senate, it is necessary to examine the initial legislative step of December 2005 when the House of Representatives passed H.R. 4437 (the Border Protection, Anti-Terrorism and Illegal Immigration Control Act). The bill introduced by conservative Republicans meant to increase law enforcement at the border (and within the U.S. territory) and create new penalties for immigration violations. Above all, it made unauthorized presence on the territory a felony. As Suzanne Jonas explains: "the mere act of being in the U.S. without a visa constituted an 'aggravated felony,' a criminal violation treated far more harshly than a non violent civil offence, as it is now ...; anyone or any organization assisting or hiring undocumented migrants could also be brought up on criminal charges"[34] (a provision that made some professionals such as social workers, advocates and lawyers wonder if their work with undocumented populations was going to send them to jail if H.R. 4437 became law).

By criminalizing undocumented workers, this bill provoked huge protests among immigrant rights associations and revived a pre-existing movement. Their message was: "We are human beings endowed with inalienable rights."[35] As we shall see, this capacity among immigrants to organize politically is precisely what the U.S. government sees as a threat and, as a result, what it hopes to suppress.

In March 2006, the Senate Judiciary Committee examined a number of bills, including one supposedly comprehensive "bi-partisan" bill. From the outset, the latter was seen as more "immigrant-friendly" since it provided a path to citizenship for the undocumented. In May, after a long and acrimonious debate, the Senate passed a "compromise" bill which was soon perceived by immigrants and immigrant rights advocates as H.R. 4437 "light": S.B. 2611 combined numerous security and deportation measures, militarization of the border, English as the national language, with a temporary guest-worker program and a long tortuous path to "earned" legal status for a minority of the twelve million undocumented immigrants already in the United States. Even though it offered a path to legalization, by the time numerous

---

[33]   Ngai, *Impossible Subjects*, 5.
[34]   Suzanne Jonas, "Reflections on the Great Immigration Battle of 2006 and the Future of the Americas," *Social Justice* 33.1 (2006): 6.
[35]   Ibid.

amendments had been added, S.B. 2611 was not regarded as "immigrant-friendly" any longer.

In June 2006, the House and Senate bills moved to Conference Committee where they were supposed to be reconciled but the possibility was seemingly torpedoed by the House Republican leadership who called for public hearings at sites near the border. The November mid-term elections were looming up and the vote was postponed. However, late in June, the Supreme Court adopted the principle of *retroactivity* (retroactive punishment) "by allowing the government to use the 1996 IIRIRA to deport all immigrants who had entered the U.S. without documents after a previous deportation, even if that had occurred 20-plus years ago (long before IIRIRA) and if the immigrant had no criminal record."[36] Such immigrants would have no opportunity for an appeal either. The ruling clearly expanded the number of deportable migrants and paved the way for "mass" deportations, especially from California. Since then, Jonas concludes, all three branches of the U.S. government have been acting as if H.R. 4437 was already in effect.

Given the xenophobic mood in the United States and considering how much passion the proposed immigration reform has inflamed, it is not surprising that local anti-immigrant initiatives should have taken place. Several municipal governments have passed laws to drive unauthorized workers out of their towns. Measures go from prohibiting renting to them (imposing sanctions on landlords) to anti-loitering laws which aim at preventing day laborers from soliciting employment in public places. This wave of anti-immigrant ordinances started in April 2006 in San Bernardino, California, with a ballot initiative which sought to deny city permits and contracts to businesses that employ undocumented immigrants and ban the latter from renting or leasing property.[37] A similar ordinance was passed in the town of Hazleton, Pennsylvania, in July 2006. For the American Civil Liberties Union (ACLU) the new law created a very vague and broad definition of an "illegal" immigrant.[38] By punishing employers, landlords or anyone who did business with them, it actually criminalized undocumented migrants further and accentuated their marginalization. In effect, the mayor of Hazleton went as far as overtly equating immigration with delinquency, blaming unauthorized immigrants for developing a crime wave in his town. This example opened an avenue: more localities felt they could now act the same way. Since then, more than one hundred municipalities have proposed some form of the Hazleton initiative in twenty-nine states (it is estimated that forty of these ordinances have passed).[39]

---

[36]   Ibid., 11.

[37]   Quoted from an article by the American Civil Liberties Union, "Local Anti-Immigrant Ordinance Cases," at http://www.aclu.org, accessed on 18 April 2007.

[38]   The notion of "illegality" has only been briefly discussed here. For further discussion of this socially constructed category, see Ngai, *Impossible Subjects,* and Jocelyn Solis, "Rethinking Illegality as a Violence Against Immigrants," *Journal of Social Issues* 59.1 (2003): 15-31; Jocelyn Solis, "No Human Being Is Illegal," unpublished manuscript (CUNY Graduate Center, 2001).

[39]   ACLU, "Local Anti-Immigrant Ordinance Cases: Hazleton, Pa. Ordinance No. 2006-40," 26 December 2006, at http://www.aclu.org, accessed on 18 April 2007.

Many civil liberties and immigrant rights organizations have vigorously opposed such attempts at enforcing immigration policies at the local level. Already in October 2006, a federal judge issued a restraining order preventing the town of Hazleton from enforcing anti-immigrant legislation as a result of a lawsuit filed by the ACLU against it. At a trial in March 2007, the plaintiffs presented evidence that Hazleton's attempt at scapegoating immigrants was based on distorted facts and propaganda. More interesting from a legal viewpoint, the plaintiffs argued that "the ordinances violated the Constitution's Supremacy Clause, contravening federal law and the exclusive federal power over immigration"[40] (in addition to violating due process and equal protection rights).[41] On 26 July 2007, a decisive stand was taken, characterized as "the most resounding legal blow so far to local efforts across the country to crack down on 'illegal' immigration"[42]: a federal judge in Pennsylvania ruled the Hazleton ordinances unconstitutional and prohibited the town from enforcing them.[43] District Court Judge Munley stated that the City Council's decision had interfered with federal law and "violated the due process rights of employers, landlords and illegal immigrants." Interestingly, the judge emphasized that "illegal immigrants had the same civil rights as legal immigrants and citizens."[44] Of course, there is a chance that the Hazleton mayor will appeal the decision but the Pennsylvania ruling constitutes a notable precedent, "a legal and moral dead end."[45]

Considering how emotional the debate over immigration has been, it is no wonder that the federal decision was made in the few weeks following the defeat of the Senate bill. The void it has created calls for bold political stands by federal courts acting as an antidote to local immigrant bashing. Nevertheless, such pro-immigrant decisions remain scarce compared to the recent trend of punitive measures taking the form of raids. The case of eighty-one suspected undocumented workers that were arrested at a manufacturing plant in Pennsylvania on 21 June 2007, is just one example (they have since been placed in removal proceedings for eventual deportation). On 11 June more than 165 workers were arrested by federal agents in Oregon; similarly, they have been detained since then. Recent federal immigration raids have amplified tension in the population and protests have erupted everywhere showing the emergence of political resistance.

On 28 June 2007, rejecting President Bush's plea to move the immigration reform forward, the U.S. Senate blocked the bill by a fifty-three vote majority over forty-six. The bill supposedly called for the biggest changes to immigration law for more than twenty years. But, in spite of an "appealing" deal, many of the provisions

---

[40] The Immigration and Nationality Act of 1996 already undermines the exclusive right of federal authorities to deal with immigration by allowing the attorney general to negotiate agreements with states and localities that would permit "qualified" local officials to enforce federal immigration law. INA, §287. Kerwin and Stock, "National Security and Immigration Policy," 30.

[41] ACLU, "Local Anti-Immigrant Ordinance Cases: Hazleton, Pa."

[42] Julia Preston, "Judge Voids Ordinance on Illegal Immigrants," *New York Times*, 27 July 2007.

[43] The legal decision is called *Lozano v. Hazleton*.

[44] Preston, "Judge Voids Ordinance."

[45] Editorial, "*Humanity v. Hazleton*," *New York Times*, 28 July 2007.

and last-minute amendments made the bill a deeply flawed compromise. Worse, defenders of the bill could not deliver a unified message of support for it. No consensus was reached, even among pro-immigrant groups.

The seemingly attractive aspect of the reform was its path to citizenship, giving most of the undocumented immigrants living in the United States the possibility of gaining legal status. But the cost was high. Among other requirements, immigrants would have had to wait eight years before they could become permanent residents and at least thirteen years to become citizens. Under the bill, they were required to pay a $5,000 fine and to wait until certain "trigger" conditions on border security were met. Another disputable provision of the bill required heads of households to apply in their "home" countries, sending them on a "foolish touchback pilgrimage."[46] The *touchback* provision was already present in the STRIVE Act (Security Through Regularized Immigration and a Vibrant Economy) introduced in the House of Representatives in March 2007. Though controversial from the outset, it became acceptable to some immigrant advocates by the end of June 2007 as the demise of the bill loomed in the Senate. It did not matter so much what the cost would be, they said, arguing that "a winding and expensive path is still a path."[47] Nonetheless, according to most human rights organizations, the reform failed to protect the fundamental rights of immigrants, refugees and asylum seekers as it contains such troubling provisions as *touchback*. Requiring an applicant to leave the United States and re-enter the country to receive legal immigration status, they argued, raised not only "practical" but also "ethical" questions. The bill was seen as unworkable and unfair as it would have eroded constitutional rights of judicial review, privacy and due process. Privacy here refers to the Real ID requirement which the ACLU (among other organizations) considered as "a poison pill violating privacy through the creation of a national identification card under the guise of a driver's license."[48] Everyone would have been enrolled "in an invasive electronic employment verification system" while the bill would have failed "to provide essential due process and effective judicial review of DHS (Department of Homeland Security)[49] decisions." Also, it was said, the bill undermined "constitutional protections against indefinite detentions and failed to address provisions that denied people the right to challenge decisions regarding their immigration status."[50] Finally, the temporary worker program that the Bush

---

[46]   "The Immigration Deal," *New York Times*, 20 May 2007.

[47]   Ibid.

[48]   According to Kerwin and Stock, it would be useful to create a national identification number with biometric identifiers. From a security standpoint, it would allow the U.S. to protect the country more effectively. However, civil liberties and federalism would be endangered. Kerwin and Stock, "National Security and Immigration Policy," 37.

[49]   Ibid., 5. In March 2003, DHS came into being, incorporating the former INS (Immigration and Naturalization Services) and twenty-one other federal agencies. In one move, the U.S. immigration function became a homeland security concern.

[50]   ACLU, "ACLU Urges Congress to Create Real Immigration Reform, Not Reliance on Unworkable Real ID Poison Pill," 28 June 2007, at http://www.aclu.org. Immigration experts point to several other flaws in the bill: a proposal would have eliminated several categories of family-based immigration, and would have distributed green cards

administration was eager to implement also raised concern. Seen as a "barely
disguised" impulse to limit the number of workers, Latinos mostly, some said it only
called for the creation of a new *underclass* who would be welcome to work hard but
never allowed "to put down roots."[51] As one *New York Times* reporter posits, the
deal meant the repudiation of generations of immigrants, the weakening of families
(that would have been split apart) and the creation of a system of modern peonage
within American borders.[52]

On Democracy: A Few Remarks

Many Americans, whether experts, observers or ordinary citizens, share the
sentiment that punitive anti-immigrant strategies will only undermine the quality of
democracy for everyone living in the United States. "Strategies that violate civil
rights cannot be sustained over the long haul in our constitutional democracy,"
Kerwin and Stock conclude in their *National Security and Immigration Policy*
report.[53] It does not take civil libertarians or immigrant advocates to understand the
evidence. The fabric of society in the United States (and beyond) is damaged by the
increasing mass of undocumented migrants whose labor is essential to the U.S.
economy[54] but who have been excluded from participating in U.S. public life.

For the majority of immigrant rights advocates, the immediate goals are to
undo the damage of the 1996 and 2001 laws, to reverse the rationale of the "national
security regime" for immigrants, to provide for the legalization of populations who
have been living and working in the United States for years, even decades, and
eventually to facilitate political participation by immigrants at all levels of society.
Actually, signs of change are already showing as a growing number of legalized
immigrants have registered to vote since 2005. Even more significant in the
aftermath of the debate that had strong anti-immigrant overtones: it seems that
citizenship applications are at record levels.[55] Meanwhile, some immigrant
advocates focus primarily on how the U.S. immigration system "violates human

---

according to a point-based system giving more weight to educated and skilled workers.
This point system is of great concern to undocumented migrants from Mexico and
Central America who, in their great majority, are unskilled workers and migrate to the
United States on the basis of family ties. It also evidences the stake of the reform: the
goal was indeed to end what immigration restrictionists call "chain immigration."

51   "The Immigration Deal."
52   Ibid.
53   Kerwin and Stock, "National Security and Immigration Policy," 12.
54   It has been estimated that undocumented workers constitute 5 percent of the U.S.
      workforce, and even higher rates of workers in many industries. For example, they
      represent 25 percent of meat and poultry workers, 22 percent of maids, 20 percent of
      construction workers and 18 percent of sewing machine operators (source: "Estimates
      of the Size and Characteristics of the Undocumented Populations"). In some urban
      centers such as New York City, percentages are even higher.
55   "Behind Acrimonious Debate, Public Support High for Comprehensive Immigration
      Reform," *National Immigration Forum*, 30 July 2007.

rights and does not serve appropriate 'ends' such as predictable justice or equality under the law."[56]

From a wider angle, the question may be more about reflecting upon possible reconceptualizations of citizenship. Legal and political analysts are increasingly addressing the subject of national citizenship.[57] Linda Bosniak, a leading expert of such pressing questions, makes the following insightful remark in an essay entitled *Universal Citizenship and the Problem of Alienage.* "In an era of widespread transnational migration," she writes, "national political communities necessarily face questions of where to draw the boundary between insider and outsider. Significantly, however, these boundary questions are not confined to the territorial border; rather, they reach deep into the heart of the political national community, and profoundly affect the nature of relations among those residing within."[58] If we consider non-citizens, or aliens who reside within the liberal democratic political economy, what do we see? "Aliens" is Bosniak's answer, that is to say, people who lack the rights and status of national citizenship by legal definition, who are "outsiders to citizenship." Yet, aliens are also persons whose "presence in the community raises pressing questions about the practice of citizenship, including questions about precisely how far the rights and status of citizenship can and, should be, understood to extend."[59] Even though there may be a contradiction between human rights declarations and states' sovereignty claims (in terms of controlling borders), Bosniak posits that the distinctions between citizens and aliens can be rendered fluid and negotiable through democratic "iterations." The blurring of such distinctions would not only benefit everyone, she says, but would reaffirm democracy in the United States and beyond.

On Political Repression

The very fact that immigrants are consistently trying to assert their rights is significant. Not only is it a sign that basic rights are increasingly being denied to them, but it also points to the emergence of political organizing among immigrants that the U.S. state is unwilling to accept. In fact, both the U.S. executive and Congress are developing a strategy aimed at suppressing nascent political movements. Several legal scholars and political scientists do not hesitate to call this strategy an apparatus (of which immigration laws, detentions and deportations are a major part) designed to discipline "subordinated populations," namely immigrants and asylum seekers, and crush "threatening dissent" against what they call "U.S.

---

[56]   Kerwin and Stock, "National Security and Immigration Policy," 9. Organizations such as ACLU, or the Catholic Legal Immigration Network serve such purposes.

[57]   Citizenship cannot be developed here.

[58]   Linda Bosniak, "Universal Citizenship and the Problem of Alienage," *Northwestern University Law Review* 194.3 (2000): 967.

[59]   Ibid.

imperial policies."[60] Repression being necessary to discipline "bodies," to use Ong's words, and to target politically threatening dissent, it may seem appropriate to speak of political repression. Today a significant number of immigrants are not just socially controlled, they are politically repressed. The new form that political repression has taken (in the context of the war on terror) simply needs to be defined.

Civil liberties analysts have already brought to light similarities between the COINTELPRO operations and the Patriot Act, such as the anti-alien sentiments and tactics used to target non-citizens.[61] Even more relevant for our discussion is the contention that the end of the Cold War has seen the substitution of terrorism for communism in the U.S. state.[62] Anthropologist De Genova, who has done extensive work on the notion of "deportability" in recent years, interestingly notes: "'Terrorism' has now come to serve the same ideological role of pervasive and imminent external threat to the stability and security of the United States that 'communism' previously did during the Cold War."[63] Quoting Marilyn Young in *Cold War Triumphalism: The Misuse of History after the Fall of Communism*,[64] he adds: "In terms of public rhetoric, domestic security policies, militarization of foreign policy and culture, curtailment of civil liberties, and a pervasive sense of fear and threat, the war on terrorism is the Cold War redux."[65] It takes no historical imagination to see, in what has become a permanent war on terrorism (and by extension, as I have tried to demonstrate, a war on immigrants at least for the most vulnerable ones), a continuation of what was originally imagined as a permanent war on communism.

This war on immigrants, which some have identified as the "securitization of immigration" (a term coined by Didier Bigo in the context of migration to European countries)"[66] or the "securitization of citizenship" itself, has taken on various forms in the United States. What seems to constitute a strategic apparatus, a centerpiece of "the Homeland Security State"[67]—restrictive immigration policies, detentions

---

60   Here, I quote Sunaina Maira but many other scholars have recently referred to the United States as an imperial state. Sunaina Maira, "Deporting Radicals, Deporting La Migra: The Hayat Case in Lodi," *Cultural Dynamics* 19.3 (2007): 41.

61   For example, Nancy Chang, *Silencing Political Dissent* (New York: Seven Stories Press, 2002) and David Cole, *Enemy Aliens: Double Standards and Constitutional Freedoms* (New York: New Press, 2003).

62   Maira, "Deporting Radicals," 47.

63   Nicholas de Genova, "The Production of Culprits: From Deportability to Detainability in the Aftermath of 'Homeland Security," *Citizenship Studies* 11.5 (2007): 421.

64   Marilyn Young, "Still Stuck In the Big Muddy" in Ellen Schrecker, ed., *Cold War Triumphalism: The Misuse of History after the Fall of Communism* (New York: New Press, 2004).

65   De Genova, "The Production of Culprits," 421.

66   Ibid., 423. Here De Genova quotes Didier Bigo in "Security and Immigration: Toward a Critique of Governmentality of Unease," *Alternatives: Global, Local, Political* 27 (2002). Jef Huysmans uses the term "securitization of citizenship" in *The Politics of Insecurity: Fear, Migration and Asylum in the EU* (New York: Routledge, 2006). In his book, Huysmans examines the process of securitization, a theory he applies to analyze migration, asylum and refuge in the European Union.

67   De Genova, "The Production of Culprits," 440.

without rights of due process, mass deportations and, more recently, immigration raids—serves to produce a new regime of "migrant illegality," targeting undocumented populations in particular, emphasizing their illegality while erasing the fact that they are migrants. Only legal migrants are now called "immigrants." The legal category that now designates undocumented migrants is not even "illegal alien" for some but "deportable alien." Thus, in De Genova's view, migrant "illegality" is lived through a palpable sense of the possibility of being "removed"[68] from the space of the state, that has historically rendered undocumented labor as a distinctly disposable commodity. What has made deportability so decisive for migrant "illegality" and the policing of state borders is, he adds, that "*some are deported in order that most may remain* (un-deported)."[69]

The "profitability" of migrant illegality is both economic and political. As the targeting is selective, it enables authorities to produce certain "culprits" at specific moments: thus the labelling of Arabs and Muslims as enemy aliens in the months following the terrorist attacks of 2001. As for the category of "illegal alien" or "deportable alien" (to refer to immigrants from Mexico and other Latin American countries), it is still functioning as the concept that has long been made synonymous with "a corrosion of law and order."[70] It makes it possible for the U.S. government and immigration authorities alike to continuously subject undocumented Latinos ("a racial dimension of the war on terror") to considerable surveillance, discipline, intimidation and control, and, more generally, at a moment of intense nativism such as the post 9/11 period, to declare a majority of undocumented immigrants potential terrorists.

Among all the elements which constitute the arsenal of what can be seen as a new form of political repression, it appears that the most problematic is deportation. The logic of deportation is both economic and political for, according to Sunaina Maira, it supports U.S. policies of liberal capitalism and of political domination and repression. Deportation in the United States, she reminds us, "is not an exceptional phenomenon in response to exigencies of infiltration and invasion, but is actually part of the normative regime of controlling and disciplining bodies."[71] Deportation is a technology of subjection, many agree, "for regulating citizens, migrants and workers by a state in which repression and war, at home and overseas, are not a 'state of exception' but rather the everyday state of emergency in the U.S. empire."[72]

The detainees and deportees referred to in this article are not activists in the traditional sense of the term but they are "subjects of a political process that targets populations selectively, in accordance with political projects of intimidation and

---

[68] The Bush administration and immigration officials think removal is a more neutral term but to most liberals, the word may instead conjure up negative analogies with Andrew Jackson's Indian Removal Act of 1830.

[69] De Genova, "The Production of Culprits," 426.

[70] Ibid., 428.

[71] Here, she refers to Aihwa Ong's work, *Neoliberalism as Exception: Mutations in Citizenship and Sovereignty* (Durham, NC: Duke University Press, 2006).

[72] This analysis Maira shares with Giorgio Agamben, *State of Exception*, trans. Kevin Attell (Chicago: University of Chicago Press, 2005) and Michael Hardt and Antonio Negri, *Empire* (Cambridge, MA: Harvard University Press, 2000).

control."[73] In this light, there is a continuum between them and so-called political prisoners.

Since 9/11, repression has been revived indeed. Insidiously, as Corey Robin[74] points out, it works now on two levels to silence dissent: on a state level, through agencies such as the FBI or the DHS, but also on the level of civil society, where individuals internalize repression and censor themselves.

---

[73] Maira, "Deporting Radicals," 50.
[74] Corey Robin, "Fear, American Style: Civil Liberty after 9/11," in Stanley Aronovitz and Heather Gautney, eds., *Implicating Empire: Globalization and Resistance in the 21st Century World Order* (New York: Basic Books, 2003), 48.

FREE SPEECH VS. FEAR:
A CONSTITUTIONAL IDEAL AND
THE TYRANNY OF THE MAJORITY
IN THE AMERICAN TRADITION

Ole O. Moen

Americans like to think of their nation as an exceptional one. They are rightly proud of their Constitution, which is the oldest functioning fundamental law in the world, and the claim that the United States of America is a nation of law and a very legalistically minded one is supported by the fact that it employs between one third and one half of the world's lawyers; in fact, some foreign observers consider the United States an exceedingly litigious country and, at least on that score, are willing to accept the concept of American exceptionalism.

American constitutionalism rests on three legs: the Rights of Englishmen going back to Magna Charta, the Common Law Tradition, and the American Constitution of 1787 with its twenty-seven amendments. Although all three components have European roots, in their application they are suffused by the robust idea of American exceptionalism. The First Amendment to the Constitution provides a seemingly omnibus protection of the freedom of expression, in the broad sense of the word: "Congress shall pass no law ... abridging the freedom of speech, or of the press, or of the right of the people peaceably to assemble, and to petition the Government for a redress of grievances." The Constitution, including *The Bill of Rights*, infuses the American people with the idea that nowhere on earth are civil rights and liberties protected as well as in the United States of America.

Therefore, one does well in reminding oneself of Alexis de Tocqueville's observation: "I know no country in which there is so little real independence of mind and genuine debate as in America."[1] This statement is in fact shockingly valid today, it seems, as is the very telling heading of the section of his insightful book *Democracy in America* under which this statement was made—"The Tyranny of the Majority"—which reveals that Homo Americanus, despite his frequent declaration of his love of and dedication to stalwart individualism, has in fact always been driven by the basic instincts of a conformal pack creature. And one of the strongest of these instincts is a deep-seated, unspecified but unadulterated fear.

For in spite of the ubiquitous claim of Americans that their nation is the home of freedom in the modern world, those precious guarantees of individual liberties are easily waved aside the very moment when the national security seems threatened in any significant manner. The 230-year history of the American Republic is rife with examples of rather grim violations of those cherished civil liberties amply and frequently proclaimed in public oratory on festive occasions. In fact, one could argue that this phenomenon constitutes a large portion of that gap between ideals

---

[1] Alexis de Tocqueville, *Democracy in America*, with a critical appraisal of each volume by John Stuart Mill (New York: Schocken Books, 1961), 1:310.

and reality that Gunnar Myrdal dubbed *An American Dilemma* in his book by the
same title.[2]

The nation had hardly come of age when it passed the Alien and Sedition Acts
of 1798, which set stiff penalties for "false, scandalous, or malicious" writings about
the president, Congress, or government in general.[3] They were very unpopular Acts
imposed by the Federalists, which probably contributed significantly to the party's
demise. However, it was informed by a profound fear of a potential subversion of
the Republic, which has remained a strong undercurrent in American life ever since
the birth of the Republic. It is this basic fear that Richard Hofstadter wrote about in
his essay "The Paranoid Style in American Politics" and which he seemed to make a
constituent trait of the American national character. (It could perhaps be argued, too,
that his essay "Anti-Intellectualism in American Life" is also very relevant in this
context.)[4] Although Hofstadter describes these streaks of hysteria—or paranoid
styles, in his idiom—as minority phenomena, it seems that they could not have had
such a major impact if they had not resonated strongly in a substantial part of the
populace. This inherent fear seems to have made Americans particularly sensitive to
potential dangers or threats to both personal and national security, thus making them
particularly vulnerable to and easy targets for demagogues.

This fear is also expressed in many other ways and in many areas of American
life, for instance in the nation's obsession with guns as a protection against all kinds
of threats, or even evil. The provocative filmmaker Michael Moore seems to have a
strong case when he points to a much lower rate of fatal shootings in Canada than in
the United States despite the fact that there is a higher frequency of gun ownership
among Canadians. He blames the higher rate of deaths from gunshots among
Americans on the pervasive fear in the nation, which readily triggers a rash resort to
guns and to shooting at potentially perilous targets, often only hazily identified at the
moment of firing. Furthermore, he bolsters his hypothesis by offering Canadians'
lax attitude about locking their homes and their feeling very relaxed about it and
about personal safety in general.[5] In his book *The Culture of Fear: Why Americans
Are Afraid of the Wrong Things*, Barry Glassner elaborates further on this seemingly
endemic and pervasive national paranoia.[6]

At the same time there is a proud tradition of freedom of the press in American
history which, of course, is a very important aspect of the freedom of expression. It
goes back all the way to the Zenger case of 1735, in which John Peter Zenger, the
editor of the *New York Weekly Journal* (thanks to his lawyer, Philadelphia attorney
Andrew Hamilton) won a court endorsement of his claim that truth was a defense

---

[2]   Gunnar Myrdal, *An American Dilemma: The Negro Problem and Modern Democracy*,
        with the assistance of Richard Sterner and Arnold Rose (1944; repr., New York: Harper
        & Row, 1969).

[3]   The Alien and Sedition Acts of 1798, at http://www.yale.edu/lawweb/avalon/statutes/
        alien.htm, accessed on 29 May 2007.

[4]   Richard Hofstadter, *The Paranoid Style in American Politics and Other Essays* (New
        York: Vintage Books, 1967), 3-40.

[5]   This argument is central in his film *Bowling for Columbine*.

[6]   Barry Glassner, *The Culture of Fear: Why Americans Are Afraid of the Wrong Things*
        (New York: Basic Books, 1999).

against libel and thus established this fundamental principle of law, which soon spread to other American colonies.[7] More than two centuries later the newspapers' right to print news which may be perceived as detrimental to the interests of the political authorities was also upheld by the U.S. Supreme Court in the Pentagon Papers case.[8] And between these two court cases there were a great number of significant court decisions dealing with the freedom of expression. Nonetheless, even in the twenty-first century, the press still seems to be easily whipped into obedient silence once national security seems threatened, as in the case of CBS's handling of the controversy around the president's military service, resulting in news anchor Dan Rather's departure from his post.[9] Also the fact that *New York Times* journalist Judith Miller chose to go to jail rather than reveal her sources in connection with a leak case seems to reflect at least a trace of pluck in the contemporary press corps, although there may have been more mixed motives in that case than meet the eye, and some less admirable, behind her act.[10]

The Clear and Present Danger Criterion

The right of political association is an important aspect of the freedom of expression in the broad sense and is protected by the First Amendment: "the freedom of speech, or of the press, or of the right of the people peaceably to assemble, and to petition the Government for a redress of grievances." In the wake of World War I, the U.S. Supreme Court passed decisions in six cases involving national security and the right to express political opinions. Of special interest in this context is *Schenk v. United States* (1919), in which Justice Oliver Wendel Holmes introduced the legal standard of "clear and present danger," which has remained a dominant principle in such cases ever since.[11] The defendant was charged with the seditious act of distributing a pamphlet advocating opposition to the draft and was convicted, as his act was deemed a menace to national security. However, eight months later—in *Abrams v. United States*, a case involving criticism of the government's deployment of troops to Russia in 1918, and encouraging strikes among workers in the armament

---

[7]   Http://www.law.umkc.edu/faculty/projects/ftrials/zenger/zenger.html, accessed on 29 May 2007.

[8]   *New York Times Co. v. United States*, 403 U.S. 713 (1971). U.S. Supreme Court opinions are found on this website: http://www.findlaw.com/casecode/supreme.html.

[9]   The allegedly fraudulent document presented by the CBS anchor in the "For the Record" segment of *60 Minutes*, on 8 September 2004, related to President Bush's Texas Air National Guard Record, and was instrumental in his departure as CBS news anchor.

[10]   *New York Times* journalist Judith Wilson's role in the 2005 leak case of the Bush administration involved CIA undercover agent Valerie Plame and her husband, former Ambassador Joseph C. Wilson. The controversy was over his 2002 mission to Niger to investigate whether this African state had provided Saddam Hussein with "yellowcake" uranium for the production of an atomic bomb. The controversy came to a head with his 6 July 2003 article in the *New York Times*, "What I Didn't Find." Miller went to jail rather than disclose her sources.

[11]   *Schenk v. United States*, 249 U.S. 47 (1919).

industry—the Court's 7-2 majority moved so far away from the original "clear and present danger" standard that its author could not support the Court's opinion. In fact, Justice Holmes, supported by Justice Louis D. Brandeis, modified his previous standard to apply only to national emergencies or cases of "immediate evil." In so doing, Justice Holmes launched a constitutional theory which later was described by a scholar as "one of the sacred icons in the free speech tradition," the so-called "free trade in ideas" principle.[12]

Nevertheless, in the next case, *Schaefer v. United States*, the Court majority moved even further away from the "clear and present danger" standard. It upheld the conviction of three officers of a German-language newspaper in Philadelphia for publishing false news items with the intent of promoting the German cause and obstructing U.S. recruiting efforts by manipulating news accounts lifted from other publications. In his dissent, supported by Holmes, Brandeis chided the majority for not applying the "clear and present danger" test and for all too readily restricting free speech.[13] In the final case, *Pierce v. United States*, a recruiting pamphlet for the Socialist Party entitled "The Price We Pay," was found to represent "a tendency to cause insubordination, disloyalty and refusal of duty in the military and naval forces."[14] In a dissenting opinion joined by Holmes, Brandeis rejected the majority's willingness to make "punishable statements of conclusions or of opinion":

> The fundamental right of free men to strive for better conditions through new legislation and new institutions will not be preserved if efforts to secure it by argument to fellow citizens may be construed as criminal incitement to disobey the existing law—merely because the argument presented seems to those exercising judicial power to be unfair in its portraying of existing evils, mistaken in its assumptions, unsound in reasoning or intemperate in language.[15]

In the early 1920s, as the postwar and post-Bolshevik revolution hysteria—exemplified in the Red Scare and Palmer Raids of 1919-1920—began to subside, the pendulum started to swing away from restrictive legislation and harsh judicial rulings. In 1921 the Sedition Act was repealed and persons convicted under it were pardoned or had their sentences reduced.

However, the espionage Act remained on the statute books, and the fear of left-wing radicalism remained strong throughout the 1920s and the 1930s and was augmented by the Molotov-Ribbentrop Pact of 1939. *Gitlow v. New York* (1925) upheld the conviction of a member of the Socialist Party for having disseminated thousands of copies of his "Leftwing Manifesto," which advocated the overthrow of democratic government. Against the dissenting voices of Holmes and Brandeis, the Court articulated more clearly the "bad tendency" test, which had been in the bud in

---

12   *Abrams v. United States*, 250 U.S. 616 (1919); Rodney Smolla, *Free Speech*, 101, as quoted in David G. Savage, *The Supreme Court & Individual Rights*, 4th ed. (Washington, DC: Congressional Quarterly Inc., 2004), 28 and 119 n. 12.

13   *Schaefer v. United* States, 251 U.S. 466 (1920).

14   *Pierce v. United States*, 252 U.S. 239 at 249 (1920).

15   Ibid., 273.

previous cases, by stating explicitly that states need not prove that utterances would create "a clear and present danger," thus foreshadowing the "preemptive war" argumentation of the Bush administration of the twenty-first century:

> It cannot be said that the state is acting arbitrarily or unreasonably when in the exercise of its judgment as to the measures necessary to protect the public peace and safety, it seeks to extinguish the spark without waiting until it has enkindled the flame or blazed into the conflagration.[16]

Two years later a unanimous Court upheld the conviction under a California criminal syndicalism law of Anita Whitney, a young woman who was a member of the radical Communist Labor Party. At a party meeting, her resolution of seeking political change by means of the ballot had been defeated in favor of a more militant approach through revolutionary class struggle. Strangely enough, Holmes and Brandeis supported the judgment (because the pertinent constitutional claims had not been raised by the defendant at the trial), but their concurrency sounded more like a dissent, implying that the defendant had been convicted on the basis of guilt by association. Justice Brandeis wrote squarely that an orderly society cannot be maintained merely through fear and enforced silence, since "fear … breeds repression … repression breeds hate … [and] hate menaces stable government."[17]

However, the same year the Court majority, for the first time, overturned a state criminal syndicalism statute. In *Fiske v. Kansas*, the Court found no evidence that a preamble of a platform for the International Workers of the World (IWW, the "Wobblies") in Kansas advocated violence by their urging people to "take possession of the earth and the machinery of production, and abolish the wage system."[18] (It was not until 1969, however, in *Brandenburg v. Ohio*, that the Whitney ruling was voided, when Ohio's Criminal Syndicalism Statute, almost identical to the California law, was overruled.)[19] Ten years later, in *Herndon v. Lowry* (1937), the "bad tendency" test was abolished, which in reality signaled a return to the "clear and present danger" criterion, the Court stating: "The limitation upon individual liberty must have appropriate relation to the safety of the state."[20]

In the wake of the radical 1930s and the Molotov-Ribbentrop Pact of 1939, combined with the war in Europe, several repressive measures were introduced in the 1940s. The Alien Registration Act of 1940 (the Smith Act) required all non-citizen adult residents to register with the government and made it a crime for anyone to "knowingly or willfully advocate, abet, advise or teach the duty, necessity, desirability or propriety of overthrowing the Government of the United States or of any other State by force of violence, or for anyone to organize any

---

[16]   *Gitlow v. New York*, 268 U.S. 652 at 665 (1925).
[17]   *Whitney v. California*, 274 U.S. 357 at 376, 378 (1927).
[18]   *Fiske v. Kansas*, 274 U.S. 380 (1927).
[19]   *Brandenburg v. Ohio*, 395 U.S. 444 (1969).
[20]   *Herndon v. Lowry*, 301 U.S. 242 at 258 (1937).

association which teaches, advises or encourages such an overthrow, or for anyone to become a member or to affiliate with any such association."[21]

The three most infamous edicts in this nadir era of American politics and law were perhaps Executive Order No. 9066 of 19 February 1942, by President Franklin D. Roosevelt, authorizing the internment of some 122,000 Japanese Americans (nearly 70,000 of whom were American citizens) without any legal recourse, followed by the equally notorious decision in *Korematsu v. United States* in 1944, finding the order constitutional, and President Truman Loyalty Oath Program of 1947. There is no need for me in this forum to catalog the array of repressive political and legal tools employed by all levels of government to question people's loyalty to the Republic in the era of mass anti-Communist hysteria of the late forties and fifties. However, it is significant to underline the willingness of the legal branch to chime in. Even the U.S. Supreme Court, which after the famous "Switch in time that saved nine," in 1937 (the response by some members of the Court to Roosevelt's thinly veiled threats in his "Court-Packing Plan") had started to take a more positive view of the rights of "discrete and insular minorities," did not seem to extend that tolerance to politically unpopular minorities.[22]

In the seminal case of *Dennis et al. v. United States* (1951), the Smith Act was upheld and the Communist Party outlawed by the Court majority. In so doing, the Court plurality (Vinson, Reed, Burton, and Minton) seemed to be applying the "sliding scale" rule for the use of the "clear and present danger" test in sedition cases, which had been employed by Judge Learned Hand of the Second Circuit: "In each case [courts] must ask whether the gravity of the 'evil,' discounted by its improbability, justifies such invasion of free speech as is necessary to avoid the danger." Also, the Court majority held that the question of whether the danger involved was clearly imminent was to be decided by the trial judge, not the jury, an issue going to the heart of constitutional law.[23] In dissent, Justice Hugo Black argued that the ruling represented prior restraint and thus violated one of the basic tenets of the American constitutional tradition, the freedom of the press. And, admittedly, Chief Justice Vinson, for a Supreme Court plurality (which was supported in judgment by Justices Felix Frankfurter and Robert H. Jackson) felt a need to state the Court's commitment to the principle of freedom of speech before reaching the Court's ruling: "Congress did not intend to eradicate the free discussion of political theories, to destroy the traditional rights of Americans to discuss and evaluate ideas without fear of government sanction."[24] However, his verdict seemed to take away what he had just granted:

> Overthrow of the Government by force and violence is certainly a substantial enough interest for the Government to limit speech.... Obviously, the words

---

[21]   18 U.S.C. § 2385, at http://www.law.cornell.edu/uscode/18/2385.html, accessed on 28 February 2007.

[22]   *United States v. Carolene Products Co.*, 304 U.S. 144 n. 4 (1938).

[23]   *United States v. Dennis*, 183 F: 2d. 201 at 212 (2d Cir.1950); *Dennis v. United States*, 341 U.S. 494 at 509 (1951).

[24]   *Dennis v. United States*, 341 U.S. 494 at 502 (1951).

cannot mean that before the Government may act, it must wait until the putsch is about to be executed, the plans have been laid and the signal is awaited.[25]

In his forty-five-page concurrency, Justice Frankfurter was also careful to endorse the concept of free speech: "Suppressing the advocates of overthrow inevitably will also silence critics who do not advocate overthrow but fear that their criticism may be so construed." First Amendment rights must be balanced against the nation's need to protect itself, Frankfurter held forth, but it was up to Congress, not the courts, to reconcile this conflict.[26] Justice Robert Jackson—the Nuremberg prosecutor who there had emphasized the duty of individuals to oppose an oppressive government, was quite categorical in his concurrency in support of unconditional loyalty to the government, in fact foreshadowing the reasoning of the Bush II administration:

> The authors of the clear and present danger test never applied it to a case like this, nor would I. If applied as it is proposed here, it means that the communist plotting is protected during its period of incubation; its preliminary stages of organization and preparation are immune from the law; the Government can move only after imminent action is manifest, when it would, of course, be too late.[27]

Justice Douglas, in his dissent, reminded the Court that the defendants were not accused of conspiring to overthrow the government, only of organizing a group *advocating* the overthrow, warning his colleagues against the mistake of "treating speech as the equivalent of overt acts of a treasonable seditious character" and that never until this day had "anyone seriously thought that the ancient law of conspiracy could constitutionally be used to turn speech into seditious conduct."[28]

In keeping with the *Dennis* precedent, 121 conspiracy prosecutions followed involving mid-tier officials of the Communist Party, and in the next five years came a number of other trials against party members; in all cases convictions were secured, and the Supreme Court denied certiorari in all.[29] However, by 1957 the Supreme Court seemed to be moving away from under the cloud of anti-Communist hysteria which had held its firm grip on the nation during the McCarthy era. In *Yates v. United States* (1957), it brought an end to prosecutions under the Smith Act, but allowed to stand its earlier assessment of the constitutionality of the Act. However, it reversed the previous convictions, acquitting the defendants for lack of sufficient evidence in several cases. The acquittal was based on a narrow interpretation of the term "organize" with regard to the Smith Act, pertaining to the formation of the Communist Party. This period could not be stretched over such a long period of

---

[25]   Ibid., 509.
[26]   Ibid., 549.
[27]   Ibid., 570.
[28]   Ibid., 584.
[29]   Savage, *The Supreme Court & Individual Rights*, 163. The U.S. Supreme Court (and other appeals courts) may grant or deny a writ of certiorari, which is an appeal from a lower court to have the superior court review a lower court decision.

time: The three-year statute of limitations invalidated the charge, said the Court.[30] Furthermore, the Supreme Court held that the lower court had failed to observe the traditional distinction between advocacy of an abstract doctrine and advocacy of action: "The essential distinction is that those to whom the advocacy is addressed must be urged to do something now or in the future, rather than to believe in something…."[31] It was perhaps a sign of a changing *Zeitgeist* that the government decided to drop the charges against those who might have been retried according to the Court's verdict.

It could be argued that the courts seem most willing to protect the rights of speech, press, and association when protection is least needed. After the demise of McCarthy (and the fall of Stalin) the massive anti-Communist hysteria was subsiding. However, that the change in political and legal atmosphere was not radical is testified to by the 5-4 conviction in 1961, under the so-called membership clause of the Smith Act, of Junius Scales, director of a Communist school. This provision was seen in connection with the Subversive Activities Control Act—Title I of the Internal Security Act of 1950 (known also as the McCarran Act)—in light of the self-incrimination clause of the Fifth Amendment. The constitutionality of the Act was upheld, but against the stricter standard of evidence stated in *Yates*. However, there was a strong and articulate dissent by the Chief Justice and three Associate Justices—Warren, Black, Douglas, and Brennan—signaling a growing opposition within the Court to defer to congressional and executive pressure. And the Court majority had obviously also embarked on a course of stricter scrutiny of the measures imposed by the other two branches of government. In short, the fear that had held the nation—including the entire federal government—in a firm grip, was gradually losing its hold.

In cases before the High Court over the next few years also the majority became steadily more critical, curtailing the discretion of the other branches regarding repressive measures against forces deemed subversive, thus gradually giving the lifeblood back to the constitutional guarantees of civil liberties. In fact, one could argue that there had been a fifteen-year continual process since the early 1950s to circumscribe and weaken the hysterical mood of the late forties and early fifties. After a series of decisions chipping away at the restrictive measures of the early 1950s, the Court, in *Albertson v. Subversive Activities Control Board* (1965) and in *United States v. Robel* (1967), in effect ended the long effort by the government to force the registration of the Communist Party members.[32] In *Robel*, Chief Justice Warren, writing for the Court majority, finally decided that the ban on Party members from holding governmental jobs plainly represented guilt by association: "The statute quite literally establishes guilt by association alone, without any need to establish that an individual's association poses the threat feared by the government in proscribing it."[33] Nonetheless, in two cases decided on the

---

[30]   *Yates v. United States*, 354 U.S. 298 at 306-307 (1957).

[31]   Ibid., 326-327.

[32]   *Communist Party v. Subversive Activities Control Board*, 367 U.S. 1 (1961); *Albertson v. Subversive Activities Control Board*, 382 U.S. 70 (1965); *United States v. Robel*, 389 U.S. 258 (1967).

[33]   *United States v. Robel*, 389 U.S. 258 at 285 (1967).

same day four years later, the Court drew new and fuzzy boundaries of the authorities' right to question people about their political opinions and affiliations: On one hand, the Court stated that a lawyer must not be denied admission to the state bar solely on the basis of his refusal to answer a question about membership in an organization advocating the overthrow of government. On the other hand, a good moral character and loyalty to the Constitution may be required, including answering questions about membership in organizations of the above kind.[34]

In terms of free speech in general, a relaxation also took place in the 1960s, reflecting the easing of Cold War tensions and the general liberal atmosphere of the decade, in spite of the Vietnam entanglement with its civil liberties fall-out. The right of high-school students in Des Moines, Iowa, to wear black armbands in protest against the war was upheld in 1969.[35] However, the previous year the Court had refused to accept the burning of draft cards as a legitimate symbolic speech protest, out of national security concerns.[36]

However, in three cases involving desecration of the flag, one in 1969 and two in 1974, these actions were upheld as examples of constitutional symbolic speech.[37] Moreover, a protest play against the war, staging men in American uniforms performing symbolic killings of Vietnamese women and children, was upheld as constitutional, since the uniform was to be considered part of the performer's speech (1970).[38] Similarly, in an antiwar rally near the Washington Monument in Washington, D.C, an eighteen-year-old boy who was shortly to report for his army physical, stated vehemently: "If they ever make me carry a rifle the first man I want to get in my sights is LBJ." In a *per curiam* ruling the Court stated that his only offense was a "kind of rude offensive method of stating a political opposition to the President." In an unusual concurrency, Justice Douglas stated: "The Alien and Sedition Laws constituted one of the sorriest chapters; and I had thought we had done with them forever."[39] Interestingly, in 1989 a majority of the Supreme Court which included conservatives Antonin Scalia and Anthony Kennedy upheld the right to burn the flag. The following year the same Court majority voided a flag desecration law passed by Congress to reverse the Court decision.[40] Worth notice is that in both cases Justice Stevens joined the dissenters.

In principle, the broadest concept of freedom of speech was perhaps established in *Brandenburg v. Ohio* (1969), in which the Court upheld the rights of a KKK group to advocate the use of force or law violation unless there was an imminent danger of lawless action, thus in fact reversing its *Whitney* decision of

---

[34]   *In re Stolar, Baird v. State of Arizona*, 401 U.S. 23 (1971); *Law Students Civil Rights Research Council v. Wadmond*, 401 U.S. 154 (1971).

[35]   *Tinker v. Des Moines School District*, 393 U.S. 503 at 508-509 (1969).

[36]   *The United States v. O'Brien*, 391 U.S. 367 at 376 (1968).

[37]   *Street v. New York*, 394 U.S. 576 (1969); *Smith v. Goguen*, 415 U.S. 566 (1974); *Spence v. Washington*, 418 U.S. 405 (1974).

[38]   *Schacht v. United States*, 398 U.S 58 (1970). A *per curiam* opinion is issued by the whole court collectively and is to to be distinguished from an opinion written by any one judge (and joined by other judges to constitute a majority opinion).

[39]   *Watts v. United States*, 394 U.S. 705 at 708, 709 (1969).

[40]   *Texas v. Johnson*, 491 U.S. 397 (1989); *United States v. Eichman*, 496 U.S. 310 (1990).

1927.[41] It is probably of some relevance that no national security issue was involved in this controversy.

In 1971, the Pentagon Papers case—in which the *New York Times* and the *Washington Post* had to defend in court their right to publish a series of documents which the government alleged would cause "irreparable injury to the defense interests of the U.S"—embraced several aspects of this guarantee of press freedom.[42] On 15 June 1971, a U.S. District Court issued a restraining order on the *New York Times*, later upheld by the U.S. Court of Appeals. However, on 26 June, the U.S. Supreme Court, by a 6-3 majority, rejected the government's claim. Significantly, all nine justices wrote separate opinions, a fact which reflects the complicated nature of the issue.

Absolutists on this issue, Hugo Black and William O. Douglas, accepted no restrictions of the freedom of the press, whereas others were willing to make some concessions provided valid justification was offered. The bottom line was, though, that such justification had not been presented in this case. A vital point to Justice Byron White was his unwillingness to grant the president discretionary power to exercise prior restraint of the press in the absence of valid congressional authorization, as such a decision would mean a clear violation of the doctrine of separation of powers.[43] This point remains equally valid when we move into the twenty-first century. A relevant point in this connection is the opinion of the Court in the Watergate tapes case, *United States v. Nixon* (1974), in which the Court, by a 8-0 majority, held that the president is not above the law and that Executive Privilege has its limits.[44]

The above observation seems to be a timely reminder to the second Bush administration after the 9/11 tragedy. To a great extent, the executive branch took the lead—supported by a dazed and obedient Congress—in writing legislation that set aside many of the fundamental protections of the Constitution. The major piece of legislation in violation of the Constitution was the USA Patriot Act, introduced less than a week after the event and passed by an overwhelming majority in both chambers of Congress on 26 October 2001, without most of the traditional legislature procedures, such as committee hearings. (Admittedly, a series of other pieces of legislation related to the War on Terrorism raised many issues of civil liberties, but this omnibus act was the great symbolic stumbling block.) The Act amended more than fifteen different statutes, including the Electronic Communications Privacy Act of 1986 (ECPA), the Computer Fraud and Abuse Act (CFAA), the Foreign Intelligence Surveillance Act (FISA), and the Family Education Rights and Privacy Act (FERPA).[45]

Although many of the provisions of the original Act were struck out, modified, or severely restricted by the USA Patriot Act Reauthorization and Improvement Act

---

41   *Brandenburg v.* Ohio, 395 U.S. 444 (1969).

42   *New York Times Co. v. United States* and *United States v. Washington Post*, 403 U.S. 713 at 714 (1971).

43   Ibid., 730-731.

44   *United States v. Nixon*, 418 U.S. 683 at 692, 705, 712 n. 19 (1974).

45   Http://www.ala.org/ala/washoff/woissues/civilliberties/theusapatriotact/usapatriotact .cfm, accessed on 9 March 2007.

passed by Congress on 9 March 2006, the Act still contains many repressive measures to which civil liberties groups objected. It is quite revealing that the coalition of interest groups that had challenged the original Act in federal courts included not just the traditional watchdogs of citizens' rights such as the American Civil Liberties Union and the Electronic Privacy Information Center, but also the National Rifle Association, Gun Owners of America, the American Bookselling Foundation for Free Expression, the American Conservative Union, and even Americans for Tax Reform. Although their targets were a broad range of First, Fourth, and Fifth Amendment issues, their concern about the government's use of National Security Letters is of particular interest in our context.

The NSL, when first introduced under the Foreign Intelligence Surveillance Act of 1978 (FISA), was a sort of subpoena instrument to be used by the FBI to investigate persons that it had reason to believe were agents of a foreign power. The measure required no probable cause or judicial oversight. But the Act was amended in 1986 to compel disclosure and was further extended in 1993 to allow its use to obtain information about persons under no investigation. The USA Patriot Act of 2001, Section 505, greatly expanded the use of NSLs against U.S. citizens and visitors suspected of no wrongdoing, and the USA Patriot Reauthorization Act of 2006 in fact added penalties for noncompliance.[46]

However, the Reauthorization Act directed the Department of Justice Office of the Inspector General (OIG) to examine the FBI's use of National Security Letters and of Section 215 orders to obtain business records. On 9 March 2007, the OIG issued separate reports on the two areas of investigation. The very same day, FBI director Robert S. Mueller III released a response to the report in which he fully admitted the shortcomings of his agency—"his finding of deficiencies in our processes are unacceptable"— and stated that he was ordering "additional corrective measures to be taken immediately."[47] In his statement to the Permanent Select Committee on Intelligence of the House of Representatives on 28 March 2007, Inspector General Glenn A. Fine reported:

> Our review found widespread and serious misuse of the FBI's national security letter authorities. In many instances, the FBI's misuse of national security letters violated NSL statutes, Attorney General Guidelines, or the FBI's own internal policies. We also found that the FBI did not provide adequate guidance, adequate controls, or adequate training on the use of these sensitive authorities. In many respects, the FBI's oversight of the use of NSL authorities expanded by the Patriot Act was inconsistent and insufficient.[48]

In 2004, four Connecticut members of the American Library Association— joined by the ACLU—took the Administration to court on account of the NSL

---

[46]   Http://en.wikipedia.org/wiki/National_Security_Letter, accessed on 2 April 2007.

[47]   "Response to DOJ Inspector General's Report on FBI's Use of National Security Letters," at http://www.fbi.gov/pressrel/pressrel07/nsl030907.htm.

[48]   "The FBI's Use of National Security Letters and Section 215 Requests for Business Records," at http://www.usdoj.gov/oig/testimony/0703b/index.htm.

provision in the USA Patriot Act of 2001, 18 U.S.C. § 2709, inter alia its request of "subscriber information ... or electronic communication transactional records." On 28 September 2004, in *Doe v. Ashcroft*, the U.S. District Court found the NSL in violation of the First and Fourth Amendments, the non-disclosure provision being a clear breach of the freedom of speech, as a content-based prior restraint and in addition not narrowly enough tailored to achieve a governmental interest under strict scrutiny.[49] The Court quoted the U.S. Supreme Court's decision in *Hamdi v. Rumsfeld* (2004): "We have long ... made clear that a state of war is not a blank check for the President when it comes to the rights of the nation's citizens."[50]

On 23 May 2006, the U.S. Court of Appeals for the Second Circuit handed down its decision in the consolidated cases, John Doe I and John Doe II. Because of the passage of the revised USA Patriot Act—which permitted the recipients of NSLs to challenge the issuance in court, and which was to apply retroactively to the original Act—the Fourth Amendment-based appeal was rendered moot; hence the Fourth Amendment challenge was vacated.[51] The Court also noted that the revised version of the Act effectively affected the First Amendment challenge since it allowed recipients of NSLs to speak to an attorney to obtain legal advice.

However, the plaintiffs maintained their challenge on this point, and in response the Court declined to resolve the question under the changed circumstances (questioning its own retention of jurisdiction) and remanded the case back to the lower court to secure a thorough reevaluation of the whole complex of factors involved in light of the nature of the changes.

As to *Gonzalez v. Doe II*, in which the District Court had held that § 2709 (c) violated the John Doe II First Amendment rights as a content-based prior restraint on speech, the Appeals Court ruled that the case should move in the Connecticut District Court under the new procedures in 18 U.S.C. § 3511(b) for a modification of the terms of its § 2709 (c) non-disclosure requirements so that it could reveal its identity. The government's proposals for the handling of the case was dismissed by the Court for the reason that the government had failed to demonstrate that it was entitled to *vacatur*.[52]

One of the three panelists, Judge Cardamone, wrote a significant concurrency pointing to the unusual (although implicit) claim by the government that antiterrorism investigations are different from other investigations in that they are derivative of prior or concurrent investigations. He labeled the government argument a "mosaic theory," under which bits and pieces of innocuous information could be collated into an indictable picture. Consequently, all terrorism investigations were permanent and unending, and the government insisted that a permanent gag order was permissible under the First Amendment.

[49]   *Doe v. Ashcroft*, 334 F. Supp. 2d 471 (SD.N.Y. 2004), at http://w2.eff.org/patriot/20040929/_NSL_Decision.pdf, accessed on 19 August 2008.

[50]   *Hamdi v. Rumsfeld*, 124 S.Ct. 2633 at 2650 (2004), quoted in *Doe v. Ashcroft*, at 7.

[51]   *Doe v. Ashcroft*, at 5.

[52]   Vacatur (Medieval Latin term): it is made null and void, *Merriam-Webster Dictionary of Law* @ 1996, at http://www.findlaw.lp.com.

Judge Cardamone observed that this "endless ban on speech flies in the face of human knowledge and common sense."[53] Implicit in his phrasing was the clear inference that the government had acted in defiance of both established legal principles and common sense.

Judge Cardamone's words are very much in line with a damning statement made by Steven R. Shapiro, ACLU National Legal Director, on 11 January 2007, in response to an attack made by Cully Stimson, deputy assistant secretary of Defense, on lawyers who were willing to serve as defense attorneys to Guantanamo detainees. Stimson had said in a radio interview that he found such willingness among major American law firms "shocking," and suggested that these firms would suffer financially once that representation became known to the firms' corporate clients. In his rejoinder, Mr. Shapiro said that "what is truly 'shocking' is that a senior Administration official would demonstrate so little appreciation for the role of lawyers and the rule of law.... What Mr. Stimson condemns are precisely the values we should be trying to defend in the war on terror."[54]

On 21 December 2006, FBI director Robert S. Mueller III belatedly responded to a request (originating in the 2 May 2006, hearings before the Senate Judiciary Committee) by its chairman Arlan Specter, in which he explained why libraries should be subject to NSLs when the law as written and clarified by the Senate exempts them. Responding to Mueller's answer, Leslie Burger, president of the American Library Association commented: "Director Robert S. Mueller III again demonstrated that the Justice department fails to comprehend the role of libraries and the importance of privacy in the United States.... Why can't this Justice Department respect the wishes of U.S. citizens and the privacy of library patrons?"[55]

The Electronic Frontier Foundation is involved in a series of lawsuits with the federal government on free speech and privacy issues. After the release of the Justice Department's report in mid-March, it called on Congress to hold aggressive hearings pertaining to the FBI's access to and use of telephone, Internet, financial-credit, and other personal records of ordinary Americans. "This is not simply about errors of oversight. This is about disregard for the law. For example, FBI terrorism investigators ignored their own lawyers' advice to stop using so-called 'exigent' letters for about two years," said EFF Senior Staff Attorney Lee Tien. The Justice Department's report supplements and corroborates the inspector general's findings last year that the FBI had disclosed more than a hundred instances of possible intelligence misconduct to the Intelligence Oversight Board in the previous two years. Senate Judiciary Committee Chairman Patrick J. Leahy (D-Vt.) said that more than just a cursory examination was called for.[56]

---

53   *Gonzalez v. Doe II*, Docket Nos. 05-0570-cv(L), 05-4896-cv(CON), at 13, at http://www.eff.org/files/filenode_v_ashcroft/doevgonzalez_05232006.pdf.

54   Http://www.aclu.org/printer/printer.plp, accessed on 29 March 2007.

55   Http://www.ala.org/Template.cfm?Section=pressreleases&template=/ /contentmanagement/contentdisplay.cfm&ContentID=145760, accessed on 29 March 2007.

56   "EFF Calls for Aggressive Congressional Hearings on National Security Letter Misuse," at http://www.eff.org/deeplinks/archives/005153.php.

Another area in which repressive practices by the administration have met with resistance is in the field of immigration control. A great number of foreign scholars and artists have been barred from the country, often without adequate explanation by the authorities. A well-known case in point is the ordeal of the Swiss Muslim scholar of Egyptian descent, Tariq Ramadan, currently at Oxford University, United Kingdom. In January 2004, he was offered a position at Notre Dame University as a professor of Islamic Studies and as Luce Professor of Religion, Conflict and Peace-building. In July 2004, after having established himself and his family there, he was informed that his visa had been revoked under a provision of the USA Patriot Act, which applies to people who have "endorsed or espoused" terrorist activity. He had previously visited the United States frequently to lecture at prestigious institutions, among others Harvard, Stanford, and Princeton Universities as well as the William Jefferson Clinton Presidential Foundation. It should also be mentioned that in the United Kingdom he had been invited by the Blair government to serve on a task force fighting terrorism and extremism.[57] The U.S. government invited him to apply for a new visa, and he did so with the help of Notre Dame University. However, after three months had elapsed without any response from the government, he felt obliged to move back to Europe, resuming his activities at Oxford University and the Lokahi Foundation in London.[58]

In January 2006, the ACLU, the American Association of University Professors, and PEN American Center filed a lawsuit in his behalf, challenging the government's actions. In court, the government lawyers admitted that they could establish no connection between Dr. Ramadan and terrorist groups, but even then they maintained that the process of reevaluating his visa would take years. In June, the court ordered the government to grant him a visa or explain why it would not do so.[59]

In the fall of 2006, Dr. Ramadan received a letter from the U.S. embassy in Bern, dated 19 September, informing him that his visa had been denied. Lengthy investigations had shown no link to suspicious relationships, no meetings with terrorist groups, and no encouragement or advocacy of terrorism. However, he had made a donation to two humanitarian organizations serving the Palestinian people (a French group named Association de Secours Palestinien and its Swiss chapter, the Comité de Bienfaisance et de Secours aux Palestiniens), groups which he "reasonably should have known" provided money to Hamas. According to Ramadan, the donations ($1,336) had been made between December 1998 and July 2002, respectively, whereas the United States had not blacklisted the charities until

---

[57]   Declaration by John R. Fitzmier, Executive Director of the American Academy of Religion, before the U.S. District Court for the Southern District of New York, Case No. 06-588 (PAC), 17 February 2007, 8.

[58]   "Second Declaration of Tariq Ramadan, United States District Court for the Southern District of New York, Case No. 06-588 (PAC), 1.

[59]   Tariq Ramadan, "Why I'm Banned in the USA," at http://www.washingtonpost.com/wp-dyn/content/article/2006/09/29/AR2006092901334_pf.html.

2003, and he had himself volunteered the information about these donations to the immigration authorities.[60]

On 5 February 2007, the ACLU announced that it had filed a complaint challenging the government's continued exclusion of Dr. Ramadan from the country by means of the "ideological exclusion" provision of the USA Patriot Act. Said deputy director of the ACLU's National Security Program Jameel Jaffer: "The government is using the immigration laws as a means of censuring academic and political debate inside the United States." The ACLU argues that Dr. Ramadan's donations were not a basis of inadmissibility at the time they were made and that the current material support provision cannot be applied retroactively.[61]

Professor Ramadan is far from the only victim of the government's application of this provision. In recent months a great number of foreign scholars, writers, and activists have been excluded for reasons that appear to be ideological. In February 2006, Dr. Waskar Ari, a Bolivian historian and an outspoken advocate for the rights of indigenous peoples in Latin America, was prevented from accepting a position at the University of Nebraska-Lincoln when he was denied a visa. Similarly, John Milios, a Greek professor of Marxist economic theory, and Basque historian and activist, Iñaki Egaña, were both excluded in June 2006. In October 2006, South African Professor Adam Habib, a prominent anti-war activist, was denied access to the country and thus prevented from meeting scholars in New York, the National Institute of Health, the Centers for Disease Control and Prevention, and the World Bank. "Academic discourse relies on an open exchange of diverse ideas but that vital exchange is thwarted when the government prevents foreign scholars from coming to the United States to speak to American audiences," said ACLU Attorney Melissa Goodman. "By banning foreign scholars, the government is sending the message that America is afraid of critical thought."[62]

The ACLU has also provided legal advice to Lieutenant Ehren Watada who has refused to serve in the Iraq War because he considers the war unlawful. The ACLU takes no position on the question of the lawfulness of the war but holds that "[s]oldiers should not be court-martialed for explaining their views on important political issues when doing so does not adversely affect military functioning."[63] Lt. Watada is charged with violating two articles of the Uniform Code of Military Justice: Article 88, which prohibits the use of "contemptuous words" against the president and other top governmental officials; and Article 133, which prohibits

---

[60] He writes in his Second Declaration that he mistakenly may have stated in his visa interview that he had also contributed to the Comité de Bienfaisance et de Secours aux Palestiniens (CBSP), because he was confused about the relationship of the two organizations. He now states that the CBSP has confirmed that he has never donated any money to this organization. Http://www.aclu.org/pdfs/safefree/aar_v_chertoff _ramadan_affadavit.pdf., accessed on 19 August 2008.

[61] "U.S. Groups Renew Legal Challenge to Lift Ban on Muslim Scholar," at http://www.aclu.org/safefree/general/28248prs20070205.html (5 February 2007).

[62] Ibid.

[63] "ACLU Defends Lt. Watada's Right to Free Speech," at http://www.aclu-wa.org/detail.cfm?id=508 (15 August 2006).

"conduct unbecoming an officer" or "seriously compromises the officer's character as a gentleman."[64]

I will not address the can of worms that the Armed Forces' incarceration practices at Guantanamo and other places in and outside the United States represent, because it would go beyond the scope of my essay. Also, although free speech issues are involved here, these cases comprise a series of other questions as well, such as habeas corpus, privacy, and international law pertaining to the treatment of prisoners of war. But in all these areas of law the government's policies seem to reflect a blatant disregard for law, domestic and international, and an arrogant unilateralist attitude, both in the military and civilian leadership, which many legal scholars find abhorrent.

In the late summer of 1966, during the heat of the Vietnam War, Senator J. William Fulbright, the chairman of the Senate Foreign Relations Committee, gave a series of lectures at the Johns Hopkins School of Advanced International Studies, one of which was titled "The Arrogance of Power."[65] This speech was full of insights, many of which revealed less attractive and admirable aspects of American culture. He was mainly concerned about the dangers of arrogance, which he saw as a natural corollary of power, but he also warned about the fact that, contrary to popular belief, one of the main roots of such arrogance may be uncertainty and lack of self-confidence, rather than of omnipotence. Such a deficiency may produce paranoid traits in an individual, and likewise in a nation. Also, it may create a need for self-assertion which borders on the pathological, a demand that one's wishes are always heeded, for instance, and a loud insistence on calling all shots. Because of its superior power, America has at times succumbed to the temptation of acting overly unilaterally in its policies, said Fulbright, which has made the nation less than beloved in many quarters.

Fulbright's message seems equally valid today, since the right to act unilaterally without any concern about the views of the world community as expressed in the United Nations General Assembly, for instance, whenever American national security seems threatened has characterized American foreign policy since the onslaught on the United States on 9 September 2001. That fear and insecurity lie behind many of these actions is beyond doubt. On the eve of the Second Iraq War, the former Majority Leader of the U.S. Senate Robert Byrd (D-WV) made a damning indictment of the Bush administration action in defiance of world opinion:

> Instead of reasoning with those with whom we disagree, we demand obedience and threaten recrimination.... We say that the United States has the right to turn its firepower on any corner of the globe which might be suspect in the war on terrorism.... We flaunt our superpower status with arrogance. We treat the UN Security Council members like ingrates who offend our princely dignity by lifting their heads from the carpet. Valuable alliances are split. After the war

---

[64] Ibid.

[65] The series was published under that title as a book the same year: J. William Fulbright, *The Arrogance of Power* (New York: Vintage Books, 1966).

has ended, the United States will have to rebuild much more than the country of Iraq. We will have to rebuild America's image around the globe.... What is happening to this country? When did we become a nation that ignores and berates our friends? When did we decide to risk undermining international order by adopting a radical and doctrinaire approach to using our awesome military might? How can we abandon diplomatic efforts when the turmoil in the world cries out for diplomacy?

One special aspect of present-day America is its sensitivity to criticism, a phenomenon to which Senator Fulbright pointed in his 1966 book. And one feature par excellence is the influence of the Israel lobby, which effectively stifles debate of the Middle East situation by labeling as anti-Semitism any criticism of Israel. Professors Stephen M. Walt and John J. Mearsheimer learned that lesson after having published their pointed study of the activities of the Israel lobby groups, "The Israeli Lobby."[66]They were vilified in the mass media by a massive campaign by pro-Israel activists, led by high-profile Israel defender/apologist Alan Dershowitz.[67] It is also symptomatic that Congress gave Israel a blank check to deal with the Palestinian rebels in Lebanon, when it voted on 18 July 2006, by majorities of 410-8 and 98-0 respectively, giving its full support of punitive Israeli actions. Congressmen may be individually willing to speak off the record regarding the immense influence of the Israeli lobby in the U.S. Congress, but dare not be quoted publicly on the issue or in any way cast a vote critical of Israel. This in fact amounts to political gagging and a near-total curb on free speech.[68]

However, this is a virtual anathema in the United States, and any mention of it may trigger accusations of anti-Semitism. The encouraging thing is that it is Jewish Americans who have been most outspoken in their criticism of this taboo in current American political debate.

---

[66] The article was first commissioned by the *Atlantic Monthly*, which was unwilling to publish it when its critical tone was discovered. Unable to find a publisher in the United States, the authors had it published by the *London Review of Books* 28.6 (23 March 2006). Because of its turbulent reception in the USA, the *LRB* arranged a debate at the Great Hall of the Cooper Union, New York, on 28 September, moderated by historian Anne-Marie Slaughter with participants Shlomo Ben-Ami, Martin Indyk, Tony Judt, Rashid Khalidi, John Mearsheimer, and Dennis Ross, at http://www.lrb.co.uk/v28/n06/print/mear01_.html, accessed on 26 June 2007.

[67] Dershowitz has since then been active in demanding the removal of Norman Finkelstein, the author of *The Holocaust Industry*, from the faculty of DePaul University in Chicago. "Harvard Law Professor Works to Disrupt Tenure Bid of Longtime Nemesis at DePaul U," the *Chronicle of Higher Education*, Thursday, 5 April 2007. Significantly, Finkelstein was denied tenure by a 4-3 vote by the Board on Promotion and Tenure.

[68] Jim VandeHei, "Congress Giving Israel Vote of Confidence: Both Parties Back Ally, Court Jewish Support," *Washingtonpost.com*, 19 July 2006, at http://www.washingtonpost.com/wp-dyn/content/article/2006/07/18/AR2006071801415 .html, accessed on 26 June 2007; Stephen Zunes, "U.S. Role in Lebanon Debacle," *Worldpress.org*, 25 May 2007, at http://www.worldpress.org/Mideast/2802.cfm, accessed on 26 June 2007.

Because of traditional American rhetoric, but also on account of America's track record as a formidable force for peace and a guardian of civil liberties, the United States is held to a higher democratic standard than most countries, and it is certainly considered to be of a different order than those who committed that dastardly deed on 11 September 2001. Also, because one of the most frequent words employed by President Bush in his speeches is freedom, often in conjunction with liberty, the novel practice of a near-total disregard for human rights demonstrated by the current administration is seemingly out of character. Freedom of speech is one of the most basic criteria for defining a democratic nation. Consequently, the repeated blatant violations of this nearly sacrosanct democratic standard represent a serious breech of the code of conduct on which civilized nations have agreed. In fact, it is the very credibility of American national rhetoric—and adherence to so-called American values—that is in jeopardy.

As testified to by the history of repression of free speech that I have documented above, this trend is not entirely new. However, the breadth and degree of the violations are unprecedented, and they have occurred at a time when international standards of human rights have been developed into a robust web accepted by all civilized nations. And the roots of these violations—during the Red Scare, the relocation of Japanese Americans, the McCarthy era, and the post 9/11 excesses—seem to be the same: a basic fear of the undermining of national unity and a potential fragmentation of the Republic.

This kind of fear made Congress adopt the Tonkin Gulf Resolution—with 416-0 and 88-2 votes, respectively—in 1964 and the vote on the Authorization to Use Military Force Resolution of 18 September 2001, against one vote—without proper hearing sessions or other traditional legislative procedures.[69]

This practice of waiving constitutional requirements in times of danger may reflect both the American Dilemma of which Gunnar Myrdal spoke in 1944 and the paradox that Senator Morse warned about twenty years later, when he, as one of two senators, voted against the Tonkin Bay Resolution, which brought the nation down the slippery slope into the quagmire of the Vietnam conflict. It is indicative of that insecurity to which Senator Fulbright pointed in his timely book during the Vietnam debacle, and it reminds us that the United States is still an immature nation—which readily submits to the "strong man syndrome" and waives democratic control mechanisms whenever its national security seems to be in jeopardy—rather than being a fully fledged democracy, its frequent claims to the latter notwithstanding.

---

[69]   44 Pub. L. No. 107-40, § 2(a), 115 Stat. 224 (18 September 2001), at http://www.hamdanrumsfeld.com/GovtMotionToDismiss.pdf.

NOTES ON CONTRIBUTORS

MARÍA LUZ ARROYO (larroyo@flog.uned.es) is currently a Lecturer at the Open University of Spain (UNED) in Madrid. She has published extensively in Spanish on twentieth-century U.S. history, with particular research interests in the New Deal, American women, and diplomatic and cultural relations between the United States and Spain. English publications include "European Views of the New Deal: The Case of Spain," *Journal of Transatlantic Studies* 3.2 (2005); *History and Culture of the United States* (2007). Her current research areas include U.S.-Spanish relations, U.S. foreign policy and African-American Women History.

THOMAS CLARK (clark@uni-kassel.de) is Assistant Professor at the University of Kassel's chair for British and North American History. His primary research interests are American intellectual history and political ideas, transatlantic studies, the Revolutionary era, and popular culture. His current book project is entitled "Tocquevillian Moments: Transatlantic Visions of an American Republican Culture." Recent publications include "'Beam Me Across, Scotty': Star Trek, 'Cult' and the Mainstream," in M. Arbeit and R. Trušník, eds., *Cult Fiction & Cult Film: Multiple Perspectives* (2009) and "'The American Democrat' Reads *Democracy in America:* Cooper and Tocqueville in the Transatlantic Hall of Mirrors," in *Amerikastudien/American Studies* 52.2 (2007): 187-208.

MARK ELLIS (m.ellis@strath.ac.uk) is a Senior Lecturer in American History at the University of Strathclyde in Glasgow. His publications on America race relations around the time of World War I include articles in the *Journal of American History*, the *Journal of Policy History* and the *Journal of American Studies*. His book, *Race, War and Surveillance: African Americans and the United States Government during World War One*, was published in 2001. He is completing a monograph on the career of the white southern sociologist and government official, Thomas Jackson Woofter, Jr. (1873-1972), who was a central figure in the early work of the Commission on Interracial Cooperation in Atlanta and Howard Odum's Institute for Research in Social Science at Chapel Hill.

ADAM FAIRCLOUGH (a.fairclough@hum.leidenuniv.nl) is the Raymond and Beverly Sackler Professor of American History and Culture at Leiden University. A specialist in African American and southern history, he is the author of seven books, including *To Redeem the Soul of America: The Southern Christian Leadership Conference and Martin Luther King, Jr.* (1987); *Race and Democracy: The Civil Rights Struggle in Louisiana, 1915-1972* (1995); and *Better Day Coming: Blacks and Equality, 1890-2000* (2001). His latest book, *A Class of Their Own: Black Teachers in the Segregated South* (2007), won the Outstanding Book Award for 2008 from the History of Education Society. He is currently chairman of the Netherlands American Studies Association.

ALEX GOODALL (ag566@york.ac.uk) is a Lecturer in Modern History at the University of York, United Kingdom. He works on the history of the United States and U.S.-Latin American relations, with a particular focus on revolutionary and counter-revolutionary politics in the Western Hemisphere. His primary field of research is the history of anticommunism in the United States, particularly in the period between World War I and II. Recent publications on aspects of the cultural, political, and international history of American anticommunism have been published in the *Historical Journal* and *Journal of Contemporary History*, and he is currently working on a monograph on the subject, tentatively titled *Making Joe McCarthy: The Fall and Rise of American Anticommunism, 1917-1954*.

SYLVIA L. HILTON (slhilton@ghis.ucm.es) is Professor of U.S. and Latin American History at the Complutense University in Madrid. She has published numerous articles and book chapters on colonial North American borderlands, and on intercultural perceptions as one aspect of U.S. international relations. She serves as international contributing editor from Spain for the *Journal of American History*. She is co-author and co-editor of *European Perceptions of the Spanish-American War of 1898* (1999), *Teaching and Studying U.S. History in Europe* (2007), *Norteamérica a finales del siglo XVIII: España y los Estados Unidos* (2008), and *Gulf Nexus of Empire: Negotiating Loyalty and Identity in the Borderlands, 1760s-1820s* (forthcoming).

CATHERINE LEJEUNE (lejeunec@univ-paris-diderot.fr) is Associate Professor of American Studies at the University of Paris Diderot. Her main book publications are *Cultural Studies. Etudes Culturelles*, co-edited with André Kaenel and Marie-Jeanne Rossignol (2003); *Explorations and Borders/Frontiers in the U.S. (History-Anthropology)*, co-edited with François Brunet (1998); *"Street Cultures" in the U.S. (Hispanic Barrios)*, co-edited with Geneviève Fabre (1996). Her research interests include the concept of border in the Social Sciences, and the remapping of disciplines (cultural studies and anthropology). She is currently researching recent immigration policies and their security-oriented approach since 9/11 (with a focus on Latino immigrants and undocumented workers in the United States).

CORNELIS A. VAN MINNEN (ca.v.minnen@zeeland.nl) is Director of the Roosevelt Study Center in Middelburg, the Netherlands, and Professor of American History at Ghent University, Belgium. His books include *American Diplomats in the Netherlands, 1815-1850* (1993) and *Van Loon: Popular Historian, Journalist, and FDR Confidant* (2005). He is editor and co-editor of many volumes, most recently of *Federalism, Citizenship, and Collective Identities in U.S. History* (2000), *Nation on the Move: Mobility in U.S. History* (2002), *Frontiers and Boundaries in U.S. History* (2004), *Teaching and Studying U.S. History in Europe* (2007), and *Four Centuries of Dutch-American Relations, 1609-2009* (2009).

OLE O. MOEN (ole.moen@ilos.uio.no) is Professor of American Civilization at the University of Oslo. He received his PhD from the University of Minnesota in 1978. He has served as secretary general of the European Association for American Studies, 2002-2006, and is contributing editor for Norway of the *Journal of American History*. His most recent books are: *Race, Color, and Partial Blindness: Affirmative Action under the Law* (2001), *USA—Annerledeslandet i vest* [The USA—A Different Western Country, 2005], and *USAs presidenter—fra George Washington til George W. Bush* [U.S. Presidents—from George Washington to George W. Bush, 2008]. Ole Moen is the most frequently used academic commentator on American affairs on national Norwegian radio and television.

SERGE RICARD (serge.ricard@univ-paris3.fr) is Professor Emeritus of American Studies at the Sorbonne Nouvelle, Paris. He has published extensively on Theodore Roosevelt, U.S. expansionism and foreign policy, and Mexican-American culture. He is the editor or co-editor of numerous books and the author, notably, of *Theodore Roosevelt: principes et pratique d'une politique étrangère* (1991), *The Mass Media in America: An Overview* (1998) and *The "Manifest Destiny" of the United States in the 19th Century* (1999). He was educated at Davidson College, N.C., and at the Sorbonne, Paris, and was twice a Fulbright research scholar and many times a visiting scholar at Harvard University.

DANIELA ROSSINI (rossini@uniroma3.it) is Professor of Contemporary History at the University of Roma Tre. She spent three years at Harvard, as Fulbright scholar and fellow of the Charles Warren Center for Studies in American History. She is the author of *L'America riscopre l'Italia. L'Inquiry di Wilson e le origini della Questione Adriatica, 1917-19* (1992) and *Woodrow Wilson and the American Myth in Italy: Culture, Diplomacy, and War Propaganda* (2008). Her edited books include *From Theodore Roosevelt to FDR: Internationalism and Isolationism in American Foreign Policy* (1995), *La propaganda nella Grande Guerra tra nazionalismi e internazionalismi* (2007) and *Le americane. Donne e immagini di donne tra Belle Epoque e fascismo* (2008).

ELLEN SCHRECKER (schreckr@yu.edu) is Professor of History at Yeshiva University and received her PhD from Harvard University. She is a leading expert on McCarthyism and has published many books and articles on the subject, including *Many Are the Crimes: McCarthyism in America* (1998), *The Age of McCarthyism: A Short History with Documents* (1994, rev.ed. 2002), and *No Ivory Tower: McCarthyism and the Universities* (1986). Her most recent book is an edited collection of essays, *Cold War Triumphalism: Exposing the Misuse of History after the Fall of Communism* (2004). She is the former editor of *Academe*, the publication of the American Association of University Professors, and is currently working on a general study of political repression in America.

MELVYN STOKES (m.stokes@ucl.ac.uk) teaches American History and American Film History at University College London. His edited or co-edited books include *The State of U.S. History* (2002), *Race and Class in the American South since 1890* (1994), *The Market Revolution in America* (1996) and *The U.S. and the European Alliance since 1945* (1999). He has co-edited five books on film audiences: *American Movie Audiences* (1999), *Identifying Hollywood's Audiences* (1999), *Hollywood Spectatorship* (2001), *Hollywood Abroad: Audiences and Cultural Exchange* (2004), and *Going to the Movies: Hollywood and the Social Experience of Cinema* (2007). He has recently published *D. W. Griffith's "The Birth of a Nation": A History of "the Most Controversial Motion Picture of All Time"* (2007).

KEVERN VERNEY (verneyk@edgehill.ac.uk) is Professor in American History at Edge Hill University, United Kingdom. He has numerous publications on African American history including *Black Civil Rights in America* (2000), *The Art of the Possible: Booker T. Washington and Black Leadership in the United States, 1881-1925* (2001), *African Americans and U. S. Popular Culture* (2003) and *The Debate on Black Civil Rights in America* (2006). His co-edited book (with Lee Sartain) *Long Is the Way and Hard: One Hundred Years of the National Association for the Advancement of Colored People* (*NAACP*), will be published in 2009. He is also working on a monograph on the NAACP in Alabama, 1913-1955.

CLIVE WEBB (c.j.webb@sussex.ac.uk) is Reader in American History and Head of the History Department at the University of Sussex in Brighton, United Kingdom. He is the author of *Fight against Fear: Southern Jews and Black Civil Rights* (2001) and, with David Brown, of *Race in the American South: From Slavery to Civil Rights* (2007). Webb is also the editor of *Massive Resistance: Southern Opposition to the Second Reconstruction* (2005). Clive Webb is currently working on two projects, a study of militant white opposition to desegregation in the South and, in collaboration with William Carrigan of Rowan University, a history of the lynching of Mexicans in the United States.

ACKNOWLEDGMENTS

The essays in this book were originally presented and discussed at the Roosevelt Study Center's Eighth Middelburg Conference of European Historians of the United States on 25-27 April 2007. The conference and the publication of this volume were made possible by the generous sponsorship of the Roosevelt Study Center in Middelburg, the Franklin and Eleanor Roosevelt Institute at Hyde Park, New York, and the U.S. Embassy in The Hague.

In our capacity as organizers of the conference and as editors of this volume, we gratefully acknowledge the indispensable and most efficient services of the Roosevelt Study Center's secretary Leontien Joosse throughout the project.

Cornelis A. van Minnen and Sylvia L. Hilton
Middelburg/Madrid, April 2009